Democracy and the Welfare State

STUDIES FROM THE PROJECT ON THE FEDERAL SOCIAL ROLE

FORREST CHISMAN AND ALAN PIFER, SERIES DIRECTORS

The Politics of Social Policy in the United States
Edited by Margaret Weir, Ann Shola Orloff, and Theda Skocpol

Democracy and the Welfare State
Edited by Amy Gutmann

Democracy and the Welfare State

EDITED BY

AMY GUTMANN

PRINCETON UNIVERSITY PRESS

Published by Princeton University Press, 41 William Street,
Princeton, New Jersey 08540
In the United Kingdom: Princeton University Press, Guildford, Surrey

Library of Congress Cataloging-in-Publication Data will be found
on the last printed page of this book

ISBN 0–691–07756–8 (cloth)
0–691–02275–5 (pbk.)

This book has been composed in Linotron Sabon

Clothbound editions of Princeton University Press books
are printed on acid-free paper, and binding materials are chosen
for strength and durability. Paperbacks, although satisfactory for
personal collections, are not usually suitable for library rebinding

Printed in the United States of America by Princeton University Press,
Princeton, New Jersey

Designed by Laury A. Egan

CONTENTS

FOREWORD

This book is one of several volumes based on activities sponsored by the Project on the Federal Social Role. The Project was a nonprofit, nonpartisan enterprise established in 1983 to stimulate innovative thinking about the future directions of federal social policy.

Americans are doubtless more preoccupied than any other people with questions about the fundamental purposes and directions of their national government. In part this concern reflects a healthy political culture. We are always searching for better ideas about government and always disagreeing about which ideas are best. In part, too, our concern reflects a longstanding ambivalence about the value of national institutions. We still honor the tradition of Thomas Jefferson, which presumes against an active federal role, in an era when programs and policies emanating from Washington permeate every aspect of our lives.

But while Americans never seem to tire of arguing about the proper role of national government, systematic thinking on this subject has been neglected in recent years. Scholars have produced a great deal of excellent research about specific policies and programs. But there has been too little careful study of what effect those measures, considered as a whole, have on the American people.

This neglect of the larger issues of public policy is deeply troubling. The federal social role is more than the sum of its parts. The various policies and programs that constitute it interact with each other in a great many ways. Collectively they have a far greater impact on our future as a nation than the study of particular issues can reveal.

More importantly, the specific measures of government are all parts of a broader commitment by the American people to employ their common resources toward achieving common goals. Only a strong sense of what those goals are and what overall directions of policy are required to achieve them can ensure that so large and diverse an enterprise as the federal government serves the general welfare.

The problems that arise when basic issues of purpose and direction are neglected have been vividly demonstrated in recent years. For half a century Americans supported an almost continual expansion of the federal social role. But the growth of federal activism slowed in the late 1970s and early 1980s, and there were dire predictions that national government had exhausted its possibilities as an instrument for social betterment. A period of reassessment followed. For over a decade, virtually every aspect of the social role was closely scrutinized by politicians, scholars, and the press.

As an exercise in public education, this reassessment was undoubtedly a success. But as an exercise in policy development it was a disappointment. No clear directions for the future emerged. The federal role was neither greatly augmented nor diminished; nor was it set on any new course. The nation remained locked in political stalemate.

Although periods of national stock-taking are often healthy, prolonged stalemate is a luxury that the United States cannot afford. While national policy has been standing still, major forces of change have been at work in our social and economic life. Transformations in the nature of our economy, evolving personal lifestyles, societal aging and worsening conditions for many of the poor are the largest and most visible developments. We are no longer the nation that we were a few decades ago, and because government pervades so many aspects of our lives, we need new measures to suit our new circumstances.

The recent reassessment of public policy failed to come to grips with the forces of social and economic change in large part because it proceeded in a piecemeal fashion. Debate was confined primarily to the merits and demerits of policies and programs already in place. As a result, the nation artificially constrained its options. We failed to examine carefully enough the need for major new initiatives by the federal government and ways to make them work.

In this static and backward-looking environment, destructive myths and misunderstandings found fertile ground—most notably the myth that there are severe limits to what an activist government can achieve. This idea takes various forms, and in most of those forms it is seriously misleading. If our national history teaches us anything, it is that each generation is capable of accomplishing far more through the use of government than previous generations would have dreamed possible. History also teaches that we *must* accomplish more: that effective government is a never-ending process of responding to needs and opportunities. This requires breaking with the ideas and patterns of the past. As often as not, the social role has evolved through large measures that defied past skepticism and cut across the categories of previous thought.

But to move boldly into the future, as it must, the nation needs to raise its sights above the terms of the current debate. The American people need to understand the full dimensions of the federal social role, how it evolved and the ways in which it operates. Based on that understanding, they need to consider what they want to do with this enormously complex and valuable machine—how it should be used to meet the challenges of today and of the decades to come.

The Project on the Federal Social Role was established to shed light on basic questions of purpose and direction. Its activities were designed to raise issues that transcend the usual domains of public policy analysis and to enhance public understanding of national government. Each of the volumes that have resulted from the Project's work advances these goals in a different way. Individually and collectively, they grapple with many of the larger concerns that have been neglected during the recent period of reassessment. And they exemplify the type of informed debate that must become a larger part of our public life if the United States is to move beyond political stalemate and toward a stronger sense of common purpose.

Washington, D.C.

Forrest Chisman
Alan Pifer

ACKNOWLEDGMENTS

This book is the culmination of a collaboration that began at the meetings of a faculty seminar at Princeton University, supported by the Project on the Federal Social Role and the Woodrow Wilson School. The seminar brought together faculty and graduate students from Princeton's Departments of Politics, Philosophy, History, and Sociology and from the Woodrow Wilson School, as well as members of the Institute for Advanced Study and political philosophers from several other American and European universities. The participants shared a broad interest in rethinking the relationship between liberal democratic values and the welfare state in its American incarnation. Each session of the seminar centered on a paper that raised a new problem or called into question a conventional wisdom concerning this relationship. Because the papers were circulated in advance of the seminar, the authors were able to benefit enormously from the comments of participants.

Forrest Chisman, Alan Pifer, and Sanford Thatcher had enough confidence in our enterprise to support it and enough interest to participate in many of our sessions. In addition to acting as rapporteur for the seminar, Stephen Macedo contributed insightful comments to our discussions. Several people also deserve thanks for their extensive comments and for the papers they submitted at particular sessions: David Aladjem, Robert Amdur, Charles Beitz, Jameson Doig, Ronald Dworkin, Thomas Ferguson, Christopher Jencks, Jane Mansbridge, Michael Sandel, Nancy Schwartz, Kerry Whiteside, and Sheldon Wolin. We also thank Edna Lloyd for her secretarial help and Felicity Skidmore for her editing.

Democracy and the Welfare State

INTRODUCTION

Every modern industrial state is a welfare state. None permits natural or social contingencies fully to determine the life chances of its members. All have programs whose explicit purpose is to protect adults and children from the degradation and insecurity of ignorance, illness, disability, unemployment, and poverty. "If, as our Constitution tells us, our Federal Government was established among other things, 'to provide for the general welfare,' then it is our plain duty to provide for that security upon which welfare depends," Franklin Delano Roosevelt told Congress in 1934.[1] The duty may have been plain, but the measures passed by Congress between 1934 and 1939—unemployment compensation, old-age and disability insurance, aid to dependent children—were at the time extraordinary.

The welfare state in the United States has grown since the New Deal in both cost and complexity. Federal spending on welfare increased from 8.2 to 18.7 percent of the GNP between 1950 and 1980. The programs that today constitute the American welfare state—among them, Medicaid, Medicare, Food Stamps, public housing, student loans, and a variety of veterans' programs in addition to the New Deal programs—defy a great deal of empirical generalization. Many programs, such as Social Security (the most expensive), distribute money; many others, such as Medicare (the second most expensive), provide aid in kind. Some programs are means-tested; others are not. Programs aimed at low-income families constitute a small proportion of federal spending on social welfare—approximately one-fifth in 1980.[2] Aid to Families with Dependent Children (AFDC)—probably the single program most often identified with "welfare" in the United States—accounted for less than 2 percent of federal spending on social welfare in 1983.[3]

Roosevelt's defense of the welfare state still makes sense as a start. Yet even fifty years later, the protection provided by the American welfare

[1] Franklin Delano Roosevelt, "Message to Congress Reviewing the Broad Objectives and Accomplishments of the Administration, June 8, 1934," in Alan Pifer and Forrest Chisman, eds., *The Report of the Committee on Economic Security of 1935* (Washington, D.C.: National Conference on Social Welfare, 1985), p. 138.

[2] U.S. Bureau of the Census, *Statistical Abstract of the United States* (Washington, D.C.: U.S. Government Printing Office, 1984), pp. 368–71.

[3] General Accounting Office, *Federal Benefits Programs: A Profile* (Washington, D.C.: U.S. Government Printing Office, 1986), pp. ii–iv.

state against degradation and insecurity is only partial and is occasionally counterproductive. The welfare state in the United States therefore invites criticism of its promises and programs, perhaps more so now than at any time in its history.

Conflicting criticisms of the policies of the American welfare state have been offered by conservative, liberal, and radical theorists, and each is, on its face, credible. Conservatives suggest that instead of securing the poor more effectively against misfortune, increases in welfare benefits since the 1960s have subsidized personal and social irresponsibility. Generous welfare payments have enabled teen-agers to drop out of school, unwed mothers to raise children, and men to forgo steady employment. By securing the poor against responsibility, the welfare state creates more poverty as well as a drain on governmental resources, to everybody's detriment. "We tried to provide more for the poor and produced more poor instead," Charles Murray has claimed. "We tried to remove the barriers to escape from poverty, and inadvertently built a trap." Murray criticizes AFDC for trapping poor mothers by making it more profitable for them to raise children without being married. Like many other welfare programs, AFDC encourages "the poor to behave in the short term in ways that . . . [are] destructive in the long term."[4] The welfare state thereby fosters illegitimacy, divorce, and dependency on the dole, rather than personal or civic virtue.

A more plausible interpretation of the available evidence suggests that welfare-state policies cannot be faulted for the increasing instability of the American family. The various phenomena associated with such instability—illegitimacy, divorce, "living in sin"—have also become more prevalent among the affluent since the mid-1960s. It is true that higher levels of welfare payments are associated with higher divorce rates among poor women. But should welfare payments therefore be reduced to discourage divorce among poor women? Surely not on the grounds that higher AFDC payments make it profitable for poor women to behave in the short run in ways that are destructive in the long run. It would be rash to assume that unhappily married women are better off married than divorced (in the long or the short run). If we doubt the validity of this assumption, then we must also conclude that welfare policies should not make it difficult for unmarried women to feed, clothe, and house their children adequately.[5]

Whereas conservatives often suggest that the American welfare state has gone too far, liberals often argue that it has not gone far enough.

[4] Charles Murray, *Losing Ground: American Social Policy, 1950–1980* (New York: Basic Books, 1985), p. 9.

[5] For an argument along these lines with supporting empirical analysis, see Christopher Jencks, "How Poor Are the Poor?" *New York Review of Books*, May 9, 1985, pp. 41–49.

Citizens have a right to be treated as equals. Being treated as an equal (that is, in a way that preserves human dignity) demands greater and freer access to education, health care, employment, and income—as a matter of right—than welfare policies in the United States have ever provided.[6] Preservation of dignity also demands that the state not intrude into the private lives of poor people for the sake of fostering civic virtue or their own welfare. A truly liberal welfare state would not allow poor children to be penalized for the poverty of their parents, or poor adults to suffer because of their undeserved misfortune.

Although this liberal vision may be theoretically attractive, it is practically unworkable. To undo all the disadvantages of poverty, ignorance, unemployment, chronic illness, and comparably serious forms of misfortune would bankrupt even the wealthiest welfare state. There is no limit to what a liberal welfare state could spend to compensate children for the poverty of their parents or to compensate chronically ill adults for their physical disabilities. If the right to be treated as an equal requires that the state compensate people for their undeserved hardships, then compensation to such an extent will not elicit the commitment necessary for rights to be taken seriously. Such expansive rights may also encourage people to neglect their duties as citizens. Liberals have not yet offered a principled way of limiting welfare rights to deal with these problems.

Radicals tend to agree with conservatives that liberals demand too much of the welfare state. They also tend to agree with liberals that the welfare state has not gone far enough. But in contrast to both conservatives and liberals, they argue that the fiscal policies of a capitalist welfare state contradict their own purposes. The capitalist welfare state either temporarily succeeds in providing a safety net for its citizens but consequently fails to maintain a sound economy, or it temporarily succeeds in maintaining a sound economy but fails to protect those citizens most at the mercy of market forces. In both situations, private ownership of commercial property impedes the self-realization of citizens, especially those most vulnerable to fluctuations in the labor market and therefore least in control of their working lives. Welfare and capitalism are therefore a socially unsavory as well as an economically unstable combination.[7] Welfare capitalism systematically blocks the self-realization of all working-class citizens and deprives many (in particular the unemployed) of their self-esteem.

[6] For examples of liberal arguments for the welfare state, see Ronald Dworkin, *A Matter of Principle* (Cambridge, Mass.: Harvard University Press, 1985), pp. 181–213; and Carl Wellman, *Welfare Rights* (Totowa, N.J.: Rowman and Allanheld, 1982).

[7] See, for example, Samuel Bowles and Herbert Gintis, *Democracy and Capitalism: Property, Community, and the Contradictions of Modern Social Thought* (New York: Basic Books, 1986).

In championing full employment, preservation of self-esteem, and the self-realization of all citizens, the radical criticism of welfare capitalism promises too much. No socialist mode of economic control can promise all this—and a sound economy too. A credible criticism would require a choice among these goals, or a decision to settle for something less than the full realization of each. But such a criticism would be considerably less radical than the one just described.

These weaknesses in conservative, liberal, and radical criticisms suggest not that the welfare state is beyond criticism but that we must move beyond the conventional criticisms. The primary focus of many of the papers in this volume is not individual virtue, equality, or self-realization, but democratic citizenship. The pivotal questions are: What social institutions are necessary to encourage and protect citizenship? What rights do citizens have, and what duties are required of them? The papers are not intended to represent the range of opinion on the welfare state, nor is their aim to survey the many problems that arise in the welfare state in its American incarnation (although they do cover a broad range of problems). Rather, these authors try to develop a democratic perspective on the welfare state or to provide empirical support for such a perspective.

Those who develop a democratic perspective often point to a commonly acknowledged problem that conventional theories of the welfare state either do not focus on or fail to solve satisfactorily. Although the welfare state has improved the condition of the poor, the unemployed, and the disabled, "the poorest citizens, the unemployed and the helpless, are not significantly more independent, more responsible, more capable of shaping their own lives and joining in the common work of citizenship." Political dependency is the disappointment motivating Michael Walzer's search for ways of socializing welfare-state services (Chapter 1). The disappointment results from failure to uphold the traditional democratic ideal of a "community constituted by citizens committed to one another." But Walzer's vision of a socialized state is untraditional: "Distribution and not production will . . . be the first field of human activity to be socialized." Socialization will necessitate more voluntary organizations as well as experiments in local democracy, both of which require "a state strong enough to superintend and subsidize the work of citizens and volunteers."

The disappointment concerning dependency reflects another feature of a democratic perspective, described in J. Donald Moon's paper (Chapter 2). Democratic theorists interpret self-respect as based on the "self-understanding" of citizens. Self-respect, according to Moon's interpretation of self-understanding, depends not just on having one's rights respected by others but also on carrying out one's duties as a self-supporting member of society. The widely sensed failure of welfare-state programs to support the self-respect of poor people seems to be traceable at least in part to this understanding, which, as Moon puts it, "poses a deep dilemma for a polity that aspires to be a welfare state. For if people hold the norm that they should be independent (in the sense of self-supporting), then how can the state provide them with the means of subsistence without violating their self-respect?" Although the welfare state can be defended by extending the classical liberal list of rights to include economic security, the liberal defense typically neglects this self-understanding and therefore the practical dilemma that results from it: providing welfare but not work for the poor undermines their status as citizens in civil society.

One distinctive feature of a democratic defense of the welfare state is that it emphasizes the self-understanding of citizens, rather than a more abstract or universal understanding of persons as (for example) "free and equal" beings. Moon interprets the self-understanding of Americans to mean that they are particularly averse to societal dependency, and tries to find some means of overcoming the dependency problem. He considers several promising proposals—governmental management of a full-employment economy, universal provision of crucial social services, and social insurance to cover basic needs. But these proposals also run into problems.

Jon Elster (Chapter 3) challenges both the possibility and the desirability of guaranteeing work to all citizens—whether by state planning, subsidies to and taxes on capitalist firms, market socialism, or profit sharing. Creating an unqualified right to employment appears to be as economically infeasible as the creation of many other (similarly unqualified) welfare rights championed by liberal theorists. Even if it were feasible for the state to ensure full employment, it would not be desirable, according to Elster. Employment policies designed primarily for the purpose of ensuring self-esteem cannot be rationally pursued: "If the work one does is esteemed enough by others to provide one with self-esteem, there will be a demand for it and no need to provide it as of right. . . . Verbally expressed esteem will not generate self-esteem if people are not willing to put their money where their mouth is, both as consumers and as taxpayers."

Universal provision of social services and social insurance is the least socially stigmatizing way of providing welfare services, but it is also (as Moon points out) the most costly and the least likely to meet the many material needs of the poor. Perhaps the problem lies in part not with those services, but with the capitalist economy that sustains poverty and societal dependency simultaneously with enormous inequalities of income and wealth. If, in a property-owning democracy, inequalities in the initial distribution of physical and human capital were sharply decreased, fewer problems might be encountered in subsequent redistributions by means of welfare-state services than are encountered in America's present highly inegalitarian capitalist economy. Richard Krouse and Michael McPherson (Chapter 4) derive this argument from a reinterpretation of John Rawls's *A Theory of Justice*, which is widely regarded as a liberal defense of welfare-state capitalism. This original reinterpretation explains Rawls's claim to be defending a democratic rather than a liberal conception of equality.[8] Krouse and McPherson introduce another possible way of alleviating the dependency problem that is important for our study of the welfare state. Were physical and human capital more widely distributed, fewer citizens would be dependent on welfare-state services for their subsistence. Such services would still be necessary to protect people against disabling illness, poverty, and unemployment. Although dependency in property-owning democracies would not disappear, the problem would be more controlled than it is today.

Dependency might be still further diminished if children were assured of receiving a better education. Few people deny the importance of public schooling as a welfare good, but most discussions of equal educational opportunity place undue emphasis on the economic (as distinct from the political) benefits of schooling. Quality education alone cannot ensure a steady income or meaningful work in an economy characterized by structural unemployment, but it can help citizens to participate intelligently in the political processes that can influence the economy. Better education for the poor would tend to increase their ability to engage in effective political activity, which in turn could result in policies more favorable to their economic self-sufficiency. In addition to its potential for indirectly producing economic benefits, a better education can directly decrease social dependency and increase self-respect.

A democratic perspective focuses not only on welfare-state policies but also on the political processes that can shape those policies. In considering the distribution of public education, I argue (Chapter 5) for the authority of communities in a democracy to choose how to allocate educational resources above the threshold level that is necessary to teach children the skills and habits of citizenship. The threshold principle constrains decision making in a democracy in that it prevents communities from depriving children of the education necessary to participate in the democratic processes that determine, among other things, the distribution of social welfare. But the constraint is justified by the democratic ideal itself.

Most citizens determine the distribution of welfare only indirectly, by electing representatives who collectively create or revise (but rarely dismantle) welfare-state programs. What principles should guide represent-

[8] See John Rawls, *A Theory of Justice* (Cambridge, Mass.: Harvard University Press, 1971), pp. 74–80.

atives in shaping welfare-state programs (and citizens in judging the records of their representatives)? Dennis Thompson (Chapter 6) discovers the same serious flaw in the answers provided by both delegate and trustee theories of representation. Neither adequately copes with the temporal dimension of the representative process: "Delegate theory takes account of the need to hold representatives responsible for complex policies that reach into the future, but at the price of severing the connection with the preferences of citizens in the present. Trustee theory tries to escape the conflict between present and future preferences by relying instead on principles, but at the cost of placing those principles beyond the political choice of citizens." Thompson defends three more democratic principles that better take account of the temporal dimension of the representative process. In applying these principles (generality, autonomy, and publicity), he does not attempt to devise a single group of equitable welfare-state programs. (That goal, he suggests, would subvert a democratic theory of representation.) Rather, he views the legislative history of the New Deal, the New Frontier, and the Great Society critically in a new light, and suggests reforms—ranging from a more responsible party system to the public financing of campaigns—that would improve the political processes that can influence the welfare state.

Even the most effective democratic processes cannot ensure just policies. A democratic perspective provides new answers to some old and unresolved problems concerning the welfare state, but it also raises some new problems with regard to social welfare. Jennifer Hochschild (Chapter 7) analyzes one of the most urgent of those problems: popular opposition to many reforms that are essential to overcoming the severe and cumulative deprivations of black citizens. Hochschild suggests that there is a way, but not a democratic will, to overcome these deprivations and thereby make the United States an integrated multiracial society. "Solving the problem of cumulative inequalities . . . would require a coordinated attack on racial discrimination and poverty and political powerlessness." But there may never be a democratic will, Hochschild suggests, because such a coordinated attack threatens the economic, political, and social status of many Americans. Although Americans fully endorse the theory of equal opportunity that supports such an effort, they resist its practical demands. "At present," Hochschild concludes, "deep and mutually reinforcing problems have combined with the perverse consequences of a partially achieved but fully endorsed ideology of equal opportunity to inhibit the full development of the American welfare state. We have all the elements necessary to solve the problems of race, class, and power if we choose to do so; but thus far Myrdal's diagnosis seems more apt than his prognosis." The problem of democratic will formation highlighted by Hochschild merits further analysis.

Is there an even greater problem of democratic will formation with regard to the welfare state in general? According to many observers, the most obvious shortcoming of a democratic defense of the welfare state in the United States is that it fails to acknowledge the lack of continuous popular support for a welfare state. The election and reelection of Ronald Reagan were widely interpreted as democratic mandates to dismantle the programs of the New Deal. Stanley Kelley, Jr., demonstrates (Chapter 8) that this interpretation is mistaken. In the elections of 1980 and 1984, "many voters demanded a better performance from the economy," Kelley concludes after a careful analysis, "not revision of New Deal policies unnecessary to the realization of that demand." Countering many arguments claiming a realignment of forces in the American party system, Kelly demonstrates that New Deal issues continued to be salient among voters from 1952 (when the appropriate data first became available) through 1984, and that in every election except that of 1980, voters have favored the Democrats on New Deal issues. Even the data for the election of 1980 "provide almost no support for the view that the Reagan administration came to power as the result of an increasingly insistent popular demand for the economic and welfare policies Reagan had proposed. Of course, opposition to New Deal-like policies won some support for Reagan, but it had won support in roughly equal measure for all Republican candidates for president since 1952."

Many of the staunchest Democratic proponents of such New Deal policies, however, oppose extending the American welfare state by opening the nation's borders. The liberal democratic theory of the welfare state is often said to be based on the ideal of human equality: all people have a right to the satisfaction of their basic needs. Why, then, should the American welfare state exclude people who are anxious to immigrate, many of them much needier than Americans? Although the United States admits more immigrants each year than do all other nations combined, it admits only a fraction of the world's desperately needy people. But, as Joseph Carens (Chapter 9) indicates, the problem is not simply the lack of democratic will to open U.S. borders. Were the United States to open its borders, the immigration flow would almost certainly turn into a flood tide, drowning out welfare benefits on which many Americans rely to maintain their standard of living. Are Americans justified in restricting the flow to a slow (but steady) stream, given that they have the resources to provide for many more people, although the immigrants' standard of living must generally be lower than that to which many Americans are accustomed? Most Americans assume that some restriction of the flow of poor into their country is justifiable. Carens shares this view, but he finds no principled support for it in contemporary political theories. The conflict between common-sense morality concerning immigration and liberal democratic principles is still unresolved, and presents a challenge to a democratic defense of the welfare state.

Another unresolved problem concerns the place of women in the welfare state. Carole Pateman (Chapter 10) suggests that despite a considerable body of literature on the "feminization of poverty," most welfare-state policies in the United States are poorly designed to secure the welfare of women in their increasingly common position of both primary child supporter and primary child rearer. In some cases, welfare-state programs that were created with the patriarchal model of the family in mind may even contribute to the dependency and degradation of women. Pateman's criticism challenges democratic theorists to consider whether a different set of welfare-state programs could satisfy the special needs and preserve the self-respect of women, or whether achieving the aims of the welfare state requires transforming the basic structure of other social and economic institutions.

Democratic views of the welfare state, taken together, can help to eliminate the blind spots of more conventional political theories. They may encourage policymakers to reformulate policies, in some cases resolving old problems; they raise new challenges and reveal weaknesses in existing welfare-state programs. But almost every view has a blind spot. Robert Fullinwider (Chapter 11) points to one in discussing the relationship between democratic citizenship and welfare that is presently a concern of many democratic theorists. He suggests that the relationship may be less clearly defined than these theorists assume. The benefits of many welfare-state programs in the United States are available to resident aliens as well as to citizens. Public schooling, one of the most costly and extensive welfare-state services, is open even to children of illegal aliens. Given the many grounds upon which democratic theorists can justify the welfare state—simple humanity, the desire to maintain social harmony and develop human capital, in addition to cultivating communal solidarity—the extension of welfare services to those who are not citizens is, at least in democratic principle, relatively unproblematic.

To expect the institutions of the welfare state to cultivate communal solidarity, however, may be more unrealistic than some democratic theorists suggest. Tying welfare to a work requirement is unlikely to teach civic responsibility or to encourage independence "in the absence of supporting and enforcing lessons in all other aspects of the welfare recipient's life. In the United States, work requirements press against the tide, not with it as they do in Switzerland. And it is the tide that produces the main effects." Some democratic theorists are too eager to turn the tide toward pursuit of common goals, Fullinwider suggests, rather than settling for cultivation of those civic virtues that enable citizens of a pluralistic democracy to reach their diverse goals. At the same time that those who advance this argument criticize a certain "martial" view of democratic citizenship, they invoke another, more "liberal" view of democratic citizenship: "The role of civic education is to foster . . . habits of self-sufficiency, neighborliness, and political participation. The good citizen must subordinate private will to the common good, but the subordination is partial. In a well-ordered state, by supporting the common good, the individual supports the conditions for his own, independent good."

Even were liberal, conservative, and radical critics to agree that the welfare state should enable each individual to pursue his or her own (partially) independent good by supporting the common (democratic) good, some difficult questions would still remain: What are the elements of the common good of a democracy? What are the conditions that will enable citizens to pursue their own good in a manner consistent with pursuit of the common good? What is the proper balance between subordination and independence? How are the habits of economic self-sufficiency and political participation best taught? Merely agreeing that the problem exists, of course, does not resolve it. But such a discussion redirects attention to the relationship between democratic citizenship and welfare. Rather than defending policies that prevent poor adults (particularly single women with children) from earning a decent living, conservatives might focus on policies that encourage poor adults to act in socially productive ways while allowing them (and their children) to maintain a decent standard of living. Liberals would no longer be concerned with (defining and) defending absolute equality of opportunity, but might defend a decent minimum that would enable all adults to participate effectively as citizens in a democracy. Radicals might look for alternatives to both utopian socialism and welfare-state capitalism—alternatives that would give citizens the chance to lead productive lives, while preserving their self-respect.

Because the concern with citizenship is so widely shared, a democratic perspective has the potential to join liberal, conservative, and radical critics in a constructive dialogue. The authors of the papers in this volume set the stage for such a dialogue by developing several central elements of the democratic perspective.

1

Socializing the Welfare State

MICHAEL WALZER

I suggest that we think of the modern welfare state as a system of nationalized distribution. Certain key social goods have been taken out of private control or out of exclusive private control and are now provided by law to all (or to some subset of) citizens and residents. The distribution is paid for with public funds and organized by public officials. Social Security is an easy example. In the past, the private sector sold old-age insurance and pensions to men and women who could afford the premiums. Now the state takes over, collects the premiums in the form of a tax, and guarantees the pensions. The British national health service works in a similar fashion. Without abolishing the private sector, the state organizes and largely controls the distribution of health care, guaranteeing a minimal standard of care to everyone.

Seen in this way, the welfare state is more familiar than it might otherwise be. Nationalized distribution invites comparison with nationalized production, a common feature of the European if not the American political economy. The argument that I want to make is essentially contained in that comparison; it is an argument that works by analogy. The problems of the welfare state, I shall suggest, have been anticipated, have already been the subject of critical reflection, in the socialist debate over "nationalization," even though productive rather than distributive activities were at issue, and still are at issue, in that debate.

Spelling Out the Analogy

Nationalized distribution is obviously not a new process. The state as we know it has its origins in the nationalization of police protection and military security, both of which the feudal regime distributed privately. More recent nationalizations have come at the expense of capitalist or market distributions—without, however, supplanting either capitalism or the market. The process is infinitely variable, for even if there is only a finite number of goods whose distribution might conceivably be nationalized, there is no limit to the ways in which nationalized distributions might be organized or to the range of people for whom the provision of this or that good might be guaranteed. Most nationalizations are only partial, state distribution coexisting with other forms of distributive activity—as public education, though it is guaranteed to all citizens, coexists with private. The National Endowment for the Humanities is a typical, if minor, agency of the welfare state, it distributes funds that are only supplementary to other distributions, some of which are philanthropic in character, some market based. Nevertheless, we can say that the support of the humanities is now a national project.

The development and expansion of such projects have gone much further in some countries than in others, but it would be a mistake to arrange countries along a single continuum, as if nationalization had some necessary form or logical end point. Every welfare state has its own history and, I suppose, its own destiny. But nationalization does produce, under contemporary conditions, a characteristic set of distributive arrangements: a central administration, a new cadre of civil servants, a more or less uniform code of rules and regulations. However partial the arrangements are, insofar as they are state arrangements, they will be organized and controlled along what we might think of as Weberian lines, in accordance with some "rational/legal" ideal. The welfare state is first of all a state. The recipients of welfare stand in a necessary relationship to the state, a relationship mediated by the state bureaucracy.

The nationalization of distribution is, thus, formally parallel with the nationalization of production. Both involve state takeovers of activities that were once entirely in private hands. Production, exactly like distribution, can be made into a national project, managed by public officials, with investment capital provided, if necessary, out of tax money. Neither of these projects has a necessary form or preordained end point. Just as it is possible to take over the distribution of this social good but not that one, so it is possible to take over this industry and leave that one untouched—steel but not chemicals, chemicals but not steel. And as with any given good, so with any given industry, nationalization is commonly incomplete, no bar to small-scale (sometimes not even to large-scale) entrepreneurial activity on the side—in education or health, say, or in chemicals or steel. But whatever the extent and degree of nationalization, its characteristic features regularly reappear: centralized control, bureaucracy, uniform regulation.

If nationalized distribution characterizes the welfare state, nationalized production characterizes, or was once thought to characterize, the socialist state. Theorists of socialism have had little to say about distribution. Get the productive arrangements right, they thought, and distributive arrangements would fall readily into place. According to Marx, "any distribution whatever of the means of consumption is only a consequence of the . . . mode of production itself."[1] Curiously, though socialists in office have been far more successful when they nationalized distribution than when they nationalized production, theory has never caught up with political reality. Production is still primary in principle, and the argument over the merits of nationalization is still focused on productive activity. Another reason for the focus, of course, is the lack of success in bringing on socialism by taking over industry. Nationalized production has been a great disappointment. I shall explain the nature of that disappointment and then turn to the analogous but smaller disappointments of nationalized distribution.

It is not inefficiency that has made nationalized production disappointing. State-run industries are not (in the West) noticeably less efficient than privately run industries. Indeed, the problems of the two, and their performance in the face of those problems, have not been all that different. British steel and American steel, for example, have undergone a similar decline for similar reasons. Lack of managerial adventurousness may be one of the reasons in both cases. Why should corporate managers and state managers, recruited from the same social groups, subject to virtually identical incentives and constraints, behave differently? The possibilities for entrepreneurial initiative are no doubt more numerous in the private sector; but even there they exist on the margins, not at the center, not in heavy industry, not in the large corporate complex. The prospects for social responsibility and long-term planning are no doubt better in state-run industry; but it has proven possible to impose responsibility and to generate plans, where there is a will to do so, without nationalization. At the center, in the modern regulative state, nationalized production is not significantly different from private production—and therein, of course, lies the disappointment.

Nor is the experience of workers in state-run factories all that different; and, since nationalization was supposedly undertaken on behalf of the workers, that is another disappointment. What difference does it make if one's boss is a civil servant rather than a corporate official? In principle, perhaps, it makes a notable difference, since workers are also voters and so can take part in choosing the boss of their boss. But the political distance is too great: what is true in principle is insignificant in practice. The effective chain of command, the everyday experience of hierarchy, is not changed much by the fact of periodic national elections. The relations of production have not been transformed. To work on the assembly line of a nationalized industry is no more exciting or desirable than to work on

[1] Karl Marx, "Critique of the Gotha Program," in *The Marx-Engels Reader*, 2d ed., ed. Robert C. Tucker (New York: Norton, 1978), p. 531.

the assembly line of a privately run industry. When the worker calculates his costs and benefits, nationalization hardly comes into the reckoning.

Hence the standard left-wing critique of nationalized production goes like this. What we really had in mind was socialized production. The real alternative to private management is self-management, workers' control, some contemporary version of syndicalism—for the standard critique recapitulates much of what syndicalists, guild socialists, and other pluralist critics of the state were arguing many decades ago. If the experience of production is to be changed, it is not enough for the nation or the state to take over the process; the producers themselves must take over. The tasks of management must be shared, or the managers must be controlled, by the men and women on the line. Otherwise it is only state power, not the power of ordinary people, that is enhanced.

I shall not pursue this argument any further, but will only point out that this critique of nationalized production is relevant also to the case of nationalized distribution. The disappointment, of course, is not the same; the state's distribution of social goods actually delivers the goods—to far more people than private distributors have ever reached, and far more steadily and consistently. To some extent, the experience of welfare recipients has indeed been transformed. Now they get what they get not in the form of charity and noblesse oblige but in the form of legal entitlement, and they get it not as paupers but as citizens.

But the transformation is only partial, for it is also true that old patterns of dependency have been reconstituted as new patterns of civil clientage. Private distributors have been replaced (and, their operations, no doubt, improved upon) by state officials, but what might be called the welfare relationship has not disappeared. The position of employed workers, even relatively ill-paid workers, has been strengthened and stabilized. But the poorest citizens, the unemployed and the helpless, are not significantly more independent, more responsible, more capable of shaping their own lives and joining in the common work of citizenship. Hence our disappointment with the welfare state. The purpose of nationalized distribution was to free us from all the superfluous and degrading forms of human dependency. Now we measure the advance of the welfare state—but we can hardly measure its success—by the growing number of dependents each working citizen must support, and to many citizens these days the number seems insupportable.

The disappointment has another (related?) form. Nationalized distribution was supposed to express a sense of the nation-state as a community committed to its citizens—or, more accurately, as a community constituted by citizens committed to one another. The welfare state was imagined as a systematic form of mutual assistance, replacing the unsystematic (and unreliable) forms that had existed before. Certain historical images lie behind this conception, images interestingly contrasted with those that lie behind the idea of socialism. Socialists seek to institutionalize and perpetuate the ardor of revolutionary engagement, the solidarity of the strike meeting or the political demonstration. Their heroes are not so much workers working as workers deciding (together) on how to work. A nationalized factory run by bureaucrats is not the right setting at all. Defenders of the welfare state, by contrast, seek to institutionalize and perpetuate the helpfulness born of collective crisis, the spirit of mutuality that arises among citizens confronting a flood or a storm or even an enemy attack. British welfarism, it has been said, emerged from the ashes of the blitz. Its heroes are not almsgivers, but men and women extending a helping hand to one another. A check in the mail, though that is very important, does not quite make the proper point.

Let me now complete the analogy: What we really had in mind was socialized distribution. The preferred successor to private philanthropy is collective help—which is the work not only of bureaucrats spending taxpayers' money but also of citizens "spending" their own time and energy. It is not easy, however, to say exactly what this would involve.

What would a socialized welfare state look like? We might think about it in terms of "power to the distributors," an analogy with the old socialist slogan "power to the producers." But the distributors are mostly state officials and professionals of different sorts, and they already exercise considerable power over their clients, the men and women who receive the benefits they distribute. Then what about "power to the recipients?" But that would make a virtue out of dependency. And what will the recipients, suddenly empowered, ask for but more of what they are already getting?

Neither distributors nor recipients, as these two groups are currently constituted, seem plausible candidates for empowerment. But both groups could conceivably be reconstituted on a broader basis. That would open the way to a twofold program, which I shall explain and defend in the remainder of this paper: first, power to the distributors only insofar as many more people, amateurs as well as professionals, join in the work of distribution; second, power to recipients and potential recipients, that is, ordinary citizens at or near the point of reception, the immediate setting where goods are delivered.

The Need to Hold Nationalization and Socialization in Balance

Socializing distribution, like socializing production, requires us to find ways in which the strengths of civil society can be reflected in, and enhanced rather than overwhelmed by, the growing activism of the state. It does not require the disappearance or the replacement of the state—a utopian project and one unlikely in fact to strengthen civil society. Society's "civilians" need the state (and the bureaucracy) to defend them against their own divisiveness, to protect them when they are alone and helpless, to enforce universal standards of care and safety. But every state preys on the society it protects; that is why socialization is the necessary correlative of nationalization. The problem is to hold the two in some rough balance: central planning and workers' control, state regulation and entrepreneurial initiative, a welfare minimum and local self-help.

We can see some of the problems involved in holding the balance if we consider for a moment the organization and politics of American education—the first distributive sector to be both nationalized and socialized. Education is nationalized in that it is guaranteed by the state and its delivery is regulated, at least in some ultimate sense, by federal authorities. It is socialized in that it is organized and run on a day-to-day basis by local and elected school committees.[2] The tension generated over racial integration of the public schools—a policy imposed by federal judges and resisted by local committees—is a tension between nationalization and socialization. This has a characteristic content, which I will come to in a moment. I want to note here its characteristic political form. The conflict arises between state officials, judicial or bureaucratic appointees, who are professionally committed to national goals, and elected representatives who are parochially committed to their own constituents. One can imagine similar tensions in the field of production between, say, state planners and factory councils. But tensions of the latter sort, in the United States, at least, are only imaginary, whereas in the field of distribution they are real and even urgent. Is it odd, or is it usual (characteristic, perhaps, of left-wing thought?) that the general issue is debated with reference chiefly to the imaginary case?

The substance of the debate is readily described. It is the claims of efficiency and universality that are most often represented by national (state and bureaucratic) authority. Consider an easy example: the distribution of medical care. State officials are likely to want to impose a division of labor, concentrating expensive equipment in a small number of centrally-located hospitals whose services are readily available over a wide area and asking smaller hospitals to focus on preventive or routine care. This division makes a lot of sense, and yet a local hospital committee, serving a particular community, elected by the members of that community, might

[2] Private education, when it is organized cooperatively by voluntary associations of parents and teachers, or sponsored by religious or political groups, is also an example of socialization, but not one I will consider here. I will have something to say about the importance of volunteers later in this paper.

nonetheless seek to obtain the very latest medical technology for its own "people"—setting an example of welfare autarchy likely to be imitated.

The claims of particularity are represented by social authority, that is, by men and women closely connected to a particular place or regularly attentive to the interests and aspirations of a particular group. For this reason, socialized distribution is bound to be different in different places, reflecting the decisions of many different committees. And "different" here necessarily means unequal. Some committees function better than others, because they tax their members more heavily, spend their money more wisely, choose to provide these services rather than those. Just as factory councils are more or less successful, so school committees and hospital boards are more or less successful. When welfare is delivered socially rather than nationally, citizens receive different and unequal kinds or amounts of welfare. State bureaucrats, acting in the name of efficiency and universality, will seek (as they should) to remedy the inequalities, providing equal financial support, for example, to every school district.[3] But they cannot require, without abolishing the local committees, that the money be spent equally well.

Difference and inequality are intensified by the partial character of distributive nationalization. All sorts of voluntary organizations participate in the delivery of welfare goods and services, and it is obvious that these groups function differently in different communities, depending on the resources (time and energy as well as money) that they can command and on the skill of their leaders. Their functioning also depends on the policy commitments of their leaders; though these people are more often coopted than elected, their views are likely to reflect local opinion (subject, very often, to middle- or upper-class qualification). This sort of distributive activity belongs to civil society, even though it has never in any formal sense been socialized—that is, handed over to, or taken over by, the local citizenry. It depends upon the voluntary mobilization of (some of) the citizens. We might think of voluntary mobilization as a spontaneous or nonpolitical form of socialization: It enables (some of) the citizens to control and shape the delivery of welfare services. Of course, they control and shape it differently in accordance with their different views, and would do so even if the expenditure of tax money and bureaucratic effort were absolutely uniform across the nation.

One of the consequences of distributive nationalization in Western Europe has been to reduce the extent and scope of voluntary activity. The clearest example is the collapse of the old working-class "friendly societies" that provided their members with the earliest form of social security.

[3] Arthur E. Wise, *Rich Schools, Poor Schools: The Promise of Equal Educational Opportunity* (Chicago: University of Chicago Press, 1968), esp. chap. 10.

These groups have simply been superseded by the state, which provides for its members—that is, for everyone—a more secure security.[4] Other forms of mutual aid have only been curtailed as activists realized that the work they once did is done more efficiently, if not always more humanely, by state officials. I do not think that this curtailment has anywhere been an intended consequence of nationalization, though advocates of the welfare state have certainly intended a degree of consistency and uniformity in the provision of basic services that voluntary organizations cannot approach. They have also intended to professionalize these services, for the sake of consistency and uniformity, and to deliver them more impersonally, as entitlements rather than as gifts.[5]

State action is likely to make voluntary activity seem superfluous, if not positively wrongheaded. It certainly discourages volunteers; a number of the more advanced welfare states have in fact reported a significant drop in voluntary contributions of time, energy, and money.[6] The nationalization of distribution desocializes welfare—conceivably for good reasons. This effect is hardly visible in the United States, where nationalization is less advanced than in Europe and where voluntary activity is more highly valued. The value may, of course, help to account for the backwardness. In any case, the first represents a strength, the second a weakness in American welfarism, and the two together suggest the ambiguity of nationalization.

It was certainly not the intention of advocates of the welfare state to undercut or diminish altruistic feeling and mutual aid. On the contrary, they would say, the purpose of state action is only to guarantee a minimum above which altruism and mutuality will have free play. It appears, however, that if these two do not come into play at the minimal level, with regard to basic services, they will not come into play at all. So we need to think of ways to draw volunteers into the range of activities financed and superintended by the state; we need, as two British leftists have recently argued, a "more participative and decentralized form of service provision"—that will make room for self-help and local initiative.[7] Spontaneous socialization needs to be seconded by state-sponsored socialization, that is, the democratic transformation of state agencies at

[4] P.H.J.H. Gosden, *Self-help: Voluntary Associations in the Nineteenth Century* (London: Batsford, 1973).

[5] Noel and José Parry, "Social Work, Professionalism, and the State," in N. Parry, M. Rustin, and C. Satyamurti, eds., *Social Work, Welfare, and the State* (London: Edward Arnold, 1979), pp. 21–47.

[6] *New York Times*, July 2, 1981.

[7] Roger Hadley and Stephen Hatch, *Social Welfare and the Failure of the State* (London: Allen and Unwin, 1981), p. 111; quoted in Neil Gilbert, *Capitalism and the Welfare State: Dilemmas of Social Benevolence* (New Haven, Conn.: Yale University Press, 1983), p. 169.

the local level or the transfer of authority and resources to voluntary organizations.

This will certainly produce new inequalities, since some agencies and organizations will be bolder or more energetic than others. But the alternative is to make our peace with the disappointments of nationalization, gratefully accept the benefits that bureaucrats bring, and give up the hope of providing some of those benefits more directly, as part of the everyday activity of (some) citizens. The result would be a welfare state unbalanced by what we might think of as a welfare society.

Increasing the Number of Distributors

But (again) what would a welfare society look like? The socialization process has two aspects. The first, much discussed in the 1960s, is expanded participation in decision making; the second is expanded participation in the actual delivery of welfare services. I am inclined to think that the second is the more basic. It has no analogy in the field of production, where there already exists a mass of producers, and where socialization requires only that we find ways of introducing members of that mass into the business of management—members who already know something about what is being managed. The situation is different in distribution, where the first requirement of a welfare society is to increase the number of people, recipients and potential recipients, who are also distributors. Only when that number is increased will it be possible to give both recipients and distributors a greater say in welfare management.

There is an alternative model, drawn more strictly on the productive analogy; it is a kind of welfare trade unionism, where recipients would be organized against distributors. But this analogy fails, I think, because welfare dependency is not a "trade." Recipients are not involved in an activity over which they can claim some rights of control. They have rights as citizens, of course, and they can organize interest or pressure groups to defend those rights; sometimes that defense will have to be militant if the rights are to be enjoyed at all. But the appeal of the recipients is to other citizens; we would not want them bargaining collectively with state bureaucrats over the size and delivery of their benefits. On the other hand, there is a variety of decisions that might plausibly be made by local councils of citizens or groups of volunteers, who know something about the distribution of benefits because they are involved in it, and who are at the same time actual or potential recipients.

The involvement might be worked out either within a democratized system of state provision or through the less systematic activities of philanthropic organizations. Indeed, in any welfare state that was also a welfare society, the line between these two would probably begin to blur. It is already blurred with regard to economic resources, since philanthropic organizations, in the United States at least, effectively spend tax money; it would blur also with regard to personnel.

Consider, for example, the proposal that volunteers be paid by the state. They would receive, presumably, only nominal sums, rather as left-wing activists are paid subsistence amounts (or less) for work in the "movement." The aim is to make it possible for more people to volunteer and also to generate greater consistency over time in voluntary service.[8] Is the idea of a paid volunteer a contradiction in terms? Not so long as the individual is contributing time and energy (and, one hopes, a growing skillfulness) that would command much higher pay on the market.

Or, consider the proposal that we require a period of national service from all citizens and then direct some significant proportion of the conscripted time and energy to "helping" activities—working in hospitals, caring for the aged, and so on. There is no such thing, obviously, as a conscripted volunteer (though individual conscripts might choose the particular service they performed). But conscription would introduce large numbers of amateurs to the work of distributing welfare, thus radically shifting the proportion of citizen helpers to professional helpers, just as military conscription shifts the proportion of citizen soldiers to professional soldiers. Nor would national service succeed in the absence of some degree of philanthropic feeling, any more than military conscription could succeed (in a democratic society) if citizens were not, to some degree, patriots.[9]

National service would draw in the young, but another group, with more time if less energy, might play an even greater role in the delivery of services: the growing number of elderly and retired citizens. There seems to be no reason why they should not be helped to help one another or organized to look after infants and preschool children. The sorts of services they once "naturally" provided within the extended family now require alternative networks. State officials can probably play only a modest role in developing such networks; but insofar as they emerge, they might well be recognized within the state system—even subsidized in some small measure.

But if the measure is small, is not this sort of thing properly called exploitation? The question has arisen chiefly with regard to women, who have, over the years, constituted by far the majority of volunteers. Both

[8] Gilbert, *Capitalism and the Welfare State*, pp. 124–28.

[9] It has been suggested to me that jury duty may be a better analogy here than military conscription—since the service required might be intermittent rather than continuous, extending for weeks rather than years. Juries too, as Tocqueville argued long ago, depend upon (and also strengthen) civic sentiment.

the growing strength of the women's movement and the growing number of women in the work force help to explain the decline in volunteering. Why should some women do without pay what men (and, increasingly, other women) get paid to do? It is not likely, however, that any society can pay for all the helpfulness its members require. Nor is there any reason why it should. Helping others is a rewarding social activity, and the fact that some people make a career of it ought not bar other people—certainly, not on ideological grounds—from doing so. In the past, women have formed what we might think of as the reserve army of the welfare system.[10] It would be better, surely, to have a gender-free reserve. In a fully developed welfare society, many more citizens would be ready to help, would actually be involved in helping. They would help and be helped; helping would not be exploitative nor being helped degrading. Assuming a rough equality in other respects (most important, in opportunities for work), I do not see that it would matter much if a majority of the volunteers were women, any more than it would matter much if a majority of welfare professionals were women. These would just be interesting facts, reflecting customary behaviors slow to change, or a differential interest in nurturance, or (in the case of older volunteers) female longevity.

I have focused first on the delivery of welfare, the everyday work of distribution, in part because of the failures of "maximum feasible participation" in the welfare programs of the 1960s. The War on Poverty was indeed an effort, the most recent effort, to socialize the welfare state. But this was a socialization focused almost exclusively on decision making. Behind it lay a conception taken, perhaps unconsciously, from the literature on workers' control. Robert Kennedy made the argument as clearly as anyone in those years when he said of welfare bureaucrats in relation to their clients what socialist writers have often said of managers in relation to workers: "They plan programs for the poor, not with them. Part of the sense of helplessness and futility comes from the feeling of powerlessness to affect the operations of [the existing welfare agencies]." What was necessary was "the involvement of the poor in planning and implementing programs: giving them a real voice in their institutions."[11] But most of the arguments, and all of the failed experiments, had much more to do with planning than with implementing. The vitality of the institutions of the welfare state, Gunnar Myrdal insisted in the mid-1960s, depended on popular participation in their management and direction.[12]

[10] There must be a good book on the character of this reserve army and the feelings of its members (the ideology—and also the reality—of service or sacrifice). What is it?

[11] Quoted in Daniel Moynihan, *Maximum Feasible Misunderstanding: Community Action in the War on Poverty* (New York: Free Press, 1969), pp. 90–91.

[12] Myrdal, *Beyond the Welfare State* (New York: Bantam, 1967), pp. 43–48.

The problem was that there were no significant cadres of welfare recipients trained for the tasks of managing and directing.

So the War on Poverty turned, very often, into a different sort of war: one between radicalized professionals and middle-class organizers (joined by some local militants), on the one hand, and established professionals and lower-middle-class politicians, on the other. For neither group was it really feasible to maximize participation, though the politicians could probably have turned out more of the "people" if they were pressed. "It may be," writes Daniel Moynihan about these wars, "that the poor are never 'ready' to assume power in an advanced society: the exercise of power in an effective manner is an ability acquired through apprenticeship and seasoning."[13] And apprenticeship and seasoning, Moynihan seems to think, are acquired only through professional training and political office.

He may be right, but it seems to me at least possible that participation in the delivery of services might constitute a kind of training for participation in the management and direction of services. The War on Poverty might have fared better had there existed greater numbers of poor people with some experience of giving as well as taking. But the experience of giving, outside the family, in the wider world of hospital auxiliaries, parent-teacher associations, church-run hostels and sanctuaries, and so on, is a characteristically middle-class experience. The poor (so we are told) have no time or, once their work is done, no energy. In fact, of course, poor people have both time and energy, or else there would never have been any political protest or union organizing, or friendly societies, or radical movements. All these are the work of volunteers—some of whom, at least, are recruited from the poor. The poor could be similarly recruited today for the work of mutual help, drawn into a range of distributive activities, so that they would begin to acquire some knowledge of the social economy of welfare to supplement the knowledge they already have of their private economies—both straitened, though in different ways. Then it might be more feasible to think about maximizing participation in decision making.

But it is wrong to describe the agencies of socialized distribution as if they "belonged" to the poor (were "their institutions," as Kennedy said). Just as socialized factories belong not only to the workers but also to the people who consume their products, so welfare agencies belong not only to their consumers but also to the people who produce what is consumed. This is to say, again, that socialization balances rather than replaces nationalization. When it deals with the productive sector, the state must represent consumers; when it deals with the distributive sector, the state

[13] Moynihan, *Maximum Feasible Misunderstanding*, pp. 136–37.

must represent producers (taxpayers). In both cases, of course, it claims universality, but its officials speak first of all for those who are not present at the point of production or at the point of reception. That is why those who are present at the point have some claim to direct representation, to a "real voice" in decision making. But they have no claim to a sole voice.

The problem is to get the balance right. It makes sense, for example, to create a local governing board for a local welfare project (as in the War on Poverty programs), but it makes no sense to think that the governing board can replace the local government.[14] The two must work together; perhaps the government must be represented on the board. "Seasoned" officials alongside the unseasoned poor? All the more reason to make sure that poor people experience something other than their own poverty.

A Transformation in the Relations of Distribution

The productive sector now absorbs a declining proportion of the work force—and will continue to do so unless (more likely, even if) we find new ways of dividing and sharing work. A growing proportion of men and women is involved instead in providing, delivering, organizing, and distributing human services. Many of these people are publicly employed; that is, they are civil servants of the welfare state: schoolteachers, social workers, caretakers and administrators of many different sorts—and, in Europe today, doctors and nurses. These are the agents of nationalized distribution, and their number is steadily growing. We might think of them as professional "helpers." Their aim is not the production of commodities but the enhancement of human life. It is sometimes said, however, that they have a prior aim, namely, control of the society whose members they help. They seek the enhancement of their own lives as professional helpers, and so have an interest in the helplessness of all the rest of us. The latter is not likely to be an entirely conscious or widely acknowledged aim, but it undoubtedly does explain some of what they do.

What they do, though, they do not do by themselves; they have no monopoly on helping. They are both anticipated and seconded by private or nonprofit associations of many different kinds. The welfare state coexists with the welfare society, but the society today is relatively weak compared with the state. Extended families, friendly societies, churches, and fraternal organizations have lost their primacy in welfare provision, and no new groups have appeared to balance the triumphant civil service. The state is active—once again, for good reasons—and citizens are in-

[14] Moynihan is very good on this point; see ibid., esp. pp. 182–83.

creasingly passive (or active only in demanding state action). Hence the need, and the recurrent efforts, to socialize state action itself.

Distribution and not production will, I think, be the first field of human activity to be socialized. Since most people will not be content with a world in which they are helpless (even if they are, intermittently, helped), they will continue to find ways to help themselves and one another. The purpose of socialization is to provide new ways—a multitude of networks and institutions for mutual aid. This requires experiments in local democracy; it also requires an effort to extend the reach of voluntary organizations. At the same time, it requires a state strong enough to superintend and subsidize the work of citizens and volunteers. The greater the number of these citizens and volunteers, the more work they will do as part-time and amateur distributors of goods and services, and the more likely it is that the professional helpers will really be helpful. A lively and supportive welfare society framed, but not controlled, by a strong welfare state would represent, to return for the last time to my analogy, a fundamental transformation in the relations of distribution.

2

The Moral Basis of the Democratic Welfare State

J. DONALD MOON

The welfare state is often interpreted as a kind of compromise—of liberal and socialist principles, or of bourgeois (or middle-class) and working-class interests. If not exactly a hodgepodge, it is said to incorporate contradictory elements that its critics hope, and its friends fear, will soon or at least eventually fly apart. Some see it as a corruption of genuine liberal principles, and bemoan the failure of the "New Right" to undo the last century of social policy. For others, the welfare state is a strategic response to the dislocations of capitalism, temporarily enabling a repressive and irrational form of society to stave off fundamental change by blunting the edge of social conflict. For both, the democratic welfare state fails to meet the critical standards of their theory, and so it is judged not to have a moral basis.

Even the friends of the welfare state seem perplexed by its complexity, and offer accounts of its fundamental aims that ignore some of its most characteristic practices and institutions. In this paper I examine two such accounts, one offered by Raymond Plant and based on the idea of rights, the other offered by Ronald Dworkin and based on the idea of equality. Although welfare rights are an important aspect of the welfare state, accounts centering on them cannot explain why so many social services are provided through some kind of "insurance" scheme that includes identifiable contributions on the part of recipients. On the other hand, it is implausible to view equality as the principal objective of the welfare state, for one of the characteristic features of welfare-state programs is universality of coverage or participation. In most welfare states, unemployment benefits, pensions, education, and medical care are provided to everyone, the prosperous as well as the poor. This significantly limits the redistributive potential of these programs.

I would like to thank Brian Fay, Amy Gutmann, Jane Mansbridge, Nancy Schwartz, and Kerry Whiteside for their very helpful comments on an earlier version of this paper.

What is missing from these accounts, it seems to me, is sufficient attention to the "self-understandings" of the citizens of welfare states—to the ways in which social and political practices appear to participants in them, and the ways in which these practices express ideals and principles that give point and meaning to their lives. In particular, both neglect the value of self-respect and ignore the norms that specify what one has to be and to do to attain self-respect. Other accounts suffer similar weaknesses.

In contrast to approaches that focus on rights or equality, I will argue that we can best begin to understand the democratic welfare state as an attempt to solve a serious moral dilemma that necessarily results from the central role of markets in modern society. Because Hegel was one of the first to perceive and to diagnose this dilemma, I will begin by reviewing his formulation of it, and the failure of his proposed solutions.

The Moral Dilemma of the Market: Hegel's View

In *The Philosophy of Right* (1821), Hegel observed that the organization of economic life through the market appears necessarily to produce great poverty alongside great wealth. This poverty is a threat to the modern state—both materially in that it breeds discontent that can cause instability, and morally in that the institutions of civil society bring about undeserved and unjustifiable suffering. In Hegel's words,

> The poor still have the needs common to civil society, and yet since society has withdrawn from them the natural means of acquisition . . . and broken the bonds of the family . . . , their poverty leaves them more or less deprived of all the advantages of society, of the opportunity of acquiring skill or education of any kind, as well as of the administration of justice, the public health services, and often even of the consolations of religion.[1]

It is important to see that Hegel's dilemma involves a deep, moral contradiction, and not merely a practical problem. The justification for organizing economic life through the market is based upon a conception of the individual as an agent, capable of choice and deliberation, and entitled to certain rights and to be treated with respect. The individual must therefore be independent in the minimal sense that no private person may use the powers of another without the other's consent. More positively, there must be a fairly extensive sphere within which individuals are free to direct their energies and to use their powers to realize purposes they

[1] G.W.F. Hegel, *The Philosophy of Right*, trans. T. M. Knox (Oxford: Oxford University Press, 1952), para. 241.

have set for themselves. But this justification of the market is weakened if the normal operation of the market deprives some people—through no fault of their own—of the very means of survival, not to mention the possibility of maintaining their well-being and dignity. The significance of poverty, then, is not just the suffering it involves, though that is obviously important, but the fact that it represents an undeserved exile from society. It is the failure of libertarian arguments to recognize and come to terms with this fact that ultimately destroys their moral viability. There is something deeply and undeniably unjust about a social order that necessarily frustrates fulfillment of the promises it makes.

Unfortunately, as Hegel perceptively notes, the obvious remedy for this suffering—simply redistributing income or wealth to the poor—is not adequate. Hegel argues that since the principles of a market society are freedom and the exchange of equivalents, membership in civil society requires that one support oneself by selling one's labor power, or other assets one owns, in exchange for what one needs. Were the poor to receive support without giving anything in exchange, they would fail to observe the basic principles of civil society. Merely giving them money, therefore, would undermine their status or membership in civil society, and with that their dignity and self-respect.

As Avineri has pointed out, Hegel never solved the problem he posed.[2] Considering Hegel's rather remarkable ability to find formulas that "reconcile" apparent contradictions, or to find "meaning" in the most arbitrary and pointless practices, it is striking that he left this problem unresolved, offering only a few remarks about the need for the state to step in and regulate the market in such a way as to prevent the problem from getting out of hand.[3] But his suggestions, though they have frequently been acted upon—are hardly adequate. He proposes, for example, that the state should regulate the prices of essential commodities, which would make it possible for the poor to purchase them.[4] Such a policy is viable when temporary shortages occur, perhaps as a result of a war or natural calamity, at least for those states that have reasonably honest and competent administrations and whose citizens display a reasonable level of civic virtue. But it is not a solution for the fundamental dilemma of civil society. The policy of regulating some prices causes distortions in the market that will eventually undermine either the state or the market system, or (perhaps most commonly) both. Either the state will be forced to allocate directly more and more goods and services, thereby replacing

[2] Shlomo Avineri, *Hegel's Theory of the Modern State* (Cambridge: Cambridge University Press, 1972), chap. 7.

[3] See the discussion of police powers in Hegel, *The Philosophy of Right*, paras. 231–45.

[4] Ibid., para. 235.

the market, or black markets and other forms of evasion will develop, corrupting both the administration and the citizenry.

Hegel also suggested a system of "corporations," consisting of producer organizations in each industry or trade linking the state and civil society. The idea that many of the problems of capitalism can be solved through a system of mixed or quasi-public and private groups has had great appeal. Durkheim's vision of a just capitalist and democratic order is based upon an elaborate system of corporate groups; corporatist policies and practices are pervasive in Western Europe and, to a lesser extent, North America as well. But corporatist structures have not proven adequate to solve the problem of poverty, even when they have been given direct responsibilities for welfare. In Hegel's vision, corporations would maintain funds contributed by their members and would use them to support members in distress. Individuals who needed assistance could turn to their corporation. And they could do so without a loss of dignity because, having contributed to the fund, their receiving its benefits would not be a violation of reciprocity.[5]

But this system would work only if everyone were at least initially a member of some corporation, and if the burdens on any particular producer organization did not grow too large. In a dynamic economy, however—where some industries are in secular decline and where workers move from area to area and industry to industry—these assumptions do not hold, as Hegel himself realized.[6] Even under ideal circumstances, too many people needing help would find (and have found) the system of corporate groups inadequate to meet their needs. Since these needs cannot be met through private or quasi-public organizations, the state must take on the task of relieving the distress occasioned by the operation of the market. But we are still left with the question of how it can do so, consistent with the moral requirements of civil society itself. Is a morally coherent welfare state possible?[7]

Rights as the Moral Basis of the Welfare State: Plant's View

On the face of it, one of the most promising ways to think about the welfare state is to see it as based on an extension of the classical list of

[5] Ibid., para. 253.

[6] See, e.g., Remarks to para. 252 in ibid.

[7] Hegel offered other suggestions as well, notably colonization, private charities, and making the state the employer of last resort. But none of these is adequate to solve the problem he posed.

human rights to include "social" or "welfare" rights.[8] From this perspective, we can see the welfare state as an essentially internal development of the idea of human rights that is basic to the liberal tradition. Just as Locke asserted that a limited, constitutional state is necessary to protect our rights to life, liberty, health, and possessions, proponents of this view argue that the welfare state is required to guarantee a wider set of rights, including the "social" rights to employment, economic security, health care, and education.

This way of understanding the welfare state has been advocated not only because it provides a convenient link to a well-established tradition of political thought, but also because it is said to solve Hegel's problem. For if one has a right to certain services and benefits, then receiving those benefits should not, according to this view, be demeaning. As Plant has argued, if "the needy have a right to welfare, a right to have their needs satisfied, . . . [then] there is no reason in principle why [a] transfer made as a result of a claim to a right should embody stigma." Plant recognizes that recipients of welfare benefits may not realize that they have a right to the benefits in question and so may feel shame when they receive them, but he suggests that this would be "misplaced" because the "situation is one of equality. The recipient claims a right; the provider acknowledges an obligation to satisfy it." Thus, it might be concluded, if welfare rights can be counted among our fundamental rights as humans, then a legitimate state would have to be a welfare state, and receiving welfare benefits should no longer be a source of shame.[9]

There are many difficulties involved in developing a coherent account of human rights that would include a right to welfare, and Plant has attempted to answer them. He has argued that human needs constitute a satisfactory basis for a right to welfare;[10] that considerations of liberty, particularly the worth of liberty, and justice support such a right;[11] and that a positive right to welfare is not, at least in principle, conceptually or logically incompatible with our ordinary understanding of what is involved in possessing a right.[12]

Plant's often ingenious arguments go a long way to showing that a democratic polity can establish a right to welfare, and that there are good reasons for it to do so. Further, as I shall argue in this paper, Plant is

[8] Raymond Plant, "Welfare and the Value of Liberty," in *Government and Opposition* 20 (1985): 297–314.

[9] Raymond Plant, Harry Lesser, and Peter Taylor-Gooby, *Political Philosophy and Social Welfare* (London: Routledge and Kegan Paul, 1980), p. 23.

[10] Ibid.

[11] Plant, "Welfare and the Value of Liberty."

[12] Raymond Plant, "Needs, Agency, and Rights," in J. Donald Moon, ed., *Responsibility, Rights, and Welfare* (Boulder, Colo.: Westview Press, forthcoming).

correct in contending that welfare must be granted as a right—rather than as a matter of charity or at the discretion of state officials or private persons—if it is not to be stigmatizing. But the idea of a right to welfare is not sufficient to account for the moral basis of the welfare state.

The entire approach of analyzing the welfare state simply in terms of a human right to welfare is mistaken. Even if it could be shown that we have such rights, this approach would not solve the problem that Hegel diagnosed, because providing relief to those in need, even when they have a right to it, may nevertheless still cause them to lose status and self-respect. What is demeaning about receiving welfare is in part the invidious distinction that the receipt of welfare itself makes between those who receive it and those who do not. Even if one has a right to receive a benefit, if the need to exercise that right is a sign of failure, it will be stigmatizing to do so.

This is not to say that anyone who receives benefits will necessarily experience a loss of self-esteem. "Self-esteem" is a very broad concept; as used by social-psychologists, it means a "generally favorable or unfavorable, positive or negative, pro or con feeling toward [oneself] as a whole."[13] In this general sense, there are many bases on which one may come to consider oneself "a person of worth,"[14] including the favorable appraisals one receives from family and friends, comparisons of self with others, and attainments in areas one considers important. Since we have at least some freedom in selecting those against whom we might compare ourselves, and in selecting those values which we deem important, it is possible for some individuals to have high self-esteem, even if most people in the society hold them in little regard. For example, delinquents or criminals may take pride in qualities and activities which others condemn.

This very general concept of self-esteem is important, and has considerable relevance to an evaluation of the justice or desirability of a social and political order. But because it is so general, and because it can be affected in particular cases by so many idiosyncratic factors, it is necessary to focus on a more specific concept. Although the notion of self-respect is often used synonymously with self-esteem, in this paper I will use it in a narrower sense to refer to one's belief that one lives up to certain standards that define what it is to be a person of worth, a person entitled to respect. It is thus, for most people, a crucial component of self-esteem, but it expresses a specifically moral judgment of the self.

In using the concept of self-respect in this way, I am following Walzer, who has argued that self-respect is dependent upon one's measuring up

[13] Morris Rosenberg, *Conceiving the Self* (New York: Basic Books, 1979), p. 21.

[14] Ibid., p. 54.

to a standard.[15] It is a concept that is essentially tied to notions of worth and honor: to have self-respect is to have "proper regard for the dignity of one's person or one's position," where dignity is "the quality of being worthy or honourable."[16] Because self-respect requires that one hold and live up to standards, the concept invokes ideals of excellence and is expressed in the language of duties, rather than the language of rights. Thus, self-respect is an achievement, earned by living in a way that is worthy or honorable, not a good that one can have simply by virtue of being a person. As something to be achieved, self-respect cannot be guaranteed; it is always possible for a person to fail to measure up, and so to lose his or her self-respect.

Like the bases of self-esteem, the standards by which an individual assesses his or her moral worth are variable. Moreover, a person may come to have a sense of self-respect by selectively misperceiving one's qualities or misinterpreting the perceptions of others. But standards are at least implicit in the practices and institutions of any society; they define the kinds of character, actions, and attainments that are worthy or honorable, and specify the individuals who are subject to them. Standards are often part of the expectations of certain central or important social roles such as "mother" or "friend"; other standards are general, applying to nearly everyone irrespective of his or her particular roles.

For most people, living up to these standards is essential to their coming to have a sense of self-respect. Although there are some escape hatches, few can succeed in finding identities that do not incorporate many of these expectations into their own sense of what they must be. But even if some can escape from these social expectations, this possibility is not relevant to an account of the moral basis of the welfare state. For that purpose, we must suppose that the members of the society accept its fundamental norms and principles as valid or legitimate, and use them to define themselves and to orient their behavior. If the practices of a society are to be just, it must be possible for people to maintain their self-respect in terms of the standards implicit in these practices.

There are, it goes without saying, many standards or norms to which people must measure up if they are to achieve self-respect. Among these standards in American society is "independence," which requires at least able, working-age men to provide for their own needs and those of their family. That Americans have this expectation is a legacy of their past; it is not by any means a necessary feature of social organization as such. It is greatly affected by other institutions of American society, in particular, the family (and associated gender roles), and by the centrality of markets in

[15] Michael Walzer, *Spheres of Justice* (New York: Basic Books, 1983), p. 274.

[16] Definitions are from the *Oxford English Dictionary*.

economic life. This conception of independence both expresses and reflects social understandings of work, vocation, and other values. And the meaning of this standard changes with the changing context of practices and concepts in which it is embedded.

The expectation of independence is grounded in our understanding of ourselves as morally equal, autonomous agents, whose relationships are governed in part by a norm of reciprocity. In the context of civil society, dependence of one person on another violates the ideal of reciprocity. Often such dependence involves relationships of moral inequality, premised on the subordination of one person to another. But even when subordination is absent, the dependent person receives something without offering anything in return. As Hegel put it, for people to receive their subsistence from the state "directly, not by means of their work, . . . would violate the principle of civil society and the feeling of individual independence and self-respect in its individual members."[17] That is why the need to exercise one's right to welfare is, in American society, a sign of failure. It is certainly true that the way welfare is administered can worsen the stigma associated with receiving it; but as long as people are expected to support themselves, that stigma is inevitable.

Many of the discussions of self-respect in the field of contemporary political and moral theory neglect the fact that self-respect is something that must be achieved, and at least implicitly see it only as a matter of status and individual rights. For example, Sachs lists a number of ways in which a person's self-respect might be threatened—by having one's wishes arbitrarily disregarded, by having one's rights flouted, and by being used or degraded.[18] But if we think about how these situations threaten self-respect, we will see that they do not do so directly. One does not lose self-respect merely by having one's rights violated, but by failing to respond appropriately to such violations. It is not the improper treatment, but one's own acquiescence in it, that leads to a loss of *self*-respect. A person who has self-respect will demand to be treated with respect. To that extent, self-respect does involve questions of rights and status. But self-respect must be earned by asserting one's rights, by refusing to allow others to disregard, to use, or to degrade oneself.

In his penetrating discussion of the concept of self-respect, Walzer points out that, in our society today, to treat people with respect is to treat them as one's equal. The "democratic revolution" has created a single set of norms, where "the experience [of self-respect] is connected now to a sense of one's ability to shape and control the work (and the life) one

[17] Hegel, *The Philosophy of Right*, para. 245.

[18] David Sachs, "How to Distinguish Self-Respect from Self-Esteem," *Philosophy and Public Affairs* 10 (1981): 348.

shares with others." In a democracy, "there is one norm of proper regard for the entire population of citizens." Today, self-respect is a complex function of membership in a democratic society "and depends upon equal respect among the members."[19]

It is important not to misunderstand the role of equal respect and equal rights. Equal rights and equal respect have become necessary conditions of self-respect, but they are not sufficient. Self-respect is not a matter of having a certain status or enjoying particular rights. Rather, it requires that one perform certain duties or, better, live up to some ideal. One cannot achieve self-respect simply by having one's rightful claims recognized. Indeed, the opposite may be more nearly true: to be able to assert one's rights depends upon one's having self-respect, that is to say, feeling oneself to be worthy of exercising those rights. And that depends upon one's living up to the standards one holds. To have self-respect, we must be accorded the rights of citizens; to gain self-respect, we must perform the duties of citizens.

This poses a serious dilemma for a polity that aspires to be a welfare state. For if people hold the norm that they should be independent (in the sense of self-supporting), then how can the state provide them with the means of subsistence without violating their self-respect? Walzer describes the welfare state as an effort "to guarantee effective membership" in society, thus helping to make self-respect possible. But if self-respect requires that one satisfy one's own needs, and the needs of one's family, then how can the state meet these needs in a way that will not be degrading to the people for whom it provides benefits?

If the strategy of basing the welfare state on a general theory of human rights to welfare is inadequate, it at least points to an important truth: that the moral basis of the welfare state cannot be charity or altruism on the part of those more fortunate individuals whose taxes pay for its services. Of course, to the extent that people are altruistic, or believe themselves to have a duty of benevolence to advance the well-being of others, they will be motivated to contribute their resources to meet the needs of the disadvantaged. But, as David Miller has argued, the state may be an inappropriate instrumentality for the expression of altruism.[20] State provision is compulsory, and compulsion suggests a form of obligation that is incompatible with the idea of charity. Making charitable donations expresses one's altruistic sentiments, but paying taxes does not.

It is arguable that altruism can be squared with compulsion by viewing the problem of welfare as somehow involving public goods or, perhaps,

[19] Walzer, *Spheres of Justice*, pp. 277–78.

[20] David Miller, "Altruism and the Welfare State," in Moon, *Responsibility, Rights, and Welfare.*

high transaction costs, for voluntary efforts would then be insufficient to provide an adequate level of welfare provision.[21] But a more serious objection to seeing altruism as the basis of the welfare state is that it is difficult if not impossible to reconcile the self-respect of beneficiaries with the receipt of charity in a democratic society. In a hierarchical society, people who occupy lower-status positions might be able to receive charity from their "betters" without a loss of dignity. Their sense of self-respect depends upon their living up to the demands of their (inferior) station. The acknowledgment of inferiority need not, at least in principle, threaten one's self-respect, so long as there is no expectation of equality. But in a democracy, one may receive something gratuitously only in intimate relationships or relationships that involve a reciprocal exchange of gifts or services.

At best, then, altruism may help to explain the willingness of (some of) the advantaged to support welfare programs, but it cannot be the basis of the welfare state.[22] Thus, Plant is correct to argue that in providing services, the welfare state must be seen as recognizing the rights of its citizens. But the welfare state must do more than guarantee welfare rights if its citizens are to maintain self-respect.

Equality as the Moral Basis of the Welfare State: Dworkin's View

Dworkin offers an interpretation of the welfare state (which he identifies as the economic side of "liberalism") as based upon equality. For Dworkin, equality requires that "the resources devoted to each person's life should be equal," when their lives are considered as wholes.[23] This ideal should be distinguished from equality of welfare—which requires that everyone enjoy the same level of well-being—and from what we might call instantaneous equality, which requires that each person have access to the same (or the same level) of resources at every moment.

One problem in understanding, not to mention fulfilling, the ideal of devoting equal resources to each person's life is that resources are hetero-

[21] Ibid.

[22] Titmuss is frequently held to have advocated altruism as the basis of the welfare state, but this may be an exaggeration of his position. When he argued for the "gift relationship" as one appropriate model for social relationships in a good society, he certainly did not intend to replace uniform state provision of services by right with private charity. Rather, he was calling our attention to the ties of common citizenship, common vulnerability, and community, which—although far from relationships of personal intimacy—permit forms of mutual aid that transcend the strict reciprocity of discrete exchanges. See *The Gift Relationship* (New York: Random House, 1971).

[23] Ronald Dworkin, "What Is Equality? Part 2: Equality of Resources," *Philosophy and Public Affairs* 10 (1981): 289, 306.

geneous. Ackerman tries to evade this issue by imagining a world in which there is a single resource, "manna," that can be transformed into usable objects, but this device is manifestly unsatisfactory.[24] An important virtue of Dworkin's work is that he faces this issue squarely and tries to develop a metric that can be used to compare the value of different resources, so that we can determine whether any two persons' bundles of resources are equal. Dworkin's proposed measure is the set of prices that would be reached in an idealized market. He imagines an auction in which people with equal amounts of money bid for the resources that are actually available to them. The prices that these resources would command provide the required measure of their value: "Equality of resources supposes that the resources devoted to each person's life should be equal. That goal needs a metric. The auction proposes . . . that the true measure of the social resources devoted to the life of one person is fixed by asking how important, in fact, that resource is for others."[25] We know that the bundles of resources that people would purchase under these circumstances would be equal because this distribution would pass what Dworkin revealingly calls the "envy test." He explains that "no division of resources is an equal division if, once the division is complete, any[one] would prefer someone else's bundle of resources to his own bundle."[26]

This model is adequate only for a world in which a single decision is made to divide up existing resources among various individuals. No account is taken of the fact that resources must be transformed into usable goods, and that resources are themselves reproduced and new resources created through work. To extend this model to a world of production, we have to consider such things as risk and differences in people's willingness to bear it, differences in the quality of and type of work performed, different choices between work and leisure, and differences in people's skills and talents. If equal resources are to be devoted to different people's lives, then individuals may come to have very different bundles of goods because they make different choices regarding risk, work, and leisure.

Suppose that, after an initial auction, Smith works hard producing widgets, and is able to accumulate a great deal of money, which he exchanges for other goods. Jones, meanwhile, takes things easy and has less wealth as a result. Assuming that Smith and Jones had the same basic talents and skills, Jones cannot complain that he has been shortchanged, because his bundle includes more leisure than Smith's. The additional material goods that Smith enjoys are a measure of the social value of the time that Jones spent in leisure. By choosing not to work as much as Smith,

[24] Bruce A. Ackerman, *Social Justice and the Liberal State* (New Haven, Conn.: Yale University Press, 1980).

[25] Dworkin, "What Is Equality?" p. 289.

[26] Ibid., p. 285.

Jones showed that he did not value additional material goods as much as he valued additional leisure. The social resources devoted to each person's life are equal because the value of the time Jones spent in leisure equals the value of the material goods Smith acquired through working.

A similar argument can be made regarding risk and the quality of work that is performed. People who are willing to take greater risks or perform more onerous tasks are properly rewarded with higher incomes. As Dworkin puts it, "equality of resources requires that people pay the true cost of the lives they lead." Therefore, people who want lives of greater leisure, more security, or more pleasant working conditions have to settle for less of the other resources available to society.[27]

Up to this point the argument has rested upon the assumption that everyone has equal talents and skills, for it is only this assumption that allows us to trace the different outcomes just discussed to individuals making different choices, rather than to their having faced different alternatives. But when this assumption is not made, the concept of equality of resources becomes more complex. Dworkin invites us to think of natural aptitudes as resources (and skills as derivative from natural aptitudes), which leads to the conclusion that natural aptitudes—or the benefits deriving from them—should be distributed as equally as possible. This way of viewing natural aptitudes is based on a "distinction between those beliefs and attitudes that define what a successful life would be like, which the ideal [of equality of resources] assigns to the person, and those features of body or mind or personality that provide means or impediments to that success, which the ideal assigns to the person's circumstances." Thus, equalizing the circumstances of different people requires that something be done to compensate for natural inequalities.[28]

Since we cannot transfer these aptitudes among individuals,[29] we must discover a different way to achieve equality of resources. One possibility would be to buy and sell the use of people's bodies and skills in the same way that we would auction other resources. However, this could have the unfortunate effect of making the talented worse off than others, because talented people might have to pay so much money to secure control over their own bodies that they would be condemned to working in those oc-

[27] Ibid., p. 295.

[28] Ibid., p. 303.

[29] Given Dworkin's general argument, it would appear that such transfers would be required if the technology were available, but Dworkin rules this out: Human powers "are not . . . resources for the theory of equality in exactly the sense in which ordinary material resources are. They cannot be manipulated or transferred, even so far as technology might permit" (p. 301). Dworkin does not explain why such transfers are not permitted. But perhaps we can take this as a recognition that a person's bodily and mental powers cannot be considered part of the person's circumstances, but rather are essential aspects of that person.

cupations for which they had the special talents that enabled them to earn high incomes, even if they were not interested in doing so. Thus, they might come to envy the "bundles" available to the untalented, and so Dworkin rejects this solution.

Unfortunately, there is no perfect or even adequate solution to this problem. This theory requires that we allow (possibly quite significant) inequalities among people based upon their choices regarding leisure, risk, and the unpleasantness of different tasks, but that we eliminate all inequalities based upon differences in genetic luck. To do this Dworkin proposes a progressive income tax coupled with redistribution in the form of transfer payments to those with low incomes. The actual rates of taxation and redistribution would be set by means of a simulated insurance scheme, designed to model the choices people would make if they did not know what their own talents would enable them to earn, and wished to insure against falling below a certain level of income. Although this scheme would not, of course, equalize people's talents, its aim would be "to put [the less talented] in the position they would have been in had the risk of their fate been subjectively equally shared." The less talented would receive transfer payments that would bring their income up to the level that the average member of the society would not wish his or her income to fall below. And everyone would be willing to insure against that possibility by offering some part of his or her expected income as an insurance premium.[30]

This is an ingenious way of interpreting and defending the welfare state, or at least two of its central policies—progressive income taxation and transfer payments to those in need. But it is not an adequate account for several reasons. In the first place, the tax-transfer scheme simply is not a solution to the problem that Dworkin himself poses. Although it would somewhat equalize income differentials due to differences in talent, it would at the same time equalize income differentials due to differences in the willingness to bear risk, ambition, and the unpleasantness of tasks.[31]

[30] Dworkin, "What Is Equality?" p. 329.

[31] In this discussion I have focused principally on the reasoning Dworkin uses in explicating his notion of equality of resources. I have neglected one important question, which is whether his proposal would, if implemented, result in significant equalization of incomes. A committed egalitarian might well read Dworkin's essay as a justification for maintaining significant disparities of income—but one that tries to undercut the egalitarian position by offering a putatively egalitarian defense of these disparities. Dworkin does insist upon the desirability of disparities, and criticizes the "dogma" that egalitarianism requires strict equality in the command of material resources. Moreover, by giving pride of place to the market as a means of registering and reflecting individual choices, and by implicitly accepting some form of private property, Dworkin creates a context in which inequalities will inevitably occur, thereby posing the problem as one of *re*distribution. Arguably, this way of framing the problem makes the achievement of equality problematic. Finally, and perhaps

For when the hypothetical insurance scheme that is to be used to determine the extent of redistribution is set up, the income distribution that is used as a baseline will reflect all these factors, not merely differences in natural aptitude. A progressive income tax may be superior to schemes of flat equalization because it allows some scope for different choices regarding risk, leisure, and the amenities of the working environment, but it fails to achieve the goals Dworkin sets.

A more important shortcoming of this argument, however, is that it misunderstands the point of the progressive tax-transfer policy of the welfare state.[32] Although tax-transfer policies lead to a degree of equalization (essentially as a result of transfers), this is more a means to achieve other goals, particularly dignity and self-respect, than an end in itself. Dworkin is aware of this, for he sees equality as necessary to someone's having a "proper sense of his own independence and equal worth."[33] Indeed, he is eloquent in his criticisms of the "New Right's" economic and social policies, which appear to sacrifice the interests of the most impoverished and powerless, supposedly in order to enhance the well-being of others, including future generations. And he quite properly ties these criticisms to the question of active or meaningful membership in society. Only those citizens can properly be asked to make a sacrifice to the common good who are full participants in the community whose good requires that sacrifice.[34] Where Dworkin's argument goes wrong is in equating equality of resources, as he articulates it, with the concept of equality underlying the values of self-respect, equal dignity, and equal worth.

If it were true that persons could be distinguished from their circumstances in the way that Dworkin recommends—that is, if one could see oneself as identical with, or in some sense constituted by, one's values and attitudes, and one's body and faculties merely as part of one's circumstances—then equality might require equal shares of natural talents, or at

most important, by limiting redistribution in accordance with the choices people would make in a simulated insurance market, he offers a standard that is very indeterminate. In view of the low levels of disability insurance that people currently purchase (when they know what their place in the income order is), it is plausible to argue that most welfare systems in the West already realize the degree of redistribution that Dworkin's proposal would endorse.

[32] Strictly speaking, Dworkin offers his argument as an interpretation of the economic aspects of liberal policies, not as an interpretation of the welfare state. But since in the period that Dworkin mentions—1930s through 1960s—these policies resulted in the creation of the welfare state in America, such as it is, I do not think my more general interpretation does him an injustice.

[33] Ronald Dworkin, *A Matter of Principle* (Cambridge, Mass.: Harvard University Press, 1985), p. 211.

[34] Ibid., pp. 208–13.

least the redistribution of their benefits.[35] But that is not how we see ourselves, and it is hard to imagine how we could ever attain self-respect and a sense of equal worth if we did. If I were to identify myself solely with my will, and if my ability to make my will effectual were less than yours, then it is reasonable to suppose that I would see myself as less worthy than you. Under these circumstances, it is hard to see how I could be content with less power than you, for to the extent that one has less power than others, one is impotent and insubstantial. A world in which people did not identify their powers as part of themselves would be a world suffused with envy.

Happily, this is not our world. We do not distinguish between the person and his or her circumstances in the way that Dworkin suggests. Indeed, we do not draw a rigid line at all; sometimes we impute characteristics to the person that at other times we impute to the person's circumstances. In some contexts we identify ourselves through our relationships with others, which may extend over significant distances in time and space. But in almost all contexts we understand ourselves as essentially embodied beings. Systematically to assign "features of [one's] body or mind or personality" to one's circumstances, as opposed to one's person, would be for us a kind of madness. If we are to attain self-respect and a sense of equal worth, and if we are to live lives that are relatively free of envy, we must be able to do so in the face of significant differences and even inequalities among us. Ultimately, then, it is the extreme narrowness of Dworkin's conception of the person that causes him to miss essential features of the democratic welfare state.

The Welfare State: Ideals and Institutions

I began this paper by suggesting that the starting point of any attempt to understand the democratic welfare state should be to see it as an attempt to solve what I called "Hegel's dilemma." The welfare state must overcome poverty, which involves a kind of moral exile from society, and which results from the normal operation of the market, but it must do so in a way that is compatible with the self-respect of its beneficiaries. In the preceding two sections I argued that two alternate approaches to the welfare state—one focusing on a human right to welfare, and the other focusing on equality of resources—are inadequate. Both fail to grasp the importance of self-respect in a society where people are expected to pro-

[35] I say "might require," because it would depend upon the actual values and attitudes of the community. If, for example, the good life were considered to be a matter of the right order of the soul, of making oneself a fit vessel of the divine spirit, then equality of material circumstances might appear to be unimportant, if not actually an impediment.

vide for themselves, and where citizens demand equality not as disembodied wills, but as full persons whose claim to equality transcends otherwise important differences in their natural aptitudes and capacities. In this section I will show how the welfare state attempts to solve Hegel's dilemma by establishing certain institutions and policies, which generally conform to three "institutional principles" of the welfare state: economic management, the universal provision of services, and social insurance. But before doing that, it is necessary to explicate the ideal of moral equality, or equal citizenship, which is fundamental to the democratic welfare state.

Shortly after World War II, T. H. Marshall argued that the welfare state must be seen as part of, or as the current stage in, a long struggle for equal citizenship.[36] Modern, liberal society is distinctive in part because it is based upon the premise of moral equality, that is, that no person is inherently superior, simply as a person, to any other, and thus entitled to differential rights and privileges. By nature, as Locke put it, "all power and jurisdiction is reciprocal, no one having more than another."[37] Basic human equality requires full membership in the community—or citizenship—for all.

In Marshall's account, equal citizenship can be understood in terms of three sorts of rights: civil and legal rights, political rights, and the "social rights of citizenship." He argues that the achievement of these rights took place in three distinct stages. The first stage was the extension of civil rights to the entire population. This extension was, as Marshall argues, a corollary of the abolition of villeinage, as civil rights are simply the rights of free persons. Needless to say, the effective recognition of these rights for all is still on the political agenda, but the principle of equal civil rights was conceded long ago. The second stage was the extension of political rights. This was part of the struggle for democracy, in particular, the right to vote and to hold office. Although the struggle for political equality continues, the triumph of the principle of equal political rights was in large measure the achievement of the nineteenth and early twentieth centuries.

The achievement of the social rights of citizenship constitutes the third stage in the quest for full citizenship for all. These are the rights that the welfare state seeks to guarantee, although some of them, such as the right to a publicly provided education, preceded the development of the welfare state. That these rights are different from most traditional civil rights and, to a lesser extent, political rights has long been recognized. In partic-

[36] T. H. Marshall, "Citizenship and Social Class," in *Class, Citizenship, and Social Development* (Chicago: University of Chicago Press, 1977).

[37] John Locke, *Two Treatises of Government*, ed. Peter Laslett (Cambridge: Cambridge University Press, 1970), chap. 2, sec. 4.

ular, they do not give rise to duties on the part of individuals generally, but on the part of political society as a whole. And these duties require the provision of specific services or goods. They cannot be discharged by refraining from interference with a protected sphere of individual action, as can many (though not all) of our civil and political rights.[38]

The basis of these rights is in part, but only in part, the need to make our other rights effective. Without the ability to perform certain activities, and without some basic level of economic security, the classical civil rights such as life, liberty, freedom of conscience, are deprived of at least part of their moral significance in a person's life. I say "at least part of" because it is a mistake to denigrate them by saying they are "merely formal," and to suggest that they are of no use or even "a burden to the vast mass of the exploited and oppressed in both the developed and undeveloped worlds."[39] These rights are of immense value even for those whose positions in society are relatively disadvantaged. These supposedly "merely formal" rights are essential expressions of the moral equality of persons. To see the speciousness of arguments that discount the value of "formal" equality, one need merely consider justifications of apartheid that point to the superior levels of material well-being enjoyed by blacks in South Africa, as opposed to other African countries.

The other basis for these rights is the recognition of what Marshall calls the "equal social worth" of all members of the society. This is a notion that goes beyond the idea of making civil rights effective by providing the resources necessary to their exercise. In addition, it includes the ideal of enabling everyone to achieve full membership in the community, and to participate in what a particular society has come to regard as valued and worthwhile ways of living. It thus includes a concern with social integration, or social solidarity, with promoting enough commonality in the social experiences and ways of life of different sections of the society so that genuine equality of respect will be possible. Equal social worth is closely tied to the idea of self-respect for, as I argued earlier, equality of respect is a necessary condition for self-respect in a democracy.

The ideal of equal social worth requires that there be a "safety net," a minimum level of resources available to everyone, sufficient to enable them to maintain a place in society. This will involve some equalization of circumstances, as Dworkin argues. But even in principle, even as an ideal, it does not require that the only differences in peoples' material well-being be traceable to different choices made under identical circumstances—particularly when a person's "circumstances" are defined as in-

[38] For a comparison of traditional and "welfare" rights, see Plant, "Needs, Agency, and Rights."

[39] Anthony Arblaster, "Liberal Values and Socialist Values," in Ralph Miliband and John Sevile, eds., *The Socialist Register* (London: Merlin Press, 1972), p. 98.

cluding the person's body and natural aptitudes. Rather, this ideal anticipates a society in which the bonds of fellowship and mutual respect are as significant as the inevitable differences and inequalities that will remain. As Tawney put it,

> What is repulsive is not that one man should earn more than others, for where community of environment, and a common education and habit of life, have bred a common tradition of respect and consideration, these details of the counting house are forgotten or ignored. It is that some classes should be excluded from the heritage of civilization which others enjoy, and that the fact of human fellowship, which is ultimate and profound, should be obscured by economic contrasts, which are trivial and superficial. What is important is not that all men should receive the same pecuniary income. It is that the surplus resources of society should be so husbanded and applied that it is a matter of minor significance whether they receive it or not.[40]

The social rights of citizens and the principle of equal social worth are fundamental to the welfare state. To realize them without undermining self-respect, however, requires that the government manage the economy in an attempt to achieve full employment, ensure the universal provision of certain social services, and establish a program of social insurance to meet a wide range of needs and contingencies. Economic management, universal provision, and social insurance may be thought of as a set of "institutional principles" governing the policies of the welfare state. These principles are expressed differently in different contexts, but in general they work to enable people to exercise the social rights of citizenship in a way that is compatible with maintaining their self-respect. Thus, they enable the welfare state to solve, at least to a significant extent, the dilemma Hegel posed.

The state's management of the economy includes implementing policies of economic stabilization to secure conditions of high, if not full, employment. Although this function is an obvious one, the ability to discharge it effectively has required a long and often painful process of social learning. Heclo has analyzed the growth of the welfare state in Britain and Sweden principally in terms of a process, which enabled policymakers to understand the causes of social distress and the kinds of policies that could be effective against it.[41]

Heclo describes two episodes of social learning that were important in the development of the welfare state. In the first, policymakers came to

[40] R. H. Tawney, *Equality* (New York: Barnes and Noble, 1964), p. 113.

[41] Hugh Heclo, *Modern Social Politics in Britain and Sweden* (New Haven, Conn.: Yale University Press, 1974).

understand the macroeconomic causes of unemployment, thereby dispelling the view that unemployment was always indicative of a lack of initiative or responsibility on the part of the individual. This knowledge made it possible to provide support for the unemployed through a quasi-insurance program, since it enabled people to see that unemployment was similar to other kinds of insurable risks. Unfortunately, government action, particularly in periods of high unemployment, continued to be limited by the prevailing orthodoxy, which militated against deficit spending even in recessions. According to Heclo, the way to a full-scale welfare state was opened by the second episode of social learning, in which the work of Keynes and others made it possible to understand the techniques of aggregate demand management. Achieving this understanding meant that government programs did not have to be sharply curtailed by budgetary constraints in periods of recession. Thus, the state was able to develop welfare programs that could provide continuity of services and that could be expanded in periods of acute distress. This achievement laid the basis for the post-war period of prosperity and the building of the welfare state, though the economic conditions of the 1970s suggest that governmental capacities in the area of economic management are still critically limited.[42]

To the extent that economic management is successful, most people will usually be able to provide their basic needs for themselves. But even if we could guarantee full employment all the time, there would still be important needs that would not be met. Even in the absence of cyclical changes in employment and in economic activity, in a dynamic economy jobs will continually disappear. Even if new ones are promptly created, the period of transition will involve hardships for workers and their families. Many will suffer from illness or disabilities that impair their capacity for work, and everyone faces the need to make provision for retirement and old age. There are also certain needs that must be satisfied if one is to be able to participate in the life of the community. An obvious need is education. Although education is, from a narrowly economic viewpoint, a form of capital investment whose returns accrue mainly to the person receiving it, it is so essential to citizenship that it is never entirely left to be provided by the market.

In responding to these contingencies and needs, the welfare state is guided by the principles of universal provision and social insurance. In some areas—education is the obvious example—public provision of a (nearly) universally consumed service enables everyone to receive the service without stigma. Consuming a universally provided service, like enjoying a universally accorded right, does not, enable a person to achieve

[42] Ibid., chap. 6.

self-respect, since these activities do not involve a performance or an achievement. At the same time, when a need can be met through some form of universal provision, such programs do not threaten the individual's self-respect.

In other areas, where it is necessary to respond to differential needs, the establishment of social insurance enables people to receive differential benefits without violating the idea of reciprocity, which is fundamental to their sense of themselves as moral equals. Two obvious examples are social security and unemployment compensation. Both of these systems are set up as insurance schemes, so that those who collect benefits under them see themselves as (and, to a large extent, are in fact) receiving something to which they have a right just because they have contributed their fair share to provision of those benefits.

The observance of these principles in providing public services may be older than the welfare state itself. What is distinctive about the welfare state is the generalization of services provided on the basis of these principles to cover a wide range of needs. And that generalization is essential if citizens are to protect themselves against the contingencies of illness, disability, old age, and unemployment in a way that enables them to maintain their membership in society and their self-respect.

Economic management, the universal provision of certain services, and social insurance have enabled us to make considerable progress in overcoming the moral breach in civil society that Hegel pointed to. Many of the risks that caused some to lose their effective membership in society have been significantly socialized and their effects ameliorated—particularly the risks of adult unemployment, disability, and old age. Educational opportunities have been significantly broadened, and public education continues to represent a major area of shared social experience for Americans. In spite of the efforts of the Reagan administration to reduce public spending for social services, these programs of the welfare state continue to command strong support.

Continuing Dilemmas

Yet there continues to be poverty in the United States. To be sure, the problem is not as serious or extensive as it is often taken to be. The proportion of the population in poverty between 1966 and 1981 has varied between 12 and 15 percent, as officially measured by the Census Bureau, but this figure disguises a considerable amount of mobility between the "poor" and "nonpoor" strata of the population from year to year. A much smaller proportion of the population remains in poverty from year to year. According to one study, only 2.6 percent of the population could be classified as "persistently poor," but over 20 percent of the population experienced some period of poverty between 1968 and 1977.[43] Thus, we can say that the income maintenance system works well for a great many people who face temporary crises, enabling them to meet at least very basic needs until they can reestablish themselves.

Nonetheless, the continued existence of poverty raises the obvious question of whether the welfare state can in principle realize its own ideals—at a minimum, overcome "Hegel's dilemma." The fact that this has not yet happened in America does not, of course, show that it cannot happen; it may merely point to the need to expand the welfare state. But would such an expansion be sufficient? Are there, perhaps, inherent limits to the welfare state that prevent it, even in principle, from fulfilling its own promise?

I see two difficulties that appear to pose severe limits to the welfare state's capacity to meet its own goals. The first is the problem of achieving full employment; the second is what I shall call the problem of selectivity vs. universality.

Given the importance I have attached to the achievement of self-respect through work, the first problem is critical. The committment to full employment, stated in the 1946 Full Employment Act, has been weakened by a growing skepticism that the government can achieve full employment without creating serious threats to long-term growth and stability, particularly inflation. The inability to maintain full employment would not be so serious if it meant only that the length of time between jobs was somewhat greater than it otherwise would be. Unfortunately, in times of high unemployment, those workers whose skills and other characteristics make them less desirable to employers may be unable to find work for very long periods. Thus, they often become discouraged and drop out of the work force. The efforts to address this problem by establishing training and work experience programs have not met with uniform success, to say the least. Although there is room for further social experimentation in this area, it is certainly possible that the practical obstacles to achieving full employment through the normal labor market are insurmountable.

In the face of these difficulties, some have proposed an alternative approach: to establish a right to work and make the government the employer of last resort. People who could not find a job in the regular labor market could, under this proposal, be given employment by the state. Lester Thurow has even proposed using a guaranteed jobs program to achieve other goals as well, such as narrowing the wage gap, especially that between men and women and between highly skilled and less skilled

[43] Greg J. Duncan, *Years of Poverty, Years of Plenty* (Ann Arbor: Institute for Social Research, University of Michigan, 1984).

workers.[44] Less ambitious programs of job creation have been tried in both western Europe and the United States, and experiments have been conducted with various kinds of supported work programs.

There are serious practical obstacles to implementing these programs, especially when it comes to reaching the least advantaged groups who suffer the most from undesirable jobs and lack of job opportunities. But the most serious problem with job-creation programs is that they are self-defeating. If the point of providing people with jobs is to enable them to maintain their self-respect, then the jobs must be productive in the sense that they must produce goods and services that people wish to consume, either individually or collectively, and consumers must be prepared to pay enough to cover the costs of providing these goods and services. There is certainly scope for government action to create productive jobs that would not otherwise exist because of various institutional rigidities, or because they produce public goods that must be collectively provided. But if a job were genuinely productive, there would be no need to create it as part of a guaranteed jobs program. Because those programs provide work that is not productive, they violate the principle of reciprocity, and so fail to provide an adequate means for people to maintain their self-respect. (This issue is taken up more fully by Jon Elster in Chapter 3.)

The second inherent limit on the welfare state that I wish to address is the problem of selectivity vs. universality. I have stressed the importance of universal provision as a means of providing services to people in a way that is consistent with maintaining self-respect. I have also pointed out that the principles of social insurance and universal provision have not been extended far enough to eliminate poverty. In providing a floor under incomes, we rely largely upon selective programs in which eligibility is determined by means-testing, rather than the principles of universality and social insurance.

The problem of selectivity vs. universality reflects important structural issues facing any welfare system. One way to maintain a floor under incomes through universal provision would be to use a scheme such as a guaranteed annual income program, which could be administered through the income tax system. Everyone would be granted a certain minimum amount, which would then be added to their other sources of income and each person's total income taxed. People without other sources of income would have the minimum grant; those with other income would finance the program through their taxes.

Schemes like this have been strongly advocated for a long time, and have found champions on both the right and left. But, in general, they have not been politically popular—as George McGovern discovered to his dismay when he proposed such a program during his unsuccessful bid

[44] Lester Thurow, *The Zero-Sum Society* (New York: Penguin Books, 1981), pp. 203–7.

for the presidency in 1972. Rather than consolidating a variety of income maintenance programs in one such scheme, citizens and elected leaders have opted for a variety of programs, geared to different needs, and covering different sectors of the population. There are several reasons for this preference, quite apart from the fact that some needs, such as medical care, do not lend themselves to a pure income-transfer approach. From the perspective taken here, such schemes lack the moral appeal of a contributory program, such as Social Security, in which those who collect benefits earn them as a result of their contributions (or the contributions of members of their family). Although technically universal, a guaranteed annual income program is in fact a straight transfer program. In contrast to Social Security, only the relatively poor receive benefits under this program; those who are better off will, of course, find their taxes increased, perhaps considerably. Furthermore, many who are not poor, but who take pride in their ability to support themselves, receive transfers under such a program. Although this may be in their material interests, many resent it as a blow to their self-respect.

These schemes are also expensive—much more so than their originators had anticipated. The expenses are of two types: the effect on work incentives, and the costs of providing grants to those whose incomes are well above the income floor. The costs of income maintenance programs is an issue that has aroused widespread controversy. The majority of investigators, however, using data either from income maintenance experiments or from other studies of household behavior, have found that work effort would be significantly reduced in response to a guaranteed income.[45] In summarizing many of these findings, Aaron estimates that "for every $100 provided to male-headed families, earnings would fall $25 to $50." Aaron also points out that the effect of a guaranteed income appears to be even greater for female heads of household, wives, and single adults.[46]

What this means is that providing a guaranteed income to everyone reduces the overall size of the economic pie from which this minimum is to be provided. Of every dollar that is provided in this way, 25 to 50 cents goes to replace a dollar that the recipients would otherwise have earned themselves. In a culture that places a high value on people providing for themselves, this is not an insignificant cost, either economically or morally.

[45] See, for example, the excellent survey by Frank Stafford, "Income Maintenance Policy and Work Effort: Learning from Experiments and Labor Market Studies," in Jerry Hausman and David Wise, eds., *Social Experimentation* (Chicago: University of Chicago Press, 1985).

[46] Henry J. Aaron, "Six Welfare Questions Still Searching for Answers," *Brookings Review* 3 (Fall 1984): 13.

Nonetheless, those committed to the value of equal social worth, and aware of the kinds of jobs that people on the edge of poverty must take, might be willing to pay the costs indirectly resulting from the adverse work incentives of a guaranteed minimum. But the second set of costs—the costs of providing cash assistance to people whose income is well over the minimum—is even more significant.

If the major purpose of such assistance is to lift people out of poverty, then programs such as a guaranteed annual income or negative income tax will result in what Levitan and Taggart call low "target efficiency."[47] This is because most of the money that these programs require will be spent on people whose income is above the floor. In a world of limited resources, this may mean that we will be using social resources to meet less urgent needs. Reliance upon universality would have the effect of condemning many people to much lower levels of well-being than would be the case under a selective program that concentrated help on those most in need. Significantly, the minimum that was proposed in the ill-fated "family assistance program" in the early 1970s was well below the poverty level, which itself may be below the level necessary to attain the objectives of the welfare state.

The problem of selectivity vs. universality also arises in programs that directly provide social services, as opposed to those providing income that recipients can use in whatever way they wish. The welfare state provides services in a host of areas—including education, medical care, job training, family planning, mental health, housing, and transportation—all of which can be considered forms of social consumption. Ideally, social consumption should provide benefits that are not stigmatizing to recipients. When universally provided, they should have the additional advantage of creating areas of shared social experience, and so heighten the sense of social integration. Because the costs of these services are disproportionately borne by higher-income groups (even when taxes are somewhat regressive, as state and local taxes for education often are), collective consumption should result in some equalization of the distribution of life chances. Unfortunately, these positive effects are not always achieved in practice.

A significant problem with programs designed to provide universal services is that those most in need are often least able to take advantage of them. As Gilbert has argued, "although in theory universalism facilitates social integration of all classes, in practice the poor are often relegated to inferior services or wind up at the end of the line."[48] What Gil-

[47] Sar A. Levitan and Robert Taggart, *The Promise of Greatness* (Cambridge, Mass.: Harvard University Press, 1976), pp. 258–60.

[48] Neil Gilbert, *Capitalism and the Welfare State* (New Haven, Conn.: Yale University Press, 1983), p. 71.

bert calls the "contradictions of universalism" result from a simple model of service provision and consumption. On the consumption side, Gilbert notes that middle-class clients are more likely than lower-class clients to obtain knowledge about available services and to gain the attention of service providers. On the service side, providers will serve "less troublesome" (and therefore generally middle-class) clients before "more troublesome" clients; they will service those who can pay before those who cannot, and higher-status clients before lower-status clients.[49] These results have also been observed by other investigators; for example, LeGrand has found a similar pattern in the provision of health care, education, housing, and transport in Britain.[50] This pattern has also been found in "manpower" training programs, which often are directed to the people who are already most likely to succeed, rather than those whose lack of skills and motivation means that their "needs" may be greater.

Thus, there is good reason to believe that the welfare state cannot fully solve the dilemma that Hegel posed. Although we can, undoubtedly, do better than we have done, there appear to be inherent limits to the ability of the welfare state to alleviate poverty. Ideally, we should guarantee jobs for all who are willing to work, but both practical and conceptual difficulties stand in the way. Further, the "contradictions of universalism" limit the capacity of the state to reach those most in need of welfare services.

Conclusion

The perspective from which I have been examining the democratic welfare state has been an "internal" one. I have focused on how social and political practices appear to participants in them, and the ways in which these practices express ideals and principles that give point and meaning to their lives. I have not set out to find criteria that can be used to assess and rank alternative social structures considered as closed systems such as welfare capitalism, market socialism, and state socialism. Indeed, I have been critical of accounts of the welfare state that analyze it in terms of abstract conceptions of human rights or equality. The idea that the welfare state ought to realize a purported human right to welfare, or ensure equality of resources, neglects the critical role of self-respect in defining the problems that the welfare state faces, and in constraining the permissible solutions.

The adoption of an internal perspective has been criticized on the grounds that it is inherently conservative. Just because it is internal, it is

[49] Ibid., p. 70.

[50] See Julian LeGrand, *The Strategy of Equality* (London: Allen and Unwin, 1982).

said to bar radical criticism of a given set of practices and the principles that they (however imperfectly) embody. The internal perspective allows us to ask "how a concretely experienced form of life can be extended,"[51] by enabling us to criticize particular principles or practices in terms of other principles or values of a particular society. But because it does not offer a set of universal principles, it fails to provide a standpoint for radical change, for altering the fundamental principles of a society.

The discussion in the last section suggests how this criticism of the internal perspective might be refuted, as well as what might be done to mount a radical critique of the democratic welfare state. Although I have argued that the "institutional principles" of the welfare state enable it to go a long way in realizing the basic values of equal social worth, consistent with self-respect, I have also argued that there are internal limits to what it can accomplish. It does not seem to be possible to extend social insurance or universally provided services beyond a certain point. In part, that is a result of economic constraints; in part, it is a result of the "contradictions of universalism." The questions then become: How should we respond to these limits? Recognizing these limits, should we reject the legitimacy of the welfare state? Or, having seen the rose in the cross of the present, should we resign ourselves to the necessary imperfections of the human condition?

These are very large questions, which I cannot address here. But I would like to suggest that a rational response to them depends upon the view one takes of the alternatives to the welfare state. A critical issue is the importance attached to the use of markets in the organization of economic life. If we could organize the economy on some other basis—so that self-respect were no longer tied to work, or so that individuals could always find socially recognized and valued work, whatever their capacities or skills—then the central problem faced by the welfare state would disappear. And if this alternative form of organization could be achieved without sacrificing other, more precious values, then the adherence to an internal perspective would be no bar to radical criticism and revolutionary change.

A full vindication of the welfare state, then, requires a comparison with its alternatives. Only such a comparison can tell us how to respond to our recognition that there are limits to the ability of the welfare state to fulfill its promise. But the starting point for that comparison must be an explication of the underlying ideals of the welfare state, a task that can be performed only by taking an internal perspective.

[51] Bernard Williams, *Ethics and the Limits of Philosophy* (Cambridge, Mass.: Harvard University Press, 1985), p. 104.

3

Is There (or Should There Be) a Right to Work?

JON ELSTER

Unemployment is endemic in capitalism. So is the demand for a right to work, as a remedy for that state of affairs. Ever since the *droit au travail* was the battle cry of the workers in the French Revolution of 1848, the claim has tended to surface whenever unemployment levels have been high. In the last ten or fifteen years, in particular, the proposal to create a legal right to work has been put forward and discussed in most Western countries. Conversely, the existence of an effective right to work is widely perceived as the major argument for the centrally planned economies of Eastern Europe. If mass unemployment is the Achilles heel of capitalism, the right to a job is the backbone of socialism.

Unemployment is bad for those thrown out of work, who lose income and the nonpecuniary benefits of work. It is bad for society in general, because of the loss in production. It saps people's confidence in the economic system when, as often happens during a depression, idling plants and unemployed workers coexist. Solutions to these problems are essentially of two kinds. First, one may attempt to ensure work for the unemployed, by macroeconomic policies, institutional reform at the level of the firm, work relief programs, or the creation of a right to work. Second, one may create alternative sources of income, by unemployment assistance, unemployment insurance, or less selective schemes such as a universal, unconditional grant. I focus on the right to work, the other solutions serving mainly as a foil. Although I refer to legal and factual material from various countries, the approach is not comparative. My purpose is

This paper is part of the project "Distributive Effects of Unemployment Insurance," financed by the Norwegian Research Council for Societal Planning. I have benefited greatly from written comments on an earlier version of the paper by Robert Amdur, Joseph Carens, J. Donald Moon, and Cass Sunstein. I am also grateful for criticism and suggestions provided in seminars at Princeton University and at the Institute for Social Research, Oslo. King T. Tsao provided invaluable research assistance.

mainly conceptual; references to particular times and places are intended mainly to illustrate the general argument.

I do not have great faith in the creation of a legally enforceable right to work as a solution to the problem of unemployment. In this regard I espouse the conventional wisdom. No Western country has established any such right, presumably for reasons similar to those I discuss. Why bother, then, to argue against it? Most obviously, the recurrence of the proposal to establish a right to work makes it worthwhile to examine exactly what is wrong with it. Moreover, explaining why the right to work is not a good remedy may help us understand the merits and demerits of other solutions. Finally, the purported superiority of central planning in this respect may appear in a somewhat different light when the rationale for having a right to work is properly spelled out.

A legally enforceable right to work would be part of the broader spectrum of rights that make up the modern welfare state. It does not, however, fit the pattern of most other welfare rights. Welfare is provided either in kind or in cash. Goods in kind include health services, education, cheap housing and transportation, and food stamps. Cash transfers are usually made to people who have low earning capacity for some reason or other. Virtually all the goods that are provided in kind can also be made available by giving people the money they need to buy them at the market price. This would appear to be the best procedure, since it allows people to define their own priorities. On the other hand, one may argue for payment in kind on the grounds of justified paternalism, externalities, fairness, intrinsic meaning, or political feasibility. Work does not fit this framework. The state may have the choice between offering work and offering unemployment benefits, but the unemployed cannot use these benefits to buy work.[1]

Work and unemployment benefits may, like any other welfare benefit, be forthcoming as a legal entitlement or as a discretionary policy of a self-interested or benevolent provider. I shall consider only legal entitlements that have arisen out of democratic decision-making procedures. They are, in that sense, "democratic rights"—not to be confused with the right to democracy.

Democratic Rights

The title of this chapter reflects a distinction between two views of rights. According to one, rights exist independently of their legal codification or even of their existence in anyone's mind. Whether a right to

[1] Nor, of course, can the blind use their special benefits to buy good eyes, but this inability is matched by the government's inability to offer sight as an alternative to cash.

work exists, on this view, is an issue to be resolved by moral theory. According to the other, rights are man-made: they are legally created, legally enforceable entitlements, including the right to sue or appeal if they are not respected. Prior to effective legal codification one can, at most, speak about moral claims. The question whether there is a right to work then becomes a purely factual one. Needless to say, moral questions also arise for proponents of this view. When does an existing right have moral force? When should a new right—such as the right to work—be created?

According to the first view, the moral basis for a legal right must be that it is also, and in the first place, a moral right. This is necessarily a substantive justification. According to the second view of rights, the moral justification can be either substantive or procedural. An argument for the establishment of a new right must be in terms of substantive justice. This may, but need not, take the form of an assertion that there exists a corresponding moral claim. One might argue on rule-utilitarian grounds that it is useful to be inflexible with respect to a certain value, even though a case-by-case consideration may point in a different direction. Or one might want to protect a value by elevating it to a right because one deems that the fine-tuned flexible treatment that recommends itself on first-best grounds is politically unfeasible or likely to be distorted in practice. When arguing for the moral legitimacy of an existing right, one may in addition draw upon procedural considerations. If a right has been created according to generally accepted democratic procedures, it has moral force by that very fact. One may believe that the right has been adopted on unsound grounds, and yet feel compelled to respect it because it has been adopted in a sound way.

Rights do not fall from heaven. Nor can they be drawn from the consensus of philosophers, since there are no signs of agreement among them. For practical purposes, rights are what people, by democratic procedures, properly protected from bias and distortion, decide to be rights.[2] A simple, paradigmatic example is legislation conferring the right to vote on new groups (e.g., by lowering the voting age).[3]

[2] This is the view defended by John Ely in *Democracy and Distrust* (Cambridge, Mass.: Harvard University Press, 1980). By and large, it seems to me that his arguments survive the criticism mounted against them by Ronald Dworkin in *A Matter of Principle* (Cambridge, Mass.: Harvard University Press, 1985), pp. 57 ff.

[3] Should the nonenfranchised have the right to vote on the issue of whether they should be given the right to vote? Since any enfranchised group would be able to vote if their disenfranchisement was proposed, considerations of symmetry point to giving voting rights to the disenfranchised. In at least one case (Denmark in 1953), this procedure was adopted; but, needless to say, it had to be adopted by the already enfranchised, on pain of an infinite regress. Even if one believes that the nonenfranchised have a moral claim to be heard on this issue, one must admit that only the enfranchised and their representatives can turn that claim into a legal right.

It should be clear that by "rights" I do not mean "manifesto rights"—mere claims to something that are not also claims against someone.[4] Hence I shall not be considering a right to work that does not correspond to the duty of someone. Nor, conversely, shall I discuss the duty of an agent to provide work if it is not a duty toward specific individuals. Thus the duty of firms, in certain countries, to allocate a certain percentage of jobs to the handicapped does not allow a handicapped person to sue a firm if it does not give him a job, even if it has not fulfilled its quota. The firm may be fined by the state, but that is a different matter. Similarly, it has been said that the duty to help the poor in Victorian England was a "duty owed to the public and not to the poor person himself."[5]

The right to work is a positive right. Classical political rights are largely negative, in the sense that they protect the individual from interference by others or by the state. The right to work may thus be contrasted with the right to choose one's occupation.[6] The latter is not a right to a job in the occupation of one's choice. It is merely a negative right, protecting individuals from certain forms of state interference with employment. It protects the individual from being directly or indirectly coerced into a job: directly, as in the press-gang system, or indirectly, as would be the case if the state imposed an ability tax on individuals in order to force them to develop and deploy socially valuable skills.[7] The distinction between negative and positive rights does not coincide with the distinction between claims-against and claims-to. Although many positive rights are mere manifesto rights, others are legally enforceable claims against the state or against an employer.[8]

I have mentioned one respect in which rights (as I understand them here) and duties are correlative: the right of X to A is logically linked to the duty of Y and B.[9] Are there any correlative duties of X? Specifically,

[4] For this distinction see Joel Feinberg, *Rights, Justice, and the Bounds of Liberty* (Princeton, N.J.: Princeton University Press, 1980), chap. 7.

[5] Ivor Jennings, as cited in T. M. Marshall, *The Right to Welfare and Other Essays* (London: Heinemann, 1981), p. 84.

[6] A similar distinction can be made with regard to one's place of residence: the classical right to choose where to live may be contrasted with the positive right to live in a specific place. Regional policy in some countries rests on what almost amounts to a positive right to a specific residence.

[7] For arguments against the ability tax, see Jon Elster, "Self-realization in Work and Politics," *Social Philosophy and Policy* 3 (1986): 97–126.

[8] James W. Nickel, in "Is There a Human Right to Employment?" *Philosophical Forum* 10 (1978–1979): 149–70, notes that, among the classical political rights, the right to a fair trial is a positive, enforceable right. This refutes, and on their own grounds, the arguments of libertarians who believe that the government never has an obligation to provide anything to citizens beyond protection against third parties.

[9] Actually, the matter is more complex, as shown by David Lyons in "The Correlativity of Rights and Duties," *Nous* 4 (1970): 45–55.

does X's right to A impose on him a duty to A? In general, this is of course not the case. The right to free speech certainly does not imply a duty to talk. There are examples, however, of such a correlation. Under feudalism, the serf's right to stay on his plot went together with a duty to do so. In Australia and in some other countries, the right to vote goes together with a legal obligation to vote. Even in countries where voting is not a legal duty, it is usually thought of as a moral obligation, in recognition of the fact that without a sense of civic duty most people would not vote.[10] The right to vote presupposes the institution of voting, which can hardly be viable unless most people actually vote, which in turn—given the free-rider problem that otherwise arises—presupposes that most people feel an obligation to vote. To a lesser extent, the argument could even apply to the right to free speech. The institution of public debate is a public good that might wither away unless some people actually exercise their right to free speech.

A partially analogous argument applies to the right to work. Assume that everyone had the right to choose between guaranteed work and a guaranteed income without working. Clearly, it would be self-defeating if all or most people tried to take the latter option, since all income is ultimately generated by work.[11] Perhaps only a minority would in fact take that option. Most people might still want to work, in order to obtain nonpecuniary benefits and to earn more than the guaranteed income. One might nevertheless, on grounds of fairness, want to foreclose the free-rider option. The argument in fact has a wider application. With or without a positive right to work, the right to a minimal income (e.g., in the form of unemployment benefits) presupposes the duty to take work that is offered, subject to conditions of acceptability.

An analogy from education might be thought to provide an additional argument for linking the right to work and the duty to work. In all countries recognizing a right to education, there is also compulsory schooling. Education is provided as a right because the result of education is thought to be highly valuable. The right is also enforced as a duty because otherwise the tendency to seek short-term gratification might prevent many from exercising their right. (There may be a free-rider problem here as well.) Children must be forced, in their own interest, to exercise their right to education. Similarly, as I argue below, work as a source of social contacts and as a vehicle for self-realization also involves deferred grati-

[10] See, e.g., Brian Barry, *Sociologists, Economists and Democracy*, 2d ed. (Chicago: University of Chicago Press, 1979).

[11] Compare the comment by Marx on the absurdity of "the idea of converting all the capital into money-capital, without there being people who buy and put to use the means of production," in *Capital*, vol. 3, *The Process of Capitalist Production as a Whole* (New York: International Publishers, 1967), p. 377.

fication, which, in the presence of myopia, might seem to provide a rationale for an obligation to work. A decisive objection to this view is that workers are not children. They have a general right to be protected from paternalistic interference. Yet if one can argue on other grounds that any right to work (or to unemployment benefits) must go together with an obligation to work, because of the free-rider problems that would otherwise arise, the prevention of myopic behavior is a welcome side benefit.

Welfare: Benevolence, Social Control, or Justice?

To explain or justify the welfare system one may proceed in three ways.[12] On one view, "welfare payments are never a matter of legal entitlements of the recipients, but only an expression of collective benevolence by the transferrers."[13] Presented here as a possible justification of welfare, the benevolence argument has also been offered as an explanation of income transfers in the age of classical capitalism.[14] This view of welfare payments is similar to a widespread conception of economic aid to less developed countries: a matter of humanity, not of justice. On a second view, welfare payments and services are essentially a form of social control—a preemption of revolutionary demands and movements, a means to protect the health and safety of the affluent classes, a way of generating legitimacy for an essentially unjust system of production and distribution, and a method of cementing social inequalities.[15] This view is usually offered to explain the welfare system, rarely if ever to justify it. On the third view, the welfare state is based on democratic rights. Procedurally, these rights are grounded in a political process involving recipients as well as donors. Substantively, the rights rest on the needs of recipients, not on the benevolent or self-interested motives of the donors, except to the extent that they themselves are potential recipients.[16] This view has been advanced both to explain and to justify the welfare system.

Before the introduction of universal suffrage, benevolence and fear

[12] I am grateful to Cass Sunstein for pointing out to me the need to distinguish justification and explanation, which were confused in an earlier draft of this paper.

[13] Richard A. Epstein, "A Common Law for Labor Relations: A Critique of the New Deal Labor Legislation," *Yale Law Journal* 92 (1983): 1361.

[14] See notably Karl Polanyi, *The Great Transformation* (Boston: Beacon Press, 1957), pp. 165–66. His argument shades over into that of self-interested social control.

[15] See Michel Foucault, *Surveiller et Punir* (Paris: Gallimard, 1975); and, following him, Mary Hawkesworth, "Workfare and the Imposition of Discipline," *Social Theory and Practice* 2 (1985): 163–82.

[16] See Marshall, *The Right to Welfare*; Albert Weale, *Political Theory and Social Policy* (London: Macmillan, 1983); Carl Wellman, *Welfare Rights* (Totowa, N.J.: Rowman and Littlefield, 1982).

were probably the main motives of well-to-do voters and their representatives when they decided to provide some services for the nonenfranchised poor. The relation between donors and recipients in that era is in some respects similar to that between rich and poor countries today. Nobody has yet proposed in earnest that people in poor countries be given the right to vote concerning the amount to be transferred to them by rich countries; benevolence and fear still seem to be the main considerations. In one important respect, however, the relation is different. By and large, rich countries do not today depend for their wealth on the exploitation of poor countries. To the extent that they do not, the moral claim of poor countries to a transfer cannot be defended by the argument that they are just getting back part of what has been extracted from them. By contrast, the upper classes of classical capitalism did depend, for their affluence, on the exploitation of the workers. The welfare system was the partial undoing of an injustice, although it was not, of course, defended as such.

In most West European countries, the right to welfare was demanded increasingly with the extension of suffrage. The story is complex, and I have neither the space nor the competence to tell it here. Some features of the process may be noted, however. Initially, recipients of welfare were often disqualified from voting. Although as voters they may have been instrumental in setting up the welfare system, they could not benefit from it without losing their right to vote. Welfare was not yet seen as a form of collective self-insurance, created to protect people from the hazards that routinely arise in a complex industrial market economy. The notion of "there but for the grace of God" was seldom part of the motivation. At this stage, the needy had the right to welfare in the sense, previously noted, that the state or the municipality had an obligation to provide it, but they did not have the right to sue or to appeal. Later they got the right to appeal (through administrative channels). The final stage of incorporation was reached when they were given the right to sue (in adversarial hearings).[17] Democratic rights, rather than benevolence and fear, had become, and are now, the basis of the welfare state.

In practice, matters are somewhat more complex, because of the imperative that welfare be provided to all those and only to those who need it (and whose need, moreover, has not arisen as a deliberate adaptation to the requirements for receipt). The administration of the modern welfare state is riddled by three anomalies that, in the eyes of welfare recipients, conspire to make it appear more like the nineteenth-century system. They all arise because of certain features of the criteria that are used to define conditions of eligibility. The criteria are frequently (1) subject to

[17] Marshall, in *The Right to Welfare*, chap. 6, presents a brief overview for Britain and Scandinavia.

discretionary interpretation, (2) manipulable, and (3) complex in ways that risk defeating their purpose. Not all facets of a welfare system are equally vulnerable to all of these anomalies, but most are subject to at least one. Moreover, an attempt to eliminate any one of them, when it arises, often leads to the creation of another.

Legal and physical conditions of eligibility can usually be stated in explicit criteria that leave little scope for discretionary interpretation. A person either is or is not married, blind, or more than sixty-five years old. Other criteria are inherently vague, such as the requirements that a person be "involuntarily unemployed" and "genuinely looking for work" in order to receive unemployment benefits. They relate to unobservable attitudes and intentions, not to physical characteristics that can be observed or to legal statuses that can be documented. The first anomaly arises, therefore, when the applicant for welfare is unable to convince the welfare officer or social worker that he is eligible for benefits.

The second anomaly arises when the recipient has the opportunity and the incentive to manipulate the criteria of eligibility. Accelerating the age process is impossible. Self-mutilation to get a disability pension, although possible, is presumably rare. The deliberate breakup of a marriage (or the deliberate refusal of a parent to marry) for the purpose of obtaining certain benefits that are reserved for single parents is more widespread. In addition, the decision to have children in the first place might in part be due to a desire to get these benefits. Having children and marrying are both manipulable criteria. To limit the incentive to make oneself eligible for welfare, supervision and policing have been instituted to a large extent to ensure, for instance, that the breakup of a marriage is real and not merely formal. Churchill said that, in a democracy, a knock on the door early in the morning is the milkman. In the democratic welfare state, it has sometimes been the social worker, checking to see whether there is a "man in the house."

The third anomaly arises when, in order to overcome either of these difficulties, the rules are made so complex that they prevent some of the eligible from getting their due. Stories abound of Catch-22 cases in which the ability to understand the rules de facto ensures that one is not eligible under them.[18] This problem is exacerbated when the rules are constantly evolving. The second anomaly creates the opposite problem: it allows ineligible individuals (including people who, in the absence of the rule, would not have satisfied the conditions of eligibility) to get the benefit. The first anomaly can pose both problems. Vagueness cuts both ways:

[18] The following excerpt from *The Observer* (February 17, 1980) is relevant here: "A one-legged man seeking a state mobility allowance had to struggle up four flights of stairs to the room where a tribunal was to decide his claim. When he got there the tribunal ruled that he could not have the allowance because he had managed to make it up the stairs."

some applicants may be able to exploit the system, whereas others may unjustly be made victims of suspicion.

To avoid these anomalies, welfare criteria should be clear, nonmanipulable, and simple. Paradigms in this respect are old-age pensions and assistance to people who suffer in unforeseeable natural disasters. Note, however, that there is no guarantee that criteria that have these desirable properties will also satisfy the fundamental condition of channeling benefits to all and only those who need them. Ideally, many welfare services should be means-tested, so that more welfare can be provided to the really needy. In practice, simple and automatic criteria are often preferable, for several reasons. Some are derived from the outcome of applying more complex criteria; others result from the process of applying them.

By virtue of their vagueness or complexity, means-tested services may fail to reach those who really need them, while still benefiting some who do not. One should attach more weight to a failure to provide welfare to an eligible person than to provision of welfare to an ineligible individual. Money spent on the needy is so efficient in generating utility that some waste is acceptable. Income transfers that reduce the total wealth of society may increase the total utility. Even when utilitarian calculations point in a different direction, they are overridden ("trumped") by the right to welfare.[19] Utilitarian arguments may or may not have been among the reasons for establishing the right to welfare, but they should not affect its administration. (They could, of course, be reasons for abolishing it, if the right turns out to be much more expensive to implement than foreseen when it was adopted.)

The anomalies of the welfare state cannot, however, be reduced to the costs of providing benefits to some people who do not qualify and of not providing them to some who qualify. There is an additional cost imposed on those who do qualify and who do get the benefits, but as a result of a process that they experience as degrading and humiliating. Legitimate recipients of welfare easily come to feel stigmatized if they are treated as potential liars and deceivers. To them, it may indeed appear that welfare benefits are provided out of suspicious paternalism or are a form of social control. A symmetric cost is imposed on those who do not qualify and do not get the benefits, after applying for them in good faith, or, more generally, on those who are denied benefits as the result of a procedure that does not respect their rights to privacy and participation.

The dilemma of the democratic welfare state, then, is the following. From the point of view of applicants and recipients, the services do not

[19] As suggested by Jerry L. Mashaw, *Due Process in the Administrative State* (New Haven, Conn.: Yale University Press, 1985), p. 122, this second argument could also be expressed in terms of "demoralization costs—that is, a denial of what was thought to be a secure entitlement."

appear to be entitlements unless the criteria of eligibility are clear and simple. Vague and complex criteria lead to what appears at best to be meddlesome paternalism and at worst a Kafkaesque nightmare. From the point of view of the taxpayers, the legitimacy of the welfare services depends on the extent to which they are (1) nonmanipulable; (2) if manipulable, subject to strict supervision; and (3) allocated on the basis of either individualized discretion or complex and explicit criteria, to ensure that all and only the needy benefit.

The representative citizen is torn, therefore, between two tendencies. As a potential future applicant for welfare services, he has an interest in minimizing the cost of not providing benefits to those who qualify and the stigma cost. As a current taxpayer, he has an interest in keeping the cost of financing the welfare state as low as possible, that is, in minimizing the cost of providing benefits to those who do not qualify. The outcome of these opposing tendencies is in general indeterminate, although in particular cases there may be reasons for thinking that one or the other will prevail. I shall not attempt here to show why.

The Value of Work

Not all good things in life can be provided as of right. This is sometimes true for goods taken individually, and often true for goods taken collectively. The impossibility of providing goods as of right may be explained on both conceptual and empirical grounds: (1) It is conceptually impossible to create a right to love or to happiness. (2) It is empirically impossible (at present) to provide everyone with the right to a high-level, unconditional grant. (3) It is conceptually impossible to grant everyone the right to the full fruit of his labor and a basic right to welfare. (4) It might be possible to provide everyone with the right to free, high-quality education or with the right to free, high-quality health services, but it is empirically impossible to provide both at the same time.

To show that a good ought to be provided as a right, one has to argue that it is feasible to do so and that the good is sufficiently important to take priority over conflicting rights that one might also want to create. The question of feasibility is discussed later. Here I want to consider the value of work, to see whether the right to work passes the second test. The alternative to work being unemployment, I also consider evidence concerning the disutility of being out of work. I discuss only the nonpecuniary benefits of working, since these are what might justify a right to work, as distinct from a right to income.

Work—having a regular job offering an income—can provide a number of nonpecuniary benefits. It can be an opportunity for self-realization. It can be a source of the esteem of others and hence of self-esteem. It can provide a social environment, an escape from isolation. It can impose structure on everyday life, an escape from limitless and alienating freedom. Against this positive assessment, one may offer two observations. First, work can be monotonous, degrading, isolated, and unstructured. Second, even when work does provide some of the cited benefits, they may still be less highly valued than the leisure foregone. At equal monetary incomes, the individual might prefer leisure to work.[20]

To see the limits of the second observation, imagine that workers were free to vary the length of the workweek, without any loss of income. Any relatively minor reduction in the workweek would have little immediate impact on most work-related benefits. A worker would not lose friends or their esteem by working slightly less, and he would gain some leisure. He might well prefer the reduction. Yet the cumulative long-term damage to his social life and self-esteem may be more substantial, and outweigh the short-term gain in leisure. Each hour absent from work creates losses for future periods, by loosening his insertion into the web of social relations and reducing the sense of his own worth.[21] Thus, although the worker would overall be better off in all weeks by working full time in all weeks, in any given week he can increase his welfare by taking some time off from work.[22]

Consider now work as an opportunity for self-realization.[23] The temporal utility pattern of self-realizing activities is typically "one step backward, two steps forward": an initial painful effort is followed by a reward. Work, at its best, is neither mere drudgery nor pure amusement.[24]

[20] When contrasting work and unemployment, I tacitly assume that, within the budgetary constraint, an unemployed worker is "free" to devote all of the newly acquired time to leisure and consumption activities. But for women who have or plan to have children, this assumption is misleading. Having and raising children can be a source of both esteem and self-esteem, and it imposes (an often unwelcome amount of) structure on everyday life. It tends to reduce the opportunities for wider social contacts. It cannot (or should not) be a vehicle for self-realization, as I define that notion.

[21] As a useful contrast, consider the person who regularly works overtime, each time truthfully (let us assume) saying to himself that, within a given period, the extra income offsets any damage done to the quality of family life. Over time, the net effect could be negative.

[22] For an interpersonal analogue to this intrapersonal dilemma, consider the problem of work motivation when workers are paid according to need rather than contribution. Although all workers are better off if all of them work hard, any worker can increase his welfare by working less.

[23] The discussion in this paragraph draws upon my "Self-realization in Work and Politics." The basic idea is taken from R. Solomon and J. Corbit, "An Opponent-Process Theory of Motivation," *Psychological Review* 81 (1974): 119–45. See also F. J. Landy, "An Opponent Process Theory of Job Satisfaction," *Journal of Applied Psychology* 63 (1978): 533–47.

[24] Karl Marx, *Grundrisse* (Harmondsworth: Penguin Books, 1973), p. 611.

The temporal utility pattern of consumption activities is the exact opposite: an initial enjoyment is followed by withdrawal symptoms. Moreover, these patterns are reinforced by repetition, as shown in Figure 1.[25] With discounting of the future, consumption activities might be preferred over self-realizing activities, even if the latter have a higher undiscounted value. The argument reinforces the conclusion of the preceding paragraph. Even when work provides more satisfaction than leisure or consumption, the latter may be preferred for reasons variously referred to as myopia or weakness of will.

Most forms of work are obviously superior to leisure with respect to structuring everyday life. Although vacations have their own structure, being unemployed is not like being on holiday. It is an open-ended mode of existence that is difficult to fill even at the best of times (that is, even if the requisite material resources are available). Beyond a certain point, the expansion of the "realm of freedom,"[26] that is, of free time, ceases to be liberating. Freedom needs constraints within which alternatives can be compared and meaningful choices made. Conversely, the need to work enhances the value of leisure. For the unemployed, who have fewer resources than usual and more time in which to use them, the result can be deeply alienating.[27]

Let me turn to the observation that the value of work depends on the way in which it is organized. Not all forms of work offer social contacts, opportunity for self-realization, or self-esteem, but almost all forms of work impose structure on everyday life, in the sense that the worker is rarely free to decide whether to work or not. If he does not have an employer, he has customers that keep him in line. The bank or the landlord must be paid; his family must be supported. For most people, these expectations and sanctions add up to a very firm structure indeed. Providing a framework for living is the minimal nonpecuniary benefit, as it were, offered by work.

For work to be a main arena of social life, two conditions must be fulfilled.[28] First, the physical layout and organization of the work must be such as to allow workers to talk and otherwise interact with each other. This requirement might not be satisfied for various reasons. Sometimes

[25] The idea that all consumption has an addictive aspect is not essential for the argument. The main point is that consumption has decreasing marginal utility across episodes, not that each episode has an increasing negative component.

[26] Marx, *Capital*, 3: 820.

[27] Peter Kelvin and Joanna Jarrett, in *Unemployment: Its Social Psychological Effects* (New York: Cambridge University Press, 1985), chap. 5, make many important observations and theoretical conjectures.

[28] The following discussion draws upon the analysis of solidarity in my *Making Sense of Marx* (New York: Cambridge University Press, 1985), chap. 6.2.

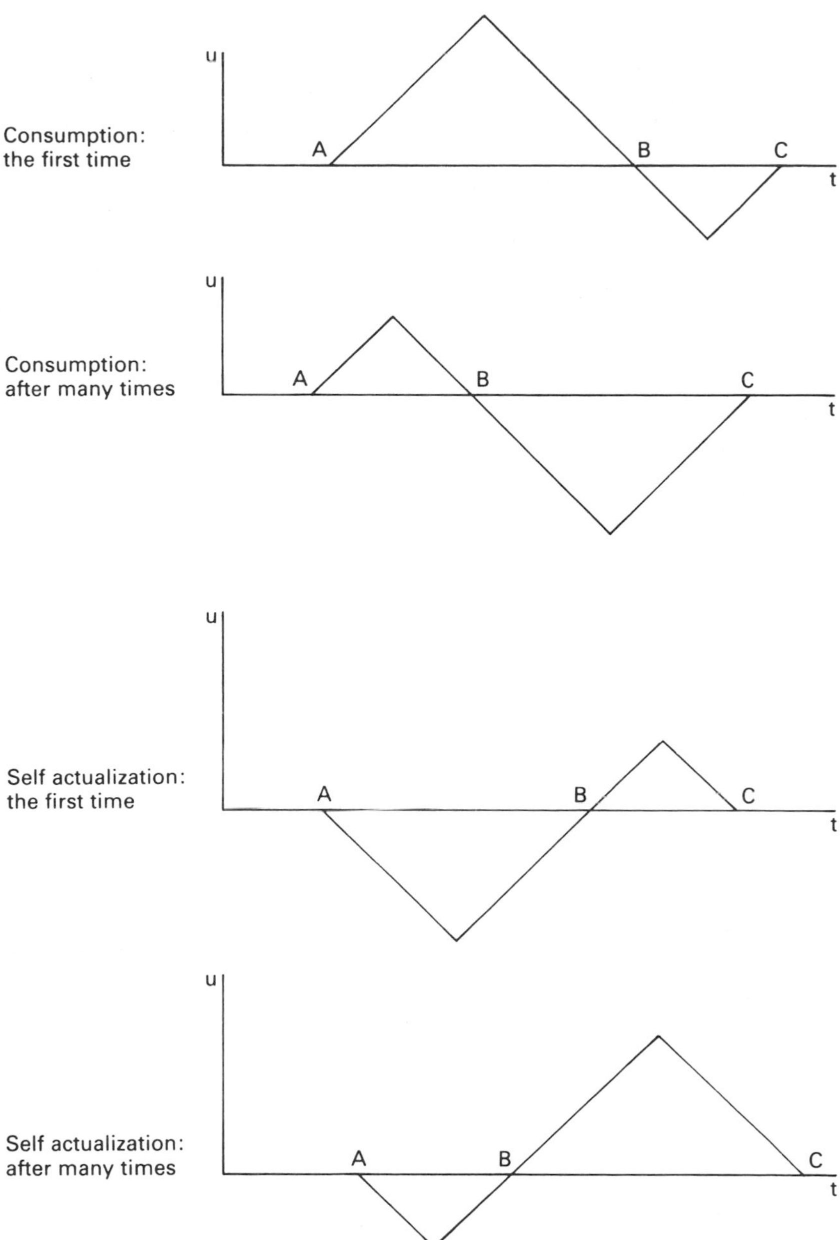

FIGURE 1. Temporal patterns of utility corresponding to single episodes of consumption or self-actualization, at early and later stages. (From Jon Elster, "Self-Realization in Work and Politics: The Marxist Conception of the Good Life," *Social Philosophy & Policy* 3, no. 2 [Spring 1986]: 105, published by Basil Blackwell for the Social Philosophy and Policy Center, Bowling Green State University. Reprinted courtesy of the publisher.)

working conditions are deliberately designed by employers to prevent interaction among employees; sometimes the work is intrinsically isolating, as in the case of traveling salesmen. Second, there must be a minimum of stability and continuity in the work force, so that relations among workers can develop into enduring friendships. There must be actual stability, without which there would be no time for growth and development, as well as expected stability, without which the emotional investment necessary for the growth and development would not be made.[29] This condition might be frustrated for extrinsic or intrinsic reasons. An employer might intentionally engineer a high turnover of the work force to prevent the formation of horizontal bonds. Seasonal work, such as in the construction industry, undermines the stability of interpersonal relations.

Consider next, work as a vehicle for self-realization—the self-externalizing and self-actualizing development and deployment of one's powers and abilities. Although in one sense this is the most important work-related value, in another sense, it is the most peripheral. It is important in that successful self-realization is among the most gratifying experiences one can have. It is peripheral in that working conditions for most people in contemporary industrial societies—capitalist and communist—do not lend themselves to fulfillment of this goal. By and large, self-realization is more easily achieved when there is decentralized production and a relatively unchanging technology. It is no accident that the artisan, the artist, and the scientist are the usual exemplars of self-realization. The scope for self-realization can be increased by making changes in industrial production, but to what extent is still unclear.[30] As I argue later, it is surely utopian to claim that people could have a legally enforceable right to self-realization in the workplace.

Consider finally, work as a source of self-esteem. Although the notion of self-esteem is somewhat elusive, it may most usefully be characterized not as something that has value, but as that without which nothing else has much value. Self-esteem is needed for the motivation to go on with the business of living. Thus, when we say that a depressed person suffers from low self-esteem, we mean that it is the cause of the suffering, not its object. Work can provide self-esteem insofar as it serves as a vehicle for self-realization, but in Western societies this is an exception. More commonly, work generates self-esteem by resulting in production of a good or service that others value enough to purchase (as consumers or taxpayers) at a price that allows the worker to earn a living that is decent by the

[29] An analogous argument is made with respect to the family in Gary Becker, *A Treatise on the Family* (Cambridge, Mass.: Harvard University Press, 1981).

[30] For a useful discussion of this possibility, see G. E. O'Brien, "The Centrality of Skill-utilization for Job Design," in K. D. Duncan, M. M. Gruneberg, and D. Wells, eds., *Changes in Working Life* (New York: Wiley, 1980), pp. 167–87.

standards of the society. Self-esteem is undermined by the belief that one is parasitic on others. If true, this claim implies that highly and visibly subsidized work or make-believe work, like digging ditches and filling them up again, is not a source of self-esteem. The self-esteem of people who are living on unemployment insurance may be damaged because they feel they are being parasitic, but they would not be happier if they performed work that visibly was not paying its way. I offer some illustrations in support of this claim later. Here I want to emphasize that if work does not provide self-esteem, it cannot—if I am right in believing self-esteem to be a necessary condition for the enjoyment of life in general—provide any of the other cited benefits either. In this sense, self-esteem is the most important of all the work-related values.

The other side of the coin is the harm that unemployment does to the unemployed and their dependents. We can distinguish four effects: the direct loss of income caused by the loss of a job (which I do not consider here); the nonpecuniary suffering caused by the loss of a job; the indirect loss of income caused by the experience of unemployment itself; and the indirect and delayed effects on other people.

Since the pioneering work by Marie Jahoda and Paul Lazarsfeld on Marienthal (1933), there have been a number of studies on the psychology of unemployment, which have been admirably summarized by Peter Kelvin and Joanna Jarrett. They emphasize the withdrawal of the unemployed from social life, not only because of stigma but also and mainly because of "the sheer, progressively exhausting effort needed to keep going at all, just oneself and one's family; and . . . the unemployed individual's frequent debilitating dislike of himself."[31] They note the obsessive preoccupation with time—"with the extent of it, with the inability to make use of it, with the sense that one is therefore merely 'killing' it."[32] The unemployed of the 1970s and the 1980s spend much time watching television, which imposes even less structure on life than did visits to the cinema for the unemployed in the 1930s. This is not necessarily a picture of the average unemployed person. Rather, it depicts a worker with a long history of employment and bleak prospects of finding a job in the near future, often with a family to support. The description does not fit the young, unmarried worker who drops out of the labor force not because jobs are unavailable but because they are unattractive.

If unemployment induces changes in people, it would not be surprising to find that some of the changes make it more difficult for them to find new employment. Whether this is in fact so is a controversial issue. There are two explanations for the finding that the probability of getting a job

[31] Kelvin and Jarrett, *Unemployment*, p. 54.

[32] Ibid., p. 68.

declines with the length of unemployment. One is that some people are inherently less employable than others; that is, their (unchanging) probability of getting a job is low. As a consequence, their average period of unemployment is longer, thus accounting for the observed regularity. The other is that although all people begin their unemployment with the same chance of getting a job, the employment chances of those who do not draw the lucky ticket decline over time, either because they lose self-confidence or because employers subscribe to the first explanation. There is much qualitative evidence for the second explanation,[33] as well as some econometric evidence.[34] The second explanation, if correct, would foster a "there but for the grace of God" view of unemployment, with important policy implications.

The hysteresis effects of unemployment may go beyond that of a cumulative decrease in the chances of finding a job. Even when the unemployed person has found a job, his further career and income profile (and that of his dependents) may be adversely affected by the stretch of unemployment. To my knowledge, there have been no systematic studies of this problem, perhaps because of the lack of longitudinal, individual-level data. Some casual evidence follows. The Beveridge Report on unemployment refers to an employer who said (in 1886) that "we have always found, as to the artisan, that if he happens to be out of work for 3 months, he is never the same again."[35] (Presumably such beliefs enter into the explanation of why reemployment probabilities decline over time.) Stephan Thernstrom found that the cohort of Bostonians born in the first decade of the twentieth century who held unskilled and semiskilled jobs around 1930 never recovered from the Great Depression. Once the depression was over they got jobs, but their careers progressed slowly compared with the normal career pattern.[36] The aftereffects of unemployment may also

[33] Ibid., pp. 32ff., 91ff.; A Sinfield, *What Unemployment Means* (Oxford: Martin Robertson, 1981), p. 89.

[34] A. McGregor, in "Unemployment Duration and Reemployment Probability," *Economic Journal* 88 (1978): 693–706, finds that the second explanation, in terms of cumulative inertia, dominates the first. A broadly similar conclusion is reached by T. Lancaster and S. Mickell, "The Analysis of Reemployment Probabilities for the Unemployed," *Journal of the Royal Statistical Society* 143 (1980): 141–65; and by S. Nickell, "Estimating the Probability of Leaving Unemployment," *Econometrica* 47 (1970): 1249–66. Kelvin and Jarrett, in *Unemployment*, p. 21, suggest a possible synthesis of the two views: individuals may have different initial reemployment probabilities, but as time goes by and they fail to find employment, they may become more and more similar, with their reemployment probabilities converging. "There must come a point or period of transition, such that an individual's prior personal characteristics (his 'personality') largely cease to shape his response to unemployment, and instead he is himself shaped by that unemployment."

[35] Quoted from Kelvin and Jarrett, *Unemployment*, p. 35.

[36] Stephan Thernstrom, *The Other Bostonians* (Cambridge, Mass.: Harvard University Press, 1973), pp. 59, 233. This is the only exception he finds to an otherwise amazing reg-

extend to the descendants of the worker, who might be forced to leave school early to help their families.[37] There is also some evidence that an increase in unemployment tends to create, with a lag of several years, an increase in the number of welfare recipients.[38]

Underlying these issues are three different views of human nature. According to the first, peoples' preferences and motivation levels are essentially stable over time. Whether they are employed or unemployed, peoples' attitudes toward work are the same. The second view is that people are marked irreversibly by their experiences. Once they have been exposed to work, they may acquire an ineradicable taste for it. Once they have been exposed to continuing unemployment, their self-esteem and belief in their employability may be permanently weakened. According to the third view, people are reversibly marked by their experiences. Exposure to work develops a taste for work; exposure to unemployment induces a taste for leisure. Both the first and the third views are rather shallow. In the crude version just stated, the first view seems just plain wrong. Although more sophisticated versions have been constructed to account for phenomena like addiction and habit formation,[39] they tend to be somewhat Ptolemaic. The core of truth in the third view is that people often rationalize defeat by adapting their preferences to the feasible set ("sour grapes"). I submit, however, that it is jejune to assume that these adaptive preferences are on a par with the taste for work induced by an exposure to work.

A Right to Work?

There have been several discussions—some critical, some favorable—of the proposal to create a statutory, legally enforceable right to work.[40] Before I enter the fray, I shall briefly sketch the background against which

ularity in career mobility patterns: in less severe depressions, nobody suffered durably; and, in the Great Depression, only the unskilled and semiskilled did.

[37] Alexander Keyssar, *Out of Work: The First Century of Unemployment in Massachusetts* (New York: Cambridge University Press, 1986), p. 172.

[38] P. Albin and B. Stein, "The Impact of Unemployment on Welfare Expenditures," *Industrial and Labor Relations Review* 31 (1977): 31–44. See also Helen Ginsburg, *Full Employment and Public Policy: The United States and Sweden* (Lexington, Mass.: Lexington Books, 1983), pp. 95 ff.

[39] George Stigler and Gary Becker, "De Gustibus non est Disputandum," *American Economic Review* 67 (1977): 76–90.

[40] Advocates of the right to work include Nickel, "Is There a Human Right to Employment?"; Peter Townsend, *Poverty in the United Kingdom* (Harmondsworth: Penguin Books, 1979); M. Rustin, "A Statutory Right to Work," *New Left Review*, No. 137 (1983), pp. 48–67. For a critical argument, see B. Hepple, "A Right to Work?" *Industrial Law Journal* 10 (1981): 65–83.

the proposal can be evaluated. First, I shall distinguish between several different interpretations of the right to work, corresponding to different conceptions of who has the duty to provide work. Next, I shall distinguish between different ways of implementing full employment.

The right to work can be a right against the state, against an employer, or against a trade union. My main concern is with the first of these. But I shall comment briefly on the others, beginning with the last. The "right-to-work" laws that have been passed in about twenty U.S. states forbid an employer to set up a "closed shop," a "union shop," or an "agency shop"—arrangements that require workers to be or become members of a union, or at least to pay their share of the costs of collective bargaining.[41] This terminology is pure demagogy. These laws do not guarantee income for anyone. Given the clause in the Wagner Act specifying that the employer has an exclusive duty to bargain only with the union, where one exists, they amount to legal protection for free riders. They are abhorrent not only from the unions' perspective but also from the perspective of those taking a consistent libertarian position, since they block certain free, voluntary, mutually beneficial agreements between an employer and the employees. If the goal were really to protect the freedom of the individual to remain outside the union, it would be more logical to attack the Wagner Act itself. Within the framework of the act, that freedom might be protected by requiring nonmembers to pay an amount equivalent to membership dues to some charitable organization, thus sorting out the conscientious objectors from the would-be free riders.

The right to work, as defined against an employer, can at most be the right to retain a job that one already holds. It is nearly impossible to imagine how there can be a legally enforceable right to acquire a job. Even the right to retain a job is subject to serious reservations. According to the classical contract-at-will doctrine, the employer has complete freedom to terminate the employment relation, with no need to show due cause. When introduced, the right to sue against dismissal without due cause did not amount to a right to work, since the successful plaintiff was usually awarded damages rather than reinstatement in the job. The legal doctrine against requiring specific performance excluded the possibility that an employee could have the right to be employed by someone who did not want to employ him.

Later the doctrine was abrogated, and workers could now sue for rein-

[41] For the legal situation, see J. R. Eissinger, "The Right-to-Work Imbroglio," *North Dakota Law Review* 51 (1975): 71–96; and T. R. Haggard, "Right-to-Work Laws in the Southern States," *North Carolina Law Review* 59 (1980): 29–69. For the (apparently minor) economic effects of such laws, see W. Moore and R. Newman, "The Effects of Right-to-Work Laws: A Review of the Literature," *Industrial and Labor Relations Review* 38: 571–85.

statement. Yet even this right falls short of a full property right to the job, for two obvious reasons. First, a worker can still be dismissed if the employer shows due cause. Second, and more important, the employment can never be more secure than the job itself. The worker cannot be legally protected against layoffs. Usually, a conditional right is one that depends on some properties of the right-holder. The right to work in the presently discussed sense would be anomalous, in being conditional upon the material possibility of providing the object of the right. To avoid confusion, it seems preferable to speak of workers as having an unconditional right against unfair dismissal rather than to confer on them this strangely conditional right to a job. In any case, no amount of job security will create jobs for the unemployed. If they are to have a right to work, it must be a right against the state.

The state, however, does not have to take the legal approach to full employment. It can hold that work for all, although an all-important value, is not one that can or should be implemented by granting a specific right. It can try instead to promote full employment by using other measures, which I shall divide in three categories: traditional, radical, and moderately radical.

The traditional measures take the ownership and decision-making structure of private capitalist firms as given. Within this framework the state can offer wage subsidies or impose layoff taxes. It can stimulate demand and protect firms against foreign competition. It can help the unemployed to set up new firms. And it can provide some jobs itself, by establishing work relief programs. All of these measures may have some effect on unemployment, although there seems to be little agreement among economists as to how well they work under various conditions. For present purposes it is sufficient to note that they certainly do not create a de facto guarantee of full employment. For this, one will have to look elsewhere.

Radical measures—the substitution of public for private ownership—might look more promising. It is well known that Soviet-type economies have very good employment properties. The unpredictable supply situation in such economies creates an incentive for enterprises to hoard everything, including labor.[42] Yet, although labor in centrally planned econo-

[42] See Jan Adam, *Employment and Wage Policies in Poland, Czechoslovakia, and Hungary Since 1950* (London: Macmillan, 1984), chap. 2. There are signs that, in the Soviet Union, full employment is beginning to be seen as an obstacle to economic modernization. In an article published in *Sovetskaya Kultura* on January 4, 1986 (and reported in *The New York Times* on January 9), a government economist writes that the economic modernization program could force anywhere from 13 million to 19 million in the industrial sector temporarily out of work, creating a need for massive retraining programs and for transitional benefits. See also J. L. Porket, "Unemployment in the Midst of Labour Waste," *Survey* 29

mies is fully employed, it is very far from fully deployed. Although the official ideology celebrates the dignity of work, in actual practice labor is underutilized and degraded. If the system offers self-esteem, it must be with a pronounced element of cynicism.

By moderately radical solutions I mean measures aimed at making changes that retain the basic features of a capitalist economy or, at the very least, of a market economy, but impose new modes of ownership and decision making, such as work sharing, profit sharing, and workers' self-management. Work sharing—dividing existing jobs among more workers—does not even look good on paper as a solution to the unemployment problem, and is likely to meet with resistance from the unions. Labor-managed firms are well known to have undesirable employment properties. Since their aim is to maximize net earnings per worker, they usually have no incentive to dilute earnings by taking on more workers. To ensure full employment, an economy of labor-managed firms would have to rely very heavily on the creation of new firms.

Martin Weitzman has recently offered a powerful argument ("best idea since Keynes," according to the *New York Times*) to the effect that unemployment can be eliminated overnight if firms and workers agree to bargain over their relative share of the net product instead of over the wage rate, as they do now.[43] At a given percentage share, management will always have an incentive to hire an extra worker, since the firm will retain part of the additional net product created. In the "share economy," firms are like sponges, soaking up all available labor and thus doing away with unemployment. The objection has been made that the proposal represents an unstable halfway house between capitalism and market socialism (or codetermination).[44] In an economy of full employment, the bargaining power of the workers would be enhanced to such an extent that it is hard to imagine they would not demand a say in the decisions of the firm—especially the decision whether to hire more workers and thereby reduce wages.

Another, related objection is relevant also to the proposal to create a right to work. In a situation of full employment, individual workers would be in a strong position, even in the absence of collective bargaining. They could shirk at little risk to themselves, since if they were detected and laid off, they could easily get a new job at the same wage. As

(1984): 19–28, for a discussion of underemployment and unemployment in the U.S.S.R. in the 1980s.

[43] Martin Weitzman, *The Share Economy* (Cambridge, Mass.: Harvard University Press, 1984).

[44] D. M. Nuti, "The Share Economy: Plausibility and Viability of Weitzman's Model," European University, Florence, Working Paper no. 85/194 of the Department of Economics, 1985.

Carl Shapiro and Joseph Stiglitz have shown, in a capitalist economy, some unemployment is required for work discipline:

> To induce its workers not to shirk, the firm attempts to pay more than the "going wage"; then, if a worker is caught shirking and is fired, he will pay a penalty. If it pays one firm to raise its wage, however, it will pay all firms to raise their wages. When they all raise their wages, the incentive not to shirk again disappears. But as all firms raise their wages, their demand for labor decreases, and unemployment results. With unemployment, even if all firms pay the same wages, a worker has an incentive not to shirk. For, if he is fired, an individual will not immediately obtain another job. The equilibrium unemployment rate must be sufficiently high that it pays workers to work rather than to take the risk of being caught shirking.[45]

Weitzman's share economy would be vulnerable to the problem of workers' opportunism without having available to it unemployment as a "solution." It would probably, therefore, exhibit some of the sluggish features of Soviet-type economies, in which workers can shirk and get away with it since they know that, if fired, they will always be hired by another firm.

Thus far we have not met any way of ensuring de facto full employment that is not beset with serious problems. Let us now consider whether the establishment of a de jure right to work would be a superior option. Such a right could be implemented in various ways. The state employment agency could subsidize private or public employers, or it could directly create jobs itself. The state would always have to be the employer of last resort, but only when other measures had failed. Whichever measure or combination of measures were used, the following issues would be crucial. Who would have the right to work? To what kind of work? For how long? Where? At what pay? The answers to these questions have implications both for the cost of the measures and for their expected benefits.

Before we consider the problem of cost, I want to make two general observations. The first concerns the implications of the Shapiro-Stiglitz argument about the necessity for some unemployment. If the establishment of a right to work led to effective full employment, the following problem would seem to arise. Private employers would feel it necessary to raise the wages of their workers, to reduce their incentive to shirk. This would have two consequences: on the one hand, the public-sector jobs would be a less desirable alternative, serving as a deterrent for workers; on the other hand, private employers would demand less labor, thus cre-

[45] Carl Shapiro and Joseph E. Stiglitz, "Equilibrium Unemployment: A Worker Discipline Device," *American Economic Review* 74 (1984): 433.

ating a need for more public-sector jobs. If the state employment agency raised the wages of public-sector jobs to avoid the stigma that would otherwise attach to them, private employers would have to follow suit, again raising wages and reducing the demand for labor. Theoretically, the process would go on until all private firms were driven out of business. In other words, it would seem that in a capitalist economy, full employment can only be achieved at the expense of creating a second-rate work force that is paid lower wages than private-sector workers performing the same tasks. In capitalism, either some workers are unemployed or some workers are paid less than other workers doing the same job. Any attempt to escape this dilemma will have the same result: the state will be the sole employer, and all labor will be underemployed.

The second observation concerns the relation between the right to work and self-esteem. If one agrees with Rawls that self-esteem is the most important primary good—that without which nothing has much value,[46] and if in addition one believes that work is the most important source of self-esteem, there would seem to be a strong case for creating a right to work. Consider, however, the following *reductio ad absurdum* argument. Love, although not the most important thing in life, is certainly a very important value, without which many other strivings lose their point. For many people, marriage is the main source of love. One ought to create, therefore, the right to a spouse.

The analogy is far from complete, but it points us in the right direction. To create the right to a spouse for the purpose of promoting love would be self-defeating, since love, as we understand it, must be freely given. It would be similarly self-defeating to create a right to work for the purpose of promoting self-esteem, because self-esteem depends essentially on the freely accorded esteem of others.[47] Work that has no purpose other than ensuring self-esteem would also fail in that regard. To engender self-esteem, work must first of all result in production of a good or service that is valued by consumers or taxpayers. Self-esteem, like happiness, dignity, or innocence, belongs to the class of states that are essentially by-products.[48]

It follows that if the purpose of work is to promote self-esteem, a right to work that was visibly realized by heavy subsidies would be self-defeating. This proposition needs careful qualification. First, there may be independent grounds for offering subsidies. Farmers in many countries are subsidized to the point where it would be cheaper to pay them a full in-

[46] John Rawls, *A Theory of Justice* (Cambridge, Mass.: Harvard University Press, 1971), p. 440.

[47] A similar point is made by J. Donald Moon in Chapter 2 of this volume.

[48] For a discussion of this notion, see chap. 11 of my *Sour Grapes* (Cambridge: Cambridge University Press, 1983).

come for doing nothing. If such subsidies have not led to any visible degradation of their self-esteem, it is in part because there is an independent justification for supporting farming, such as the desire to maintain settlement in certain regions or the need for military preparedness.

Second, the argument is intended to apply only to permanent subsidies. Temporary subsidies can be a rational solution to the problems of sectors facing a predictably temporary failure of demand. In particular, state intervention may be necessary when the capital required is so large that private financial institutions are deterred by risk-aversion.

Third, the visibility condition should be stressed. Frequently, what farmers or industrial workers in backward regions object to are not subsidies as such. Rather, they resist being subsidized in ways that make it obvious that they do not make any productive contribution. This is probably why the "farmers of West Germany favor a subsidy through price over a direct subsidy of income although this involves astronomical deadweight losses and will certainly turn against them since it cannot be maintained."[49] Similarly, it is a well-known fact of Norwegian political life that it is (politically) feasible to maintain regional employment by subsidizing capital, but not by directly subsidizing labor.[50] The aluminum industry in Western Norway demands and gets huge subsidies in the form of cheap energy, partly because the workers do not want wage subsidies. The government has tried to offer the fishermen in Northern Norway direct labor subsidies, only to be met with the response that they prefer subsidies to be given to shipowners. In both cases, observers emphasize, accepting wage subsidies is perceived to be like begging. Workers in the textile industry, where direct wage subsidies are given, envy the aluminum industry because its energy requirements justify less transparent—although much less efficient—income transfers. Whether these curious and irrational reactions are due to self-deception, or something else, they seem to illustrate the thesis that I am defending: there is something inherently self-defeating about job subsidies whose sole and explicit purpose is to maintain the self-esteem of the recipients.

The American work relief programs during the Great Depression also provide some support for this proposition. As Kesselman has pointed out,

> the political economy of work relief placed a web of constraints on the productive factors, the technology, the organization, and the type

[49] Ekkehart Schlicht, "The Emotive and Cognitive View of Justice," manuscript, Institute for Advanced Study, Princeton University, September 1985.

[50] For an explicit recognition of this fact of political life, see J. Serck-Hanssen, "Subsidiering av Kapital i Utbyggingsomradene" (Capital subsidies in development areas), *Statsøkonomisk Tidsskrift*, 1972, pp. 140–66. Since there is a paucity of written sources on this subject, I have largely relied on verbal communications from Hilde Bojer and Jens Chr. Andvig.

> of products. These constraints affected the social value of the outputs. Not only was the efficiency of work relief operations forced below that of comparable contract projects, but the political forces of a private enterprise economy restricted projects to being noncompetitive. The restriction of project types was probably the more serious factor in reducing the value of output. The nonpecuniary benefits to be derived from work relief—maintenance of morale, skills, and work habits—themselves hinged critically on the value of output.[51]

I do not want to place heavy emphasis on these scattered empirical observations. The argument is, above all, a conceptual one, about the kinds of policies that can be rationally and publicly pursued. Self-esteem, although supremely important, is not the kind of benefit that can be ensured by creating a right to work. If the work one does is esteemed enough by others to provide one with self-esteem, there will be a demand for it and no need to provide it as of right. If there is no demand for it, so that it has to be provided by a separate right, it cannot promote self-esteem. This equating of esteem and demand, although likely to be controversial, is deliberate. Verbally expressed esteem will not generate self-esteem if people are not willing to put their money where their mouth is, both as consumers and as taxpayers.

Consider next, work as a source of social relations. To the extent that the right to work is motivated by this value, it sets constraints on the kinds of work that can realize it. In particular, the work has to be, and be expected to be, of some duration. It will not do to have the unemployed providing community services for the elderly one year and cleaning up the parks the next. Seasonal work and construction projects are also unsuitable for this purpose. More generally, this value rebels against the idea of having the unemployed perform the work that at any given time is most needed. I am not saying that this could not be a sensible practice. It would be less costly for the community and could, if the argument in the preceding paragraphs is correct, for that very reason bolster the self-esteem of workers employed in such tasks. If, however, the underlying purpose is to prevent social isolation by inserting people into the work community, stable jobs are required. To provide these jobs could be very costly and, if my reasoning is correct, for that reason would be destructive of self-esteem.

Consider finally work as a means of self-realization. The references to

[51] J. R. Kesselman, "Work Relief Programs in the Great Depression," in John L. Palmer, ed., *Creating Jobs: Public Employment Programs and Wage Subsidies* (Washington, D.C.: Brookings Institution, 1978), 215 (italics supplied). For comments on the value of output of subsidized work, see Robert H. Haveman, "Direct Job Creation," in Eli Ginzberg, ed., *Employing the Unemployed* (New York: Basic Books, 1980), pp. 152–53.

the "right to the free choice of employment" and to the right to "just and favorable working conditions" in the Universal Declaration of Human Rights could, if taken together with the right to work, be understood as asserting the right to self-realization through work. Whether or not this is intended, there can be no such right. Individual self-realization will, of necessity, be constrained by the social need to maintain a balance between the activities that consume scarce resources and the activities that generate them. If society tried to underwrite the right of each and every individual to pursue his chosen means of self-realization, chaos would ensue. More generally, the decision to allocate scarce resources to a given means of self-realization must be a social one. No individual can have a right to direct epic color films, even if this should be his preferred path to self-realization.

Cost considerations enter here as well. Typically, jobs that are conducive to self-realization must be stable and allow for long-term planning. In addition, they typically require a great deal of capital per worker. If self-realization were seen as the central value of work, it would be pointless to offer unskilled, labor-intensive jobs of the kind often associated with job-creation projects. Needless to say, the provision of stable, capital-intensive jobs could be very expensive and, for that reason alone, destructive of self-esteem.

Conclusion

I conclude that any right to work that could feasibly be created is not a right to work that is worth having. It would be self-defeating to create work whose main purpose was to enhance self-esteem. Unless the main purpose of the work is the efficient production of socially useful goods or services, it will not be a source of self-esteem. To achieve efficiency, other work-related benefits would have to be sacrificed. If one deliberately set out to promote work as a source of social contact and a means of self-realization, subsidies per job would probably have to be so large as to undermine the work—as a source of self-esteem. This, in turn, would undermine the other work-related benefits the worker could derive from a job. Thus the problem is not one of a trade-off between self-esteem and other benefits. If the work does not generate self-esteem, it cannot provide the other benefits either.

This is a purely conceptual argument that holds for any level of unemployment. In addition, there is an empirical argument that comes into play in the face of mass unemployment. To provide a large number of the unemployed with stable, meaningful jobs may require resources in excess of the total supply or in excess of what is left over after the satisfaction of other, more urgent needs.

Thus, both the conceptual argument and economic constraints suggest that work that could be established as of right will have to be relatively unskilled, labor-intensive, and of short duration. Moreover, the salaries of these jobs would have to be lower than those of similar jobs in the private sector, since otherwise workers in that sector would have no incentive to avoid shirking. This difference would, in itself, tend to reduce the self-esteem one could derive from work made available as of right. In addition, many of the unskilled jobs provided by the state employment agency would be held by skilled workers who had lost their jobs. It is highly implausible to assume that one can maintain the self-esteem of a skilled worker by offering him an unskilled job at a lower wage than what is paid to unskilled workers in the private sector.

There are good reasons, then, for the methods used in most countries for dealing with unemployment, by a combination of selective job creation and unemployment benefits. This is not to say that existing systems are perfect. Reforms ought to be guided by the assumption that people want work once they have been exposed to it. This has two main implications. First, a high priority should be given to creating jobs—"real jobs"—for the young. They might even have the right to be the last to be fired in the event of layoffs, contrary to the present practice, which is largely based on seniority. Second, one could and should raise the level of unemployment benefits for experienced workers, without worrying too much about incentive effects. Higher benefits probably induce more unemployment, by reducing the opportunity cost of leisure and of searching for new jobs, but it is ridiculous to interpret this fact, supposing it to be one, as reflecting a preference for paid leisure over paid work. Both work and leisure offer nonpecuniary benefits. At the moment a worker becomes unemployed, the benefits of leisure may be preferable to those of work, but in the long run "any suggestion that these two non-financial items are offsetting is totally unjustifiable."[52] Raising the level of unemployment benefits to or toward that of sick pay would entail some loss of production, as do most redistributive measures, but it would also bring substantial benefits by removing some of the overtones of punishment associated with the present system, which act as deterrents to job seeking. To remove the remaining overtones, workers should have the right to refuse work that is not closely related to their qualifications, subject to an obligation that they undergo retraining if changes in demand or technology have made their skills obsolete.

[52] Richard Hemming, *Poverty and Incentives: The Economics of Social Security* (New York: Oxford University Press, 1984), p. 109.

4

Capitalism, "Property-Owning Democracy," and the Welfare State

RICHARD KROUSE AND MICHAEL McPHERSON

There has been much debate over whether Rawlsian justice in political economy is more compatible with private ownership or with social ownership of the means of production—debate no doubt inspired in part by Rawls's stated agnosticism on the issue. But there is broad if not universal consensus that, in affirming the possibility of a just private property market economy, *A Theory of Justice* offers "a philosophical apologia for an egalitarian brand of welfare-state capitalism."[1]

In our view, this consensus is misleading in two important respects. First, in labeling Rawls's idealized private property system "capitalist," the consensus view underestimates the degree of equalization of property holdings that Rawls's conception of just private property requires, and hence also the distance that separates his ideal from existing examples of

We are indebted to Richard Arneson, Alan Blinder, J. Donald Moon, George Marcus, John Rawls, Michael Weber, and members of the Seminar on the Welfare State, held at Princeton University during the fall of 1985, for valuable comments on an earlier draft of this paper.

[1] Robert Paul Wolff, *Understanding Rawls: A Reconstruction and Critique of "A Theory of Justice"* (Princeton, N.J.: Princeton University Press, 1977), p. 195. A partial list of those who see Rawls as offering a defense of welfare-state capitalism would include, in addition to Wolff, Brian Barry, *The Liberal Theory of Justice* (New York: Oxford University Press, 1973); Allen Buchanan, *Marx and Rawls: The Radical Critique of Justice* (Totowa, N.J.: Rowan and Allanheld, 1982); Barry Clark and Herbert Gintis, "Rawlsian Justice and Economic Systems," *Philosophy and Public Affairs* 7 (Summer 1978): 302–25; Norman Daniels, "Equal Liberty and Unequal Worth of Liberty," in Norman Daniels, ed., *Reading Rawls* (New York: Basic Books, 1975); Amy Gutmann, *Liberal Equality* (New York: Cambridge University Press, 1980); Carole Pateman, *The Problem of Political Obligation: A Critical Analysis of Liberal Theory* (New York: Wiley, 1979); Alan Ryan, *Property in Political Theory* (New York: Basil Blackwell, 1984); and David Schweikert, "Should Rawls Be a Socialist? A Comparison of His Ideal Capitalism with Worker-Controlled Socialism," *Social Theory and Practice* 5 (Fall 1978): 1–27. The only author, to our knowledge, who explicitly views Rawls's ideal as noncapitalist is Arthur Di Quattro; see "Rawls and Left Criticism," *Political Theory* 2 (February 1983): 54–78.

welfare-state capitalism. Indeed, if one follows Smith, Marx, and Weber in identifying capitalism as a social formation that divides society into propertied and propertyless classes (rather than defining all private property systems as capitalist), then Rawls's ideal regime should not be called capitalism at all. For the sake of clarity, we shall refer here to Rawls's ideal private property regime as "property-owning democracy," reserving the term "capitalism" for regimes (including welfare-state regimes) that accept deep inequality in the underlying distribution of property, however much they use taxes and transfers to redistribute incomes. The terminology does not matter much, but if in fact Rawls's ideal, unlike familiar versions of welfare-state capitalism, requires substantial equalization of property holdings, then that is an important and, in our view, attractive feature of his formulation.

Our second dissent from the consensus concerns the role of the welfare state in Rawls's theory. Rawls, we shall argue, is much less enthusiastic about using welfare-state taxes and transfers to redress income inequalities than many commentators suppose. This is partly because he wants to reduce the need for income transfers by making property holdings more equal. But Rawls's resistance to welfare-state measures goes beyond what can be justified by the need for more equal background conditions—and in our judgment he goes too far.

It should be stressed at the outset that we confine our discussion for the most part to the question of which private property system is best, without considering whether something else might be better. Rawls claims that justice cannot determine the choice between ideal private property and ideal socialist regimes. We will not systematically assess this claim, although we shall note in conclusion some possible problems with even an ideal private property regime that might argue for the superiority, on Rawlsian grounds, of a market socialist regime or perhaps of a system combining elements of property ownership and socialism. It should also be noted that, following Rawls, we focus principally on characterizing the ideal regime, and only secondarily on how to get there from here. We think it is illuminating to note that Rawls's ideal of just private property presupposes that ownership of productive property will be quite widespread. In this regard, it is important to ask (1) whether such a regime, once in place, could be prevented from unraveling over time; and (2) what strategies might be effective in promoting such a regime, assuming the initial existence of great inequality in property holdings. How one answers these difficult questions will affect one's conclusions about whether a Rawlsian just private property regime is an ideal worth pursuing. We address these questions, quite incompletely, in the Conclusion.

This attempt to characterize and assess Rawls's conception of an ideal private property regime has two main aims. First, given the prominence of Rawls's position in contemporary discussions of economic justice, we think it important to dispel what we see as a pervasive misconception about the kind of political economy he advocates. Second, we believe that Rawls's idealized private property system has considerable advantages (as well as some drawbacks), and we hope that a clear statement of its institutional requirements and way of operating will advance substantive discussion of justice in political economy.

Rawls's View of Just Property Institutions

Rawls's theory is based on two principles of justice. His first principle, which takes priority over the second, guarantees such liberty to each as is consistent with a like liberty for all. His second principle establishes that social and economic inequality should be to the greatest benefit of the least advantaged (called the difference principle), and that offices should be open to all under conditions of fair (rather than merely formal) equality of opportunity.

Though he maintains that these principles can at best provide the foundation for a just political economy, Rawls in all cases insists upon two conditions: (1) a regime of competitive markets, and (2) state intervention both to correct market imperfections (e.g., to supply public goods and to correct negative externalities) and to ensure the background conditions essential to distributive justice. Rawls favors a competitive market economy partly, of course, on standard efficiency grounds. But more important, markets provide an essential means of ensuring equal liberty and fair equality of opportunity. In particular, markets protect the "important liberty" of free choice of occupation, since "in the absence of some differences in earnings as these arise in a competitive scheme, it is hard to see how . . . certain aspects of a command society inconsistent with liberty can be avoided."[2] More generally, by decentralizing the exercise of economic power, markets protect free association and other important liberties of political opposition. Thus, for Rawls, the priority of both liberty and fair opportunity straightforwardly eliminates bureaucratic or state (i.e., nonmarket) socialism as a means for securing justice in political economy.

A crucial additional virtue of markets, closely related to the preceding considerations, is that it is only through their use that the problem of distributive shares can be handled as a case of "pure procedural justice."

[2] John Rawls, *A Theory of Justice* (Cambridge, Mass.: Harvard University Press, 1971), p. 272. For an illuminating discussion of the special circumstances under which equality of income can be combined with standard market efficiencies and freedoms, see Joseph Carens, *Equality, Moral Incentives, and the Market* (Chicago: University of Chicago Press, 1981).

With market allocation, the state can avoid having to keep track of the endless variety of circumstances and changing relative positions of particular persons, and the bureaucratic encumbrance this inevitably entails.

But, as Rawls emphasizes again and again, pure procedural justice requires that competitive markets be set within a framework of "appropriate background institutions." A just basic structure requires a background of legal and political institutions that regulate the overall trend of economic events and preserve the necessary social conditions. Only when markets are set within such a framework can justice, as Rawls tellingly puts it, "be left to take care of itself."[3] In more recent unpublished work, Rawls recognizes the need for sustaining appropriate background conditions by characterizing the ideal as that of "pure adjusted procedural justice."[4]

What are these "appropriate background institutions?" We discuss them more fully in the course of our argument. Here it is sufficient to note that these institutions must enforce (in order of priority) (1) fair value of political liberty, (2) fair equality of opportunity, and (3) the difference principle. Fair value of political liberty is required by Rawls's first principle; fair equality of opportunity and maximization of the life chances of the least advantaged are required by the second.

We may, on the basis of these fundamental requirements, immediately eliminate laissez-faire capitalism, or the "system of natural liberty," as a means for securing justice in political economy. Restricting the discussion for the moment to the second principle, we can say that the system of natural liberty ensures only formal (as opposed to fair) equality of opportunity; in permitting the competitive determination of total income (in accordance with only the weak requirement of efficiency), it presumptively violates the difference principle. In both respects, it permits distributive outcomes to be governed by natural and social contingencies that are arbitrary from a moral point of view. A just political economy must subject these contingencies to an appropriate scheme of legal and political regulation.

Although he thus eliminates both state socialism and laissez-faire capitalism as means for securing justice in political economy, for Rawls the two essential requirements—markets and appropriate background institutions—are compatible in principle with both private and social ownership of the means of production. Rawls is plainly not committed to the view that any existing system of political economy—property-owning or market socialist—is just. To the contrary, existing property regimes are

[3] Rawls, *A Theory of Justice*, p. 87.

[4] Rawls, "The Basic Structure as Subject" (revision), n.d.

"riddled with grave injustices."[5] No example of a market socialist society with political liberties exists, and no capitalist welfare state comes close to meeting the distributive requirements that appear, on the basis of plausible empirical assumptions, to follow from Rawls's commitments to fair value of liberty, fair equality of opportunity, and the difference principle. "Because there exists an ideal property-owning system that would be just," Rawls writes in the spirit of Mill, "does not imply that historical forms are just, or even tolerable. And, of course, the same is true for socialism."[6]

Nevertheless, as we have observed, Rawls's description of an ideal property-owning system in *A Theory of Justice* has been widely assumed, by critics and defenders alike, to be a reformed or idealized version of welfare-state capitalism. This assumption is, however, very dubious because the ideal property-owning regime described by Rawls is arguably not a form of capitalism at all.

Borrowing James Meade's idea of a "property-owning democracy," Rawls outlines an ideal system of private ownership in which "land and capital are widely though presumably not equally held. Society is not so divided that one fairly small sector controls the preponderance of productive resources."[7] Meade describes an economic system with, inter alia, strongly egalitarian inheritance laws limiting the intergenerational transmission of wealth; financial arrangements that would significantly boost the returns and opportunities available to small savers; and a strong governmental commitment to promoting equal opportunity in education. In Meade's judgment, such institutions would ensure that most people would start life with substantial property income, and that opportunities to invest in physical and human capital would be substantially equalized. There is plainly a question whether Meade's institutional proposals are sufficient to produce these egalitarian background conditions—a question we touch upon in the Conclusion. But clearly Rawls's view presupposes that widespread ownership of productive property would result, and if it did, the distinction between laboring and capitalist class would disappear. Thus, even though it would involve private ownership in the means of production, a "property-owning democracy" could not be described as "capitalist" in the classic Marxian sense.

It is particularly important, for our purposes, to note the differences, emphasized by Meade, between welfare-state capitalism and property-owning democracy. Both seek to subject the natural and social contingencies reflected in market outcomes to a just scheme of legal and political

[5] Rawls, *A Theory of Justice*, p. 86.

[6] Ibid., p. 274.

[7] James Meade, *Equality, Efficiency, and the Ownership of Property* (London: Allen and Unwin, 1964); Rawls, *A Theory of Justice*, p. 280.

regulation. But welfare-state capitalism (as commonly understood) accepts severe class inequality in the distribution of physical and human capital, and seeks to reduce the consequent disparities in market outcomes through redistributive tax and transfer programs. Property-owning democracy, by contrast, aims at sharply reduced inequality in the underlying distribution of property and wealth, and greater equality of opportunity to invest in human capital, so that operation of the market generates smaller inequalities to begin with. Thus, the two alternative regimes exemplify two alternative strategies for providing justice in political economy: Welfare-state capitalism accepts as given substantial inequality in the initial distribution of property and skill endowments, and then seeks to redistribute income ex post; property-owning democracy seeks greater equality in the ex ante distribution of property and skill endowments, with correspondingly less emphasis upon subsequent redistributive measures.

Although *A Theory of Justice* is not entirely unambiguous in its characterization of an ideal private property regime, we believe the work provides ample warrant for ascribing to Rawls the broad view of property-owning democracy developed here.[8] More important, there are good reasons to believe that the argument from the two principles shows property-owning democracy to be superior to welfare-state capitalism from the standpoint of Rawlsian justice.

The Two Principles and the Role of Unequal Endowments in a Just Property-Owning Regime

In this section we shall consider three requirements of the two principles, in the order of priority assigned to them by Rawls: fair value of political liberty, fair equality of opportunity, and the difference principle.

Fair Value of Political Liberty

A standard criticism of Rawls, which has come from the left, is that the meaningfulness or effectiveness of the formally equal civil and political rights guaranteed by the first principle would be systematically undermined by the (substantial) inequalities of income, wealth, and power sanctioned by the difference principle—thus violating the priority that

[8] Rawls's discussion of just political-economic institutions relies heavily on Meade (*Equality, Efficiency*). It is significant that Rawls never refers to his ideal property-owning regime as "capitalist." Rawls has indicated to us in private correspondence that he did intend in *A Theory of Justice* to endorse property-owning democracy in preference to welfare-state capitalism.

Rawls himself accords to the equal liberty principle. We shall contest this view, but we begin by noting its very real textual basis.

That basis is most notably Rawls's notorious distinction between liberty and the worth of liberty. Equal liberty requires only formal equality of liberty; unequal worth of liberty refers to inequalities in the capacity for the effective exercise of liberty.[9] Thus it appears that, for Rawls, the equal basic liberty required by his first principle is perfectly compatible with the indefinitely large inequalities permitted in theory by the difference principle.

But it is plain that matters cannot be left here. Rawls's response to this possible reading, even in *A Theory of Justice* but more explicitly in his later writing, is to argue that the worth or usefulness of many personal and civil liberties is not too seriously affected by the degree of inequality permitted under the difference principle, but that there are strong reasons to take special steps to further limit the unequal worth of political liberty—because political liberty is necessary to secure just legislation and because its worth is largely determined by the degree of inequality.[10]

Whether or not Rawls should build in more protection for the worth of liberties other than political liberty, he is almost certainly right that strict equality in the worth of liberty is not a feasible or desirable goal. Since individuals cannot be equalized, either in their material resources or in the talents, skills, and motivations that they bring to the exercise of formally equal rights, it is difficult to see how some inequality in the worth of liberty can be avoided. The basic notion behind Rawls's definition of justice as fairness—that some inequalities should be permitted because they are in the mutual interest of all—surely applies here.[11] Moreover, to effect this complete equalization would almost certainly involve decreasing the autonomy of the family and, arguably, manipulating the natural endowments of persons as well—"egalitarian collapse," unacceptable from a Rawlsian, and more broadly liberal, perspective. (We shall return to this issue when we discuss fair equality of opportunity.)

Although he rejects equal worth of liberty as a possible or in any case desirable goal, Rawls insists on measures to secure the "fair value" of political liberty. By this he means approximate equality, or at least the absence of severe inequality, in the resources and capacities essential for the effective achievement of formally equal political liberty—in other words, approximate equality in the worth of political liberty. The question we need to answer is, what kinds of institutional arrangements are needed to secure the fair value of political liberty? Rawls in effect consid-

[9] See especially the criticism of Rawls in Daniels, "Equal Liberty."

[10] Rawls, "The Basic Liberties and Their Priority," in *The Tanner Lectures on Human Values* (Salt Lake City: University of Utah Press, 1982), p. 43.

[11] Ibid., p. 44.

ers two alternative strategies to this end: (1) insulating the state from the influence of underlying inequalities in economy and society, and (2) eliminating those inequalities.[12]

At certain points he appears to rely heavily if not exclusively upon the former strategy. What is crucial, if the fair value of political liberty is to be secured, is that political parties, and by implication the political process more generally, "be autonomous with respect to private demands." Rawls insists upon insulating the political process from underlying inequalities in the economic and social system through public financing of political parties, provision of government moneys on a regular basis to encourage free discussion, and the like. In the absence of these measures, he argues, private interests with greater resources come to acquire "a preponderant weight in settling social questions"; the political forum is "so constrained by the wishes of the dominant interests that the basic measures necessary to establish just constitutional rule are seldom seriously presented."[13]

Are such measures, necessary to secure the fair value of liberty, sufficient? Rawls is often read as assuming that, through such prophylactic measures alone, the liberal democratic state could be rendered fully autonomous vis-à-vis underlying inequalities of income, wealth, and power. Note that from this it would follow that such a fully autonomous liberal democratic state could, even when superimposed upon an otherwise untransformed capitalist economy, uphold distributive justice through more or less standard tax and transfer, welfare-state programs.[14] R. P. Wolff charges that "Rawls has no theory of the state"—that is, he appears to believe that a reformed liberal democratic welfare state could achieve distributive justice "painlessly, cooperatively, harmoniously, and within the present framework of private enterprise."[15] And Alan Ryan sympathetically assumes Rawls to have demonstrated that "anything which can be done by a government under socialism can apparently be done by a government under capitalism, when it operates vis-à-vis the tax and welfare system."[16]

We deny that Rawls holds these views attributed to him, which are, in any case, implausible. It would be naive indeed to believe the strategy of insulation just outlined sufficient to secure the fair value of political liberty and the autonomy of the state in the face of severe class inequality in

[12] James Fishkin, *Justice, Equal Opportunity, and the Family* (New Haven, Conn.: Yale University Press, 1983).

[13] Rawls, *A Theory of Justice*, pp. 225–26.

[14] Or could, in other words, combine any system of production with any system of distribution.

[15] Wolff, *Understanding Rawls*, pp. 202, 207.

[16] Alan Ryan, *Property in Political Theory* (New York: Basil Blackwell, 1984), p. 190.

the ownership and control of productive resources. For, as work by both mainstream and Marxian theorists suggests, capitalist economies impose significant structural constraints upon the range of policy options available to the liberal democratic state—which depends for its tax revenues and overall political viability upon a healthy process of capital accumulation, and hence upon the private investment decisions of those who own and control productive resources.[17] This dependency raises the gravest doubts about the ability of liberal democratic regimes operating in capitalist environments to maintain the fair value of political liberty or, more generally, to promote distributive justice. Fair value requires, as well, the elimination of at least the most severe underlying economic and social inequalities if the political process is (through public financing of political parties, etc.) to be insulated from the inequalities that remain. This theme figures prominently in *A Theory of Justice*, and bears upon the choice between welfare-state capitalism and property-owning democracy.

Rawls states the point most straightforwardly as follows: "There is a maximum gain permitted to the most favored on the assumption that, even if the difference principle would allow it, there would be unjust effects on the political system and the like excluded by the priority of liberty." Under extant capitalism, "disparities in the distribution of property and wealth that far exceed what is compatible with political equality have generally been tolerated by the legal system."[18] Again and again he emphasizes that if the fair value of political liberty is to be maintained, background institutions for upholding distributive justice must prevent excessive accumulation of property and wealth.[19] The institutional means by which this widespread dispersion of property and wealth is to be achieved are discussed more fully later in this paper. Insofar as it is precisely this widespread dispersion in the ownership of property and wealth that most sharply differentiates property-owning democracy from welfare-state capitalism, the Rawlsian commitment to the priority of liberty, including the fair value of political liberty, lends decisive support to the former system over the latter as the ideal version of a private property market economy.[20]

[17] Charles Lindblom, *Politics and Markets: The World's Political-Economic Systems* (New York: Basic Books, 1977); and Lindblom, "The Market as Prison," in *Journal of Politics* 44 (May 1982): 324–36.

[18] Rawls, *A Theory of Justice*, pp. 81, 226.

[19] Ibid., pp. 73, 225, 278, e.g.

[20] Although we have emphasized here the value of political liberty, the importance of equalized property holding to some forms of personal liberty can also be argued. Meade, in *Equality, Efficiency*, says of property-owning democracy: "The essential feature of this society would be that work had become rather more a matter of personal choice. The unpleasant work that had to be done would have to be very highly paid to attract to it those whose tastes led them to wish to supplement considerably their incomes from property. At the

Fair Equality of Opportunity

Background institutions that ensure fair equality of opportunity are an essential feature of a just scheme of legal and political regulation. Formal equality of opportunity, or "careers open to talents," is necessary but not sufficient. There must in addition be "roughly equal prospects of culture and achievement for everyone similarly motivated and endowed. The expectations of those with the same abilities and aspirations should not be affected by their social class."[21]

What this requires, above all else, is equal educational opportunity for all. The system of educational provision must "even out class barriers," which at a minimum entails ensuring equality of resources for those born into less privileged social positions and having fewer native assets. Indeed, in order to treat all persons equally, it might be necessary, under the principle of redress, to devote more attention and resources to those born into less favorable social positions or with fewer native assets.[22]

However, fair equality of opportunity, like equal worth of liberty, can at best be imperfectly realized. This is so, at least, as long as the autonomy of the family—required, arguably, by the priority of liberty—is respected. The degree to which natural talents reach fruition is and will remain deeply influenced by this institution. A fortiori, moreover, the ideal of fair equality of opportunity accepts the distribution of natural endowments as given. Despite their moral arbitrariness, it does not seek (through genetic engineering, for example) to even out their distribution.

Thus, so long as the institution of the family exists and natural endowments are accepted as given, neither perfectly fair equality of opportunity nor perfect equality in the worth of liberty can ever be achieved—even under conditions of "simple equality."[23] But the degree to which both fair value of liberty and fair equality of opportunity can be approximated will be significantly influenced by the degree of underlying economic and social inequality. Just as fair value of liberty can never be fully insulated from great disparities of property and wealth, fair equality of opportunity will be undermined by these inequalities (transmitted through the institution of the family). Rawls draws the parallel explicitly, arguing that severe inequalities of property and wealth threaten both values simultaneously: Institutions whose aim is to ensure fair opportunity "are put in jeopardy when inequalities of wealth exceed a certain limit; and political

---

other extreme those who wished to devote themselves to quite uncommercial activities would be able to do so with a reduced standard of living, but without starving in a garret" (pp. 40–41).

[21] Rawls, *A Theory of Justice*, p. 73.

[22] Ibid., pp. 73, 100–101.

[23] Michael Walzer, *Spheres of Justice: A Defense of Pluralism and Equality* (New York: Basic Books, 1983).

liberty tends likewise to lose its value, and representative government to become such in appearance only."[24]

Thus, fair value of liberty and fair equality of opportunity both require constraints upon the permissible degree of underlying inequality. To this end, Rawls—following Meade—places great emphasis upon restricting the intergenerational transmission of unequal property and wealth. It is the explicit purpose of the first section of the "distribution branch," in Rawls's structure of governmental institutions, to ensure that public finance prevent concentration of property and wealth incompatible with fair value of liberty and fair equality of opportunity—significantly, by means of a steeply progressive scheme of inheritance and gift taxation.

Thus, fair equality of opportunity, like fair value of liberty, decisively supports property-owning democracy over welfare-state capitalism as the ideal private property market economy. To combat the effects of unequal family circumstances, a state requires far greater equality in the distribution of physical capital, of initial property endowments, than has been achieved by any capitalist welfare state, or that indeed seems compatible with the idea of capitalism. Likewise, the egalitarian system of educational provision required by the idea of fair opportunity would, by substantially equalizing opportunities to invest in human capital, substantially reduce inequalities in initial skill endowments. This, too, is integral to the ideal of a property-owning democracy. And although there is no reason in principle why an ideal welfare-state capitalism could not attempt substantially greater equality of education provision, the system's necessarily greater inequality in the distribution of property and wealth would (given the autonomy of the family) again seem to make it, ceteris paribus, a less promising environment for the fullest possible realization of fair equality of opportunity.

It is interesting to note that the first principle, combined with the priority of fair equality of opportunity in the second (that is, minus the difference principle), gives *A Theory of Justice* considerable egalitarian bite. Although the difference principle could in theory permit indefinitely large inequalities, fair value of liberty and fair equality of opportunity powerfully constrain any such inegalitarian implications. In the next section we consider what role, assuming that the background institutions required by these two principles are in place, the difference principle plays in Rawls's institutional scheme.

The Difference Principle

Most discussions of the difference principle have, in our view, been significantly impaired by lack of attention to the exchange environment (or

[24] Rawls, *A Theory of Justice*, p. 278.

initial distribution of endowments) in which the processes of market exchange plus state intervention would operate. They have, more precisely, assumed that, in a property-owning regime, the difference principle would be implemented in an exchange environment defined by the institutions of welfare-state capitalism.

Thus, it is generally assumed, the processes of market exchange—reflecting an initially unequal distribution of physical and human capital—will generate a highly unequal pretax distribution of wealth and income. It is then the role of the welfare state, through a more or less extensive system of tax and transfer programs, to redistribute income in accordance with the requirements of the difference principle (consistent with equal liberty and fair opportunity).

How extensive a program of egalitarian redistribution would the difference principle, applied under these conditions, require? Very extensive, it is sometimes assumed. Wolff, as we have seen, criticizes Rawls for failing to understand that the liberal democratic welfare state, operating in a capitalist system, could not generate "the very considerable political power [necessary] to enforce the sorts of wage rates, tax policies, transfer payments, and job regulation called for by the difference principle." Clark and Gintis similarly stress the substantial redistributive effort implied in applying the difference principle under capitalist conditions, because of the arguably insupportable "strains of commitment" that these redistributive requirements would impose.[25]

We freely concede that the egalitarian potential of the difference principle would face powerful constraints, both political and economic, when the principle was applied in a capitalist system. Thus, if Rawls did presuppose some version of welfare-state capitalism as the political and economic environment in which the difference principle is to be implemented, then the incoherence ascribed to his position by critics such as Wolff or Clark and Gintis would be real. But his argument includes no such presupposition. To the contrary, it emphasizes in the strongest possible way the alternative strategy of creating institutions that will ensure a more equal underlying distribution of physical and human capital, or property and skill endowments, so that the market will generate less unequal results to begin with. The idea is to develop a system of rules—themselves not overly intrusive upon the everyday working of the economy—that would prevent development of undue concentrations of economic and political power, or at least would dissolve them fairly rapidly

[25] Wolff, *Understanding Rawls*, p. 202; and Barry Clark and Herbert Gintis, "Rawlsian Justice and Economic Systems," in *Philosophy and Public Affairs* 7 (Summer 1978): 302–25.

after they occur. Strong measures to promote the intergenerational redistribution of property would be a necessary part of such a scheme.[26]

This stress on underlying equality is, we believe, crucial for Rawls. Several times in *A Theory of Justice* he insists that, if the appropriate background institutions are in place, pure procedural justice operating through market institutions "will tend to satisfy the difference principle" (p. 87). "In a competitive economy (with or without private ownership) with an open class system, excessive inequalities will not be the rule. Given the distribution of natural assets and the laws of motivation, great disparities will not long persist" (p. 158). "Although in theory the difference principle permits indefinitely large inequalities in return for small gains to the less favored, the spread of income and wealth should not be excessive in practice, given the requisite background institutions" (p. 536).

Thus, the exchange environment within which Rawls envisions the difference principle operating is intended to provide considerably more equality in the underlying distribution of property than many commentators have supposed. But this equalization plainly will be sufficient to accomplish what the difference principle requires. The government, acting through its "transfer branch," must ensure an "appropriate social minimum."

To get a clearer idea of just what this responsibility amounts to, it is useful to examine the impact of the institutions of property-owning democracy on disparities in labor incomes. In the Rawlsian ideal version of a property-owning democracy, full employment is maintained by the "stabilization branch"; formal equality of freedom in the choice of occupation is rendered effective by strong aggregate demand and tight labor markets. Moreover, with most workers deriving part of their income from the ownership of property, and an appropriate social minimum guaranteed, there would be no class of workers who were forced to sell their labor power in order to survive.[27] When "exit" is a viable option, the bargaining power of labor is strong. The "worst aspects of so-called wage slavery are removed" (p. 281).

Although these policies would raise the income floor, what is crucial to closing the income spread is fair equality of opportunity. By equalizing opportunities to invest in the acquisition of human capital, fair equality

[26] Necessary but presumably not sufficient. Power could concentrate in large firms even if widespread share ownership kept personal inequality in check, and further political regulations of economic life to control such power might well be justified. At the same time, the effectiveness of a strategy for promoting underlying equality presupposes that intergenerational redistribution will not itself face insuperable economic or political obstacles. This presupposition is further discussed in the concluding section.

[27] The importance of this point is stressed by Meade in *Equality, Efficiency*, p. 39.

of opportunity would increase the number of persons equipped with various forms of currently market-scarce skills (e.g., medical training), and hence reduce the amount of economic rent accruing to those forms of human capital. As the supply of persons endowed with such skills increased relative to demand, the incomes of those jobs would be bid down; and as the supply of persons compelled by lack of training to accept unskilled jobs (e.g., as hospital orderlies) decreased relative to demand, the price of those jobs would be bid up. Thus with "many more persons receiving the benefits of training and education, the supply of qualified individuals is much greater. When there are no restrictions on entry or imperfections in the capital market for loans (or subsidies) for education, the premium earned by those better endowed is far less. The relative difference in earnings between the more favored and the lowest income class tends to close" (p. 307). Differentials that remained would tend to be compensatory, reflecting differences in the cost of training for and the attractiveness of different sorts of jobs.

This increasingly compensatory aspect of the difference principle under fair equality of opportunity can be seen in the changing relative weight given to two of the common-sense precepts of justice: "to each according to his contribution" weighs less heavily, whereas "to each according to his effort" weighs more heavily. Thus, for example, if there were greater equality in the distribution of initial skill endowments, "to each according to his education and training," considered a special case of the precept of contribution, would receive less weight. At the same time, since individuals would still choose to invest differentially in human capital (because of different preferences regarding time rate of investments, different consumption-leisure trade-offs, and the like), differential rewards to cover the "costs of training and postponement" (p. 306), considered now a special case of the precept of effort, would still receive some weight. Various present disutilities of work (such as intensity, duration, risk, responsibility, dirt, danger, and boredom)—also considered special cases of the precept of effort—would receive compensating or equalizing wage differentials, since otherwise the jobs would simply go unperformed.

Indeed, Rawls sometimes writes—quite unjustifiably in terms of his underlying theory—as if under ideal conditions, all wage differentials would be compensatory. In a perfectly competitive economy with a just basic structure, "in equilibrium the relative attractiveness of different jobs will be equal, all things considered" (p. 305). That is, under these circumstances, there will be an equalization of net advantages between jobs—net advantage being defined as the sum of monetary and nonmonetary advantages minus the sum of monetary and nonmonetary disadvantages.[28] This is striking. It suggests, for example, that under ideal conditions, the difference principle would correspond perfectly with Ronald Dworkin's idea of equality of resources—all wage differentials would be "ambition sensitive" as opposed to "endowment sensitive."[29]

But equalization of net advantages between jobs holds only under the special condition of identical natural talents. And Rawls explicitly affirms that "persons have different natural abilities" (p. 307). Thus he either contradicts himself or fails at times to recognize that, even in a perfectly competitive economy with a just system of property and widespread opportunities to acquire skills, persons with scarce natural talents (e.g., professional athletes) will often command wages that far exceed the amount necessary to compensate them for any disutility associated with their work—or, indeed, any additional amount needed to provide incentives for the development and use of these talents. We shall argue in the next section that this discrepancy helps explain Rawls's otherwise rather puzzling opposition to progressive income taxation and, more broadly, leads him to understate the necessary role of welfare-state taxes and transfers in mitigating the arbitrariness of the natural lottery.

This discussion of wage inequality in a property-owning democracy should be related to Rawls's analysis of the role of government's "transfer" branch in securing a social minimum. To do so, it is helpful to replace Rawls's unacceptable claim that such wage inequalities would be fully compensatory with the empirically plausible (if still contestable) claim that existing noncompensatory wage inequalities are not totally due to differences in natural assets. Such inequalities could be substantially reduced by putting in place the background institutions of property-owning democracy. The government's task of securing the social minimum would then be a modest one; the transfer branch would be a supplementary rather than a central social institution. Rawls's underlying assumption is that the distribution of natural assets is sufficiently equal that it would not upset the ability of a competitive economy, with a just basic structure, to avoid great disparities in the (pretax) distribution of income and wealth. That is to say, it underscores his belief that the institutions of a property-owning democracy could—by ensuring greater equality in the initial distribution of property and skill endowments—satisfy the difference principle without the need for extensive subsequent redistribution by the cumbersome (progressive) tax and transfer programs of the welfare state.

[28] B. J. McCormick, *Wages* (Baltimore: Penguin, 1969), p. 22; quoted in Joseph Carens, "Compensatory Justice and Social Institutions," *Economics and Philosophy* 2 (1985): 21.

[29] Ronald Dworkin, "What is Equality? Part 2: Equality of Resources," in *Philosophy and Public Affairs* 10 (Fall 1982): 283–345.

We criticize Rawls in the next section, as we have indicated, for underestimating the need for a range of important redistributive policies. But given the inherent political and economic constraints upon the ability of welfare-state capitalism to achieve egalitarian redistribution, it is important to underscore the basic appeal of the idea of property-owning democracy and of the strategy it uses to achieve greater equality in the distribution of initial property and skill endowments—as opposed to subsequent redistribution of highly unequal incomes—as a desirable means to achieve the fullest possible realization of the difference principle. Thus the ideal type of property-owning democracy more nearly approximates the ideal private property market economy, from a Rawlsian perspective, than does the ideal type of welfare-state capitalism.

The Role of Welfare Provision in a Just Property-Owning Economy

Thus far, we have argued that there are inherent political and economic limits upon the ability of welfare-state capitalism to ensure fair value of liberty and fair equality of opportunity, and to apply the difference principle; and that the ideal private property market economy, from the standpoint of these Rawlsian values, is one that is founded on the institutions of property-owning democracy. In so doing, we have focused upon one of the two broad strategies previously identified—equalization of initial property and skill endowments, as opposed to (intergenerational) redistribution of initially unequal market results—as the preferred means of realizing Rawlsian justice in political economy.

We now wish to argue, however, that Rawls's views on institutional design suffer from too exclusive an emphasis upon the "equalization of initial endowments" approach as exemplified by property-owning democracy. Far from relying predominantly if not exclusively upon the redistributive tax and transfer programs of the welfare state, as is most often alleged, Rawls's approach is insufficiently redistributionist and, therefore, is an inadequate justification for certain legitimate forms of welfare-state provision. Rawlsian justice in political economy reflects a predominant, but not exclusive, emphasis upon the equalization of initial endowments approach embodied in the idea of a property-owning democracy. It requires, as well, the continuing redistribution of market outcomes (within as well as between generations) by the institutions of the welfare state—to a greater extent, we claim, than envisaged or explicitly affirmed by Rawls.

Perhaps the central intuition of *A Theory of Justice* is the belief that both social contingencies and natural fortune are "arbitrary from a moral point of view" (p. 72). Because no one can be said to deserve his or her starting point in the distribution of social contingency or natural fortune, an appropriate set of background institutions will permit unequal entitlements to flow from these initial endowments only insofar as they satisfy the two principles of justice.

Rawls places great emphasis, moreover, upon the symmetry of social contingency and natural fortune. Any conception of justice that seeks to redress the moral arbitrariness of one but not the other is theoretically unstable: "For once we are troubled by the influence of either social contingencies or natural chance on the determination of distributive shares, we are bound, on reflection, to be bothered by the influence of the other. From a moral standpoint the two seem equally arbitrary" (pp. 74–75).

Thus Rawls argues that both because equality of opportunity can at best be imperfectly realized (so long as the institution of the family exists), and because distributive shares will in any case be influenced by the outcomes of the natural lottery, we need a further principle—the difference principle—to redress the morally arbitrary consequences of social contingency and natural fortune. And it is the difference principle—which prohibits the competitive determination of total income and requires instead the provision of an adequate social minimum—that is widely presumed to provide the Rawlsian justification for egalitarian redistribution through the tax and transfer programs of the welfare state.

Yet, as we have already suggested, there is good reason to believe that Rawls fails adequately to heed his own injunctions regarding the moral symmetry of the various forms of social and natural contingency. This can be seen more fully by identifying four such forms of contingency, all equally arbitrary from a moral point of view: initial endowments of natural talent; initial endowments of property (or physical capital); initial endowments of skill (or human capital); and brute market luck ("such chance contingencies as accident and good fortune," p. 72).

Whereas welfare-state capitalism accepts substantial inequality in each of these four dimensions, and seeks to mitigate the moral arbitrariness of social contingency and natural fortune through ex post measures of redistribution, ex ante equalization of initial property and skill endowments is, as we have seen, central to the idea of property-owning democracy. But even if this equalization could be perfectly realized (which, of course, it cannot), two of these four contingencies would still exist: natural talent and brute market luck. Thus, as Rawls correctly emphasizes, we require a principle for correcting the consequences of these residual sources of inequality.

Although this is precisely the role assigned by Rawls to the difference principle, he sometimes shrinks from enforcing it. This can be seen clearly in his opposition to progressive income taxation as a means of upholding the difference principle—opposition predicated upon the belief that the pretax distribution of income will, under conditions of fair opportunity, already be (approximately) just.

Though progressive income taxation is permissible in principle if necessary to preserve the fair value of liberty or fair equality of opportunity, it would not in his view be necessary under ideal circumstances to uphold the difference principle. (Its application as a second-best alternative is another matter.) His clear preference is for progressive inheritance taxation across generations, proportional taxation of income (or, better, expenditure) within generations. Rawls prefers proportional taxation both because it is in his view fairer (assuming that income is fairly earned) and because it is likely, because it interferes less with incentives, to be more efficient.

As we have noted, Rawls sometimes suggests that most—perhaps all—wage differentials would, under conditions of fair opportunity, be compensatory. And, on the plausible assumption that compensation for disutility would under these conditions function as a necessary incentive for the performance of essential social tasks, such differentials would clearly satisfy the difference principle.

But we have also pointed out that, even under conditions of fair opportunity, those with scarce natural talents—or the brute market luck to have invested physical or human capital successfully—would still command returns well above those necessary as compensation for disutility (effort, risk, etc.). Are these returns justified by the difference principle? Yes and no. The difference principle is not, despite Di Quattro's assertion, a purely compensatory conception of justice; it encompasses compensatory considerations, but not to the exclusion of other considerations.[30] According to Rawls, "the premiums earned by scarce natural talents . . . are to cover the costs of training and to encourage the efforts of learning, as well as to direct ability where it best furthers the common interest" (p. 311). "The function of unequal distributive shares is to cover the costs of training and education, to attract individuals to places and associations where they are most needed from a social point of view, and so on" (p. 315). Thus, if and to the extent that the disciplined and dedicated performance of essential social tasks requires differential rewards above and beyond those plausibly necessary as compensation for disutility, those rewards, too, are justified by the difference principle. The difference principle, that is, would appear to justify paying those with scarce natural talents their transfer price (i.e., the amount necessary to prevent them from switching to a socially less desirable use of their talents)—even if that price includes an element of economic blackmail.

[30] Arthur Di Quattro, "Rawls and Left Criticism," in *Political Theory* 2 (February 1983): 54–78.

By the same token, however, the difference principle does not permit the payment of economic rent, above this transfer price, to those with scarce natural talents (or who enjoy brute market luck). Thus, if and to the extent that such premiums could, without having an unduly adverse effect on incentives, be transferred to the least advantaged through a scheme of progressive taxation, such a tax and transfer policy would clearly be required by the difference principle. Hence, Rawls's stated opposition to progressive taxation as a means of upholding the difference principle seems to contradict his own affirmation of the difference principle as a necessary means of mitigating the moral arbitrariness of social contingency and natural fortune.

Rawls's opposition to progressive taxation would appear to rest upon several debatable empirical assumptions. He appears either to assume, incorrectly, that under fair equality of opportunity, all wage differentials will be compensatory (and therefore justified by the difference principle); or, less implausibly but still controversially, that inequalities in the distribution of natural talent (and market luck) will not in fact be so great as to disrupt an otherwise approximately just pretax distribution.[31] The argument also rests upon assumptions regarding the adverse impact of progressive taxation upon incentives that are plausible given the prior assumption of an approximately just pretax distribution (i.e., the absence of rents to compensate for scarce natural talents), but controversial if this prior assumption is dropped. Given these assumptions, and given the assurance of an adequate income floor through the guarantee of an appropriate social minimum, Rawls's opposition to the ceiling provided by progressive taxation of income is perhaps understandable. But there seems no good reason to embrace the empirical assumptions in the first place. More reasonable assumptions would lead to the conclusion that Rawlsian justice requires the progressive taxation of income.[32]

Thus far, we have criticized Rawls for failing, in his views on institu-

[31] Technically, Rawls's endorsement of proportional taxation would be supportable if the fraction of earnings that represented economic rent was the same at different income levels. But it seems more logical to suppose that incomes reflecting a high return to natural talent or brute market luck would be concentrated toward the upper end of the scale.

[32] It must, however, be conceded that there is an important sense in which this line of criticism is mooted by another aspect of Rawls's views on institutional design. Though Rawls, in presenting his theory of the ideal private property market economy, opposes progressive income taxation as a means of upholding the difference principle, he also affirms that progressive inheritance and income taxation are permissible in principle if necessary to maintain the fair value of liberty and fair equality of opportunity (though his stress is on inheritance taxes). And since, as we have seen, these requirements serve as a constraint upon inequalities that would be permissible in theory under the difference principle, we may suppose that they supply the warrant for progressive income taxation that Rawls denies to the difference principle standing by itself.

tional design, to pursue fully the logical implications of the difference principle. There is, however, another crucially important form of welfare-state redistribution for which the logic of the difference principle provides an inadequate justification: redistribution to those with differential basic needs.[33]

Rawls's theory is determinedly "resourcist" as opposed to "welfarist": "Justice as fairness . . . does not look behind the use which persons make of the rights and opportunities available to them in order to measure, much less to maximize, the satisfactions they achieve" (p. 94). But by refusing to look behind these resources to consider their impact upon the distribution of welfare, Rawls, in applying the difference principle, fails adequately to consider the differential needs of the sick, the handicapped, and so on. He appears to believe that the provision of an adequate social minimum, in accordance with the requirements of the difference principle, answers adequately the claims of need; he assumes, for example, that such a social minimum will somehow incorporate "special payments for sickness" (p. 275). But this stipulation regarding medical care seems purely ad hoc. What the difference principle requires is that we maximize the long-run expectations of the representative least well-off person; it precludes the targeting of social provision to those with special needs. Thus, although the difference principle seems reasonably well suited to ensure the satisfaction of an important range of essentially nondifferential basic needs (e.g., food, clothing, shelter), it is quite ill-suited to ensure the protection of an equally important range of differential basic needs (e.g., medical care or legal services). The difference principle as such quite simply fails to provide an adequate justification for several crucially important forms of welfare-state provision—it fails to ensure adequately against a great deal of debilitating social and natural distress.

The failure of the difference principle to consider the claims of special need appears inconsistent with the central intent of justice as fairness. For from the perspective of the original position, risk-averse agents would surely want, above all else, to ensure the satisfaction of (differential as well as nondifferential) basic needs. The precise reformulation of the two principles required to address these considerations—that is, to incorporate certain basic welfare rights—need not concern us here. The point is that the logic of Rawls's own theory requires greater continuing scope for certain important forms of welfare-state provision than the two principles, in their present form, provide.

There are at least two distinct senses in which Rawls's theory provides

[33] In the following two paragraphs, we rely heavily upon Barry, *The Liberal Theory of Justice*; Gutmann, *Liberal Equality*; and A. K. Sen, "Equality of What?" in *Choice, Welfare, and Measurement* (Cambridge, Mass.: MIT Press, 1982), pp. 353–69. See also Carens, *Equality, Moral Incentives*, pp. 186–87; and Meade, *Equality, Efficiency*, pp. 72–73.

insufficient scope for certain important forms of redistribution by the institutions of the welfare state: a sense in which Rawls's own views on institutional design fail to carry through on the logic of the difference principle, and a sense in which the logic of the difference principle is itself defective.

This reading of Rawls leads us to a view of his theory that is at odds with prevalent interpretations. Rawls has, for different reasons, been consistently criticized from both the right and the left for excessive reliance upon the redistribution of market outcomes by welfare-state institutions. We have argued that these criticisms are fundamentally misguided—that Rawls, to the contrary, focuses heavily upon achieving a more equal initial distribution of property and skill endowments. And given the inherent political and economic limits upon the redistribution of initially unequal market outcomes, we have endorsed Rawls's basic strategy.

However, it is also clear that exclusive reliance upon the equalization of initial-endowments strategy (or even Rawls's high degree of reliance on it) is no more promising a formula for achieving justice in political economy than exclusive reliance upon the redistribution of highly unequal market outcomes. We cannot, nor should we, altogether eliminate the impact of certain morally arbitrary social and natural contingencies upon the market's distribution of rewards. Therefore, even under conditions of an ideal property-owning democracy, justice requires more continuing redistribution of market outcomes by welfare-state institutions than Rawls's formulations permit.[34] We thus arrive at the paradoxical conclusion that Rawls's own views on institutional design, and his two principles in their present form, are insufficiently, not excessively, redistributionist or "welfare-statist."

Conclusion

We have sought to establish two principal points. First, a regime that establishes and preserves widespread ownership of productive property and limits the concentration of property over time is superior from the standpoint of Rawlsian justice to one that accepts deep inequality in the ownership of productive property and corrects the results of those inequalities through welfare-state income redistribution. In our shorthand, Rawlsian justice ranks property-owning democracy over welfare-state capitalism. This judgment, we have argued, is supported both by Rawls's statements and by logical reasoning from Rawls's principles of justice.

[34] Indeed, James Meade recognizes this point in noting that his proposals for creating a property-owning democracy are needed "to supplement rather than to replace the existing Welfare-State policies" (*Equality, Efficiency*, p. 75).

Second, Rawlsian justice requires that even a property-owning democracy establish a nontrivial role for welfare-state redistribution, to enable the state both to share fairly the fruits of natural talents and to respond to differential needs. Here our argument aims to amend Rawls's statements. We claim that the difference principle calls for differential taxation of rents according to natural ability, which Rawls sometimes neglects, and that the underlying rationale for Rawls's view should lead him to modify the difference principle to take better account of differential needs.

This analysis provides, we think, a fair description of the distributive arrangements required by the private property variant of the ideal Rawlsian just society, for it highlights the importance of preserving an adequately egalitarian underlying distribution of property. It thus throws into sharper relief some basic questions about the character and implications of this private property ideal, among them the following:

- What institutional means are required to preserve this egalitarian distribution over time (should it at some time be achieved), and indeed can adequate means be described?
- What would life in a property-owning democracy be like? Would the combination of (relatively) egalitarian property ownership and competitive markets produce a society that was acceptably "well-ordered," harmonious, and stable?
- Can a theory of justice illuminate the choice between the best private property regime—property-owning democracy—and the best socialist arrangements for providing justice?
- How can this characterization of the ideal property-owning democracy help to guide the process of reform in existing, nonideal, private property societies?

Limitations of space and of our understanding preclude us from fully answering these four broad questions. But we shall conclude by offering some observations, keyed to those questions, that may put further deliberation about them in a useful context.

First, Rawls follows Meade in supposing that the key institutional means of preserving widespread property ownership in a property-owning democracy are (1) inheritance laws and taxes that encourage wide dispersal of property at death,[35] (2) encouragements to saving for families

[35] Meade advocates a so-called accessions tax, a progressive tax on an individual's lifetime receipt of gifts and inheritances above a threshold. Unlike confiscatory estate taxes, which bring property under government control, an accessions tax creates incentives for the wealthy to avoid concentrating gift donation on just a few individuals; the tax is avoided by

of modest means, and (3) public policies that promote equal opportunity in education. One might object to this institutional scheme either on grounds that it would not be adequate to preserve widespread property ownership or on grounds that the necessary arrangements would have negative side effects. Thus, the effectiveness of these measures might be challenged because they do not eliminate property inequalities that arise within generations, or because even widely dispersed inheritances would not reach many propertyless individuals. Negative side effects might include a tendency for the wealthy to consume their property before death, thus undermining economic growth, or to avoid taxes by making large gifts to foundations and charitable organizations, which would gain excessive power.[36]

It would be too much to expect a theory of justice to incorporate detailed responses to all such objections. A society that was trying hard to preserve widespread property ownership would experiment with and try to improve its institutions, but the best arrangements cannot be specified in advance. The real question is whether any objections can be identified that are clearly insuperable.

A proper investigation of that issue would have several aspects. We would have to examine whether the causal claims underlying the objections hold up. For example, although taxing inheritances might discourage saving, this effect might be offset by the fact that nobody would start life with a large inheritance and savings by the "middle class" would thus be encouraged. The net results are not clear. We would also have to weigh the seriousness of the flaws uncovered. Wealth inequalities within a generation are acceptable on Rawlsian principles if they contribute to the general good and are compatible with fair value of political liberty and fair equality of opportunity. Finally, we would need to consider modifying the institutions to correct for serious defects. To discourage excessive accumulations in charitable institutions, the government might tax their receipts or limit their size. Or if private savings are too low, the government might run a budget surplus to generate national saving. Excessive wealth accumulations within generations might be taxed; the government might provide endowments of property to those who would otherwise be propertyless. Obviously, if necessary interventions multiply, the whole institutional structure becomes shaky: at some point the notion that a society is ensuring "pure adjusted procedural justice" by maintaining back-

---

spreading gifts widely. The economics of such a tax are discussed by C. T. Sanford, J.R.M. Willis, and D. J. Ironside, *IFS: An Accessions Tax*, publication no. 7 (London: Institute for Fiscal Studies, 1973); and Lester C. Thurow, *Generating Inequality: Mechanisms of Distribution in the U.S. Economy* (New York: Basic Books, 1975).

36 We have benefited from Richard Arneson's discussion with us of these (and other) objections.

ground institutions starts to wear thin. But it is hard to form a firm judgment about these matters without more knowledge about societies that have tried hard to preserve some measure of equality in property holding.

The second question is whether the combination of egalitarian property holdings and a competitive economy is a sociologically stable mixture. This goes deeper than the first set of concerns, since it is a question not just of the means for preserving a property-owning democracy but of the character of that sort of society. The worry is that the members of such a society, in effect starting afresh in every generation, would be left extremely insecure and would therefore tend to become very competitive and aggressive in order to establish their place. The structured inequalities of American society have at least the virtue of providing some security of social position and possibility. An egalitarian property-owning society, one might worry, would remove that support without putting anything in its place.[37]

About this concern two things might be said. First, economic institutions are not the whole of a society. Supportive institutions of other kinds—family, religious institutions, local communities—would be present in a property-owning democracy, and they might help provide a sense of place. Second, welfare institutions would provide some security against the worst outcomes and would express, at the social level, some sense of fellowship and commonality.

Nonetheless, it is true that these welfare institutions would be fairly distant and abstract expressions of community. The desire to bring more sense of membership to the immediate economic life of an egalitarian society is one strong reason to consider introducing some socialist element into the Rawlsian ideal. Seeking to ensure that a substantial portion of the work force could belong to cooperative enterprises—whether socially or worker owned—would be an obvious way to encourage a sense of membership and a more favorable sociology.

Plainly this is just one consideration that would have to be weighed in assessing the merits of a property-owning democracy compared with a socialist ideal from the standpoint of Rawls's principles. Among other considerations are efficiency, the possibility of rights to worker control and rights to contract for wage work, and the relative compatibility of alternative systems with democratic politics.[38] We suggest, however, that bringing socialist alternatives into the picture should not affect our argu-

[37] Jon Elster, "Comments on Krouse and McPherson," in *Ethics* 97 (October 1986): 146–53.

[38] For further discussion, see Schweikert, "Should Rawls Be a Socialist?" and Richard Krouse and Michael McPherson, "A 'Mixed' Property Regime: Liberty and Equality in a Market Economy," *Ethics* 97 (October 1986): 119–38.

ments about the ranking of property-owning democracy and welfare-state capitalism. Moreover, comparisons with socialist or mixed regimes would be facilitated by a clearer idea of the property-owning ideal.

Our final comment concerns nonideal theory. Perhaps the most important point is that there is no reason to suppose that simply implementing the kinds of measures needed to preserve a property-owning democracy would be enough to produce one; certainly one would not result in short order. Any rapid movement toward an egalitarian scheme of property holding would probably require some sort of once-and-for-all redistribution of property holding, accompanied by institutional reforms along the lines suggested by Meade to keep the redistributed property from becoming reconcentrated.[39] A movement of this kind would obviously encounter determined and powerful opposition, and could only occur in extraordinary political circumstances.

Recognition of the considerable distance that separates American society from property-owning democracy may help prevent a fairly common and misleading reading of Rawls. As previously noted, R. P. Wolff has suggested that Rawls's attention to reformed private property arrangements encourages "the myth that income redistribution can be achieved painlessly, cooperatively, harmoniously, and within the present framework of private enterprise."[40] The effect of such redistribution, Wolff alleges, is to diffuse the energies needed in the struggle for democratic socialism. But whatever one's judgment about the relative attainability of democratic socialism and of property-owning democracy, there is no reason to think that we are close to either, or that Rawls's receptivity to the latter should encourage us to acquiesce in existing arrangements, or that only modest change is needed. By comparison with either ideal property-owning democracy or ideal democratic socialism, American society is deeply unjust.

But what implications, short of radical rearrangement of property holdings, does our analysis have for policy? Most obviously, we should push for serious taxation of inheritances and for other measures to encourage intergenerational redistribution of wealth. In the United States, heavy nominal taxes used to be levied on inheritance that were, in practice, not effective. The government has attempted to decrease this conflict between theory and practice by reducing nominal taxation, when justice required it to go the other way. It is important to make the case that the free transmission of inequalities across generations is unjust, whether its aim is only to defend short-run reforms or also to lay the groundwork for

[39] For the possible outlines of such a program, see Hugh Stretton, *Capitalism, Socialism, and the Environment* (New York: Cambridge University Press, 1976).

[40] Wolff, *Understanding Rawls*, pp. 206–7.

a more basic challenge of property inequalities at some future point. (Plainly, this advocacy need not and should not come at the expense of support for welfare-state redistribution, particularly in view of our argument that a just private property regime should give substantial scope to welfare provision.)

Although the short-run prospects for implementing any redistributive agenda appear poor, a political strategy that emphasizes intergenerational redistribution has one potential dynamic advantage over a strategy that concentrates primarily on income redistribution. The latter is likely to encounter increasingly severe political opposition over time if the redistributive impact of taxes on current income grows; the widening gap between pretax and after-tax income is a standing invitation to combat. But a strategy of gradually introducing rules that enforce dispersal of property will have a tendency to dissolve opposition as its implementation proceeds. One is less likely to regret the absence of an inheritance one never got than to bemoan the exactions of the annual tax collector. Inheritance taxation seems to have at least some potential for evolving this way, if the program is artfully designed and persuasively presented.

Whatever the prospects of attaining its standards in the short run or the middle run, further theoretical exploration of the ideal of property-owning democracy is in our view imperative. It is increasingly obvious that there are inherent fiscal limits upon the degree to which the welfare state, operating in a capitalist environment, can redistribute income and wealth through its tax and transfer programs. It is increasingly held, by both the right and the left, that welfare-state capitalism is in "crisis"—that either the welfare state, or capitalism, must go. Much if not most of this discourse reflects an unstated assumption: that welfare-state capitalism represents a unique "middle way," the sole form of political economy intermediate between laissez-faire capitalism and bureaucratic state socialism. Recent discussions of socialism and the market have done much to open up this intermediate terrain. But there has been considerably less—indeed, almost no—discussion of other possible intermediate alternatives consistent with the idea of a private property market economy. Hence the importance of further theoretical exploration of the ideal of property-owning democracy.

There is a sense in which the idea of property-owning democracy is already in the air. Several thoughtful Marxists have recently argued that any socialist ethic that includes liberty and efficiency among its values must permit "clean" acts of capitalist accumulation.[41] At least one

[41] John Roemer, "Are Socialist Ethics Compatible with Efficiency?" in *Philosophical Forum* 14 (1983): 369–88; and Elster, "Comments on Krouse and McPherson." For a powerful statement of such a view from the perspective of a non-Marxian socialist, see Alex Nove, *The Economics of Feasible Socialism* (London: Allen and Unwin, 1983).

thoughtful libertarian has emphasized the justice of greater equality at the starting gate.[42] Both, in their emphasis upon limiting the intergenerational transmission of inequality, sound increasingly like James Meade and John Rawls. Certainly exploration of the role of alternative private property institutions in a market economy with a welfare state ought to rank high on the agenda of anyone concerned with distributive justice—Rawlsian or otherwise—in political economy.

[42] Allen Buchanan, *Marx and Rawls: The Radical Critique of Justice* (Totowa, N.J.: Rowman and Allanheld, 1982).

5

Distributing Public Education in a Democracy

AMY GUTMANN

Public education was a welfare good long before the United States was a welfare state. The legitimacy of governmental support for elementary and secondary education is rarely if ever challenged these days, but how much money governments should spend on education and on whom they should spend it remain open and controversial questions. In searching for a standard to guide the distribution of schooling, Americans typically invoke the ideal of equal educational opportunity. The ideal has many meanings, which may account for its popularity. But for its promise to be fulfilled, we need to determine which, if any, of those meanings provides a defensible standard for distributing democratic education.

Interpreting Equal Educational Opportunity

In its most liberal interpretation, the principle of equal educational opportunity offers a theoretically simple rule to solve all distributional problems concerning education. The liberal state should devote as many resources to elementary and secondary schooling as necessary, and distribute those resources, along with children themselves, in such a way as to maximize the life chances of all its future citizens.[1] Call this interpretation of equal educational opportunity *maximization*. A second, more common (and less consistently liberal) interpretation of equal educational opportunity requires the state to distribute educational resources in such a way as to increase the life chances of the least advantaged child so that they approximate, to the maximum extent possible, those of the most advantaged. Call this interpretation *equalization*. A third, and per-

I thank the members of the Princeton Seminar on Democracy and the Welfare State and Christopher Jencks for helpful comments.

[1] For a popular statement and defense of this interpretation of the opportunity principle, see John W. Gardner, *Excellence: Can We Be Equal and Excellent Too?* (New York: Harper and Brothers, 1961).

haps the most common, interpretation requires the state to distribute educational resources in proportion to children's demonstrated natural ability and willingness to learn. Call this interpretation *meritocracy.* If we understand the strengths and weaknesses of each interpretation, we can develop a more democratic standard for distributing elementary and secondary schooling.[2]

Maximization

Maximization requires the state to devote as many resources to education as necessary to maximize children's life chances. "Our kind of society," John Gardner argues, "demands the maximum development of individual potentialities at every level of ability, . . . [so] that each youngster may achieve the best that is in him."[3] If the United States is a purely liberal society, then Gardner's claim is correct. Maximization supports the fundamental liberal values of free choice for citizens and neutrality of the state regarding different ways of life, and distributes the chance to benefit from these values as equally as possible among all citizens.[4] But if the United States is also democratic, then we must look more carefully and critically at maximization.

The hidden weakness of maximization is what might be called the problem of the moral ransom. The rule offers us something morally valuable on the implicit condition that we give up everything else that we value. The state could spend an endless amount on education to increase the life chances of children. Yet its resources are limited. Police protection, public parks, baseball stadiums, and stereo systems are also valuable. The price of using education to maximize the life chances of children is foregoing these other goods.

Someone sympathetic to maximization might try to avoid this criticism by adding a proviso that the state must devote as many resources to education as necessary to maximize children's life chances provided that the increase in life chances is not trivial. However reasonable, this proviso does not save maximization from the problem of the moral ransom. Even if the proviso establishes a reasonable theoretical limit to investment in

[2] Although each of these interpretations has been repeatedly offered as a distributive standard in the literature on education, none is plausible, once one draws out the practical implications. My aim in elaborating the implications of each interpretation in its pure form is not to belabor this critical point, but to be constructive: to demonstrate the need for a more complex and credible standard, and (more important) to begin developing one.

[3] Gardner, *Excellence*, pp. 74–75.

[4] Note that this liberal understanding does not identify the improvement of life chances simply with an increase in income, social status, or political power. Life chances include all opportunities to develop and exercise our human capacities.

education, there is still no practical limit in sight to what we can now collectively spend to increase substantially the life chances of future citizens. Most parents are not willing to make such a sacrifice even for their own children. Perhaps parents should be willing to sacrifice more than they now do to increase their children's life chances, but there is no good reason to obligate parents to maximize the life chances of their children at the expense of minimizing the other, noneducational pursuits that they currently value. Nor is there good reason to obligate citizens collectively to invest so much in education to maximize the life chances of the next generation.

A more promising way to defend maximization is by arguing that it requires many social commitments beyond improving schools, raising teachers' salaries, and funding more educational research and development. Maximization commits the state to provide children and their parents with many other opportunity goods, such as police protection, housing, and health care, without which education could not perform its function of maximizing life chances. Because most cultural goods—public parks and museums, perhaps even stadiums and stereos—are also educational, maximization commits the state to their provision as well. As the number of goods included in maximization increases, the price of its hidden ransom decreases. The reformulated offer, a dedicated liberal could agree, is one that we can but ought not refuse.

The more inclusive maximization becomes, however, the less guidance it gives for making hard choices among the many valuable opportunity goods, all of which the state cannot possibly provide. There is no limit in sight to the amount the state can spend on improving schools, teachers' salaries, the arts, or popular culture to expand children's choices later in life. Nor is there an apparent limit to the amount the state can spend on police protection or health care to increase children's chances of living a longer life. If proponents of maximization make it into an inclusive good, analogous to the Aristotelian or the utilitarian conception of happiness, then they must be willing to accept less than the maximum of the many goods—such as better schools—that it includes. Only inclusive goods are plausibly worth maximizing, but they require us to accept less than the maximum of the many valuable goods they include. Should the state invest in school buildings or stadiums, or neither, leaving parents with more money to spend on travel? If an answer seems obvious, it is not because maximization provides it.

The right answer is not obvious, or at least the same right answer is not obvious to all citizens (no answer is intuitively obvious to me), nor has anyone found a way to derive a single correct answer from some self-evident philosophical principle (or set of principles). These are the conditions under which democratic determination of our social priorities makes most sense. Even if maximization is correct, it needs to be supplemented by a democratic standard: States should use fair, democratic processes to determine how to increase the life chances of their future citizens.

But maximization is wrong. It relies on a general misconception: that we should strive to maximize the goods that we value most. No exclusive earthly good—not even educational opportunity, broadly understood—is so valuable as to be worthy of maximization. If the state need not be committed to using education to maximize children's life chances, then democratic citizens should be free to decide the priorities, not only among all the goods that expand educational opportunity but also between educational opportunity and all the other goods that it excludes.

Equalization

One way of avoiding the many problems with maximization is to become less liberal and more literal. Equal educational opportunity might be interpreted to demand only equalization: use education to increase the life chances of the least advantaged so that they approximate (to the maximum extent possible) those of the most advantaged. The scope of the equal opportunity principle is now significantly narrowed. The principle now says nothing about how much a state should spend on education relative to other goods, or on the education of any child except in relation to what it provides for other children. This may already be an important, albeit implicit, liberal concession to democracy. The liberal silence concerning how to determine the distribution of education relative to other social goods leaves room for a democratic determination of priorities, even if it does not demand it. I shall develop the implications of such a democratic principle when I examine the case of school financing.

According to equalization, the educational attainment of children should not (if possible) differ in any systematic and significant way according to their genetically or environmentally determined characteristics.[5] Rightly distributed, education should be used to overcome all environmental and natural causes of differential educational attainment, since these causes of social inequalities are beyond people's control, and therefore "arbitrary from a moral perspective."[6] If "even the willingness to make an effort, to try, . . . is itself dependent upon happy family and so-

[5] See James S. Fishkin, *Justice, Equal Opportunity, and the Family* (New Haven, Conn.: Yale University Press, 1983), p. 32. Fishkin takes only native characteristics, not environment, to be illegitimate correlates of life chances, although both are equally arbitrary from the moral point of view that he is describing.

[6] John Rawls, *A Theory of Justice* (Cambridge, Mass.: Harvard University Press, 1971), p. 74.

cial circumstances,"[7] then equal educational opportunity must aim also to equalize effort, or the results of unequal effort.

One sympathetic critic of equalization takes it to be a proper moral ideal. In the absence of any competing moral demands, he suggests, the state should try to eliminate all inequalities in life chances that result from morally arbitrary differences. But the presence of other moral demands, he argues, renders the price of realizing the ideal too high. To equalize educational opportunity, the state would have to intrude so far into family life as to violate the equally important liberal ideal of family autonomy.[8] Liberals cannot simply reformulate the principle of family autonomy to permit as much intrusion as necessary to achieve equalization, because the necessary amount would eliminate one of the life chances that citizens value most—the freedom to educate their own children.

Intuitionism seems to be a plausible way of handling the problem of conflicting liberal ideals. Aware of the weakness of maximization, we can conceive of equalization as just one of several liberal ideals, none of which must be fully realized to satisfy the demands of liberal justice. Liberalism, so conceived, consists of "ideals without an ideal." "How its principles are to be balanced remains an open question to be faced in particular cases as they present themselves."[9]

To be faced by whom? Because it offers no answer to the question of whose intuitions will do the balancing, intuitionism avoids rather than solves the political problem of balancing conflicting ideals. Our polity contains a variety of conflicting moral principles and conflicting moral intuitions. Invoking "our" intuitions therefore cannot resolve the conflict between equalizing educational opportunity and respecting family autonomy. Our intuitions on this issue differ, as recent controversies over school financing and busing suggest. How the principles should be balanced will depend upon whose intuitions should do the balancing.

One might doubt even the more limited claim that equalization is in itself a worthy moral ideal, among other equally worthy ideals, such as family autonomy. Completely realized, equalization requires the state to devote all its educational resources to educationally less able children until they reach the same level of educational attainment as the more able, or the highest level that they are capable of attaining.[10] Given limited educational resources and unlimited capacity for educational innovation,

[7] Ibid.

[8] See Fishkin, *Justice*, pp. 51–67.

[9] Ibid., pp. 10, 193.

[10] Alternatively, equalization could be interpreted as minimizing the variance among educational attainments. The unattractiveness of this ideal is apparent when one imagines a policy that actively attempts to suppress intellectual achievement among some students to decrease the variance.

this time may never come, and the state will be able to provide no educational resources to the more able.[11] This consequence is unacceptable because equality of life chances is not in itself a sufficiently important value to outweigh the value of enabling all children to develop their talents to some, socially acceptable, degree. Thus, even if equalization did not conflict with other liberal ideals, we have good reason to choose its incomplete rather than its complete realization.

A thought experiment can help us see why equalization takes equality too seriously. Suppose we know that every difference in the educational achievement of children is beyond their control and correctable by some expensive but finite amount of remedial education. Must we then create an educational system that eliminates all systematic and significant relationships between children's undeserved attributes and their differential educational attainment? I think not, and not because equalization would be socially inefficient. We have good reason to accept many differences in educational attainment. The good reason is that many such differences can be eliminated only by eradicating the different intellectual, cultural, and emotional dispositions and attachments of children. Some children are more proficient at (and interested in) cultivating friendships and having fun than they are at learning what schools teach. That variety makes their lives as well as ours rich and interesting. Many children, moreover, will live better lives in an environment where the competition to become a professional is not universal, but is limited partly by their predispositions to academic achievement, which (whether culturally or genetically created) are undeserved. A competitive society, stripped of such diversity, would be a less desirable place to live—for children, parents, and probably even teachers.

Not all variety, however, is valuable in a society where children who lack a certain level of learning do not have a reasonable chance to participate in making democratic decisions. The democratic truth of equalization is that all children should learn enough to be able not just to live a minimally decent life, but also to participate effectively in the democratic processes that socially structure individual choices among good lives. A democratic state, therefore, must take the steps that it can to avoid those inequalities in educational attainment that deprive children of an intellectual ability adequate to enable them to participate in the democratic political processes that socially structure individual choices.

[11] If we assume more than two levels of talent, the rule is to raise the educational accomplishment of the least talented to the level of the next least talented, and so on. On this assumption, even the average child might be deprived of any educational resources. Cf. Christopher Jencks, *Inequality: A Reassessment of the Effect of Family and Schooling in America* (New York: Basic Books, 1972), p. 109.

MERITOCRACY

The democratic truth of equalization reveals the flaw in meritocracy. A meritocracy is dedicated to distributing all educational resources in proportion to natural ability and willingness to learn. In principle, therefore, meritocracy must give the least educational resources and attention to those children who have relatively few natural abilities and little inclination to learn and the most to those children who have relatively many natural abilities and high motivation.

In practice, few meritocrats accept the full implications of the standard that they profess to uphold. They typically invoke the meritocratic interpretation of equal educational opportunity to argue not against providing an adequate education for all children, but for providing a better education for gifted children instead of concentrating resources on the "average" child and the slow learner. A meritocratic distribution of educational resources, they argue, would give intellectually gifted children what they deserve and also give society what it needs: a larger pool of human capital to increase social productivity. The case for meritocracy seems strongest when resources are so used, but the meritocratic standard still proves too much for all but the most ardent meritocrat to accept. In principle, meritocracy does not require—it may even preclude—educating less talented and motivated children until they attain a socially basic level of literacy. Furthermore, nothing in the meritocratic interpretation of equal educational opportunity secures an education adequate to ensure democratic citizenship for children who happen to have (whether by nature, nurture, or their own free will) little intellectual ability or motivation.

The democratic truth of equalization—that states must secure an education for all children that is adequate to enable them to participate in democratic political processes—does not rule out a restricted form of meritocracy in which educational resources above the level that is adequate for democratic citizenship are distributed in proportion to children's demonstrated intellectual ability and willingness to learn. A democrat might defend a limited meritocracy on grounds of just deserts: Once all children are guaranteed enough education to enable them to participate in the political process, those who demonstrate greater intellectual ability and greater motivation deserve to be provided with more education than those who demonstrate less.

A more egalitarian democrat might reasonably challenge this claim: Why do more gifted or motivated children deserve more education if they have done little or nothing to deserve their greater intellectual gifts or motivation? The less egalitarian democrat might reply: Because intellectual ability and motivation are appropriate bases for judging who deserves education, even if they are not themselves deserved. Courageous soldiers deserve Medals of Honor, even if they do not deserve their courage. Similarly, intellectually talented children and highly motivated children deserve more education, even if they do not deserve their greater talents and motivation.[12]

This response still is insufficient to support even a more restricted meritocracy, where education above the "threshold" level necessary for democratic citizenship *must* be distributed, as a matter of justice, in proportion to intellectual merit. Rewarding merit is a reasonable way to distribute educational resources above the threshold level, but surely it is not the only reasonable way. A good case could also be made for the use of education above the minimum to compensate less gifted and motivated children for their undeserved disadvantages. Another good case could be made for using educational resources above the threshold to develop new skills and interests in all children, which might be useful to society as well as satisfying to citizens in the future. Yet another case could be made, on grounds of social utility rather than of desert, for concentrating resources on those students who are both intellectually gifted and motivated: the welfare of society as a whole may be better advanced in this way.

Suppose I made each case fully, compared them, and concluded that the case for rewarding merit above the threshold is, on balance, the best. Suppose also (for the sake of argument) that I am right. I still cannot conclude that my policy preference should politically dominate a democratic one, provided the democratic one does not violate the principled constraints on democracy. Being right is neither necessary nor sufficient grounds for commanding discretionary political authority, by either liberal or democratic standards.[13]

When reasonable alternatives are recognizable, meritocracy is put in its proper, democratic place. If democratic institutions allocate educational resources above the threshold level so as to reward intellectual merit, then a limited meritocracy is properly part of society's democratic standard for distributing education. The democratic interpretation of meritocracy does not hold that education above the threshold must be distributed according to desert (regardless of democratic preferences) but that it may be so distributed (depending on the results of fair democratic processes).

12 Robert Nozick argues that "the foundations underlying desert needn't themselves be deserved, all the way down." See *Anarchy, State, and Utopia* (New York: Basic Books, 1974), pp. 224–27. See also Michael Sandel, *Liberalism and the Limits of Justice* (New York: Cambridge University Press, 1982), pp. 82–95.

13 For two different defenses of this conclusion, see Michael Walzer, "Philosophy and Democracy," *Political Theory* 9, no. 3 (August 1981): 379–99; and Amy Gutmann, "How Liberal Is Democracy?" in Douglas MacLean and Claudia Mills, eds., *Liberalism Reconsidered* (Totowa, N.J.: Rowman and Allanheld, 1983), pp. 25–50.

The Democratic Standard Stated

The standard of democratic distribution developed thus far consists of two principles. Call the first the *democratic authorization principle.* It recognizes the mistake in maximization by granting authority to democratic institutions to determine the priority of educational goods relative to other social goods. Call the second the *democratic threshold principle.* It avoids the mistakes in both equalization and meritocracy by specifying a threshold below which educational inequalities are unjustified; inequalities in the distribution of educational goods can be justified if, but only if, they do not deprive any child of the ability to participate effectively in the democratic process (which determines, among other things, the priority of education relative to other social goods). The democratic threshold principle thus places principled limits on the legitimate discretion of democratic decision making established by the authorization principle. The threshold principle establishes a realm of what one might call nondiscretionary democratic authority. It does so by imposing a moral requirement that democratic institutions allocate sufficient resources to education to provide all children with an ability adequate to participate in the democratic process. Democratic institutions still retain the discretionary authority to decide how much more education to provide above the threshold established by the second principle.

Although education above the threshold may rightly be democratically distributed according to meritocratic principles, education below the threshold may not. Democratic decision making may still be the most effective way to determine the threshold. Whether it is will depend partly on an empirical assessment of how we can best guarantee all children an adequate education and partly on a normative assessment of what is adequate. Since educational adequacy is relative and dependent on the particular social context, the best way of determining what is adequate may be a democratic decision-making process that follows public debate and deliberation. But to say that the threshold requirements are more likely to be satisfied by democratic institutions that facilitate public debate and deliberation than by nondemocratic institutions is not to say that democratic institutions have the moral discretion to decide whether to provide an adequate level of education for all citizens.

The distinction between the nondiscretionary and discretionary realms of democratic authority is already incorporated in the rationales for some of our educational policies. In passing Public Law 94-142, in 1975, Congress mandated an "appropriate" rather than an optimal education for handicapped children, leaving states and local school districts free to provide more (but not less) if they wish. The educational provisions of some state constitutions suggest a threshold requirement. The New Jersey Supreme Court has interpreted Article IV of the state constitution as requiring the state to guarantee "that educational opportunity which is needed in the contemporary setting to equip a child for his role as a citizen."[14] In establishing so-called Foundation Programs, many states invoke the ideal of providing an adequate educational foundation for school-age children in all school districts, although in practice (and perhaps even in political intent) most Foundation Programs are funded at levels so low as to leave property-poor districts with far fewer resources than they would need to satisfy any reasonable estimate of the demands of the democratic threshold. Although many of our schools fall short of satisfying those demands, implementing the two-part democratic standard does not require a revolution in our way of thinking about education. Rather, it requires a more self-conscious understanding of the implications of the standard for effective educational reform. I pursue only one aspect of that understanding in this chapter. It is, however, an aspect that poses a great challenge to the idea of a democratic threshold: its implications for educating the handicapped.

Educating the Disadvantaged

Democratic states may be incapable of providing enough schooling to enable students who are socially and biologically handicapped in a variety of ways to reach the threshold, or enough may be so expensive as to call into question the moral requirement of preparing all handicapped children to participate effectively in the democratic process. Is the democratic threshold an appropriate standard for judging the adequacy of education for such students?

Consider two cases. The first is that of six-year-old Rebecca Paul.[15] Rebecca's mother and father separated when she was two. She lives with her mother in an inner-city slum. Her father, a foreman, makes modest child support payments. Rebecca's older sister lives at home; her older brother is a drug addict and has spent time in jail and in a drug rehabilitation center. Rebecca's mother, who works as a door-to-door saleswoman, is often not home when Rebecca returns from the local public school, where she is in the first grade. She already has difficulty keeping

[14] 1875 amendment to Art. IV, Sec. 7, Para. 6 of the New Jersey Constitution of 1844: "The legislature shall provide for the maintenance and support of a thorough and efficient system of free public schools for the instruction of all children in this state between the ages of five and eighteen years."

[15] This case study is taken from Donald H. Clark, Arlene Goldsmith, and Clementine Pugh, *Those Children* (Belmont, Calif.: Wadsworth, 1970), pp. 9–39. The authors of the study changed some details to preserve the privacy of the child and her family, but tried to preserve the essential facts of the case.

up with her class, a "slow group," and is a discipline problem. (Her misbehavior includes hitting, biting, and poking objects at her classmates.) Rebecca's IQ is reported to be over 115. Rebecca's school spends considerably more than the average per child, by both state and national standards.[16] But Rebecca receives no special services.[17]

The second case is that of Amy Rowley.[18] Like Rebecca, Amy is six years old and attends a regular first-grade class in a public school. Her IQ is reported to be 122. But there the similarity ends. Amy's parents are deaf, and so is Amy. She reads at above the second-grade level and is highly motivated to learn. Before Amy entered kindergarten, members of the school staff met with her parents and agreed to assess Amy's special educational needs for the year. Several teachers and administrators took a minicourse in sign language interpretation, and a teletype phone was installed in the school to communicate with Amy's parents at home. At the end of the assessment period, the school district's Committee on the Handicapped (consisting of a psychologist, teacher, doctor, and parent of a handicapped child) recommended that Amy be provided with an FM wireless hearing aid, the daily services of a certified teacher of the deaf, and the weekly services of a speech therapist. Amy's school provided her with these services beginning in the first grade.

Are Rebecca and Amy receiving an adequate education by democratic standards? The conventional wisdom, supported by the democratic threshold standard as it applies in typical cases, is that schools must do more to help children who are hard to teach than they must do to help more talented or more motivated children. Doing more often means spending more. It almost always means spending more for seriously handicapped children, because they need special services, specially trained teachers, and more expensive teaching aids than average children to learn even the basic skills. Amy's case supports the conventional wisdom. The special services of the speech therapist, for example, make it possible for Amy to acquire the basic skill of normal speech. We know that before public schools provided such special services, deaf children were taught very little unless their parents could afford, and were motivated enough to provide, a private education (although even money and

[16] The case study provides no facts about the amount of resources spent at Rebecca's school. I have stipulated above-average spending to help clarify the democratic standard of equal opportunity. The stipulation is reasonable, since Rebecca's school is probably in New York City.

[17] None except those diagnostic services that were part of compiling the case study. All the clinical specialists who interviewed and tested Rebecca were paid for by the study.

[18] All the details of this case study are factual. They are taken from *Rowley* v. *Bd. of Ed. of Hendrick Hudson et al.*, 483 F. Supp. 528 (1980); and 632 F.2d 945 (1980).

motivation could not institute mainstreaming, which many public schools now provide).

Given her intelligence and motivation, perhaps Amy could do even better were her school to spend still more on her education by, say, providing her with a full-time sign interpreter.[19] Let us suppose Amy would learn more with a sign interpreter. Is her school morally required to provide her with one? The threshold principle suggests that it is not. Although Amy's school does not maximize or equalize her educational achievement or reward her extraordinary effort, the education it provides cannot reasonably be considered inadequate for democratic participation. Were Amy's parents to judge her education unacceptable, their dissent would be insufficient to defeat the claim that Amy's education lies within the bounds of discretionary democratic judgment. Amy was learning as much and as quickly as the average child in her class. This fact would be insufficient to sustain the school's policy unless it could be shown that the average child in Amy's school was being adequately educated. If this claim were credible (as it was in the actual case), then the court's judgment would be defensible on democratic grounds. The threshold principle permits but does not require Amy's school district to spend more on her education as long as it is not thereby depriving other children in the district of the threshold level of learning.

Amy's case is not simple; but Rebecca's case is still harder to judge because we know much less about what it would take for her to behave better and learn more. The panel of psychiatrists and social workers who diagnosed Rebecca's case recommended family counseling. The pediatrician recommended that she take an amphetamine (Dexedrine) daily to control her hyperactivity. The authors of the case study recommend that Rebecca's teacher try a variety of teaching techniques to help both Rebecca and her classmates get along better; but they also suggest that because she is so deeply troubled, "it is unlikely that a teacher will be able to help Rebecca directly." They conclude that a perceptive teacher "might sense that this child is deeply troubled and refer her for psychological consultation, where she might be kept on a waiting list while children who are more clearly 'emergency cases' receive treatment."[20]

[19] Amy's parents made this case to their school board, then to the independent examiner, next to the state commissioner of education, and finally, when these appeals failed, to the courts. The Rowleys won their case against the Hendrick Hudson Board of Education in the U.S. District Court and the Appeals Court. The case ended in the U.S. Supreme Court, which reversed the Appeals Court's decision upholding the local school board's right not to provide Amy with a full-time sign interpreter. See *Board of Education of the Hendrick Hudson Central School District* v. *Amy Rowley*, 458 U.S. 176 (1982). Justice Rehnquist wrote the majority opinion. Justices White, Brennan, and Marshall dissented.

[20] Clark, Goldsmith, and Pugh, *Those Children*, p. 38.

What, then, must Rebecca's school do to help her learn? On reading Rebecca's case study, one is struck not—as in Amy's case—by how much her school must spend to educate her, but by how little her school can do to overcome the problems that stand in the way of her learning. Perhaps an inspired teacher could achieve a breakthrough and solve Rebecca's problems, but no mass educational system can depend on hiring miracle workers. And there are many more Rebeccas than Amys in our public schools. Rebecca's case reminds us that democratic states cannot rely upon schools alone to help children reach the threshold of learning. States must provide access to a wide range of other goods and services—decent housing, job training and employment for parents, family counseling, day-care and after-school programs for children—without which schools cannot possibly succeed in their educational missions.

But schools are not therefore freed from responsibility to help children like Rebecca. They can still help by diagnosing learning problems, developing better teaching techniques for coping with these problems, hiring and training better teachers, and referring parents to people outside the school who can help even more. Given Rebecca's learning problems and the fact that her school provides her with no special services, it is as implausible to claim that her education is adequate by democratic standards as it is to claim that Amy's education is inadequate. Both children require special services (of different sorts). Because such services cost money, schools must spend more on Amy and Rebecca than they spend on children who do not have learning disabilities, just as teachers must pay more attention to those children who are less motivated to learn.

Rebecca poses a much greater challenge to her school than Amy does to hers, and not primarily because Rebecca's problem is more common and therefore more costly to solve by social policy. The primary obstacle to solving Rebecca's educational problem is not insufficient spending on schools. Without a well-developed welfare state, which provides ample economic, medical, and social services for disadvantaged families, the special services that schools can provide children like Rebecca will almost inevitably fall short of enabling them to reach the threshold. Critics of the underdeveloped welfare state often fail to recognize that lowering our expectations is consistent with increasing our demands. The more government spends on nonschool services, the better able schools will be to teach with any set of resources. The less government spends on such services, the more schools must spend to help disadvantaged children learn, if spending helps at all.

Does spending help at all? In the wake of the 1966 *Report on Equality of Educational Opportunity* (the Coleman Report)[21] and Christopher

[21] James S. Coleman, Ernest Q. Campbell, Carol J. Hobson, James McPartland, Alex-

Jencks's subsequent study, *Inequality*,[22] many have doubted the value of spending more on schooling for poor children. The Coleman Report found that differences in spending on and by schools could not account for the differences in the average educational attainment of students attending those schools. The Jencks study went one step further: "Eliminating differences between schools would do almost nothing to make adults more equal. Even eliminating differences in the amount of schooling people get would do relatively little to make adults more equal."[23] These findings were frequently cited as evidence that spending more on schools would not equalize opportunity or improve the life chances of children. Jencks explicitly recommended that "we think of school life as an end in itself rather than a means to some other end."[24] "[S]tudents' and teachers' claims on the public purse are no more legitimate," Jencks argued, "than the claims of . . . manufacturers of supersonic aircraft who want to help their stockholders pay for Caribbean vacations."[25]

Despite its methodological flaws, the Coleman Report has stood up well under reanalysis, but it does not support the policy conclusion that spending more on schooling for the disadvantaged is futile.[26] The report only measured differences in spending on and by school districts (and in teacher characteristics in these schools). It did not look at how districts distribute their resources among children within schools. We therefore cannot use its findings to conclude that significant changes in the internal organization of schools—for example, assigning the most experienced and highly paid teachers to the least advantaged children—would make no difference.[27] We cannot even use its findings to account for the variation that currently exists in the achievement levels of disadvantaged children within different schools or classrooms.

The most striking finding of the Jencks study—that income inequality among men with the same family background, cognitive skills, educa-

ander M. Mood, Frederic D. Weinfeld, and Robert L. York, *Report on Equality of Educational Opportunity* (Washington, D.C.: U.S. Government Printing Office, 1966).

[22] Christopher Jencks, Marshall Smith, Henry Acland, Mary Jo Bane, David Cohen, Herbert Gintis, Barbara Feyns, and Stephan Michelson, *Inequality: A Reassessment of the Effect of Family and Schooling in America* (New York: Harper, 1973).

[23] Ibid., p. 16.

[24] Ibid., p. 256 (italics supplied).

[25] Ibid., p. 29.

[26] Nor does Coleman himself claim that it does.

[27] For further cautions about extrapolating policy recommendations from the Coleman Report, see Eric A. Hanushek and John F. Kain, "On the Value of Equality of Educational Opportunity as a Guide to Public Policy," in Frederick Mosteller and Daniel P. Moynihan, eds., *On Equality of Educational Opportunity* (New York: Vintage Books, 1972), pp. 116–45. See also Richard J. Murname, *The Impact of School Resources on the Learning of Inner City Children* (Cambridge, Mass.: Ballinger, 1975), pp. 8–10.

tional attainment, and occupational status was "only 12–15 percent less . . . than among random individuals"[28]—tells us that we should not expect to decrease income inequality significantly by increasing educational equality. It does not tell us that Amy and Rebecca will have the same capacity for deliberation about or participation in the democratic process if they learn less in school as they will if they learn more. Nor does it justify the conclusion that schooling is a consumer good, like any other, which is valuable only if it makes life for children better in the present, not "better in the hereafter."[29]

The appeal of this conclusion stems, I think, from a truncated conception of what counts in the "hereafter" and of how opportunity should be understood. A school that teaches Rebecca how to communicate civilly and Amy how to communicate effectively with their peers would make both their lives better in the hereafter, even if it does nothing to increase their income or to affect their choice of occupation. Educational opportunity is measured not by level of income (above a certain decent minimum) but by the capacity to deliberate and participate in the democratic process.[30] Although the latter is less susceptible to precise measurement, it is not therefore less important. *Inequality* provides evidence that schooling is an ineffective means of equalizing income, not that it is an ineffective means of distributing democratic opportunity.

The Coleman and Jencks studies neither refute nor support the conclusion that better schooling for disadvantaged children will increase their educational opportunity. Subsequent studies have made it appear likely that better schooling makes a difference. Richard Murname's study of the classroom experiences of 875 inner-city black children demonstrates that "teachers have a critical impact on student achievement."[31] The most effective teachers are costly because they are experienced, yet they are not necessarily the most experienced and therefore the most costly.[32]

[28] Jencks et al., *Inequality*, p. 226.

[29] Ibid., p. 29.

[30] It is important to note that educational opportunity is only a part of the more inclusive democratic good of opportunity. The more inclusive good requires that all citizens be guaranteed a decent minimum income—to the extent possible through a full employment policy. Schooling is therefore a limited, but not an ineffective, means of equalizing opportunity for the disadvantaged. In a state that lacks a full employment policy and a decent minimum wage policy, even the best schooling for the least advantaged will leave some able people unemployed or earning less than a decent minimum. Equal educational opportunity is only part, albeit an important part, of equal opportunity.

[31] Murname, *The Impact of School Resources*, p. 77.

[32] Murname found that the most effective teachers were those who had taught for three to five years, and not longer. He rightly warns against concluding that teaching experience beyond five years does not increase effectiveness. An equally plausible conclusion is that many of the best teachers leave inner-city schools after five years, or leave the profession. See Ibid., pp. 78–80.

In his three-year study of children in twelve secondary schools in London's inner cities, Michael Rutter found that schools "varied markedly with respect to their pupils' behavior, attendance, exam success and delinquency . . . even after taking into account differences in their intake," and that these differences in outcome "were systematically and strongly associated with the characteristics of schools as social institutions."[33] Some of the most costly characteristics—such as the school's physical plant, its student-teacher ratio, and the size of its administration—did not correlate with higher achievement. Rutter notes that many characteristics that did correlate—such as the degree of academic emphasis, teacher participation in lessons, their use of incentives and rewards (rather than punishment), and the extent to which students were encouraged to assume responsibility—could be changed by the school staff without additional cost.[34] They could be changed, that is, by a staff perceptive enough to realize that they should be changed and capable enough to know how to change them. If, on the other hand, worse schools tend to have worse teachers and if higher salaries are necessary to attract better teachers to such schools, then improving schools along the lines Rutter suggests is likely to be quite costly.

These studies and others converge in concluding that better schools—and more specifically better schoolteachers—increase the educational achievement of poor children.[35] What they do not tell us, however, is whether schools must spend more to become better than they now are for poor children, or how much better they must become for the education of those children to reach the democratic threshold. The best studies all caution against making policy inferences from their research conclusions.[36] The most that we can conclude with confidence from these studies is that (1) better schools do not necessarily spend more than worse ones, and (2) it is likely that schools could improve were they able to pay more for better teachers.

This may seem inconclusive. It is, for good reason. Whether schools must spend more (and how much more) to teach disadvantaged children depends not only on whether reaching the threshold requires more spending, but also on whether citizens choose to reach the threshold by redis-

[33] Michael Rutter, Barbara Maughan, Peter Mortimore, Janet Onston, and Alan Smith, *Fifteen Thousand Hours: Secondary Schools and Their Effects on Children* (Cambridge, Mass.: Harvard University Press, 1979), p. 205.

[34] Ibid., pp. 178–79.

[35] See *Do Teachers Make a Difference?* (Washington, D.C.: U.S. Government Printing Office, 1970); see also Eric A. Hanushek, *Education and Race* (Lexington, Mass.: D.C. Heath, 1972): and Martin T. Katzman, *The Political Economy of Urban Schools* (Cambridge, Mass.: Harvard University Press, 1971).

[36] See, e.g., Murname, *The Impact of School Resources*, pp. 15, 21, 78–79; and Ritter et al., *Fifteen Thousand Hours*, pp. 180–82.

tributing the money already spent on schooling or by spending more to increase the achievement of disadvantaged children. We are not morally free to choose neither to spend more nor to improve the use of existing resources. Democratic principles leave citizens with discretion to decide how but not to decide whether to improve the education of disadvantaged children whenever it falls below the democratic threshold.

Even spending substantially more on education, however, is not an adequate alternative for helping those children who are so severely handicapped that no amount of education will raise them to the threshold, or for those whose behavior so disrupts the education of other students that trying to educate them is incompatible with educating other students in the same classroom or perhaps even in the same school. What must democratic states and schools do for such children? We have already considered the case of a "troubled" child and concluded that the state should provide her (and her family) with access to noneducational services that might improve her classroom behavior as well as her motivation to learn. One need not be pessimistic, however, to recognize that for some children, it is too late for such help. Public schools may not be able to teach the vast majority of children unless they are permitted to place children who are disruptive in special classes, even if doing so diminishes their chances of learning. Because their interests are in this sense sacrificed to preserve the educational opportunity of other children, disruptive children should be isolated only in a "supreme educational emergency": they must present a clear and substantial threat to the education and safety of other children.

Children with brain damage pose a different problem, because the best social services coupled with the best schooling may not provide them with the capacity to deliberate and to participate effectively in the democratic process. We cannot owe such children the same democratic opportunities that we owe other children, but we can owe them a good life relative to their capacities—a life that we judge to be good for them (not simply convenient for us). A substantial amount of special education is likely to be a necessary but not sufficient condition for their leading what we judge to be a good life for them. We therefore need not educate brain-damaged children to the limits of our capacity. Who knows what those limits are? The frontiers of education as a science are ever expanding. How much and what kind of education we owe such children depends on their capacities to learn and on our willingness to provide them with noneducational services as they grow older. This standard leaves room for democratic discretion in deciding on the particular combination of schooling and noneducational services to provide brain-damaged children. Any adequate combination, however, is bound to be much more costly and demanding than providing average children with a threshold-level education.

The education of handicapped children (even those who are not severely retarded) is so costly that we cannot expect states to bear it by themselves (even if the richer states should). Education, according to democratic principles, is the responsibility of all levels of government, not just the state and local governments, although we have traditionally vested more responsibility in state and local governments. The case of handicapped children (and disadvantaged children more generally) has (relatively recently) become and should continue to be an exception to this tradition. If substantial federal aid is not earmarked for their education, handicapped children are unlikely to be adequately educated. The federal government therefore should play an important financial role in protecting those children.

In passing the Education for All Handicapped Children Act (Public Law 94-142) of 1975, Congress began to assume such a role. But the federal government has subsequently assumed much less than full financial responsibility for educating the handicapped; one study estimates that its greatest contribution since 1977 was only 6 percent of the total cost.[37] At the same time it has assumed much more than financial responsibility. Public Law 94-142 imposes many regulations and reporting requirements on local schools: It requires them to provide each handicapped child with an "appropriate" education in the "least restrictive educational environment," to create a detailed "individualized education program" (IEP) for each child, to follow certain procedural guidelines in setting up the IEP, and to establish appeal procedures for parents who are dissatisfied with their child's IEP.

Critics of Public Law 94-142 correctly argue that "fairness is costly" and that federal regulations designed to ensure fairness bureaucratize schools.[38] But they often recommend remedies that are morally worse than these problems, such as eliminating the protections of due process.[39] Before procedural safeguards were instituted, most handicapped children

[37] John C. Pittenger and Peter Kuriloff, "Educating the Handicapped: Reforming a Radical Law," *The Public Interest*, no. 66 (Winter 1982), p. 87.

[38] Ibid., pp. 89–90; and Arthur E. Wise, *Legislated Learning: The Bureaucratization of the American Classroom* (Berkeley: University of California Press, 1979), pp. 27–28.

[39] In support of their critique of due process, Pittenger and Kuriloff report that half of the parents (of fifty handicapped children) who asked for due process hearings said that they "would not willingly go through such an experience again, even if they knew it would improve conditions for their children." But it is hard to know what to conclude from this fact. Half of the parents said they would go through the experience again. Pittenger and Kuriloff also neglect to consider the preventive effect of these procedural safeguards: Schools probably treat most handicapped children (whose parents never ask for due process hearings) better than they otherwise would.

were denied anything approaching an adequate education.[40] Because handicapped children are a particularly needy minority whose education is costly and demanding, they must be provided with protection not due to other children (such as the gifted and talented).[41] Because the educational needs of handicapped children are complex and individualized, they are generally better protected by instituting procedural rather than substantive safeguards at the federal level. The most effective procedures are those that hold local schools accountable to parents, professionals, and other citizens who are motivated to protect the special educational needs of the handicapped. Procedural safeguards are rarely sufficient to secure justice, but they are often, as in this instance, necessary. Instead of eliminating the procedural safeguards, the federal government should alleviate the burden on schools by paying more to support the educational programs for which it is responsible.[42]

But more money will not make schools less bureaucratized. The reporting requirements are probably the greatest single source of bureaucratization in Public Law 94-142 (and of complaints against that law). If all of those requirements were essential to accomplishing the purpose of the law, then we would face a hard choice between improving the education of handicapped children and avoiding the bureaucratization of schools. We probably do not face such a hard choice here, because telling teachers how (rather than whom) to teach is often counterproductive. Good teaching requires flexibility and imagination, which the writing of detailed blueprints discourages.[43] The more detailed the blueprints must be, the less time teachers have for teaching (or for recuperating from its strains). Moreover, federal policymakers possess no special knowledge about how to teach handicapped children, and we have little reason to believe that they will learn much more by gathering the data that they require local schools to supply.[44]

[40] See David Kirp, William Buss, and Peter Kuriloff, "Legal Reform of Special Education: Empirical Studies and Procedural Proposals," *California Law Review* 62, no. 1 (January 1974): 42–58, 117–55.

[41] Pittenger and Kuriloff criticize the procedural safeguards for handicapped children because they are part of an ongoing "procedural revolution" that "has extended due process protections to the gifted and talented, and already one hears it said that any child ought to be able to challenge the fairness of any major educational decision affecting him. Where will it end? And with what consequences for public 'education'?" ("Educating the Handicapped," pp. 89–90). Unlike violent revolutions, the procedural one can be stopped—democratically—at some socially acceptable point. A good case has yet to be made for the slippery slope argument that our only choice is between granting all children or none the fullest range of due process.

[42] For an extended case study that supports this conclusion, see Richard A. Weatherly, *Reforming Special Education: Policy Implementation from State to Street Level* (Cambridge, Mass.: MIT Press, 1979), esp. pp. 142–48.

[43] Pittenger and Kuriloff, "Educating the Handicapped," p. 90.

[44] Wise, *Legislated Learning*, pp. 53–58.

One critic of bureaucratization suggests that the federal government therefore concern itself with "equity" and leave concerns of "productivity" to the schools.[45] Although this distinction points in the right direction, it may be misleading. Increasing the educational achievement ("productivity") of handicapped children is an important part of what democratic justice ("equity") demands. Congress should concern itself with deciding whether its legislation is likely to improve the educational achievement of the handicapped. It should not, however, simply assume that detailed federal regulations, which generate an enormous amount of paper work at the local level, are an effective means to such improvement. Democratic theory establishes a presumption against bureaucracy.[46] This presumption means that if schooling is to be democratic, policymakers should not impose regulations and detailed reporting requirements on local schools unless they have good evidence that educational equity cannot otherwise be realized. Good evidence was lacking in the case of Public Law 94-142. Congress would have done better had it provided more money and fewer regulations.[47]

By assuming major responsibility for funding the education of the most disadvantaged children, the federal government can help make schooling more democratic. This claim may seem implausible, since centralization is generally not the most effective means to democratization. But the generalization does not hold here, for reasons to which I have already alluded. Local school districts should be required to educate every child up to the threshold, but they should also be free to spend more money on education than the threshold demands. States are better equipped to provide local school districts with the funds necessary to educate average children up to the threshold than they are to provide the funds necessary to educate the most disadvantaged children. This is because of the high cost of providing such children with a threshold-level education, and because the constituency for supporting special education is more likely to be effective federally than in fifty separate states. If the federal government contributed more financially to ensuring that the education of disadvantaged children reached the threshold, then state and local govern-

[45] Ibid., esp. pp. xiv–xv, 52–53, and 206–7.

[46] See Dennis F. Thompson, "Bureaucracy and Democracy," in Graeme Duncan, ed., *Democratic Theory and Practice* (New York: Cambridge University Press, 1983), pp. 235–50.

[47] This is not to say that Congress should have provided all the money and established no regulations. Requiring states to direct some of their own money to disadvantaged children (in order to receive federal funds) can encourage economy. Some regulations are necessary to ensure fulfillment of the law's purpose. See Weatherly, *Reforming Special Education*, p. 120.

ments would be freer to decide what priority to give education above the threshold.

"Education is so special," Secretary of Education T. H. Bell announced on leaving office in 1984, "that it ranks in priority alongside and possibly ahead of the Department of Defense."[48] Not until the federal government contributes more to financing education for the disadvantaged, however, can the priorities of majorities at the state and local levels be morally translated into democratic politics. The claim that "education is to state government what defense is to the Federal Government"[49] must be qualified for this reason. Like defense, education is a national responsibility. The federal government therefore must not let states and local school districts neglect the educational needs of any children. Unlike defense, education may be best controlled and distributed locally. The federal government should therefore limit its role to the protection of otherwise underserved students, and, if possible, limit its protection to providing money and instituting procedural safeguards (at least initially at the local level) to prevent the money being misused. Were the federal government to assume this responsibility, state and local governments would be free to determine how much (more) they want to spend on schooling and how they want to distribute education above the threshold.

Lessons for the Welfare State

Democratic principles do not require that we equalize either the "inputs" or the "outcomes" of education. We need not spend the same amount on every child's education, or produce equal educational results in all children—individuals or groups. The democratic interpretation of equal educational opportunity requires instead that all children be given an education that enables them to participate effectively in the democratic process. What constitutes an education adequate for democratic participation will vary over time as well as between democratic societies. But that should not stop us from trying to determine what the democratic standard demands of the United States today. The demands of the threshold principle are considerable. Federal and state governments should take greater responsibility for financing elementary and secondary education, the federal government should give local schools more money for educating handicapped children, and local school districts should assume responsibility for using federal and state money well. The authorization principle permits democratic institutions to determine how much to spend and how to distribute education above the threshold. The demands

[48] *New York Times*, Friday, November 9, 1984, p. 1.

[49] *New York Times*, Sunday, December 2, 1984, p. 40.

of this principle are primarily procedural. Federal agencies and courts should not assume more control over school politics than necessary to satisfy the threshold principle; state politicians should place school finance more firmly on the political agenda; local school districts should have the option of spending more on their children's education.

The democratic standard demands that federal agencies and courts do more than control what is commonly considered "school politics." The success of schools in providing children of the poor with an education that satisfies democratic threshold requirements depends significantly on the success of the welfare state in doing more for poor parents—creating more jobs and providing better housing, more community services, better child care, and so on. Schools cannot compensate for society, but they are not therefore relieved of all responsibility when other institutions let children down. To the considerable extent that schools can still make a difference in supporting democratic education, they must.

I have said nothing here, because I could not possibly say enough, about the implications of democratic principles for distributing children among and within schools. Children are one another's educational resources.[50] The quality of their education depends importantly on how they are distributed among and within schools. Adequately educating most black children may require racial integration of schools and classes within schools if, as many studies suggest, thoroughgoing integration is the educational means that most effectively increases the academic achievement of black students and decreases racial prejudice among white students.[51] Critics of court-ordered busing who accept the urgency of these educational ends sometimes suggest that noneducational means of accomplishing them would be preferable. Better to redistribute income, they say, or to integrate neighborhoods by redeveloping inner cities and building more low-cost housing in affluent suburbs, or both. Where there is a way, however, there is often not a will. The democratic standard suggests that schools must compensate black students as best they can for the racial discrimination that they have suffered and will continue to suffer, until other institutions compensate them in other equally or more effective ways.

[50] Michael Walzer, *Spheres of Justice* (New York: Basic Books, 1983), p. 215.

[51] For a summary and analysis of these findings, see Jennifer Hochschild, *The New American Dilemma: Liberal Democracy and School Desegregation* (New Haven, Conn.: Yale University Press, 1984). See also Willis D. Hawley, "Increasing the Effectiveness of School Desegregation: Lessons from Research," in Adam Yarmolinsky, Lance Liebman, and Corinne S. Schelling, eds., *Race and Schooling in the City* (Cambridge, Mass.: Harvard University Press, 1981), esp. pp. 150–52; and Robert E. Slavin and Nancy A. Madden, "School Practices that Improve Race Relations," *American Educational Journal* 16, no. 2 (Spring 1979): 169–80.

Might the democratic standard serve as an appropriate model for the distribution of welfare goods other than education? Consider briefly the problem of distributing health care in the United States. Like education, health care satisfies a basic need, not just a want, of American citizens. Politicians as well as philosophers have therefore claimed that all American citizens have a right to "equal access" to health care. But the standard of equal access to health care poses many of the same difficulties as the standard of equal educational opportunity. Those who interpret equal access to mean maximizing health (or minimizing infirmity) run into the problem of moral ransom: There is no limit to how much society can spend to maximize the health of its citizens. Those who adopt the equalization interpretation are committed to giving absolute priority to the health care needs of the sickest citizens, regardless of cost, even if it means spending $30,000 each year on every citizen who suffers from end-state renal disease, for example. Few people today defend a purely meritocratic interpretation of equal access,[52] but defenders of a market in health care sometimes suggest that the financially prudent deserve the best medical treatment that their money can buy, even if the basic medical needs of the less prudent consequently go unmet.

To the extent that these interpretations of equal access share similar weaknesses with the corresponding interpretations of equal educational opportunity, a more democratic standard for distributing health care recommends itself. The standard would presumably consist of a threshold principle requiring the state to ensure adequate health care for all citizens and an authorization principle leaving legislatures free to determine distributions above the threshold. In further defining and applying the threshold and authorization principles, questions analogous to those posed by equal educational opportunity would arise: What constitutes an adequate level of health care for the United States? What is the best process by which to determine the priority of health care relative to other goods? If the analogy with education holds, we should not expect to answer the first question without analyzing our specific social understandings of what constitutes adequate health care, nor the second without evaluating the results of our present methods of financing health care.

The analogy of other welfare goods, such as unemployment insurance, to education is weaker. Some goods that have historically become identified with the American welfare state are more difficult than education or health care to defend as necessary welfare goods in the United States. Why should the state be obligated to provide only temporary economic

[52] See Plato, *The Republic of Plato*, trans. Allen Bloom (New York, 1968), bk. 2, ll. 406c–7a. Plato suggests (consistently with the foundations of this theory) that medical care may be justly denied to a sick carpenter who, if he were kept alive by medicine, could no longer perform his trade.

security, and only to those citizens who have recently lost their jobs? A strong case can be made for an obligation to guarantee a threshold level of financial security to all citizens who accept the obligations of citizenship (which include the willingness to work if one is able). The strongest case for requiring a threshold level of unemployment insurance is, by contrast, relatively weak. Rather than constituting an exception to the democratic standard of being justified as a welfare good, this example demonstrates the critical potential of that standard. The democratic standard requires us to criticize our society when it fails to secure a level of welfare for all citizens that is adequate, judged by our best understanding of adequacy. We can hold ourselves and our government responsible for securing the basic welfare, based on this understanding.

6

Representatives in the Welfare State

DENNIS F. THOMPSON

If the welfare state is to be democratic, the legislators who make its policies must be responsible to the citizens affected by them. Responsibility requires that legislators explain their actions to the citizens they represent. Giving reasons is part of what being responsible means, and part of what being reelected requires.[1] But the nature of welfare itself poses a dilemma for democratic responsibility. To justify decisions about welfare, representatives must consider the preferences of citizens. But those preferences at any particular time are not adequate grounds for a justification of welfare policy. Orthodox theories of representation provide no way to cope with this problem; a satisfactory theory, must take a different approach. Instead of looking for justifications solely in the preferences of citizens at a particular time, we should look at the legislative process in which the justifications are made.

Welfare policy, more than most other kinds, is grounded in the preferences of citizens. The reasons that representatives give for other kinds of policies, such as civil rights or cultural development, should not follow preferences so closely. When justifying these policies, representatives might not count some preferences as reasons at all (those based on racial prejudice, for example), and might regard other reasons as decisive (those based on individual rights or ideals of excellence). But when welfare is in question, what citizens say should count for more. Citizens may be mistaken about their own welfare, but at some point they must be taken as competent judges of it. A welfare policy that makes citizens better off without their ever knowing it is a logical, but neither a feasible nor a desirable, possibility in a democracy. To justify disregarding the prefer-

[1] On the concept of political responsibility, see John Plamenatz, *Democracy and Illusion* (London: Longman, 1973), pp. 80–81, 87, 98, 110, 114, 177–78, 199; and J. Roland Pennock, *Democratic Political Theory* (Princeton, N.J.: Princeton University Press, 1979), pp. 260–308. On the political significance of giving reasons, see John W. Kingdon, *Congressmen's Voting Decisions*, 2d ed. (New York: Harper and Row, 1981), pp. 47–54; and Richard F. Fenno, *Home Style: House Members in Their Districts* (Boston: Little, Brown, 1978), pp. 136–70.

ences of citizens in the area of welfare policy, representatives usually appeal to other preferences—either the preferences of the same citizens in the future or the preferences of other citizens now.

But welfare policy is not adequately grounded in the preferences of citizens at any particular time. Its effects are more temporally extensive than those of most other kinds of policies. It directly affects more people for a longer period (from cradle to grave). It comprises many different programs, which begin and end at different times. Welfare policy is more likely to consist of what Madison called a "train of measures," which have "gradual and perhaps unobserved" instead of "immediate and sensible" consequences.[2] Because the policies that promote welfare are multiple and because their effects extend over time, the citizens who judge the policies now may not be in the best position to assess the policies fully and fairly. They may not be the citizens who benefit from or pay for them later. Federal policy on unemployment, for example, cannot be identified with a single bill adopted at one time; its effects must be assessed and reassessed over time. Even comprehensive legislation such as the Social Security Act of 1935 or the Economic Opportunity Act of 1964 cannot be appraised within a single electoral cycle or in isolation from prior and subsequent measures.[3] Representatives thus seem to be justified not only in disregarding the present preferences of citizens in favor of their future preferences, but also in disregarding preferences altogether in favor of principles that do not depend so much on time.

Delegates and Trustees

The conflict between these demands—that representatives should and should not consider the preferences of citizens—recalls the opposition between the two traditional theories of representation. A delegate considers the preferences as expressed at some particular time, whereas a trustee refers to the principles to which preferences should conform. But this contrast is too simple. Delegates are not strictly bound to consider preferences expressed at any particular time, and trustees are not completely free to ignore even momentary preferences. In their more plausible forms,

[2] *The Federalist*, no. 63, pp. 423–24; no. 52, pp. 355–56; and no. 57, p. 386. Madison is credited with introducing the term "responsibility" into political theory [Douglass Adair, *Fame and the Founding Fathers* (New York: Norton, 1974), p. 257n]; his analysis of the concept, though brief, recognizes a form of the tension (he calls it a paradox) that I discuss here. In a discussion of the optimal lengths of terms for representatives, Madison suggests that shorter terms strengthen responsibility (by binding representatives more closely to their constituents), but that longer terms also strengthen responsibility (by holding representatives accountable for the "train of measures").

[3] See National Conference on Social Welfare, *Report of the Committee on the Economic Security of 1935* (Washington, D.C.: National Conference on Social Welfare, 1985).

both theories recognize both demands, but in doing so they undermine democratic responsibility. They provide no coherent basis on which representatives can justify their actions to citizens. If we understand how even the modified versions of these theories fail, we can begin to appreciate the need for a different approach.[4] Although welfare policy stands most clearly in need of a new approach, other kinds of policies to some degree raise the same problem.

Most delegate theorists would not bind a representative in advance to a specific mandate or set of policies. Rather, they would make a representative responsible for policies after they had been adopted. The reasons that representatives give for policies at any particular time relate to the preferences that citizens can be expected to have at the next election. That familiar creature of contemporary political science, the retrospective voter, makes this modification of delegate theory possible.[5] Whether voters look at past performance as such or at past performance as a basis for future actions, they do not commit representatives in advance to any particular policies or results of policies.[6] This modification thus allows representatives more room for leadership and innovation than does pure delegation theory, but they are still assumed to be delegates because they follow the ends set by constituents. Political scientists who espouse this theory typically assume that the ends and means of policy can be distinguished, and that representatives are free to choose the means but not the ends of policy.[7] Delegates choose the means that will best satisfy the preferences that citizens will come to have at some time in the future.

But even this small modification regarding the preferences of citizens subverts the democratic basis of delegate theory. The distinction between ends and means cannot limit the discretion of representatives in the way that delegate theorists wish. The means that representatives choose now shape the ends that citizens can choose in the future. Once the welfare programs of the New Deal were in place, for example, citizens could no longer so easily choose policies based on laissez-faire principles. By the time these welfare programs were ready to be evaluated retrospectively, citizens could not readily dismantle them, and most did not want to.[8] Whether citizens developed this satisfaction with the programs on their

[4] We would miss this implication if, following Hanna Pitkin, we were to treat the concepts of delegate and trustee as polar opposites. See *The Concept of Representation* (Berkeley: University of California Press, 1967), p. 166.

[5] Morris Fiorina, *Retrospective Voting in American National Elections* (New Haven, Conn.: Yale University Press, 1981), pp. 193–211; V. O. Key, *The Responsible Electorate* (New York: Vintage Books, 1966); and Anthony Downs, *An Economic Theory of Democracy* (New York: Harper and Row, 1957).

[6] Fiorina, *Retrospective Voting*, p. 201.

[7] See, e.g., ibid., pp. 197–98.

[8] See the paper by Stanley Kelley, Jr., Chapter 8 in this volume.

own or as a result of the persuasion of their representatives, they were surely influenced by their experience of the programs. If choosing the means of policy can in this way help create the desire for new ends of policy, then representatives create the preferences of citizens as much as they anticipate them. Yet delegates are not accountable for this creation of preferences. They do not have to refer to the principles guiding the change of preferences, because their role presumes that they are merely giving effect to preferences that citizens already have.

Trustee theory does require representatives to invoke principles to justify their actions. Trustees appeal, for example, to principles of justice, which are independent of the preferences citizens have at any time, even their hypothetical preferences. The difficulty is that representatives and citizens reasonably disagree about what those principles should be. We are no longer so confident as Burke was that there are objective principles on which citizens and representatives should agree.[9] Even within the liberal tradition, the principles that philosophers urge upon representatives conflict in fundamental ways. Utilitarians tell representatives to maximize the social welfare, or at least the welfare of their constituents.[10] Their representatives would not necessarily act in accordance with the expressed preferences of citizens, but they would not give any independent weight to justice. Theorists of justice instruct representatives to vote their "opinion as to which laws and policies best conform to principles of justice."[11] According to which principles, then, should trustees act?

It will not do to say that each representative should act on the basis of the principles he or she believes to be right, and then let citizens choose at the next election. This would turn trustees into delegates—delegates of principle, to be sure, but no less vulnerable to the objection already raised to delegate theory. It is true that trustees (and their theorists) assume that citizens will eventually come to accept the principles on which trustees act, or at least the policies based on those principles. Even that arch trustee Burke believed that in time his constituents would concur with him: "I aim to look, indeed, to your opinions; but such opinions as you and I must have five years hence."[12]

But the validity of the principles does not depend on the concurrence

[9] On Burke's assumption about objective interests, see Pitkin, *The Concept of Representation*, pp. 180, 189.

[10] J.J.C. Smart, *Utilitarianism: For and Against* (Cambridge: Cambridge University Press, 1973), esp. pp. 67–74, 135–50; and Amartya Sen and Bernard Williams, *Beyond Utilitarianism* (Cambridge: Cambridge University Press, 1982).

[11] John Rawls, *A Theory of Justice* (Cambridge, Mass.: Harvard University Press, 1971), p. 361.

[12] Edmund Burke, "Speech at the Conclusion of the Poll," cited in James Hogan, *Election and Representation* (Cork, Ireland: Cork University Press, 1945), p. 189.

of citizens. The justification of a principle is not that citizens will accept it, but that it is the right principle to accept, now as well as in the future. The point of trustee theory is not simply that representatives should act independently of citizens, but that they should act rightly. Any particular trustee theory offers substantive principles that representatives are supposed to follow. To accept a trustee theory is to accept one set of substantive principles, and to reject competing sets of principles. By the terms of their trust, representatives are bound to act on the basis of certain principles, and exclusively those principles, when they conflict with principles that other theories uphold.

Building consideration of substantive principles into the role of the representative, though necessary in any trustee theory, undoes its democratic legitimacy. Trustee theory in effect places the choice of fundamental principles outside the political process. Representatives are to obtain their principles from some other source—typically, a philosophical theory. But even if we could show that one set of principles is philosophically superior to others, we would not be warranted in concluding that representatives should act exclusively on the basis of those principles. The principles must actually be accepted at some time by citizens. If the acceptance is to involve a genuine choice, citizens or at least their representatives must have the option of choosing other principles. The other principles cannot be excluded either from the deliberation in the legislature or from the menu of principles on the basis of which responsible representatives can act. Without such a process of choice, there is no ground for saying that they are the principles of a particular society. To settle such questions in advance in defining the duties of the trustee is to make political choices by philosophical fiat.

This is so even if trustee theory does not require representatives to adopt exclusively a complete set of principles but only places certain principled constraints on their conduct. The theory might, for example, hold only that representatives should not violate any rights of citizens.[13] The problem is that the definition of what is to count as a right in the society is itself a question that, to some extent, should be determined in the political process, including the deliberations and votes in the legislature. A principle that tells legislators not to violate certain (existing) rights is not much help when they are considering whether to support legislation that would establish new rights. The growth of the welfare state has often been explained and defended as a progressive recognition that the government should provide certain benefits (positive rights) in order to prevent harm being done to citizens (negative rights). But its opponents claim that

[13] For an example of such a theory, see Alan H. Goldman, *The Moral Foundations of Professional Ethics* (Totowa, N.J.: Rowman and Littlefield, 1980), pp. 24, 76, 88–89.

the welfare state violates the negative rights of some citizens (property owners, for example). We expect legislators, among others, to resolve such disputes; in doing so they do not merely observe, but sometimes change, the prevailing boundaries between positive and negative rights.

These objections to trustee theory are quite general in their implications. They apply to any theory that attempts to limit the role of a representative to acting in accordance with the dictates of any single substantive theory of fundamental values, such as a theory of liberty, equality, or the common good. The choices among these values are among the most important decisions that legislatures make, and the choices should not be predetermined by the role of the representative. There must be some moral constraints on that role, but they must not prevent representatives (and ultimately citizens) from choosing from a range of substantive theories.

Thus, neither delegate theory nor trustee theory succeeds in resolving the problem that welfare policy poses for the role of the representative. Delegate theory takes account of the need to hold representatives responsible for complex policies that reach into the future, but at the price of severing the connection with the preferences of citizens in the present. Trustee theory tries to escape the conflict between present and future preferences by relying instead on principles, but at the cost of placing those principles beyond the political choice of citizens.

The Significance of Process

The root of the problem is that conventional theories of representation misconceive the nature of political time. In all of them, whether pure or modified, time seems divided into discrete units—isolated moments of responsibility when representatives stand accountable for their actions. Representatives give reasons at particular times, and the reasons they give connect their actions to the attitudes of their constituents at particular times. Delegate theory provides no way to reconcile the conflicts that inevitably occur at different times. Trustee theory either assumes that citizens will accept representatives' choice of principles at some future time or removes the choice of principles from political time completely.

Missing is a recognition of the continuous nature of representation. Representation takes time. What representatives do during that time is an important part of what citizens should hold them responsible for. To avoid the conflict in the role of the representative, we must understand representation not as a relationship between constituents and representatives at particular political moments, but as a *process* in which the relationship between citizens and representatives continues over time.[14]

[14] Fenno (*Home Style*) is one of the few political scientists who emphasize the idea of

Representation can involve changes not only in the preferences of constituents (as trustee theorists appreciate), but also in the principles acted upon by representatives. The process is also affected by interactions among representatives in the legislature, which in turn affect the roles that representatives adopt in relation to their constituents. The concept of process thus allows for change not only in preferences and principles but also in the identities of constituents and their representatives. The concept therefore provides a more satisfactory way of confronting the temporal problems that welfare policy and similar issues pose for representation.

The legislative process (understood broadly to include not only lawmaking but the wide range of political activities in which legislators typically engage) best exemplifies the process of representation. Accordingly, the requirements we impose on the reasons representatives give to justify their choices should refer to the legislative process. The most promising sources of such requirements are the criteria that philosophers have suggested to define moral discourse. Since a principal purpose of democratic responsibility is to hold officials accountable for choosing fundamental values for society, the reasons that officials give to justify these choices should be judged according to some standards of moral deliberation. The legislative process should facilitate discussion of such values, and the explanations of legislators should qualify as contributions to that discussion. The problem is to find criteria that do not build into the process of deliberation a bias in favor of the fundamental values of an exclusive political theory.

Three constraints on what should count as a reason in moral discourse can, with some modification, serve as the criteria for what should count as a reason in political discourse that is concerned with democratic responsibility. The criteria are drawn from what some moral philosophers call the conditions of the "moral point of view" or the "formal constraints of the concept of right."[15] They require that a reason be general, public, and autonomous.[16] Together, the criteria are meant to define a

representation as process. But he concentrates on what occurs in the constituency more than on what happens in the legislature. Pitkin (*The Concept of Representation*, pp. 221–22) is one of the few contemporary political theorists to notice the significance of process, but she never specifies any standards by which we might assess its patterns, and scarcely discusses the legislative process itself.

[15] Rawls, *A Theory of Justice*, pp. 130–36; and Kurt Baier, *The Moral Point of View* (Ithaca, N.Y.: Cornell University Press, 1958), pp. 187–213. For further references, see W. K. Frankena, "Recent Conceptions of Morality," in H. N. Castaeda and George Nakhnikian, eds., *Morality and the Language of Conduct*, (Detroit: Wayne State University Press, 1965), pp. 1–24.

[16] The criteria correspond roughly to four of Rawls's five formal constraints (*A Theory of Justice* pp. 131–35). My use of "generality" could be understood as combining and simplifying his conditions of generality and universality. "Publicity" follows closely his condition of the same name, and "autonomy" is meant to capture the most relevant political element

discourse that does not exclude claims that express any genuine moral perspective (at least any held in modern liberal democracies), but does exclude claims that express only self-interests or group interests.

It may not be possible, even theoretically, to specify necessary and sufficient criteria for a moral reason, but it ought to be possible, even with a less systematic set of criteria, to establish the contrast we need to make between kinds of reasons that representatives should give in political practice. The difference should be clear between reasons based solely on political power and reasons based on moral principle, even if the philosophical nuances of the distinction remain controversial, and even if the actual motives of the persons who give the reasons remain questionable.

The contrast will become clearer as we trace the implications of the criteria for the legislative process. As usually stated in moral philosophy, the criteria are excessively formal. They refer to the form of reasons or principles, not to the conditions in which persons present them. Yet in the context of political judgment, each of the criteria presupposes the existence of certain institutional structures. The process itself is supposed to structure political discussion to make possible moral deliberation about the fundamental values that citizens and their representatives share or come to share while participating in the process.

The Particulars of Generality

A general reason is one that is universalizable: if it applies to one case, it applies to all cases that are similar in relevant respects.[17] The philosophical foundation of this idea owes most to Kant, whose various versions of the categorical imperative determine what is to count as an acceptable moral principle. If a principle cannot "stand the test of the form of a general law of nature," Kant writes, "then it is morally inadmissible."[18] Kant thought that this test would rule out the basic principles of many other moral theories, including utilitarianism, but most modern philosophers reinterpret it as a necessary condition that any moral principle, including the principle of utility, can satisfy.[19] In this form, the test

in his requirement of "ordering" (that the ordering of conflicting claims be independent of the capacity to intimidate and coerce). His condition of "finality" does not seem necessary for or appropriate to the legislative process.

[17] One of the most lucid discussions of universalizability in the vast literature on the subject is that of J. L. Mackie, *Ethics: Inventing Right and Wrong* (New York: Penguin, 1977), pp. 83–102.

[18] Immanuel Kant, "Critique of Practical Reason," in *The Philosophy of Kant*, ed. C. J. Friedrich (New York: Random House, 1949), chap. 2, p. 259.

[19] See, e.g., R. M. Hare, *Freedom and Reason* (Oxford: Clarendon Press, 1963), pp. 7–50.

provides an approximate criterion for generality in a theory of responsible representation.

Although the requirement of generality by itself does not exclude very much from legislative deliberation, it does exclude enough to create a problem for representation. By its nature, representation presupposes that representatives have some special responsibility to a particular group of citizens—their constituents.[20] This responsibility need not be as specific as delegate theory implies, but it must be specific enough to distinguish those whom a legislator represents from those whom the legislator does not. Even Burke recognized that he owed more to the electors of Bristol than to the electors of Warwick or Stafford.[21] Some special relationship between legislators and constituents must be assumed in any theory of representation in which a legislator stands for election by district, and by any theory that permits a legislator to speak for or answer to a particular group of citizens rather than to all citizens. Even in a legislature that seeks to ensure the general welfare through moral deliberation, the common good does not result from a sudden, simultaneous insight of all the legislators. It emerges only as each legislator expresses the views of particular groups within society (usually those to whom he or she is electorally accountable), and it must be defended to particular groups by the legislators who represent them.

If a representative may legitimately act for particular citizens, how can we insist that the representative give reasons that are general? The natural answer is that reasons that refer to the welfare of constituents *are* general in the sense that we can universalize the principle that each representative has a special responsibility for the welfare of his or her constituents. No representative claims any special privilege not granted to other representatives. But the appeal of this answer lies not so much in the formal test it satisfies as in the substantive assumption it makes: that a process in which representatives primarily act for parts of the whole functions to the benefit of the whole. The particular is thus justified by its consequences for the general.

What can justify this assumption? Neither of the familiar justifications seems plausible, though legislators seem to act (and theorists seem to write) as if one or the other were true. The first is the claim that there is

[20] Even at-large representatives elected nationally stand in a special relationship to those who voted for them, as John Stuart Mill imagined they would. See Mill, "Considerations on Representative Government," in *Essays on Politics and Society*, vol. 18 of *Collected Works*, ed. J. M. Robson (Toronto: University of Toronto Press, 1977), chap. 7.

[21] "Speech on the State of the Representation," in *Burke's Politics*, ed. Ross J. S. Hoffman and Paul Levack (New York: Knopf, 1959), p. 229. But Burke also assumes that a representative owes some special obligation to those districts such as Birmingham, which do not yet have M.P.s but whose citizens share some "interests" with those of Bristol.

an objective common good, on the definition of which the judgments of representatives and citizens will, in due time, converge. This we have implicitly rejected in criticizing trustee theory. The second justification is that the common good is the sum of particular interests. Even if this were an adequate conception of the common good, it would not provide the link we need to move from the particular to the general. The most single-minded advocate of this conception himself recognizes this problem. According to Bentham, the only way to determine what is in the public interest is for each representative to express the views of his constituents. But since these views may be mistaken, representatives must also be able to express their own view of the public interest. Bentham resolves these contradictory demands on the representative by means of one of his characteristically mechanical devices: The representative is to *speak* for what he views as the public interest but to vote in accordance with the views of his constituents.[22]

Despite its obvious inadequacy, Bentham's proposal contains an important insight—one that does not depend on his assumption that the public interest is simply the sum of particular interests. Speaking for the public interest is not just a way of fulfilling the duty to the public; it can also "have the effect of working a change in . . . [the] opinion" of constituents, and "on a later occasion causing them to concur with" their representative.[23] The public interest does not emerge either from the discovery of an objective good or from the aggregation of subjective preferences; it must be created in the legislative process. We can think of this creation as occurring in an iterated, four-step process: representatives express particular views, modify their own views in light of what other representatives say, act on the modified views, and then seek to justify them to constituents. The process begins again with the new views of the constituents if they have been persuaded, or their original views if they have not.

In this kind of legislative process, we could count as a reason a particular claim of an individual representative, *provided* that it can be justified as consistent with a legislative process that seeks a common good. There are, of course, many notions of the common good, and many ways the process can fail to pursue it. With respect to the criterion of generality, however, the most fundamental problem concerns the nature of the legislation. The more general the legislation, the more legislators may be encouraged to give general reasons to justify their views of it.

The requirement resembles Rousseau's stipulation that the general will

[22] Jeremy Bentham, *Constitutional Code*, ed. Frederick Rosen and J. H. Burns (Oxford: Oxford University Press, 1983), vol. 1, VI.1.A11, p. 44.

[23] Ibid.

should consider "all subjects collectively and all actions in the abstract; it does not consider any individual man or any specific action."[24] But it differs from Rousseau's by permitting legislation to use concrete terms to describe particular categories when they can be shown to be necessary to formulate a policy that promotes the general goals. The point is not that the language of the legislation or even its topics should be perfectly general, but rather that legislators can justify the purpose of the policy, as reflected in the legislation, from a general perspective. The legislation might be replete with particular categories, as were most of the eleven titles of the original Social Security Act (the categories included old-age and survivors, unemployed, dependent children, blind). But the legislation can still be said to satisfy the criterion of generality because it, or its legislative history, demonstrates a substantial relation of these categories to the general purposes of the legislation.

Even this modest requirement is more controversial than might at first appear, however. Some political scientists have argued that if we take any such requirement seriously, we should reject many of the recent policies of the welfare state. Consider the claim that whereas the "old welfare" (instituted in the New Deal) meets the requirement, the "new welfare" (established by the New Frontier and Great Society Programs) does not.[25] For Theodore Lowi, the most vigorous proponent of this claim, the Social Security Act of 1935 and the Economic Opportunity Act of 1964, respectively, exemplify these two kinds of welfare policy. "In contrast to the Social Security statute," he writes, the Economic Opportunity statute avoids "the identification and definition of categories and . . . cumulation of these into some kind of interrelated package. The most important sources of standards in old welfare—definitions, lists of examples, exceptions, exclusions, prerequisites—are almost absent here."[26] Instead of the explicit attention that the old welfare gives to the relation between particular categories and general rules, the new welfare employs open-ended categories; they are almost always introduced with "not limited to" or "such as."[27]

These differences in the language of the statutes reflect different conceptions of the role of the legislature. In the old welfare, Congress decided

[24] Jean-Jacques Rousseau, *The Social Contract*, ed. M. Cranston (New York: Penguin, 1968), bk. 2, chap. 6, pp. 80–81.

[25] The argument is made most forcefully and influentially by Theodore Lowi in *The End of Liberalism*, 2d ed. (New York: Norton, 1979), esp. pp. 198–236. For a more dispassionate discussion of the distinction between the two kinds of welfare, see Charles E. Gilbert, "Welfare Policy," in *Policies and Policymaking*, vol. 6 of Fred I. Greenstein and Nelson W. Polsby, eds., *Handbook of Political Science* (Reading, Mass.: Addison-Wesley, 1975), pp. 157–73.

[26] Lowi, *The End of Liberalism*, p. 213.

[27] Ibid., p. 214.

the main elements of the policies in advance. Although the legislature allowed administrators and the states considerable discretion, it did not leave open many important political questions, such as the level and kinds of aid or the qualifications necessary for receiving it. In the new welfare, Congress deliberately left key elements of the policy to be decided by local authorities, including some of the recipients themselves organized in the Community Action Programs. The new welfare assumed that the poor should have a say about the causes and cures of their poverty; it mandated "maximum feasible participation" of the poor in the planning and conduct of the programs designed to reduce poverty.

The War on Poverty, declared by the 1964 act, had neither defeated poverty nor improved participation by the time it officially ended three years later.[28] Lowi and other critics of that war blame its failures partly on the delegation of power—which they see as equivalent to the refusal of Congress to state general standards for the policies. In their view, Congress abdicated its responsibility to identify the causes of poverty and to establish general programs to attack those causes directly. Legislators refused "to make moral choices and set clear legislative standards."[29] By delegating the authority to make policy, Congress encouraged battles over control of the local programs instead of attacks on poverty itself.

It is by no means clear that the delegation of power and the provisions for more popular participation contributed to the failure of the poverty programs. The kind and extent of participation varied greatly from city to city, and often when a community action agency threatened to become effective in mobilizing the poor, the established local authorities reorganized the agency or cut off its funds.[30] The relatively modest sums of money appropriated in the three years of the program could hardly have had a major effect on either participation or poverty. But even if the critics are correct that the delegation of power as practiced under these programs contributed to the failure of the War on Poverty, they are not necessarily correct that delegation as practiced in any form cannot serve to promote welfare.

Lowi and his fellow critics seem to assume that delegation and generality are incompatible.[31] But they are not. If the legislature can justify

[28] For sympathetic critiques of the War on Poverty, see John H. Strange, "Citizen Participation in Community Action and Model Cities Programs," *Public Administration Review* 32 (1972): 655–59; and J. David Greenstone and Paul E. Peterson, *Race and Authority in Urban Politics* (New York: Russell Sage, 1973).

[29] Lowi, *The End of Liberalism*, p. 216.

[30] See Strange, "Citizen Participation," p. 655ff.

[31] When Lowi writes that the "principle of representation" on which delegation is based is "antithetical to the principle of administration" (p. 212), he implies that representation is inconsistent with responsible legislation that establishes the rules for administration.

delegation as the best means to promote the general purposes of welfare, then delegation not only satisfies the criterion of generality but may do so to a greater extent than does nondelegation. The justification itself can be perfectly general even if the reasons express the needs of the particular groups in society who are granted more political power.

Both the critics and the defenders of the new welfare, however, neglect time. Any justification of programs of this kind must be part of a continuing process of deliberation. The process should not be conceived of as a one-time decision, which initiates or terminates the delegated authority. Arguably, the problem of the War on Poverty was not that Congress delegated authority to local groups, but that Congress did not regularly review and revise the terms of the delegation in light of the responses of the participants and the deliberations of representatives. The justifications that generality requires cannot be accepted or rejected once and for all. They call for continual consideration of the relation between the general purposes of legislation and the exercise of power by particular representatives—whether that power is delegated or not.

From this perspective, the legislative process that sustained the old welfare does not necessarily look better than the one that supported the new welfare. For more than thirty years, the policies of the old welfare (and many of its administrators) remained unchanged and mostly unreviewed.[32] The aid to dependent children title of the 1935 act (now the AFDC Program) grants states wide discretion to set the levels of support, and some states have set the levels so low that they may undermine the general purposes of welfare policy.[33] There may be good reasons to allow some differences among states, but democratic responsibility, even according to a loose interpretation of the criterion of generality, requires legislators to present and discuss the reasons in a national forum. Neither the old nor the new welfare should escape the requirement of continuing deliberation about the general purposes of legislation, and the fundamental values that support those purposes.

The Autonomous Legislator

When representatives legislate, they should consider the legislation on its merits. This principle seems simple enough, and most legislators (at least in public) claim to act on it. The reasons they give to justify their

[32] Gilbert, pp. 159–60.

[33] The differences between states in recent years have ranged from about $30 to $170 per month per person (1981 figures). Variations in cost of living in different regions account for only a part of these differences in levels of support. See James E. Anderson, David W. Brady, Charles Bullock III, and Joseph Stewart, Jr., *Public Policy and Politics in America*, 2d ed. (Monterey, Calif.: Brooks-Cole, 1984), pp. 138–39.

actions generally refer to the welfare or the rights of citizens, not to the pressures of lobbyists or the influence of campaign contributors. The principle plainly excludes bribery and extortion, in which legislators act on the basis of reasons related more to the money they receive than to the purposes of the legislation they support. But extended beyond such clear cases, the principle creates many puzzling situations.

Like most people, congressmen often rationalize their conduct; the reasons they give may not be their real reasons. Their rationalizations are rarely the crude kind popularly ascribed to politicians. Congressmen do not typically keep their true reasons to themselves and give another set of reasons to the public. Nor are they inclined to fool themselves by accepting reasons that are not their real reasons for taking a position. Based on careful interviews with many congressmen, John Kingdon concluded that most "like to believe that they are going through some sort of rational consideration which is connected to the issue of public policy they are deciding. They do not enjoy seeing themselves as being manipulated or pushed and pulled by forces beyond their control. . . . [The congressman] must seize on some sort of argument that will justify his vote to himself and to others. For some congressmen, this is reinforcement; for others, persuasion."[34]

Even when this search for reasons takes place and affects the votes of representatives, it can hardly allay all our suspicions about the nature of the reasons that representatives give. One of Kingdon's examples shows why. Tobacco-area congressmen, he suggests, could not have brought themselves to vote against the cigarette advertising bill if they believed that smoking caused cancer. They arranged lengthy hearings to try to refute the evidence presented in the Surgeon General's Report. They finally gathered enough seemingly respectable testimony to convince themselves that a causal link between smoking and cancer had not been established, and thus to allow themselves in good conscience to vote against the bill.[35]

These congressmen may have been sincere; under the circumstances, citizens might have had reasonable doubts. But it is not the sincerity of representatives or even their conscious motives that should be at issue. Both are difficult enough to appraise in personal interactions. In the distant and mediated relations of political life, they can hardly be the basis for reliable judgments of responsibility. If we are trying to establish whether reasons are relevant to the merits of legislation, we should focus on the conditions under which representatives give reasons, rather than on the connection between the reasons that representatives give and their motives in particular cases. We should judge differently the legislative

[34] Kingdon, *Congressmen's Voting Decisions*, pp. 266–67.

[35] Ibid., p. 267.

conduct of congressmen who depend on tobacco interests for most of their campaign contributions and congressmen who do not. The more independent congressmen may still vote for tobacco subsidies—perhaps to protect the jobs of workers in their district. But their voting decision could be understood as a choice between the values of health and employment, because they might be less influenced by pressures unrelated to these values.

More generally, a theory of responsibility should focus on the conditions under which representatives give reasons, because they constitute the only reliable basis on which citizens can continually assess the actions of their representatives. Representatives must enjoy discretion, not only in their choice of policies but also in their choice of roles, and citizens may not be able to judge the results of these choices for many years, if ever. What citizens are in a better position to assess are the circumstances in which the representatives make the choices. Citizens may reasonably assume that some circumstances will prevent genuine deliberation and will produce undesirable legislation. Among the circumstances that bear directly on the reasons that responsible representatives should give are those in which there is improper influence. The criterion of autonomy is intended to preclude such influence.

Representation does not readily accommodate autonomy, however. The tension between the two would be impossibly acute if we were to adopt any of the leading philosophical standards of autonomy. If autonomy were thought to rule out, as Kant argued it should, any kind of desire as a basis for action, it would have little relevance to political life.[36] Even Rawls's concept ("acting from principles that we would consent to as free and equal rational beings") seems an inappropriate standard for representatives. It would "force [representatives] to consider the choice of principles unencumbered by the singularities of the circumstances in which [they] find themselves."[37] Some special obligation to a constituency is one singularity of circumstance that representatives cannot fail to consider; they must, after all, stand for reelection. Nearly as inescapable in modern politics is the obligation to a political party.[38]

The criterion of autonomy therefore cannot demand, even as an ideal,

[36] Kant, *The Metaphysical Elements of Justice*, trans. John Ladd (Indianapolis: Bobbs-Merrill, 1965), pp. 15–16.

[37] Rawls, *A Theory of Justice*, p. 516.

[38] Even Burke recognizes a special duty to party. He condemns any representative who "abandons the party in which he has long acted, and tells you it is because he proceeds upon his own judgment; and that he acts on the merits of the several measures as they arise; and that he is obliged to follow his own conscience" (*Burke's Politics*, p. 42). To accomplish anything in politics, Burke reminds us, representatives must act in concert, and that means they must be open to influence from members of their party.

a wholly unencumbered legislator, one who acts utterly unswayed by political pressures and partisan loyalties. It can, however, place some constraints on the kinds of reasons that representatives give to justify their conduct. Such a criterion would require that a representative's reasons for acting be relevant to *either* the merits of the legislation *or* the means necessary for adopting the legislation, where the means are consistent with a legislative process in which representatives generally consider legislation on its merits. According to this criterion, legislators may still trade votes on measures they think less important in order to win passage of measures that are more important, but not if such logrolling prevents consideration of the most important measures on their merits. Reelection and party loyalty can also count as reasons, if they can be kept from impairing the process of deliberation. In the case of reelection, what the criterion of autonomy demands should be clear in principle. The electoral connection has become a pecuniary connection. The most pressing problem is the influence of private money, and one of the most promising solutions is the public financing of campaigns. Although laden with practical difficulties, this reform presents fewer theoretical problems for the criterion of autonomy than does the role of political parties.

The Place of Party

Can loyalty to party be a reason that responsible representatives give to justify their actions? Such a reason seems on its face to abandon autonomy. Rather than acknowledging responsibility, this reason seems to shift responsibility to others. The party, not the representative, is to blame. The appeal to party, furthermore, seems even less general than a reference to constituency. A political party may be just another particular group within society. Constituents at least have some claim on a representative since they elected him or her (often with little regard to the program of the national party[39]). William Graham Sumner expressed the doubts of several generations of American observers of the party system: "I cannot trust a party; I can trust a man. I cannot hold a party responsible. I can hold a man responsible. I cannot get an expression of opinion which is single and simple from a party; I can get that only from a man."[40]

Behind these doubts about party lies a worthy conception of the legislative process. The connection between the doubts and that conception can be seen most clearly in the work of a more systematic theorist who opposed party government. Writing even before party discipline had be-

[39] Gary C. Jacobson, *The Politics of Congressional Elections* (Boston: Little, Brown, 1983), pp. 81–86.

[40] William Graham Sumner, *The Challenge of Facts and Other Essays*, ed. A. G. Keller (New Haven, Conn.: Yale University Press, 1914), p. 367.

come firmly established in Britain, John Stuart Mill objected to party government because it constrains deliberation in the legislature. It does so in two ways. First, it artificially reduces the number of voices in the legislature. It is wrong that "all the opinions, feelings and interests of all members of the community should be merged in the single consideration of which party shall predominate."[41] Second, party government arbitrarily restricts the possibility of change. It keeps those voices that do gain a hearing in the legislature from changing their tune. With highly disciplined parties, no amount of discussion could normally convince legislators to alter their views, and no independent representative (or the legislative leader) can have much influence.[42]

A conception of the legislative process that emphasizes diversity and change certainly supports autonomy. But accepting this conception does not entail rejecting party government. We may be able to find a place for party while preserving the virtues of diversity and change in the legislature. It is certainly worth trying because, contrary to what their critics claim, parties can promote responsibility.

Party loyalty may qualify, under the proper conditions, as a reason that a responsible representative can give. Representatives act autonomously if they acknowledge personal responsibility for choosing a party, and explain their actions in relation to what the party has accomplished or failed to accomplish. Autonomy is the opposite of the individualistic behavior that many congressmen now display. When congressmen "run *for* Congress by running *against* Congress," they do not give reasons that connect their actions to the legislative process of which they are a part.[43]

Party loyalty, furthermore, may count as a general reason if the policies of the party express a more general perspective than that of individual legislators. A party can serve as an instrument to help a representative take into account the views of other similarly situated representatives—a step toward fulfilling the more difficult duty of taking into account the views of all representatives, however differently situated they may be.

[41] J. S. Mill, *Speech on Personal Representation*, speech delivered in the House of Commons, May 29, 1867 (London: Henderson, Rait, and Fenton, 1867), p. 12.

[42] Mill, *Considerations on Representative Government*, chap. 6.

[43] Fenno, *Home Style*, pp. 167–68. The condemnation of this kind of conduct is the closest that contemporary political scientists come to affirming a normative canon on political representation. See also Fiorina, *Retrospective Voting*, pp. 210–11; Fiorina, "The Decline of Collective Responsibility," *Daedalus* 109 (Summer 1980): 26, 39, 40; Kingdon, *Congressmen's Voting Decisions*, pp. 51–53; David Mayhew, *Congress: The Electoral Connection* (New Haven, Conn.: Yale University Press, 1974), pp. 114–22; and James L. Sundquist, *The Decline and Resurgence of Congress* (Washington, D.C.: Brookings Institution, 1981), pp. 451, 455. For earlier statements, see Woodrow Wilson, *Congressional Government* (Boston: Houghton Mifflin, 1885), p. 318; and James Bryce, *Modern Democracies* (New York: Macmillan, 1921), 2: 494–95.

Moreover, the party provides a way of locating responsibility for the Madisonian "train of measures." A party manifests greater temporal continuity than does any individual representative or even the legislature itself, whose programmatic identity changes as its membership changes. In this sense, the appeal to party generalizes a reason not only with respect to constituencies and policies at any particular time but also with respect to both over time.

To satisfy the requirements of responsibility, therefore, a party system should promote two different practices in the legislature. It should encourage representatives to relate their own actions to the actions of their party and to engage in legislative deliberation. These two practices usually conflict; thus any party system that seeks to enforce one is likely to sacrifice the other.

The proposal for a "more responsible two-party system" illustrates the first practice.[44] It encourages representatives to take responsibility for the collective actions of the party, but it would make deliberation difficult if not impossible. Because the party is committed to programmatic coherence and electoral victory, sustained discussion and persistent dissent are not likely to be welcomed. In the legislature, there would be little scope for members to change their minds, and little room for independent legislators to play a prominent role.[45]

A party system such as that imagined by Ostrogorski illustrates the second practice. He believes that the "party as a wholesale contractor for the numerous and varied problems, present and to come, should give place to special organizations, limited to particular objects and forming and reforming spontaneously, so to speak, according to the changing problems of life and the play of opinion brought about thereby."[46] In a system like this, citizens would find it difficult to call representatives to account for comprehensive programs such as welfare policy. The "train of measures" might never leave the station. There is no reason to suppose that the shifting coalitions within parties would produce the set of interrelated policies

[44] Committee on Political Parties, American Political Science Association, "Toward a More Responsible Two-Party System," *American Political Science Review*, vol. 44, supplement (September 1950). See also Gerald M. Pomper, "Toward A More Responsible Two-Party System? What Again?" *Journal of Politics* 33 (November 1971): 916–40; and J. Harry Wray, "Rethinking Responsible Parties," *Western Political Quarterly* 34 (December 1981): 510–527. The call for "collective responsibility" also usually includes a plea for strong "responsible" parties (e.g., Fiorina, "Decline of Collective Responsibility," pp. 28–39). Also see David E. Price, *Bringing Back the Parties* (Washington, D.C.: Congressional Quarterly Press, 1984), pp. 104–16.

[45] For criticisms of the idea of a responsible party system, see Charles Lindblom, *The Intelligence of Democracy* (New York: Collier-Macmillan, 1965), pp. 318–19.

[46] M. Ostrogorski, *Democracy and the Party System in the United States* (New York: Macmillan, 1926), p. 441.

that citizens should reasonably expect from any group that claims to govern. If a party happened to succeed in formulating a comprehensive program, its coalitions probably could not hold together long enough for the necessary legislation to be passed in both houses, especially if legislative discussion extended over several sessions. The parties may not even form in the first place without some strong leadership in the legislature, and they would not be likely to persist without some incentives for members who dissent from parts of the party's program.

Neither of these concepts of a party system satisfies the requirements of responsibility. A truly responsible party system would combine aspects of both. Following the first concept, a responsible party would stand for a general program, a comprehensive set of measures. And in accordance with the second, the party would not be an organization dedicated to winning power regardless of the issues its legislative members favored. Representatives would stand for election on the party's record, but through discussion in legislative caucuses they could substantially modify the party's program. Legislative leaders would have considerable power to reward party loyalists, but legislators could change parties with less cost than at present. Party voting would be more regular than it has been in recent Congresses, but party membership would be more fluid. The party leadership would have greater authority over what are called "control" committees (such as Appropriations and Ways and Means), but would grant considerable freedom to other committees and subcommittees so that individual members could more readily challenge the dominant opinion in the party.

A complete model of a party system of this kind calls for an empirical analysis better conducted by political scientists than by political theorists. But the approach suggested here—combining in one party system aspects of the two conflicting practices—provides a framework for the empirical analysis, as well as for formulation of an ideal party system that favors legislative responsibility. Such a system would support a legislative process in which representatives give general and autonomous reasons for the comprehensive and long-term measures that constitute welfare policy. This system would be more likely to sustain the kind of political parties to which representatives could responsibly pledge their loyalty.

The Necessity for Publicity

It was Kant who first emphasized the deep connection between morality and publicity. He presented the criterion of publicity as a fundamental test of morality, equivalent to one version of the categorical imperative. "All actions which relate to the right of other men are contrary to right and law, the maxim of which does not permit publicity."[47] That a reason can be made public is not sufficient to make the reason moral, but it is necessary. If a reason must be kept secret, it is because the reason cannot be generally and freely accepted. In this sense, publicity is a test of the other requirements of responsibility—generality and autonomy. Representatives cannot publicly justify a lie by invoking the principle that they will tell the truth except when they believe it will jeopardize their reelection. Making that justification public would defeat its purpose. That the reason must be kept secret shows that it is not general enough (it favors the representative), and that it would not be chosen freely by others (the representative presumes their ignorance).

Because Kant considered the criterion of publicity to be "an experiment of pure reason," abstracted from all actual conditions, he did not insist that justifications in fact be made public.[48] This formality prevents his criterion, in its original form, from serving as a requirement of political responsibility. Especially in politics, the actual process of publicizing reasons differs significantly from the hypothetical process. Facing an audience, politicians are more likely to take into account arguments they have not previously considered; they also are more likely to change their minds if they cannot answer those arguments. Moreover, before an audience, they have the opportunity to change the minds of other people. As Mill stressed, publicity can "compel deliberation and force everyone to determine, before he acts, what he shall say if called to account for his actions."[49]

Unlike the other two criteria of responsibility, the requirement of publicity does not directly conflict with representation. The practice of representation does not license secrecy as it legitimizes particularity and dependency. On the contrary, representation seems to require that citizens know as much as possible about the conduct of their representatives. This is all the more true if we accept the earlier argument that representatives must have considerable discretion in deciding how to interpret their role. The more discretion they have, the more citizens must know about their decisions.

[47] Immanuel Kant, "Eternal Peace," in *The Philosophy of Kant*, ed. C. J. Friedrich (New York: Random House, 1949), p. 470.

[48] Ibid. Rawls's interpretation of the condition of publicity is also hypothetical in the sense that it is meant to constrain choices in an "original position," in which the agents do not know their particular circumstances. But part of his rationale for the condition refers to its consequences for actual political life: publicly known principles "support the stability of social cooperation" (Rawls, *A Theory of Justice*, p. 133).

[49] Mill, "Considerations on Representative Government," p. 214. Sissela Bok emphasizes the importance of actual publicity as a criterion of morality: see Bok, *Lying* (New York: Random House, 1979), pp. 99–108; and Bok, *Secrets* (New York: Pantheon, 1982), pp. 112–115.

The problems that publicity creates come instead from conflicts with generality and autonomy. The more public the activities of legislators, the more pressure they may face to support particular interests, and the more dependence they may develop on outside groups. We do not have to assume that legislators are political cowards who give in to pressures whenever they have to make decisions in the open. The problems of publicity persist even if legislators act conscientiously; indeed, they result partly from the legislators' effort to observe the other two criteria of responsibility. When legislators must always act in the glare of publicity, they are forced to justify their conduct continually. They enjoy no escape from the demand for explanation. Consequently, in giving justifications, legislators focus more on immediate issues and on more momentary audiences. Legislators are less likely to consider the "train of measures" that Madison saw as essential to responsible government, and they are more likely to respond to the citizens who have the most direct access to their attention. Both tendencies run counter to the criterion of generality (which considers the legislative process as a whole continuing over time), and to the criterion of autonomy (which prescribes deliberation on the merits of the issues).

That publicity sometimes conflicts with these criteria, however, does not justify rejecting it as a requirement of responsibility. The existence of conflict itself provides a reason not only for preserving publicity but also for granting it status equal to the other criteria. The conflicts among the criteria reflect disagreements about the relative importance of the fundamental values presupposed by both processes and policies. Is it more important to let citizens know what is happening in the Conference Committee, or to leave the members free to deliberate without citizens looking over their shoulders?

Even if legislators rightly choose secrecy over publicity in certain circumstances, they should make that choice openly. The decision must be justified to citizens, and that can only be done in public. To be sure, it can only be done by giving reasons that are also general and autonomous. But to judge whether the reasons are general and autonomous, citizens must know what they are. No less than the other criteria, publicity is a necessary condition for deciding how much weight we should assign to each criterion—including publicity itself—and for deciding whether in certain circumstances we should disregard any criterion, also including publicity.

The Secrets of Legislatures

It may hardly seem necessary to urge the importance of publicity in the U.S. Congress, generally regarded as the most open legislature in the world. Indeed, the problem of publicity, in the judgment of some observers, is that there is too much of it. In the early 1970s, as part of a general effort of self-reform, the House opened all committee meetings to the public (including television audiences), and decided that names and votes should be recorded in virtually all voting. The House Select Committee on Committees later criticized these "sunshine" provisions, complaining that they inhibit candid discussion of controversial issues, discourage changes of opinion, hamper efforts to reach compromises, and subject members to greater pressures from lobbyists.[50]

Some of these effects could subvert responsibility, and could indeed provide justifications for limiting publicity. But such justifications, tailored to fit each case or type of case, can be presented and debated in open session. This is an approach that neither the Select Committee nor most other critics of publicity seriously consider. In justifying secrecy, moreover, its advocates would have to distinguish between the need to keep the proceedings closed and the need to keep the records of the proceedings confidential. The argument for closed sessions is more compelling than the argument for confidential records; but the former argument is often mistakenly assumed to establish the conclusion of the latter argument, thereby extending indefinitely into the future the secrecy that may be warranted only in the present. Citizens may reasonably refuse to accept a justification for closed sessions unless they can inspect records of the sessions at some future time. Even if secrecy is warranted now, the further question should always be asked: *When* may citizens learn what happened? If the temporal nature of responsibility implies that citizens should in some cases wait to judge what their representatives have done, it also requires that representatives should not fail to provide citizens with the information they need when the time comes to judge.

Secrecy does not always take the form of closed meetings or concealed records, however. Even in the legislative sessions of so open an institution as the Congress, public policy can be made without the public knowing much about it. Sometimes the ignorance is the fault of citizens themselves, who do not demand to know. Their representatives are only accessories, guilty of failing to enlighten their constituents. But at other times legislators, out of perfectly benign motives, deliberately prevent an issue from receiving wide public discussion, and pass laws without the benefit of the reactions that such discussion might bring. This strategy is especially tempting when the welfare of citizens is at stake, and the motives of representatives are genuinely benevolent.

A case in point is the policy on public financing of treatment for kidney disease. According to one observer, the debate on this policy in the early

[50] Arthur Maass, *Congress and the Common Good* (New York: Basic Books, 1983), pp. 62–66.

1970s was conducted sotto voce. It was "carried out mainly within the inner councils of the medical-scientific community and the political-governmental system. . . . Both opponents and proponents were reluctant to have this issue fully considered in public debate, fearing that it was too divisive for the polity to handle."[51] Some political scientists would endorse this reluctance, arguing that policies that put a price on human life, such as those that allocate scarce medical resources, should not be the subject of open discussion. One can imagine the "perfectly 'rational' congressman" trying to justify the legislature's decision to limit expenditures for medical care: "Mrs. Jones, I share your grief about the plight of your husband, but we simply cannot afford to spend $30,000 per year to keep him alive when people are dying elsewhere who could be saved for much less." Such candor threatens the "life-preserving norm that decent societies should respect."[52] Similarly, one scholar would encourage policymakers to pretend that they are not putting a price on human life even though they are in fact doing so: "the polite fiction might just be enough to protect people's self-respect."[53]

These arguments posit a gap between representatives and citizens that is neither plausible nor desirable. Why should we assume that representatives are any more capable than their constituents of rationally considering questions about the value of life? In allocating funds for treatment of kidney disease, legislators did not in fact act like rational economists. Congress committed far too many financial resources to one disease and one group of victims, thus diverting funds from programs that could help a larger number of people who suffered from other diseases.

But even if legislators could in secret strike the right balance between efficient allocation of resources and respect for the "life-preserving norm," they would have to make sure that citizens did not understand their real reasons for the balance they struck. Perhaps Mrs. Jones does not at this moment want to hear a cost-benefit analysis of her dying husband's treatment, but neither would she want to hear lies from her congressman. The rational representative may exhibit a lack of sensitivity, but the benevolent representative exhibits a fault much more dangerous in the character of a public official in a democracy—a lack of candor. If citizens cannot know the reasons for the actions of representatives, they cannot judge the way in which representatives act. Judging the way that representatives act, we have seen, may be the only way that citizens can

[51] Richard Rettig, "The Policy Debate on Patient Care Financing for Victims of End-State Renal Disease," *Law and Contemporary Problems* 40 (Autumn 1976); 212–30.

[52] Steven E. Rhoads, "How Much Should We Spend to Save a Life?" in Steven E. Rhoads, ed., *Valuing Life: Public Policy Dilemmas* (Boulder, Colo.: Westview Press, 1980), p. 304.

[53] Robert Goodin, *Political Theory and Public Policy* (Chicago: University of Chicago Press, 1982), pp. 120–21.

hold representatives accountable for many policies, especially policies intended to promote the welfare of citizens.

No less troublesome is the argument that representatives should quietly suppress consideration of some controversial questions. Some political scientists look back nostalgically to the late nineteenth century, when congressional leaders "put the lid on" discussion of many issues of intense concern to their constituents, such as the controversial issue of bilingual education. Similarly, they praise the House Rules Committee for keeping the question of aid to parochial schools off the congressional agenda in 1961, and wish legislative leaders now would do the same with the question of abortion funding.[54]

There may be good reasons for legislatures to avoid such issues, but they are not reasons of responsibility. More precisely, responsibility requires that legislators give reasons for refusing to consider these issues. Nothing in the legislative process is more important than the agenda; therefore, nothing is more important in the explanations that representatives give than the reasons for setting that agenda. If leaders can keep the agenda clear of questions that should not be discussed, they can also keep it clear of questions that should be discussed. The leaders of the Democratic party have abused the power to control the agenda; for more than a century, they kept Congress from seriously confronting the question of racism.[55] Legislators stand guilty of similar abuses insofar as they refuse to consider, or to explain why they refuse to consider, pressing questions of welfare policy, however divisive such questions may be.

Publicity, like generality and autonomy, focuses our attention on the conditions under which representatives make decisions for citizens. All the requirements of responsibility emphasize the temporal dimension of those conditions. Representation takes place in a legislative process that takes time, and citizens need to judge what representatives do during that time.

This need is all the more critical because none of the standard theories of the role of the representative can serve as a foundation for the responsibility of representatives. None is adequate because none encourages citizens to judge the part that representatives play in the legislative process as a whole. A theory that emphasizes the legislative process does not necessarily place a higher value on the process than on its results. Nor does it make the rightness of a process a sufficient test of the rightness of policy. We judge representatives by the process they keep because that is the

[54] Fiorina, "Decline of Collective Responsibility," p. 41.

[55] Ibid., p. 44. Since Fiorina himself considers this an abuse, he clearly does not favor letting legislators "put the lid on" all controversial issues. But he does not indicate how we should distinguish the issues that should be suppressed from those that should not; nor does he suggest that such distinctions should be discussed in the legislature.

best way to hold them accountable for fundamental choices of value about which we disagree. At least, it is the best way if the choices involve consideration of a "train of measures" that, like welfare policy, join many different issues and stretch many years into the future.

Responsibility requires that representatives justify their conduct to citizens now but also that their justifications speak to citizens in the future. Welfare policy poses the dilemma in an acute form since its justifications refer directly to the preferences of citizens now but its effects extend into the distant future. Democratic representatives are supposed to defer to the preferences of citizens at some point in time, but at any moment in political time they may have good reason to disregard those preferences. This conflict has no final resolution. But we stand a better chance of coping with its consequences in the welfare state if we adopt a theory of representation that emphasizes, as most such theories do not, the significance of the legislative process.

7

Race, Class, Power, and the American Welfare State

JENNIFER L. HOCHSCHILD

Why is racial inequality in America so hard to eradicate? I propose a new answer to that old question, starting with the seemingly paradoxical claim that race policy concentrates too much on race. Recognizing how much racial inequality is entangled with inequalities of economic class and political power would, in my view, enable us to design more appropriate policies to deal with the problem. But such a recognition would also force us to confront the magnitude of the problem and the amount of change necessary to solve it. It is not at all clear that Americans are willing or able to tackle such changes. In fact, it may be that the very realization of their magnitude would dishearten reformers and encourage standpatters. Thus we face a situation in which a new analysis is analytically necessary but politically risky in our continuing efforts to solve "the problem of the Twentieth Century . . .—the problem of the color line."[1]

I explore these claims in this paper. The cumulative inequalities of race, class, and power are clear and relatively easy to demonstrate; I do so very briefly in the first section. The more difficult questions are whether the United States can in fact take the steps necessary to alleviate these cumulative inequalities, and whether it is likely to do so. In the second section I examine those questions, although I cannot fully answer them. They, in turn, raise the most important and difficult issue: Can America's partial welfare state correct its own worst shortcomings? Can the United States move from a society in which the very ideal of equal opportunity for all

My thanks to the National Academy of Education for the Spencer Foundation Fellowship, which supported this research, and to Deborah Baumgold, C. Anthony Broh, Elizabeth Bussiere, Thomas Cavanagh, Jameson Doig, Robert Fullinwider, Amy Gutmann, Jane Mansbridge, Daniel Monti, David Pavelchek, Paul Peterson, Clarence Stone, Alan Wertheimer and the members of Princeton University's faculty Seminar on Democracy and the Welfare State for their very helpful comments on various drafts of this paper.

[1] W.E.B. Du Bois, "The Souls of Black Folk," in *Three Negro Classics* (New York: Avon Books, 1965), p. 209.

inhibits its provision for some, to a society in which ideals and practices are made to concur through the operation of the welfare state? The paper is least definitive on this most important question, but I hope at a minimum to demonstrate that the issue of alleviating racial inequality is crucial to its answer.

To address these questions, I need to define my terms. I begin with Carole Pateman's statement in Chapter 10 of this book: a welfare state "gives social meaning and equal worth to the formal juridical and political rights of all citizens." In the United States, at least, those rights derive from classical liberal theory. They include the right to be treated as an individual, popular sovereignty and political equality (usually defined as majority rule), equal freedom and opportunity to pursue one's goals, protection of self and property against unwarranted interference, and only as much government as is needed to ensure these freedoms and rights. This list enables us to make Pateman's language more precise. The American welfare state is a set of policies (mostly public and mostly emanating from the federal government) that operate within the restrictions of some liberal rights in order to make possible the exercise of others. More particularly, it is a set of policies intended to grant just enough political material and resources to make tenable the promise of equal opportunity for all, even in the modern world of large, impersonal markets and "mass society."

The dimension of *race* as I use it here is a social and psychological phenomenon. People identify themselves and others as "white" or "black,"[2] and they hold views and take actions as a consequence of those identifications. Races may not be biologically distinct; what matters here is that, to a greater or lesser degree, people perceive blacks and whites as different and act accordingly.

The dimension of *class* refers to the fact of economic stratification into groups that are relatively self-perpetuating, and that shape one's work, family and social life, and expectations. Classes may not be fixed, inherently conflictual, and impermeable; I claim only that, to an important degree, one's position in the economic structure is affected by one's origins, affects one's future, and has broad consequences beyond the workplace.

The dimension of *power* is the most amorphous. It refers to political

[2] For the sake of keeping complexity to a manageable level, in this paper I ignore ethnic and racial groups other than blacks and whites (defined broadly as including all ethnicities except Hispanics and Asians.) This exclusion is substantively defensible for two reasons: (1) the histories of Asians and Hispanics now living in the United States are distinctive and deserve separate treatment; and (2) the problems between blacks and whites historically and currently eclipse the problems of integrating successive waves of non-Anglo immigrants. See the last section of the paper for a discussion of the latter reason.

control, at least in having some say over an organization's or other people's actions, and at most in determining those actions. "Organizations" and "other people" are typically governmental officials and agencies, but they may be so-called private entities such as corporations, foundations, and social clubs.

These definitions are neither unusual nor precise, but they do not need to be. I am seeking here to probe the problems of the American welfare state as most citizens intuitively understand it, rather than to explore new meanings of liberalism and welfare, or the relation between them. Similarly, I am seeking to understand how race, class, and power relate to one another, rather than to explore the internal workings of any one of the three. Depth, in short, is giving way to breadth.

Race, Class, and Power in American Life

Inequalities of race, class, and power cumulate, and their combination worsens the disparities created by each dimension alone. Furthermore, although the status of blacks has improved in obvious and deeply significant ways since the early 1960s, progress in eradicating cumulative inequalities is neither certain to continue nor universal in its reach.

Race

It may be beating a dead horse to assert the persistence of racial discrimination; nevertheless, symmetry of presentation and occasional counterassertions[3] require at least a brief recital of the evidence about racism.

Blacks now enjoy prospect-regarding equal opportunity, defined as the legal right to pursue a goal and to use the means allowed to others in its pursuit.[4] For most whites, the realization of prospect-regarding equal opportunity suffices. Most whites believe and profess to be glad that blacks

[3] Thomas Sowell, *Ethnic America* (New York: Basic Books, 1981); William Bradford Reynolds, "A Defense of the Reagan Administration's Civil Rights Policies," *New Perspectives* 16, no. 1 (Summer 1984): 34–38; Walter Williams, *America: A Minority Viewpoint* (Stanford, Calif.: Hoover Institution Press, 1982).

[4] Douglas Rae, Douglas Yates, Jennifer Hochschild, Joseph Morone, and Carol Fessler, *Equalities* (Cambridge, Mass.: Harvard University Press, 1981), pp. 64–81. Prospect-regarding equality of opportunity is distinguished from means-regarding equality of opportunity, which calls for ensuring that people have equal means or resources to achieve their chosen goal. Some argue that blacks do not yet enjoy prospect-regarding equal opportunity—therefore the need to mandate desegregation and affirmative action programs. I see those programs as moving beyond prospect-regarding to substantive or means-regarding equal opportunity, but that is another discussion.

are no longer second-class citizens. They increasingly reject prejudice and discrimination in principle, and believe them to be declining in practice. Overall, they are increasingly optimistic about the general situation of blacks.

But many blacks may as well inhabit a different nation, they disagree so much with whites. Blacks are generally pessimistic about changes in their situation in the long run, and they perceive much lingering prejudice and discrimination.[5]

Who is right? Both, to some degree; racial prejudice and discrimination are declining, but have not disappeared. More disturbing is evidence that they will not decline to the point where they no longer matter. For example, although most whites now reject any expression of prejudice, some do not.[6] And it is at least possible that the willingness to express racial prejudice does not reflect the full extent of racism. Some psychologists argue that although "old-fashioned racism" has become socially and emotionally unacceptable to most whites, "modern [or symbolic] racism" persists; many whites continue to "resist . . . change in the racial status quo based on moral feelings that blacks violate such traditional American values as individualism and self-reliance, the work ethic, obedience, and discipline."[7]

[5] Thomas Cavanagh, *Inside Black America* (Washington, D.C.: Joint Center for Political Studies, 1985), pp. 3–9; Louis Harris and Associates, *A Study of Attitudes toward Racial and Religious Minorities and toward Women* (New York: Louis Harris and Associates, 1978); Philip E. Converse, Jean Dotson, Wendy Hoag, and William McGee III, *American Social Attitudes Data Sourcebook, 1974–1978* (Cambridge, Mass.: Harvard University Press, 1980); Howard Schuman, Charlotte Steeh, and Lawrence Bobo, *Racial Attitudes in America* (Cambridge, Mass.: Harvard University Press, 1985); CBS News/*New York Times* Poll (conducted by telephone February 16–19, 1978), "The Kerner Commission—Ten Years Later," I. A. Lewis and William Schneider, "Black Voting, Bloc Voting, and the Democrats," *Public Opinion* 6, no. 5 (October-November 1983); Alphonso Pinkney, *The Myth of Black Progress* (Cambridge: Cambridge University Press, 1984).

[6] Harris and Associates, *A Study of Attitudes*, pp. 3–16; Schuman et al., *Racial Attitudes*, chaps. 5, 6; the Harris Survey, "Poll Results Contradict Claims that Prejudice Is Increasing," press release, February 18, 1985, p. 3; Converse et al., *American Social Attitudes*, p. 61; Lewis and Schneider, "Black Voting," Table 1; Tom Smith and Glenn Dempsey, "The Polls: Ethnic Social Distance and Prejudice," *Public Opinion Quarterly* 47, no. 4 (Winter 1983): 584–600.

[7] See John B. McConahay, "Self-Interest versus Racial Attitudes as Correlates of Anti-Busing Attitudes in Louisville," *Journal of Politics* 44, no. 3 (August 1982): 692–717; John B. McConahay, "Modern Racism, Ambivalence, and the Modern Racism Scale," in John Davido and Sam Gaertner, eds., *Prejudice, Discrimination, and Racism* (New York: Academic Press, 1986), pp. 91–125; Douglas S. Gatlin, Michael Giles, and Everett F. Cataldo, "Policy Support within a Target Group: The Case of School Desegregation," *American Political Science Review*, 72, no. 3 (September 1978): 985–95; David Sears, Richard Lau, Tom Tyler, and Harris Allen, Jr., "Self-Interest vs. Symbolic Politics in Policy Attitudes and Presidential Voting," *American Political Science Review* 74, no. 3 (September 1980): 670–84; Donald Kinder, "The Continuing American Dilemma," *Journal of Social Issues* 42, no. 2 (1986): 151–71.

What about the more important question of racial discrimination? On the one hand, wage discrimination has declined considerably for most workers and entirely for some, and some apparent wage discrimination is actually unrelated to race. On the other hand, even after controlling for a wide range of non-race-related differences, black men's wages remain about 10 to 20 percent below white men's wages. The monetary return for an additional year of education or labor market experience remains noticeably lower for blacks than for whites, and the black under- and unemployment rate has remained at least twice that of whites since the 1950s. Black youths are especially hard hit by unemployment, despite the fact that, on average, they are becoming more and better educated.[8]

Even successful blacks hold lower-status jobs and are perhaps less likely to be promoted than successful whites. "Overall, black occupational advancement in the 1970s is not particularly impressive. . . . Although a higher proportion of blacks could be found among the professional and technical occupations in 1980 than in 1972, they were concentrated in jobs at the lower end of the professional pay scale." In addition, black professionals' pay increases were small relative to those of whites; the black-white ratio of earnings for white-collar workers actually declined in the 1970s from 91 percent in 1973 to 86 percent in 1980.[9]

Despite their expressed preference for integrated neighborhoods, wealthy blacks continue to be less likely to live in suburbia than middle- and low-income whites.[10] This fact is particularly important given evidence that "it is the suburban rather than city blacks who were the recipients of most of the occupational upgrading during the 1970s."[11]

In sum, by all measures of economic success, blacks as a group do less

[8] Reynolds Farley, *Blacks and Whites: Narrowing the Gap* (Cambridge, Mass.: Harvard University Press, 1984); R. Price and Edwin Mills, "Race and Residence in Earnings Determination," *Journal of Urban Economics* 17 (1985): 1–18; Michael Reich, *Racial Inequality* (Princeton, N.J.: Princeton University Press, 1981); U.S. Commission on Civil Rights, *Unemployment and Underemployment among Blacks, Hispanics, and Women* (Washington, D.C.: U.S. Government Printing Office, 1983); College Entrance Examination Board, *Equality and Excellence: The Educational Status of Black Americans* (New York: CEEB, 1985); Richard Freeman and Harry Holzer, eds., *The Black Youth Unemployment Crisis* (Chicago: University of Chicago Press, 1986); Richard McGahey and John Jeffries, *Minorities and the Labor Market* (Washington, D.C.: Joint Center for Political Studies, 1985).

[9] Diane N. Westcott, "Blacks in the 1970's: Did They Scale the Job Ladder?" *Monthly Labor Review* 105, no. 6 (June 1982): 29–38.

[10] James A. Davis and Tom W. Smith, *General Social Surveys, 1972–1983: Cumulative Codebook* (Chicago: University of Chicago, National Opinion Research Center, 1983); Michael White, *Neighborhoods and Residential Differentiation* (New York: Basic Books, forthcoming); Reynolds Farley and Robert Wilger, "Recent Changes in the Residential Segregation of Blacks from Whites" (Ann Arbor: University of Michigan, Population Studies Center, 1987).

[11] Westcott, "Blacks in the 1970's," p. 33.

well than whites. More important, blacks in general are less able than whites to translate some success into further success. More education is not leading to more and better jobs for teenagers; professional jobs do not necessarily lead to higher-level professional jobs; wealth is only very slowly leading to acquisition of the residential perquisites of wealth. Black pessimism is at least as warranted as white optimism.

Class

Pointing out that blacks as a group continue to face psychological and economic discrimination is only part of the story. To enrich and deepen its meaning, we must add a new plot line—a consideration of the relationship between race and class.

Consider attitudes first. When the stigma of the "wrong" race accompanies the stigma of poverty, white Americans able to do so are eager to distance themselves from those who (they hope) are so different from them. Rejection of poor blacks may even drive them to accept middle-class blacks. For example, after presiding for ten years over a school desegregation case, one judge wrote a plan that desegregated outlying regions of a large school district but left the central city ghetto almost untouched. He did so, he explained (in private), because he realized that middle-class whites would accept middle-class blacks in their schools, but would not put up with ghetto children. His political judgment may have been too pessimistic (although subsequent events suggested that, if anything, he overestimated whites' tolerance), and it may even be constitutionally suspect. But the point here is that he, the person who knew the circumstances of the case better than anyone, saw the real dividing line falling between well-off and poor blacks rather than between blacks and whites.

Other school desegregation plans have produced the same outcome, although their authors have seldom had such a clear-eyed understanding of why.[12] The only systematic survey data I know on this point confirm the judge's intuition. Even a majority of a group of whites deeply committed to integration were willing to desegregate professions, neighborhoods, apartment buildings, and workplaces only with middle-class blacks.[13]

[12] Lillian B. Rubin, *Busing and Backlash* (Berkeley: University of California Press, 1972), pp. 45–49; Janet Schofield, *Black and White in School* (New York: Praeger, 1982), pp. 182–211.

[13] No data are reported on respondents' views about poor whites; Judith Caditz, *White Liberals in Transition* (Holliswood, N.Y.: Spectrum, 1976), pp. 56–81. For an ambiguous but intriguing set of data on people's beliefs about the relationship between race and class,

Being poor and black generates not only disfavor but also worse outcomes than those experienced as a result of being "only" poor or black. Poor black children perform worse on achievement tests and the Scholastic Aptitude Test than poor children of other ethnicities.[14] They are sometimes harmed by desegregation in liberal, middle-class white schools, even when middle-class blacks, on average, benefit.[15] Poor black schools have traditionally received fewer resources and have had less experienced teachers than wealthier black schools or white schools of all classes.[16] Most important, many poor blacks are poorer than their white counterparts; almost one-fourth of black children live below 50 percent of the poverty line, compared with less than one-twentieth of white children.[17]

Whether we should conclude that the economic penalties for being black are growing stronger or weaker depends on which blacks one looks at. On the one hand, full-time working women, well-educated young men, and professional couples have recently become indistinguishable in the aggregate; blacks in these categories now earn what comparable whites earn.[18] On the other hand, black poverty is deepening and spread-

---

see Diane Colasanto and Linda Williams, "The Changing Dynamics of Race and Class," *Public Opinion* 9, no. 5 (January-February 1987): 50–53.

[14] Sue Berryman, "Integrating the Sciences," *New Perspectives* 17, no. 1 (Winter 1985): 20, Table B; U.S. Bureau of the Census, *Education in the United States, 1940–1983* (Washington, D.C.: U.S. Government Printing Office, 1985), Table 3-3; Leonard Ramist and Solomon Arbeiter, *Profiles: College-Bound Seniors, 1985* (New York: College Board, 1986), pp. 37, 47, 57, 76.

[15] Robert L. Crain, Rita E. Mahard, and Ruth E. Narot, *Making Desegregation Work* (Cambridge, Mass.: Ballinger, 1982), pp. 144–47. Conversely, middle-class whites may thrive in otherwise poor black schools; see George Noblit and Thomas Collins, "Cui Bono? White Students in a Desegregating High School," *Urban Review* 13, no. 4 (Winter 1981): 205–16; Margaret Orr and Francis Ianni, "The Impact of Culture Contact and Desegregation on Whites of an Urban High School," *Urban Review* 13, no. 4 (Winter 1981): 243–60.

[16] Harold M. Baron, "Race and Status in School Spending: Chicago 1961–1966," *Journal of Human Resources* 6, no. 1 (Winter 1971): 3–24; Rubin, *Busing and Backlash*, p. 45; Bill Olds, "Are Minority Pupils Shortchanged? Intra-District School Financing" (Hartford, Conn.: Civil Liberties Union, 1982); *Hobson* v. *Hansen*, 269 F. Supp. 401 (1967); Gary Orfield and Howard Mitzel, *The Chicago Study of Public Schools* (Chicago: University of Chicago, Committee on Public Policy Studies, 1984); Lydia Chavez, "Two Bronx Schools: Study in Inequality," *New York Times*, July 2, 1987, p. A1ff.

[17] U.S. Bureau of the Census, *Characteristics of the Population Below the Poverty Level, 1984*, Series P-60, no. 152 (Washington, D.C.: U.S. Government Printing Office, 1986), pp. 5, 23–24.

[18] Farley, *Blacks and Whites*; James Smith and Finis Welch, "Black-White Male Wage Ratios, 1960–1970," *American Economic Review* 67 (June 1977): 323–38; Bernard E. Anderson, "Economic Patterns in Black America," in National Urban League, *The State of Black America* (New York: National Urban League, 1982), p. 29; U.S. Bureau of the Census, *The Social and Economic Status of the Black Population*, Series P-23, no. 80 (Washington, D.C.: U.S. Government Printing Office, 1978); James Smith and Finis Welch, *Closing the Gap: Forty Years of Black Economic Progess* (Santa Monica, Calif.: Rand Corporation,

ing. The proportion of children born to unmarried women is increasing for both races, but much faster for blacks; the number of people in poor families headed by women is rising for both races but much faster for blacks. The number of black men in the labor force is declining much more rapidly than the number of potentially working white men.[19] These problems reinforce one another. As the number of "marriageable males" declines in the inner cities, the likelihood of female-headed households increases, thereby increasing the number of black children in poverty and, perhaps, decreasing the number of marriageable males in the next generation.[20]

More formal measures of intergenerational mobility tell a similarly dual story. Black upward mobility across generations today, compared with that in the past, is clearly increasing. However, whites still are advancing farther than blacks from their father's occupational position and, of course, whites start from a much higher position.[21] In addition, " 'class factors' are becoming more important in explaining the distribution of occupational status in the black population" but less important in explaining the occupational status of whites.[22] Thus both cross-sectional and longitudinal data suggest that the bifurcation between wealthy and poor blacks will continue to increase.

Adding the dimension of class to that of race, then, complicates the story considerably. Although all blacks continue to operate at a disadvantage in the demographically and psychologically white American society, some operate at a much greater disadvantage than others. Whites dislike poor blacks more than they dislike well-off blacks or poor whites; public policies sometimes harm poor blacks while benefiting wealthy blacks;

1985). However, the level of black wealth holding remains dramatically below white wealth holding, even for people with the same income. See U.S. Bureau of the Census, *Household Wealth and Asset Ownership, 1984*, Series P-70, no. 7 (Washington, D.C.: U.S. Government Printing Office, 1986), pp. 42, 199.

[19] U.S. Bureau of the Census, *Statistical Abstract of the United States, 1986* (Washington, D.C.: U.S. Government Printing Office 1985), p. 392; U.S. Bureau of the Census, *Money Income and Poverty Status of Families and Persons in the United States, 1985*, Series P-60, no. 154 (Washington, D.C.: U.S. Government Printing Office, 1986), p. 23.

[20] William J. Wilson and Kathryn Neckerman, "Poverty and Family Structure," in Sheldon Danziger and Daniel Weinberg, eds., *Fighting Poverty* (Cambridge, Mass.: Harvard University Press, 1986).

[21] David Featherman and Robert Hauser, *Opportunity and Change* (New York: Academic Press, 1978), pp. 313–84; James Davis, "Up and Down Opportunity's Ladder," *Public Opinion* 5, no. 3 (June–July 1982).

[22] Featherman and Hauser, *Opportunity and Change*, pp. 329, 335; Michael Hout, "Occupational Mobility of Black Men, 1962 to 1973," *American Sociological Review* 49 (June 1984). 308–22; Wayne Villemy and Candace Wiswell, "The Impact of Diminishing Discrimination on the Internal Size Distribution of Black Income, 1954–74," *Social Forces* 56, no. 4 (June 1978): 1019–34.

black poverty is expanding and deepening. The problem of race in the United States is, in sum, not really one problem. If we do not take the complicating implications of class into account, racial inequality will remain an intractable problem for policymakers and citizens alike.

Power

Our story needs a further plot line—the dimension of power—if we are fully to understand the nature of DuBois' "problem of the Twentieth Century." In brief, blacks are disproportionately powerless, as they are disproportionately poor and socially disfavored. But just as some blacks have achieved economic parity with some whites, so some blacks have achieved political power.

This complexity has, however, yet another wrinkle. Blacks who have "made it" economically are often socially and politically isolated, since economic success may entail moving into a largely white community, working in a largely white corporation or entering a largely white profession. Conversely, blacks who have attained political power often do so in disproportionately poor minority communities, especially central cities, or Southern rural parishes. Thus we have to keep in mind at least three complications: the addition of power to the dimensions of race and class; the disparities in power holding among blacks; and the fact that for blacks, social and economic success correspond with political success less often than they do for whites. Let us consider these complications.

Citizens' beliefs about the distribution of power provide one type of evidence for the assertion of black powerlessness, since power depends partly on perceptions of who holds power. Blacks feel less politically efficacious than whites do and see the government as less responsive to their needs. Furthermore, black alienation has increased since the 1960s and black feelings of efficacy have declined at a faster rate than those of whites.[23] Yet blacks are increasingly interested in politics and are proportionately more likely than whites to engage in campaign activities.[24] These two findings combined suggest that black alienation and feelings of inefficacy result not from lack of involvement, but rather despite it.

Survey data also suggest that one reason why blacks feel powerless is whites' resistance toward (potentially) powerful blacks. The number of whites who profess willingness to support a qualified black presidential

[23] Warren E. Miller, Arthur H. Miller, and Edward J. Schneider, *American National Election Studies Data Sourcebook, 1952–1978* (Cambridge, Mass.: Harvard University Press, 1980), pp. 274, 279; the Harris Survey, "Feelings of Alienation Drop from Last Year's High," press release, May 10, 1984.

[24] Cavanagh, *Inside Black America*, p. 11; Sidney Verba and Norman Nie, *Participation in America* (New York: Harper and Row, 1972), pp. 149–73.

candidate has risen dramatically, but whites are nowhere near unanimity (even assuming that claims of support are trustworthy).[25] For example, whites praised Jesse Jackson's personal attributes during the 1980 presidential campaign; but his endorsement of Walter Mondale and Geraldine Ferraro led almost twice as many to reject the Democratic ticket as to endorse it.[26] Neither the Democratic party, the media, nor the other candidates have treated Jackson as a serious contender for the presidential nomination.[27]

Of course, Jesse Jackson is not the only black candidate, and whites have good reasons to oppose him besides his race. Whites do vote for black candidates, as Mayors Wilson Goode, Tom Bradley, and others can attest. And black constituents are gaining political clout even in voting districts with white majorities; conservative Southern Republicans are joining liberal Democrats in Congress in efforts to distance themselves from the South African government and from old-fashioned American racism.[28] Most important, of course, is the fact that the number of black elected officials has increased fourfold since 1970.[29] So here, too, progress is incontrovertible and important.

But here too we cannot assume that progress will continue. The astonishing rise in the number of black elected officials has increased blacks' share of elected offices from nonexistent to minuscule (just over 1 percent),[30] and the rise in the number of black officeholders may slow drastically if typical voting patterns persist. Several factors lead to this observation. First, redistricting to give blacks a majority of voters in a given district is largely responsible for the recent rise in the number of black elected officials.[31] Simple arithmetic implies a ceiling on that means of

[25] Cavanagh, *Inside Black America*, pp. 63–65; Schuman et al., *Racial Attitudes*, pp. 76, 81–82.

[26] Joint Center for Political Studies, "JCPS Releases In-Depth Survey of Black Political Attitudes" (Washington, D.C.: Joint Center for Political Studies, 1984), Table 4.

[27] C. Anthony Broh, *A Horse of a Different Color* (Washington, D.C.: Joint Center for Political Studies, 1987); William Crotty, "The Presidential Nominating Process and Minority Candidates: The Lessons of the Jackson Campaign," paper presented at conference on The 1984 Presidential Election and the Future of Black Politics, Joint Center for Political Studies, Washington, D.C., April 30, 1985.

[28] Francis X. Clines, "A Fledgling Protest Movement Gathers Steam," *New York Times*, August 5, 1985, p. B4.

[29] Joint Center for Political Studies, *Black Elected Officials* (New York: Unipub, 1986).

[30] Ibid.

[31] Thomas Cavanagh, "Black Mobilization and Partisanship: 1984 and Beyond," paper presented at conference on The 1984 Presidential Election and the Future of Black Politics, Joint Center for Political Studies, Washington, D.C., April 30, 1985, p. 7; Thomas Cavanagh and Denise Stockton, *Black Elected Officials and Their Constituences* (Washington, D.C.: Joint Center for Political Studies, 1983), pp. 16–21 and citations therein; Albert Kar-

increasing black power, although I know of no calculations that indicate how far we are from that ceiling. Second, the campaign to increase the number of black registrants and voters, although conducted with vigor and success, also has obvious arithmetic limits, given the vastly larger number of potentially mobilizable whites. Third, for black candidates as for white ones, the chances of success increase dramatically with an increase in personal and supporters' resources. But blacks, on average, are poorer than whites, and districts with a significant number of black voters on average are much poorer than mainly white districts.[32] These factors suggest that race, class, and power combine generally to handicap blacks in their pursuit of office and, more specifically, to restrict blacks' power to localities where there are too few resources to do much with it. The number and real power of black elected officials are not likely to increase dramatically so long as racial attitudes and economic circumstances remain roughly what they are in the 1980s.

What happens when blacks attain political office? Can they use their power to increase their own or other blacks' power? Yes, to some degree: Black mayors hire more blacks for both professional and blue-collar public service jobs than white mayors do.[33] But except for that fact, the data are ambiguous. Two explanations for the absence of dramatic changes when blacks attain political office are not hard to find. First, whites are much less likely to vote for blacks if they think that electing a black mayor will lead "them" to take over "our" city; "white voting in instances where blacks approach a majority tends to be determined . . . by the perceived balance of power between blacks and whites as a group."[34] Thus

nig, "Black Resources and City Council Representation," *Journal of Politics* 41, no. 1 (February 1979): 134–49.

[32] Cavanagh, *Inside Black America*, pp. 3–4, 11–13, 17–20; Adolph Reed, *The Jackson Phenomenon* (New Haven, Conn.: Yale University Press, 1985), p. 26. Albert Karnig, "Black Representation on City Councils," *Urban Affairs Quarterly* 12, no. 2 (December 1976): 233. Charles Bullock III, "The Election of Blacks in the South: Preconditions and Consequences," *American Journal of Political Science* 19, no. 4 (November 1975): 735–37. See also Richard Nathan and Paul Dommel, Statement to U.S. Senate, Committee on Governmental Affairs, "Needed—A Federal Safety Net for Communities," for evidence that poverty and minority proportion of the population increased together during the 1970s.

[33] Peter Eisinger, "Black Employment in Municipal Jobs: The Impact of Black Political Power," *American Political Science Review* 76, no. 2 (June 1982): 380–92; Thomas Dye and James Renick, "Political Power and City Jobs: Determinants of Minority Employment," *Social Science Quarterly* 62, no. 3 (September 1981): 480–81; Albert Karnig and Susan Welch, *Black Representation and Urban Policy* (Chicago: University of Chicago Press, 1980), pp. 131, 137, 138. But see also Kenneth Mladenka, "Comments on Eisinger: Black Employment in Municipal Jobs," *American Political Science Review* 76, no. 3 (September 1982): 645–47.

[34] Schuman et al., *Racial Attitudes*, p. 204. See also Raphael Sonenshein, "Biracial Coalition Politics in Los Angeles," *PS* 19, no. 3 (Summer 1986): 591–97.

in general, blacks who seek white support must make the implicit or explicit promise that they will use their power only minimally to aid their black constituents. Alternatively, a black leader may favor black constituents, but he or she thereby risks incurring the enmity of, and withdrawal of resources by, powerful whites.[35] The problem of balancing competing claims is not, of course, unique to black mayors, but it does suggest a further impediment to expanding black power through the electoral process.

A second reason that the election of black mayors seldom has dramatic effects is that significant change usually requires slack and therefore discretionary resources—a scarce commodity indeed in the central cities and rural parishes where most black officials are attaining power. This point, too, is racially neutral; political initiatives ranging from workfare to the Strategic Defense Initiative succeed or fail depending on whether the government puts its money where its mouth is. Nevertheless, in minority-dominated cities suffering from the results of declining tax bases and "municipal overburden," mayors are able to do little more than marginally shift budgetary stringency from one agency to another. Thus political power that does not vary with economic power is likely to have more symbolic than substantive impact.

If electoral power has seemingly inexorable limits, what about other avenues to power? Here too, the progress of the 1970s and 1980s is neither unambiguous nor inevitable. Some blacks argue that efforts to integrate blacks into white society, thereby increasing black power, have had the unintended effect of reducing it.[36] For example, proponents of community control of ghetto schools see centralization in large, desegregated school districts as simply a transfer of power from black neighborhoods to distant, white-controlled bureaucracies.[37] These claims are not idle. When school districts are consolidated for desegregation, typically the

[35] For other discussions of the relative lack of power of black elected officials, see Karnig and Welch, *Black Representation and Urban Policy*, pp. 150–53; Adolph Reed, "The Black Urban Regime" (New Haven, Conn.: Yale University, Department of Political Science, 1987); Clarence Stone, "Race, Power, and Political Change," in Janet Boles, ed., *The Egalitarian City* (New York: Praeger, 1986), pp. 200–223.

[36] American Enterprise Institute for Public Policy Research, *A Conversation with the Reverend Jesse Jackson* (Washington, D.C.: American Enterprise Institute, 1978), p. 5; Derrick Bell, ed., *Shades of Brown* (New York: Teachers College Press, 1980); "Meredith: Integration Is a 'Con Job'," *Washington Post*, February 23, 1985, pp. G1, G7.

[37] Marilyn Gittell, "Community Control of Education," in Marilyn Gittell and Alan Hevesi, eds., *The Politics of Urban Education* (New York: Praeger, 1969), pp. 363–77; Robert Maynard, "Black Nationalism and Community Schools," in Henry Levin, ed., *Community Control of Schools* (Washington, D.C.: Brookings Institution, 1970), pp. 100–111; Raymond Wolters, *The Burden of Brown: Thirty Years of School Desegregation* (Knoxville: University of Tennessee Press, 1984), p. 206.

school board and administrators of the black district lose their positions or are demoted. Between 1963 and 1971—during the height of desegregation efforts—the number of black high-school principals decreased by two-thirds in ten Southern and border states, even though white principals were being hired to fill vacancies.[38]

A different dynamic, with the same effect of retarding the growth of black political power, is apparently developing among "successful" black business people and professionals. Since we normally assume that social status, wealth, and power covary (and since their absence certainly covaries), we would expect that blacks who have attained economic success would also wield considerable power. Although the evidence on this point is largely anecdotal or self-reported (to my knowledge), it suggests that this expectation does not always hold. High-ranking corporate blacks feel isolated, marginal, and at risk for their very jobs.[39] Wealthy blacks moving into white suburbs find their life "sometimes lonely and troubled," and "so far . . . [have] not become involved in local politics."[40] This phenomenon, even if widespread, may be temporary and may not be unique to blacks. But at least for now we should not assume that blacks are finding nonelectoral power easier to attain and use than electoral power.

Up to this point, I have reviewed evidence allowing us to conclude that inequalities of race, class, and power cumulate, that cumulative inequalities worsen the inequalities of each dimension alone, and that blacks are more constrained than whites in translating achievement in one dimension into further achievements in that or other dimensions. The evidence does not permit more precision; I cannot say, for example, that class matters more (or less) than race, or that the race-power nexus is more (or

[38] Board of Education, Ferguson-Florissant School District, Report to the Court, October 15, 1977, pp. 1–8; Daniel Monti, "Administrative Discrimination in the Implementation of Desegregation Policies," *Educational Evaluation and Policy Analysis*, 1, no. 4 (1979); John W. Smith and Bette M. Smith, "Desegregation in the South and the Demise of the Black Educator," *Journal of Social and Behavioral Sciences*, 20, no. 1 (Winter 1974): 33–40. See also Everett Abney, "A Comparison of the Status of Florida's Black Public School Principals, 1964–65/1975–76," *Journal of Negro Education* 49, no. 4 (Winter 1980): 398–406.

[39] See, for example, Jonathan Hicks, "Black Professionals Refashion Their Careers," *New York Times*, November 29, 1985, p. 1ff.; Ernest Holsendolph, "Tough Road Forecast for Highly Trained Blacks," *New York Times*, December 28, 1982, p. A20; Claudia Deutsch, "The Ax Falls on Equal Opportunity," *New York Times*, January 4, 1987, p. F1ff.; Bart Landry, *The New Black Middle Class* (Berkeley: University of California Press, 1986); George Davis and Glegg Watson, *Black Life in Corporate America* (New York: Doubleday, 1985).

[40] Lena Williams, "To Blacks, the Suburbs Prove Both Pleasant and Troubling," *New York Times*, May 20, 1985, p. A1ff. See also Lena Williams, "Black Youths in Suburbs: Many Say They Feel at Home," *New York Times*, May 21, 1985, p. B1ff.; and James Banks, "An Exploratory Study of Assimilation, Pluralism, and Marginality: Black Families in Predominantly White Suburbs," University of Washington, Seattle, 1984.

less) intractable than the others. That is, in short, a preliminary sketch, with all the appropriate caveats. But it gives us enough foundation, I believe, to go on to look at the second set of questions—whether the United States can, and will, seek to solve a problem that is as complex as it is devastating.

Alleviating the Cumulative Inequalities of Race, Class, and Power

Can Americans reduce the cumulative inequalities of race, class, and power? Are they likely to do so? To address these questions, I must first answer another: What should be the goal of the American welfare state with respect to questions of race?

Earlier, I defined the American welfare state as the set of policies intended to grant citizens the resources they need to exercise liberal rights of political equality and equal opportunity. I can now specify the crucial right of equal opportunity more precisely: All citizens must have enough resources (such as education, access to desirable positions, and money) so that they have a realistic possibility of overcoming the obstacles posed by cumulative inequalities of race, class, and power. That notion implies significant improvement in the position of those at the wrong end of more than one dimension of inequality, even if it means depriving those at the top of relative position or absolute shares. It implies in addition that the range from rich to poor among blacks and the share of black officeholders should resemble the range among and share of whites (using wealth and political office as surrogates for all socially valued and distributed goods). Thus the difference between top and bottom must be *lessened* and the links between race, class, and power must be *loosened* in order for the American welfare state to be able to claim that it provides full equality of opportunity.[41]

I see three plausible arguments about the likelihood of the American welfare state providing such opportunity in the future. First, these cumulative inequalities are lessening and loosening and will continue to do so; the United States is an imperfect society that its citizens can and will improve—too slowly, perhaps, but surely. Second, these cumulative inequalities are and will remain deep and entrenched; American society has a fundamental structural flaw that cannot be eliminated without radical

[41] The discussion of equal opportunity is, of course, only a starting point because achieving the form and level of equal opportunity described here would require considerable change in American methods of education, job recruitment, property transfer, choosing political leaders, and so on. Thus equality of opportunity blurs, in commonly understood ways, into equality of results, and the whole question becomes part of the more general issue of amelioration versus structural transformation.

changes in pluralist politics and capitalist economics. Third, these cumulative inequalities can be alleviated but at a cost that Americans are not willing to incur; the problem could be solved but Americans probably will not choose to do so.[42] Note that these arguments do not represent the standard three choices between two extremes and one midpoint. The third argument lies between the first two in diagnosis, but is, if anything, more stark in its prognosis and less clear in its prescription. 

The argument for slow but steady progress is essentially empirical. It is a claim that public policy in the United States has significantly improved the status of blacks since the 1960s and will continue to do so. More precisely, the claim has three parts. First is the fact that blacks now enjoy formal, legal equality in all public and many private spheres of life. Equality before the law is necessary, even if not sufficient, for achieving the other promises of liberalism. It did not exist in 1960 but its existence is now incontrovertible. It was achieved mainly through the conventional means of court decisions, congressional legislation, and agency regulations. Thus the American welfare state has been able to reform itself enough to ensure, at a formal level, the liberal rights of equal freedom and opportunity for all individuals.

The second part of the slow but steady progress argument is that cumulative inequalities of race, class, and power have in fact lessened and loosened. Whites are less prejudiced and discriminate less than they used to. Schools, workplaces, and neighborhoods are less segregated. Blacks receive more education, and are obtaining professional jobs and attaining middle-class life styles. In the aggregate, black incomes are beginning to approximate white incomes. Blacks increasingly run their own communities and receive whites' votes in racially mixed districts. All this progress has occurred without permanent disruption of politics as usual. Thus the American welfare state has succeeded in moving closer to the substantive, not merely formal, grant of liberal rights of individual treatment and the exercise of free choice.

Third, there are no logical or empirical breaking points in the move from cumulative, deep inequalities to lesser, dispersed inequalities. Whites can (and presumably will) continue to feel less prejudice and to behave with less discrimination, especially as a generation of desegregated children replaces older whites in the workplace and the political arena. Blacks can and will continue to attain education and to obtain nontraditional jobs, especially as their desegregated children grow up and as black rural-to-urban migrants become assimilated.[43] The political gap

[42] My thanks to Robert Fullinwider for this three-part formulation.

[43] Jennifer L. Hochschild, *The New American Dilemma* (New Haven, Conn.: Yale University Press, 1984), pp. 178–87.

will narrow as whites grow accustomed to black public officials and blacks cement biracial coalitions. And so on. The point here is not that this bright future necessarily will come, but that there is no inherent reason why it cannot come. Nothing in American practices prohibits it, and everything—as Gunnar Myrdal pointed out—in American ideals prescribes it.

The second argument—that the cumulative inequalities of race, class, and power constitute a fundamental structural flaw—challenges the first argument empirically and logically. According to the structuralist argument, the changes just extolled are superficial, and the efforts necessary to produce deeper changes would unacceptably disrupt existing practices and institutions. The flawed American welfare state cannot perfect itself through actions available within pluralist political and capitalist economic structures. This argument too has several parts.

A structuralist would argue that the legal equality so proudly cited by proponents of slow but steady progress came first because it was relatively easy to achieve and relatively costless to whites. This claim does not deny the extraordinary efforts and excruciating sacrifices involved in forcing equal access to lunch counters, voting booths, and interstate buses. It emphasizes, however, that these efforts and sacrifices eventually succeeded because they did not ultimately threaten—in fact, they strengthened—America's inegalitarian social order. Once the very high ramparts of simple racism were breached, whites as well as blacks benefited from the introduction of new customers, clients, and constituents. Prospect-regarding equality for all accords perfectly with capitalism and political pluralism.

In response to the second part of the slow but steady progress argument, a structuralist concedes that means-regarding inequalities have declined, but places the changes in a different context.[44] White prejudice persists; the shift from old-fashioned to modern racism represents increasing sophistication as much as increasing racial acceptance. Black poverty persists and is deepening, and black professionals encounter unarticulated but real limits to advancement. The number of black elected officials is growing slowly at best; black power is often no more than symbolic; and black leaders seem increasingly ineffective and distant from ordinary black citizens. In short, the structuralist views progress in lessening and loosening cumulative inequalities since the 1950s as more illusory than real.

That the dispute over progress is more than a question of whether the

[44] A few structuralists do not make even this concession; see Pinkney, *The Myth of Black Progress*; and Manning Marable, *How Capitalism Underdeveloped Black America* (Boston: South End Press, 1983).

glass is half full or half empty becomes apparent in the structuralist response to the third part of the slow but steady progress argument. The United States cannot continue to redress cumulative inequalities, for the same reasons that progress heretofore has been so halting. Here is where the battle is really joined.

In the structuralist view, changes thus far have occurred on the margins, without disrupting the existing political and economic hierarchies; that is why progress has been so literally marginal. Once legal barriers were toppled and overt racism began to decline, white Americans were able to incorporate a few blacks significantly, and most blacks slightly, into their workplaces, schools, and politics. White employers have found it useful to hire a few well-trained members of the newly available labor pool, although those employees remain isolated in both unions and management. School systems have been able to integrate the most academically proficient blacks into schools that remain dominated by white administrators and students, and politicians have learned to appeal to some new voters and to make alliances with the most resourceful black organizations. But the key here is "some" or "a few." American political and economic processes are not closed to new participants—as evidenced by lessening and loosening inequalities. However, argue the structuralists, incorporation can be expected to stop at the point at which marginal change begins to shade into real transformation. The trajectory of the 1980s suggests that the United States is reaching that point.

Thus, in this view, the future will not continue the slow but steady progress of the past. In particular (to focus on only one strand of the argument), most residents of black ghettos cannot be brought into the American mainstream without drastic structural reform. Overall improvement in the economy and increasing rates of employment do not touch this population.[45] Industries are moving to the suburbs or to farming areas, away from the central cities where blacks increasingly live.[46] As the nation's economic base shifts from manufacturing to service and technology, poorly educated inner-city blacks have even fewer chances to get a first job than they used to.[47] The combination of urban demography

[45] Rebecca Blank, *Disaggregating the Effect of the Business Cycle on the Distribution of Income*, Discussion Paper no. 780-85 (Madison: University of Wisconsin, Institute for Research on Poverty, 1985).

[46] See Reed, "The Black Urban Regime," and citations therein. But see also Mark Hughes, "Moving Up and Moving Out" (Princeton, N.J.: Princeton University, Woodrow Wilson School, 1986), for evidence that this formulation misspecifies the problem of urban black un- or under-employment.

[47] See the surprisingly candid and gloomy comments of Secretary of Labor William Brock in "Altering the Face of Work," *Washington Post*, November 30, 1986, p. H1ff.; John D. Kasarda, "Urban Change and Minority Opportunities," in Paul Peterson, ed., *The New Urban Reality* (Washington, D.C.: Brookings Institution, 1985), pp. 33–67; and John Ka-

and Supreme Court decisions on the sanctity of metropolitan boundaries makes more school desegregation almost impossible. Black families are increasingly headed by increasingly poor women, so more and more black children are spending more and more of their childhood in deeper and deeper poverty. Cities are crumbling physically, and black ghettos appear to be crumbling psychologically and culturally as well.[48]

Since these problems involve economic and political institutions as much as race relations, say the structuralists, they cannot be solved without drastic changes in laws, practices, and allocations of resources. Solutions would be expensive—perhaps so expensive that some public and private goals, such as improving productivity, paying Social Security, and strengthening national defense, would have to be significantly curtailed.

More seriously, solutions would require reformulation of corporate capitalism. Some structuralists argue that a capitalist economy needs an underclass to absorb excess production, fill the secondary labor market, and provide a negative reference group for workers. The underclass need not be black—it is Turkish in Germany, Hispanic in California, and was (until recently) white in Great Britain. Nor need this argument be cast in Marxist terms; the classic sociological language of structural functionalism serves just as well.[49] An underclass may even be, not a requirement of corporate capitalism but an undesirable and inevitable byproduct. But if advanced capitalism either requires or inadvertently creates an underclass, the latter cannot be eliminated without changing the former.

Alternatively, even if corporate capitalism had nothing to do with creating an underclass, once it exists it cannot be eliminated in a democratic polity because the market "imprisons" the polity. In this view, political actions that threaten profits or economic stability—as would a program expensive enough to solve the problems of the ghetto—will automatically elicit defensive reactions by businesses. These reactions, in turn, will induce the citizens to throw the rascals out and bring in a new set of political leaders who will work to restore a "sound business environment."[50] Thus even well-meaning political leaders cannot act to affect black pov-

sarda, "Contemporary U.S. Migration and Urban Demographic-Job Opportunity Mismatches," Statement Prepared for the Joint Economic Committee, September 18, 1986.

[48] For one example of fear about the "social dislocations of the inner city," see William J. Wilson, "The Urban Underclass in Advanced Industrial Society," in Peterson, *The New Urban Reality*, pp. 129–60. See also Erol Ricketts and Isabel Sawhill, "Defining and Measuring the Underclass" (Washington, D.C.: Urban Institute, 1986); and *Chicago Tribune* staff, *The American Millstone* (Chicago: Contemporary Books, 1986), for very different types of analysis making essentially the same point.

[49] Herbert Gans, *More Equality* (New York: Random House, 1973), pp. 102–26.

[50] Charles E. Lindblom, "The Market as Prison," *Journal of Politics* 44, no. 2 (May 1982): 324–36; and Fred Block, "The Ruling Class Does Not Rule," *Socialist Revolution*, no. 33 (May–June 1978), pp. 6–28.

erty significantly because such actions would also unacceptably disrupt the economy.

These points raise another problem—the unlikelihood that there will be enough well-meaning political leaders. Since most whites see blacks' problems as largely solved or of their own making, most whites are unlikely to reward their elected leaders for spending vast amounts of energy and money on poor blacks. And, as I argued in the previous section, poor blacks themselves lack enough political power to reward elected officials for extensive action on their behalf and enough material resources to enable those officials to have much maneuvering room in any case. Structuralists often add the argument that political leaders serve the interests of corporate capitalism rather than the interests of the working class. Whether or not such a claim is true, it is unnecessary. The simple fact of the electoral connection suffices to suggest limits to action aimed at bringing most poor blacks into the economic and political mainstream.

What about black politicians? In the structuralist view, four features of the American political landscape imply a natural limit to the growth of black political power: a majoritarian system for choosing officeholders, a majoritarian system of legislative decision making, a small racial minority, and a large racial majority that generally prefers representatives of its own race. In these circumstances, the minority's political power will be severely limited. Blacks may achieve proportional electoral power and even disproportionate electoral power if some whites vote for blacks. But it is unlikely in the extreme that enough whites will vote for blacks so that blacks will win enough majoritarian elections to control majoritarian legislatures.

This argument does not assume that all policy choices divide along racial lines. Obviously they do not. Nor does it assume that white leaders never support the interests of blacks at the expense of (some) whites. Occasionally they do, as in the 1860s and 1960s. But these points are of little comfort here, since I am focusing on a problem—black poverty—that *is* likely to divide blacks and whites.

Nonetheless channels for generating and using power presumably resemble electoral channels in this regard. Whites would, other things being equal, rather be led by other whites, and whites currently lead most important organizations. Given these two points, we cannot expect blacks to make significant inroads into leadership in white communities. In fact, quite the reverse will be true if the balance of power is at all zero sum. The more blacks "encroach" on traditionally white domains, the more the remaining powerful whites (surely a majority with more resources) will resist further encroachment. The growth of black political power has natural limits so long as prejudice against a racial minority continues.

Even in the absence of white prejudice, whites will continue to win more elections and lead more organizations than blacks simply because they are wealthier. Americans have always used and will continue to use their money to gain power. Only strict limits on the use of private property in the political realm would give any hope of breaking the link between class and power; such limits are hardly to be anticipated soon. Even if most Americans supported limits (which they do not), we face a situation analogous to that of the market as prison. The wealthy are unlikely to use their political power to deny the use of wealth to attain power. In short, the weak tools of the American welfare state seem insufficient to break the links among race, class, and power.

Thus, the structuralist largely concedes the first two parts of the slow but steady progress argument, but disputes the third. The lessening of blacks' economic and political inequality in the past need not simply further progress—in fact, it implies just the reverse. The fact of massive black poverty unites with the logic of how a capitalist economy operates in a pluralist polity to produce a problem insoluble through existing political institutions and processes.

Is either argument right? Is the nature of the American welfare state such that cumulative inequalities of race, class, and power can be lessened and loosened by continuing the reform strategies initiated by the NAACP in the 1930s? Or does the dynamic of American society include a point of radical discontinuity, such that past reforms either imply nothing about future reforms or themselves inhibit further change? Or is there a more compelling third alternative?

In my view, both of those arguments are too deterministic. Americans could, if they chose, alleviate the cumulative inequalities of race, class, and power—but, other things being equal, they will choose not to do so. The structuralist view is wrong in assuming that economic and political barriers to change cannot be battered down or maneuvered around. After all, the United States has witnessed dramatic structural change, whether as a result of cataclysmic events such as depressions and world wars or through the slow accretion of small changes such as those that produced the industrial revolution and the Northern migration. Americans have even acted deliberately to change important racial, economic, or political institutions and practices. Some political leaders established, demolished, and reestablished a national bank; others established (and still others may demolish) affirmative action programs and extensive welfare programs.

The slow but steady progress argument is also wrong in assuming that most Americans want to solve their remaining racial problem strongly enough to accept the high costs of doing so. There is nothing about the problem of black poverty and powerlessness that is not amenable to considerable improvement. If Americans chose to devote their private efforts and their public resources to eradicating black poverty, they could conceivably do so. The severity of black poverty and powerlessness could at least be lessened to the level of white poverty and powerlessness. In that sense, the slow but steady progress argument is right—Americans do not, in theory, need radically to change their economic and political systems to bring practices more in line with ideals. However, thus far Americans have not chosen to take the necessary steps, and in my view they are unlikely to do so unless some new element enters the picture. Solving the problem is simply too costly, in several ways.

The first cost, again, is financial. Demonstration projects that have sought to bring welfare recipients, ex-offenders, high-school dropouts, and former drug addicts into the economic and social mainstream have had some success, but only at enormous cost.[51] Rebuilding cities, overhauling school systems, creating economically viable jobs, reducing crime rates and teen-age pregnancy—all are desirable goals in the eyes of most Americans, but so are finding cures for cancer and protecting U.S. borders against Soviet invasion. Of the many desirable things to do with inevitably scarce resources, spending a large share on poor blacks (or poor whites, for that matter) is simply not the highest priority for most Americans.

My point here differs from the structuralist claim that producing a full-fledged welfare state is too expensive for the United States to sustain. These enormous costs would, after all, be considerably offset by the great savings, in monetary and human terms, of fewer crimes and reduced prison populations, fewer welfare recipients and more workers, fewer drug addicts and lower medical costs. The issue is how the citizenry and politicians will choose to weigh (uncertain) future benefits against (certain) present costs. Americans need not, but usually do, weigh the short-term costs much more heavily than the long-term gains in making such calculations.

The second cost is organizational. Traditionally, Americans have tackled no-longer-acceptable inequalities of race, class, and power separately. Affirmative action policies challenge racial discrimination, regardless of individuals' economic or political status. The AFDC Program treats all poor alike, regardless of the implications of race for obtaining a job. Legislative reapportionment focuses on party politics and numerical balances, dividing black or working-class neighborhoods if necessary to get the numbers right. Solving the problem of cumulative inequalities, however, would require a coordinated attack on racial discrimination and

[51] Board of Directors, Manpower Demonstration Research Corporation, *Summary and Findings of the National Supported Work Demonstration* (Cambridge, Mass.: Ballinger, 1980).

poverty and political powerlessness. No feature of the American policymaking system prohibits such coordination, but every feature inhibits it.

The third cost is political. Politicians could expend—they have expended in the past—much time and effort to address the problems of blacks, the poor, and the powerless. And they have done so even though the majority of voters and of legislators is neither black nor poor. Politics is not, after all, a matter of strict numbers or of zero-sum games, as the structuralist critique implies. It is instead a matter of coalitions, historical ties, logrolling, luck, even occasionally moral commitment. So politicians could further the movement toward full equality of opportunity for all, if the electoral costs did not seem prohibitively high. But in the 1980s, at least, the electoral costs do seem too high.

The problem, then, is high costs, not impossibilities. If there were a will, Americans would find a way. However, as I see it, there is not enough will; that is, I do not think whites (and perhaps black elites) *want* to solve the problem of black poverty and impotence badly enough to find ways around these impediments. And they do not want to do so because of the very ideology that should make them want to do so—equality of opportunity.

Consider the circumstances of poor and working-class whites. Equal opportunity works as an ideology only if people believe in it—only if people believe that they (or their children) have a good chance of achieving their goals. But as the number of contestants for a fixed number of prizes increases, the chances of winning decrease. The arithmetic is simple: As blacks gain chances, whites lose certainty.

The problem, of course, is lessened if prizes increase at the same rate as contestants. That suggests, crudely, why blacks have gained the most in periods of economic growth—the late 1860s and early 1870s, the late 1940s, the late 1960s.[52] But increasing the number of prizes is not always feasible. In periods of slow economic growth or decline, a dramatic improvement in economic opportunities for blacks will worsen employment prospects for working-class whites. In all circumstances, improving political opportunities for blacks will add more contestants for numerically limited positions such as mayor or organization president. So economic prizes in some cases, and political prizes always, cannot increase enough to give all Americans the same chances for success that some Americans now enjoy.

Thus in the abstract, the belief of all whites in equal opportunity is threatened by a loosening of the links between race, class, and power. But

[52] Conversely, when the number of prizes drops or increases very slowly, players strive to reduce the number of contestants. Blacks lost ground in the depressions of the 1890s, 1930s, and 1970s.

relatively poor and powerless whites are especially threatened—or at least especially likely to *feel* threatened—by the opening of opportunities to blacks, since there are many more blacks who might compete for working-class jobs than for middle- or upper-class jobs. Why, except in extraordinary circumstances, should we expect poor white Americans to accept the costs of ending black poverty and powerlessness if their major reward is facing new competitors in the marketplace and polling booth?

The main counter to this argument is to accept its logic but to claim that the empirical consequences of admitting more blacks to the game are too slight to matter much, since blacks are a small minority. After all, the United States has frequently allowed vast increases in the number of people eligible to compete in the equal opportunity game and yet the ideology of equal opportunity seems to have survived. Whites accept, if they do not welcome enthusiastically, new competition from immigrants. The economy has always expanded (although sometimes with a lag) to accommodate the supply of workers.

I cannot disprove these contentions, but they do not convince me, for two reasons. First, in many ways the situation of blacks is not analogous to that of immigrants. The costs of attempting to solve the multiple and intersecting problems of black ghettos would be much greater than are the costs of simply liberalizing American immigration policy, especially since the United States (officially) admits only a few foreigners every year, most of whom must prove that they can and will support themselves. And these expenditures would be concentrated, in two politically problematic ways. Given U.S. budgetary politics, they would not divert revenues equally from all existing governmental programs. Instead, they would take resources mainly from social programs of particular importance to low-income citizens—such as Medicare, Medicaid, and Social Security—as well as from public education, and criminal justice. Thus even if alleviating black poverty is not unacceptably expensive in the abstract, in concrete terms, benefiting poor blacks can plausibly be seen as harming whites who are slightly less poor. In addition, blacks are geographically concentrated, so many citizens would perceive increases in aid to poor blacks as pouring their tax dollars into some other locality. But legally admitted immigrants are more scattered, so their drain on the public purse is much less visible, and the benefits of aiding them can accrue to the same community that paid for their aid.

The situation of blacks is also not analogous to that of immigrants simply because of race. Blacks' burden of slavery and discrimination is unique. (Their only rivals for this dubious honor are native Americans, but whites largely "solved" that problem by killing off most of the population and restricting the rest to reservations.) Persisting racial prejudice and current effects of past discrimination have two implications: Racist whites will be even less willing to provide resources to poor blacks than to other needy groups, and poor blacks (as we saw earlier) will need more resources to attain full equality of opportunity than other needy groups.

The second reason that the comparison of blacks with immigrants offers no comfort is that to the degree that the circumstances of blacks and immigrants *are* similar, the experience of immigrants reinforces rather than refutes my claims about the constricting implications of the ideology of equal opportunity. White citizens have in fact bitterly opposed immigrants whose number, status, and concentration appear to threaten their own political or economic position. Consider Californians' treatment of the Chinese around the turn of the century, or Bostonians' response to Irish refugees of the potato famine. More recently, New Yorkers have hardly welcomed Puerto Ricans, and Texans have killed Vietnamese shrimp fishers. Even if, as the history of most of these groups demonstrates, the American society, economy, and polity can in the long run absorb a large number of new players, that is little comfort in the short run for displaced whites or struggling immigrants. Indeed, this is exactly my point. The problem is not that the United States cannot absorb a new cohort of black workers and voters; it can. The problem is that some white workers and voters will be harmed in the process, and others fear that they will be harmed.

In short, the immigration analogy seems flawed enough not to be a potent counterargument to my claim that the ideology and practice of equal opportunity can restrict as well as expand participation in the modern American welfare state.

The preceeding discussion has focused especially on why relatively poor and powerless whites might use the ideology of equal opportunity to resist extending the practices of equal opportunity to poor blacks. Those whites are the people who need to believe in equal opportunity to retain their belief in liberal rights, and who also will be the first and most threatened by opening up opportunities to even poorer and more powerless blacks. But for successful whites, too, the ideology of equal opportunity can work against the grant of equal opportunity to blacks. This phenomenon is captured by the phrase, "the implicit right of stable expectations."

The right of stable expectations is the right to act purposively in the confidence that one has a reasonable chance to attain one's chosen goals, and that those attainments will not be arbitrarily revoked. People cannot choose which public school their child will attend, or which job they will hold, or who their neighbors will be—but normally they can move into a neighborhood within the attendance boundary of a preferred school, or train for a desired job, or buy a house in a community with desirable neighbors. The Constitution does not articulate this right, nor have the courts, but it may share the right of privacy's status as a right existing in the "prenumbra" of enumerated rights, in the Supreme Court's terminology. Stable expectations of a fair chance to attain one's goals are, after all, what equal opportunity, the rights of property acquisition and freedom of choice, and minimal governmental intervention are intended to guarantee.

Mandatory programs to break down racial barriers seem to many people to violate the right of stable expectations. "Forced busing" invalidates the right to choose a home within a certain school attendance zone; "quotas" break the link between training, fair competition, and a job. Economic transfers extensive enough to reduce black poverty even to the level of white poverty would require either an enormous shift in the use of tax revenues or an enormous increase in taxes. Transfers of power to blacks would entail the exercise of power by blacks over whites—a prospect that startles if it does not dismay most whites. The problem in these cases is not the problem faced by working-class whites—that equal opportunity is reduced to a sham through fierce competition. The problem is that, after following the rules and winning the game, one finds that the rules and prizes are suddenly transformed in apparently unfair ways. And the more one wins, the more one feels betrayed by apparently unfair changes in rules and prizes.

Note that two elements are necessary for people to feel that their right of stable expectations has been breached. The rules of the game must be changed without one's consent or support, and the changes must seem unfair.[53] People do not always resent new laws that they dislike (although new laws often include "grandfather" clauses so that people in the midst of the process that the legislation addresses are not faced with what seem to them to be arbitrary rule changes). But people resent new laws that, in their eyes, treat them unfairly or produce unfair outcomes. If whites feel prejudice against blacks, then imposed policy changes that disproportionately benefit blacks will seem to violate the political and social order. Even if whites do not feel prejudice, imposed policy changes that disproportionately benefit the poor and powerless may seem to violate property rights and political sovereignty. Not all race-related changes violate the right of stable expectations, but changes powerful enough to affect economic and political—as well as racial—inequalities are likely to betray at least one cherished norm or expectation. Again, whites' belief in equal opportunity works against blacks' achievement of it; Americans lack the will if not the way to solve the problem of cumulative inequalities.

Another way in which whites' belief in the ideology of equal opportunity reduces the chances of increasing blacks' exercise of equal op-

[53] My thanks to Amy Gutmann for this point.

portunity applies to both rich and poor and returns us to the premise of my opening paragraph. Whites have learned to incorporate racial discrimination into their belief in the United States as the land of liberty and equality. Accommodation to this realization is not easy, nor is the realization gratifying. Many admit that what Gunnar Myrdal described as the "American dilemma"—the disparity between the American creed of freedom and equality and the nation's racial practices—is "a glaring conflict in the American conscience," perhaps even "the greatest unsolved task in American democracy." But most believe, along with Myrdal, that the dilemma is on the way to being solved. In his words, "the main trend in its [America's] history is the gradual realization of the American Creed. . . . America can demonstrate that justice, equality, and cooperation are possible between white and colored people."[54] In short, Americans want to believe in the slow but steady progress argument; they can handle the problem of race without transforming or destroying their society.

However, the realization that racial inequalities are combined with inequalities of class and power is deeply troubling because this combination more severely challenges liberal ideology than does prejudice alone. Links among race, class, and power violate not only individual rights through racism, but also equal economic opportunity and political equality. Such a severe challenge on so many fronts suggests that the American dilemma is traceable to a complex, deeply rooted flaw, not a simple, shallow imperfection. That point, in turn, suggests the need for major reforms of many, longstanding institutions and practices to overcome these inequalities. Americans believe that such change, whatever its exact nature, would be risky at best and undesirable at worst. It is much safer to ignore the cumulative violations of equal opportunity and to focus on the single familiar one. Thus the very magnitude of the failure of equal opportunity makes whites cling all the more strongly to their belief that equal opportunity can succeed with only marginal adjustments. But if the evidence cited in this paper is correct, that belief is wrong.

Thus far, I have focused on why whites can be expected to resist paying the costs of eliminating cumulative inequalities. But what about blacks? They, after all, are not helpless pawns in a white world. *Pace* the structuralists, blacks do have substantial and increasing political power, especially in cities where black poverty is concentrated. The growing black middle class is evidence of substantial and increasing economic resources in the black community. And with a few unfortunate exceptions, blacks are not plagued by antiblack racism as some whites still are. Why can we not rely on blacks to save their own communities?

[54] Gunnar Myrdal, *An American Dilemma* (New York: Harper and Brothers, 1944), pp. 21, 1021–22.

I feel relatively less confident dealing with this question, so I will address it only briefly. Blacks *are* trying to help other blacks, with some success. But should whites decide that solving the problem is so expensive that it will entail considerable sacrifice on their part, it stands to reason that the smaller and poorer black population lacks sufficient resources to solve it alone.

In addition, the issue is not one of "saving their own communities." Middle-class blacks are leaving the ghetto for the same reasons that middle-class whites left the slums—for suburbia's safer streets, better schools, and more congenial life style.[55] They cannot afford—politically, psychologically, or economically—to focus too much attention on the blacks left behind. Well-off whites, after all, do not usually take on the responsibility to help all poor whites; why should well-off blacks take on such a burden?

And some argue that the class and power division within the black population has led black elites to abandon the poor and powerless masses. In this view, the NAACP and Urban League focus too much on affirmative action for corporate executives and college applicants; Jesse Jackson focuses too much on the aggrandizement of Jesse Jackson; black mayors focus too much on becoming Democratic party insiders.[56] This view is obviously controversial, but it boils down to saying simply that blacks are like whites. When push comes to shove, people believe more in using equal opportunity for themselves than in pursuing it for others.

Nothing about this interpretation of the problem of cumulative inequalities is dispositive; I have continually hedged my bets with such phrases as "other things being equal" and "the foreseeable future." As Dennis Thompson (Chapter 6) illustrates, one can imagine how legislators could use their particular political circumstances to promote the general good—in this case how they could turn their constituents' belief in the American Creed into a broad attack on cumulative inequalities. One can also imagine an economic upturn in which employers would compete for workers, wealthy blacks would be in a position to hire their less fortunate neighbors, and black mayors would be able to expand their budgets and fulfill their campaign promises. Moral commitments are made as well as broken; seemingly stable economic structures crumble; politics makes strange bedfellows. The point of all of these truisms is that we

[55] See Martin Katzman, "The Flight of Blacks from Central-City Public Schools," *Urban Education* 18, no. 3 (October 1983): 259–83; William O'Hare, Jane-yu Li, Roy Chatterjee, and Margaret Shukur, *Blacks on the Move: A Decade of Demographic Change* (Washington, D.C.: Joint Center for Political Studies, 1982).

[56] See Reed, *The Jackson Phenomenon*; William J. Wilson, *The Declining Significance of Race* (Chicago: University of Chicago Press, 1978); Dudley Clendinen, "In Black Atlanta, Affluence and Sophistication Are for the Few," *New York Times*, January 20, 1986, p. A16.

cannot predict what new factors will emerge to change the scene I have painted. After all, the status of blacks is several orders of magnitude better now than it was 150, or even 25, years ago. (As one reader of an early draft of this paper put it, "Your tone of hand-wringing angst could use a bit of seasoning. Polities usually manage to muddle through. If black folk survived slavery, they'll probably survive neoconservatism."[57])

My main point, however, is that new factors will be necessary for too many blacks to do more than survive. At present, deep and mutually reinforcing problems have combined with the perverse consequences of a partially achieved but fully endorsed ideology of equal opportunity to inhibit the full development of the American welfare state. We have all the elements necessary to solve the problem of race, class, and power if we choose to do so; but thus far Myrdal's diagnosis seems more apt than his prognosis.

[57] Comments are from a scathing but helpful set of criticisms by Thomas Cavanagh. For a set of projections as gloomy as mine (and based on similar grounds), see Anthony Downs, "The Future of Industrial Cities," in Peterson, *The New Urban Reality*, pp. 281–94.

8

Democracy and the New Deal Party System

STANLEY KELLEY, JR.

As the new presidential term was getting under way in 1985, a reporter for the *Washington Post* suggested that Ronald Reagan's presidency might "be remembered as an historic turning point for the country's politics. We may look back at these years as the end of the New Deal era."[1] What credence should one give this suggestion, a common one in the mid-1980s? Two developments make a strong prima facie case for it: (1) In its first four years, the Reagan administration brought with it substantial changes in economic and welfare policies and effected a truly striking change in the environment in which those policies are debated and enacted. To an extent unprecedented in recent history, proposals for more New Deal–like programs, or for giving more financial support to such programs, have ceased to be serious politics. (2) In and after the 1984 elections, voters moved away from the party of the New Deal and toward the Republicans in their allegiances as well as in their voting. Surveys of opinion found that a longstanding Democratic edge of fifteen to twenty percentage points in voters' identifications had either narrowed dramatically, or was gone.

Note, however, that this case for the *Post* reporter's speculation owes much of its apparent force to an assumption that the two developments just noted are connected in a particular way. Many, if not all, of those who believe that the New Deal era has ended also believe that the movement of the Reagan administration away from New Deal policies is re-

I gratefully acknowledge the helpful comments and criticisms of the members of the Seminar on Democracy and the Welfare State, of the special commentator on this paper, Thomas Ferguson, and of David Aladjem, Douglas Arnold, Thomas Cronin, Fred Greenstein, and James DeNardo. John G. Geer, James Beaubien, and Douglas Mills assisted me in my research. The data from the University of Michigan's National Election Studies were made available by the Inter-University Consortium for Political and Social Research.

[1] Robert G. Kaiser, *Washington Post* National Weekly Edition, February 4, 1985, p. 24.

sponsive to the public's growing disillusionment with them, and that the movement of voters toward the Republican party is its reward for these new directions in public policy. But does this kind of connection exist between the two developments? If not, how are they related, if they are related at all?

These questions are the central ones of this paper; they have also been central for party leaders, particularly Democratic leaders, since the 1984 election. Since then, the Democrats have been engaged in an "ideological struggle" (in the words of Governor Bruce Babbit of Arizona) between those who believe that Democrats can win elections with traditional Democratic appeals and those who believe that the party must change its message.[2] That struggle will be given a resolution of sorts when the Democrats nominate a standard-bearer in 1988. The nature of that resolution is likely to make a difference not only in the electoral fortunes of the Democratic party, but also in the choices offered American voters and in the course of public policy.

Answers to my two questions are important also for what they can contribute to an understanding of political change in democratic states. Whether the Republican party's successes in 1980 and 1984 mark a realignment of political forces in the United States is now a subject of serious debate. Although it is a subject sometimes approached in a politically millenarian spirit—some people have been waiting for realignment as others have waited for the Age of Aquarius—at its best the literature on party realignment is a thought-provoking set of ideas about the role of voters and elections in bringing change to public policy. Not surprisingly, some of those ideas are in conflict, since no realignment (or what is conventionally regarded as such) occurred at a time when popular opinion could be monitored systematically. Even if the political changes that now appear to be in progress do not deserve to be called a realignment,[3] they clearly represent a substantial change in the balance of forces supporting the two major parties. To the extent that we can trace the sources of these particular changes, we shall have made some contribution, at least, to a better general understanding of partisan change.

[2] *Washington Post* National Weekly Edition, February 18, 1985, p. 15.

[3] Because this issue turns so much on one's definition of realignment, I shall dodge it. If a political alignment is a set of forces ranged for and against a cause or causes, then it changes with any change in the number, size, composition, or cohesion of such forces, or in the cause or causes about which they contend. Although one might reasonably apply the term "realignment" to any such changed alignment, no student of the subject does. For most, realignment consists of (unspecifiedly) enduring, major change. Moreover, for some students of realignment, only changes in the composition of the contending forces, say, or changes in the cause or causes about which they contend, count as "realignments."

Interpreting Changes in Support for Parties

In a column published almost immediately after the 1984 election, George Will vigorously affirms a connection between conservative policies and the increasingly good fortunes of Republican presidential candidates. What he has to say can usefully be taken as an example of one sort of argument to that effect:

> But by now it is bizarre, if common for otherwise rational people to ask, "Are we on the verge of a 'realignment' in favor of the Republican Party?" Suppose Noah, in the 34th day of the 40 days of rain, had asked his wife, "Do you think we may get some rain?" Ye gods. At the presidential level, realignment is a fact.[4]

In support of this view, Will cites Republican victories in four of the five presidential elections from 1968 to 1984 and in six of the nine since the Truman administration, a record that he attributes to growing support among voters for conservative policies.

> The nation was moderately conservative when it chose Eisenhower over Stevenson twice. Next it barely preferred Kennedy, a moderate Democrat, over Nixon. . . . In 1968 the combined Nixon and Wallace vote was 57 percent. In 1972 Nixon got 61 percent against McGovern. In 1976 the Democrat perceived as the most conservative in the nomination contest, Carter, was nominated and narrowly defeated a conservative Republican, Ford. Then came two conservative landslides.

Johnson, the only president after Truman "with a Rooseveltian, liberal domestic agenda," Will observes, was "an accident of assassination and the perceived radicalism of his Republican opponent, Goldwater."

Will's view of what has been happening is not unreasonable, but the evidence that he adduces to support it is inconclusive at best. Facts are facts, of course. The Democrats have been losing presidential elections, and the trend in the Democratic share of the two-party vote has been downward since 1932; that trend is also evident if measured from any of several other reasonable starting points. The downward trend in the Democratic vote since 1932 has been fairly modest and punctuated by reversals, however, and it shows no striking discontinuity between the Roosevelt-Truman years and the years since 1952—the point from which Will dates the beginning of a new conservative era.[5] Will's belief that vot-

[4] *Trenton Times*, November 8, 1984.

[5] These statements about trends are based on regression analyses of the Democratic share of the two-party vote in the period 1928–1984.

ers since 1952 have preferred conservative candidates *because they were conservative* is wholly inferential; nowhere does he cite any direct evidence about the views of voters. Finally, the sizable Democratic edge in the partisan identifications of voters from 1952 through 1983 is testimony against the view that an enduring shift in voters' support for the two parties occurred in this period. Although many voters liked Ike (or Nixon, or Reagan), they maintained a preference for the Democratic party.

Because identification with a party has been thought to represent a standing and relatively stable preference, changes in voters' partisan identifications in and since 1984 are, for many observers, the most convincing evidence yet that we may be entering a period in which the major parties will compete on more even terms, if not an era of Republican dominance. On election day 1984, or soon after, several commercial polls found Democrats outnumbering Republicans by a ratio of only 1.1 to 1 (or less); the same ratio held among actual voters in the University of Michigan's 1984 National Election Study, if one lumps together declared partisans with those who said that they leaned toward a party. Michigan data also show a five-percentage-point increase in the proportion of declared partisans from 1980 to 1984, a growth in the percentage of voters who saw important differences between the parties (from 53 percent in 1976 to 65 percent in 1980 to 70 percent in 1984),[6] and unusually heavy party-line voting in 1984. Although the GOP lost some of its newly won ground in 1985 and 1986,[7] the loss was insufficient to render nugatory the observation of Thomas E. Cavanagh and James L. Sundquist that "if party identification stabilizes at or near current levels, a major equalization of the two-party competitive balance will have occurred."[8]

Will it stabilize? Consider Table 1, which reports the responses since 1937 to the Gallup Poll's question about party identification.[9] Clearly, the narrow gap in support for the two parties in 1984 is not unique in the period covered by the table. They were as close or closer to having equal support in the 1940s and early 1950s. Starting with 1937, or 1948, or 1952, the trend in the ratio of Democratic to Republican identifiers favors the Democrats, although that trend is slight. One can find a modest trend favoring the Republicans if one starts with 1964, the high point for the

[6] These figures are for voters who voted, not those who were eligible to vote.

[7] Democratic respondents to Gallup surveys in the first six months of 1986 outnumbered Republican respondents 39 percent to 32 percent, that is, in a ratio of about 1.2 to 1. See the poll release of July 27, 1986.

[8] Thomas E. Cavanagh and James L. Sundquist, "The New Two-Party System," in John E. Chubb and Paul E. Peterson, *The New Direction in American Politics* (Washington: Brookings Institution, 1985), p. 47.

[9] "In politics as of today, do you consider yourself a Republican, a Democrat, or Independent?"

TABLE 1 Partisan Identification of Eligible Voters, 1937–1984

Election	Democrats (%)	Republicans (%)	Ratio (D to R)
1937	50	34	1.5:1
1940	42	38	1.1:1
1944	41	39	1.1:1
1946	39	40	1.0:1
1949	48	32	1.5:1
1952	41	34	1.2:1
1954	46	34	1.4:1
1960	47	30	1.6:1
1964	53	25	2.1:1
1968	46	27	1.7:1
1972	43	28	1.5:1
1976	47	23	2.0:1
1980	46	24	1.9:1
1982	45	26	1.7:1
1984[a]	38	35	1.1:1
Mean	45	31	1.5:1

SOURCE: Gallup Poll release of April 25, 1985.
[a] Fourth quarter.

Democrats in these years; but to make much of that fact, we need a good reason for that choice of a starting point, and the numbers themselves do not provide one.

Of course, even an enduring shift in voters' allegiances toward the Republicans would tell us nothing about voters' attitudes toward New Deal policies. To draw a valid connection between support for those policies and support for the two parties, we need to know not just how voters have evaluated parties and candidates, but what has gone into those evaluations. If the electoral basis for the New Deal has been eroded, either recently or some time ago, voters' concern with the issues associated with it should have lessened, or voters' positions on those issues should have changed, or the relationship of those issues to voting and to voters' identifications with the major parties should have weakened or vanished. Have any or all of those things happened?

New Deal Issues and the Electorate

For the years 1952–1984, though not before, there is a good source of information about the sources of voters' evaluations of parties and candidates. In that period's presidential elections, interviewers of the University of Michigan's Survey Research Center gave voters a chance to cite up to ten things they liked and disliked about each of the major parties and each of their candidates.[10] If one examines the responses to these questions, one can see how often voters—unprompted and in their own words—invoked the issues of the New Deal in evaluating parties and candidates, and in whose favor they invoked them.[11]

In the New Deal era, controversy swirled about a particular set of conditions, policies, interests, and ideological themes. As one would expect in a party system born in the Great Depression, economic conditions—employment, wage levels, the cost of living, the goodness or badness of the times—were in the foreground of political debate. So were certain areas of policy, among them monetary and fiscal policy, agricultural and labor policy, Social Security and other welfare programs, housing, power, education, and health care. The era saw a politicizing of the interests of labor unions, farmers, the aged, the poor, and its rhetoric pitted the interests of "the common man," or working people, against those of big business, industry, and Wall Street. Ideological discourse put left and right, liberalism and conservatism, and radicalism and reaction in opposition to each other and made tests of right thinking out of orientations toward big government, states' rights, planning, governmental action to improve social conditions, and control of (or interference with) private enterprise. Accordingly, I have treated comments about these and allied subjects in voters' expressions of their likes and dislikes of candidates and parties as comments about New Deal issues,[12] have tallied the number of voters who made one or more such comments in each presidential election from 1952 to 1984, and have noted how such comments count for and against the parties and candidates about whom they were made.[13]

[10] In 1952 the questions about parties were: "I'd like to ask you what you think are the good and bad points about the parties. Is there anything in particular that you [like, don't like] about the [Democratic, Republican] Party? What is it?" The questions about candidates were: "Now I'd like to ask you about the good and bad points of the two candidates for President. Is there anything in particular about [name of candidate] that might make you want to vote [for him, against him]? What is it?" The questions for other elections were nearly identical.

[11] These responses are not only a good source of data about voters' opinions on New Deal issues, they are the only source that permits one to compare opinions on a wide range of those issues over a long period.

[12] For a more specific idea of the kinds of responses treated as comments about New Deal issues, see Appendix II, pp. 239–62, in my *Interpreting Elections* (Princeton, N.J.: Princeton University Press, 1983). The coding for the present study, obtainable on request, differs in minor ways from the coding used there.

[13] I counted a voter's comments on New Deal issues as pro-Democratic if the number of his likes of Democrats and dislikes of Republicans, added together, exceeded the number of his likes of Republicans and dislikes of Democrats. If the reverse was the case, I counted the

TABLE 2 Salience and Democratic Bias of Voters' Comments on New Deal Issues, 1952–1984

Election	Sample[a]	Salience[b]	Democratic Bias[c]
1952	1,184	85.0	60.0
1956	1,270	76.1	67.4
1960	1,413[d]	73.5	63.0
1964	1,113	77.4	66.1
1968	1,027	73.6	55.2
1972	830	74.6	58.1
1976	1,662.5[d]	75.7	62.7
1980	972	75.7	46.6
1984	1,398	83.8	52.5
Mean		77.3	59.1

[a] All samples consist of voters who were interviewed both before and after the election and who said that they had voted.

[b] Percentage citing at least one New Deal issue as something to like or dislike about the major parties and/or their candidates.

[c] Those who cited New Deal issues as something to like or dislike about the Democratic party and/or candidate, as a percentage of those who cited New Deal issues as something to like or dislike about some party or candidate.

[d] Weighted sample.

The message that this information gives us about New Deal issues in the years 1952–1984 is clear (see Table 2). In this period, about three-quarters of all voters mentioned one or more New Deal issues as something to like or dislike about the major parties and their candidates. The salience of New Deal issues stood at 85 percent in 1952, dropped about ten points in 1956, held steady for the next quarter century, and then rose in 1984 almost to its 1952 level. James L. Sundquist, who has argued that the issues arising out of the New Deal retained their hold on voters into the 1980s, is right.[14] The arguments of those who have contended that New Deal issues lost their potency in the 1960s and 1970s are unsupported by these data.[15] Note also the implication of the figures in Table 2

voter's comments as pro-Republican. For a justification of this procedure, see Stanley Kelley, Jr., and Thad W. Mirer, "The Simple Act of Voting," *American Political Science Review* (June 1974), pp. 572–91; and Kelley, *Interpreting Elections*, pp. 10–25.

[14] See James L. Sundquist, *Dynamics of the Party System* (Washington, D.C.: Brookings Institution, 1983).

[15] See, for instance, Norman H. Nie, Sidney Verba, and John R. Petrocik, *The Changing*

TABLE 3 Inconsistency between Partisan Identification and the Partisan Bias of Voters' Comments on New Deal Issues, 1952–1984

Partisan Group	Percentage of Inconsistent Identifiers								
	1952	1956	1960	1964	1968	1972	1976	1980	1984
Strong Democrat	7	3	4	3	4	7	3	12	6
Weak Democrat	16	9	12	13	18	15	13	20	17
Leaned Democratic	18	8	7	18	17	8	12	15	10
All Democrats	13	6	8	9	12	11	10	15	11
Strong Republican	9	9	7	8	8	11	7	7	4
Weak Republican	22	25	15	24	12	14	22	9	15
Leaned Republican	21	18	13	19	14	21	18	9	16
All Republicans	16	17	11	17	11	15	16	8	12
All partisans	14	11	10	12	12	13	12	12	11

NOTE: Samples and sample sizes as in Table 2.

for the Democratic bias of voters' comments on New Deal issues: If elections had turned on New Deal issues alone, the Democrats would have won all elections from 1952 to 1976 handily, but they would have lost the 1980 election by a substantial margin and would have prevailed only narrowly in 1984.[16]

Moreover, the evidence is clear-cut that New Deal issues were strongly associated with the party identifications of voters in the years 1952–1984. Table 3 shows the percentages of voters in those years whose party affiliation was inconsistent with that which the partisan bias of their comments on New Deal issues would predict for them. There is variation from year to year; but in the period as a whole, only about 12 percent of those who identified with either party showed this kind of inconsistency. As one would expect, strong identifiers were much less likely to show inconsistency than weak identifiers or leaners, but otherwise no striking trends are evident.

Table 4 shows the relationship between party identification and what I shall call "New Deal scores,"[17] which appear in the top row of each panel

American Voter (Cambridge, Mass.: Harvard University Press, 1976); they observed that "in the New Deal era, citizens cast issue votes in relation to those domestic economic issues for which the New Deal stood. By the fifties those issues faded" (p. 192).

[16] This statement assumes the application of the decision rule for voters proposed in Kelley and Mirer, "The Simple Act of Voting."

[17] The formula for a New Deal score is $(D^+ - D^-) - (R^+ - R^-)$, where D^+ is the number of pro-Democratic comments about New Deal issues, D^- is the number of anti-Democratic comments, and so on.

TABLE 4 Party Identification and New Deal Scores, 1952–1984

Year	Democratic Identification												
	New Deal Scores												
	≤ −6	−5	−4	−3	−2	−1	0	+1	+2	+3	+4	+5	≥ +6
1952	0	13	16	18	26	27	42	68	79	92	93	89	97
1956	0	0	0	3	11	21	39	61	77	86	89	91	93
1960	0	26	15	8	17	21	35	70	86	86	96	90	87
1964	0	5	10	23	19	35	53	77	83	86	91	98	89
1968	0	0	13	19	19	33	50	73	85	90	89	92	89
1972	0	13	15	13	30	24	45	65	83	84	78	92	89
1976	0	16	3	14	13	30	40	63	77	85	94	88	85
1980	4	4	11	15	16	38	53	76	82	93	98	100	100
1984	3	6	5	15	16	25	37	66	70	86	90	95	97
Year	Republican Identification												
	New Deal Scores												
	≤ −6	−5	−4	−3	−2	−1	0	+1	+2	+3	+4	+5	≥ +6
1952	100	80	76	77	69	65	47	26	17	7	7	4	3
1956	100	100	96	98	82	70	51	25	15	8	5	7	6
1960	100	74	76	93	84	73	50	19	8	9	4	0	2
1964	100	96	87	68	75	63	36	19	12	12	5	0	6
1968	100	100	80	74	77	55	36	19	12	4	6	3	8
1972	100	87	85	85	63	63	43	26	13	11	18	4	5
1976	97	84	94	79	81	58	42	24	15	9	3	10	4
1980	92	93	76	78	68	53	33	17	11	6	2	0	0
1984	94	92	86	78	69	66	47	25	17	9	9	4	2

NOTE: Samples and sample sizes as in Table 2.

of the table and range from −6 or less to +6 or more, that is, the range is from a strongly Republican position on New Deal issues to a strongly Democratic one. Arrayed in columns are the percentages of voters with a given score who identified themselves as Democrats (in the top panel) or Republicans (in the bottom) in each election.[18] The relationship between New Deal scores and party identification is ragged in places, but obviously strong. A change in score from −1 to +1, for instance, typically

[18] In Table 4, those who said that they leaned Democratic or Republican count as Democrats and Republicans, respectively.

more than doubles the probability of a Democratic affiliation. The relationship is slightly stronger than that between a voter's identification and the identification of his parents, which in turn is (much) stronger than the association of party identification with an array of social and demographic variables.[19]

In six elections (1960, 1964, 1968, 1976, 1980, 1984), University of Michigan's interviewers asked voters whether they saw important differences between the major parties and, if so, what they were;[20] responses to the second of these questions are still further testimony to the continuing relevance of New Deal issues to voters' perceptions of the parties. In these six elections, an average of about 82 percent of the differences cited as important were differences on New Deal issues. The percentage ranged from a low of 76 percent in 1984 to a high of 85 percent in 1976. Although the 1984 election marked the low point in the series, the figures show no trend; the frequency with which New Deal issues were invoked in describing the differences between the parties was slightly higher in 1980, for instance, than it had been in 1960.

It is possible, of course, that New Deal issues continued to be strongly associated with voters' partisan identifications throughout the period that we have been considering but had increasingly less influence on voting. Table 5—which shows the accuracy of predictions that all voters with negative New Deal scores would vote Republican and that all voters with positive New Deal scores would vote Democratic—rules out this possibility, however. There was a strong association between voting and voters' New Deal scores throughout the period—it was stronger in 1984, in fact, than in 1952. Indeed, the association in Reagan's 1984 landslide was almost as strong as it had been in the elections of 1960 and 1964. In this respect the 1984 election stands in sharp contrast to the Republican landslides of 1956 and 1972.

What Was Different about the Elections of 1980 and 1984?

As we have seen, throughout the period 1952–1984, the salience of New Deal issues in voters' evaluations of parties and candidates was con-

[19] A regression of the respondent's party identification on parental party identification yields an R^2 of .32. The comparable figure for a regression of party identification on New Deal scores is .34. The data used in these calculations were taken from the University of Michigan's National Election Studies for 1952, 1964, 1968, 1972, and 1980.

[20] In the University of Michigan's National Election Studies for 1980 and 1984, the questions were: "Do you think there are any important differences in what the Republicans and Democrats stand for? What are those differences?" There have been variations in the wording of these questions in other years, however, and variations also in the number of responses recorded for each respondent.

TABLE 5 Predicting the Vote from New Deal Scores, 1952–1984

Year	Accuracy of Prediction (%)
1952	80.6
1956	75.8
1960	85.7
1964	87.0
1968	84.2
1972	74.6
1976	82.0
1980	81.4
1984	85.2

NOTE: Samples as in Table 2, except for deletion of respondents who voted for third and minor-party candidates and respondents with New Deal scores of zero.

sistently high, and voters' views on those issues were strongly associated with their voting and with their partisan identifications. What changed during this period was the partisan bias of voters' comments on New Deal issues. Strongly pro-Democratic through 1976, those comments took on a Republican bias in 1980 and were nearly neutral in 1984. Table 6 shows the source of that change.

The amount and importance of the information that Table 6 summarizes justifies its complexity. The left-hand column of the table disaggregates New Deal issues into economic issues—issues about Social Security, the aged, worker's welfare programs, and so on. The remaining nine columns show, election by election, the salience and Democratic bias of voters' comments on each issue or set of issues. The first entry in the first line of the column for 1952 indicates, for example, that the salience of economic issues in 1952 was 65 percent—that is, 65 percent of those who cast ballots in that year cited one or more economic issues in evaluating the parties and candidates. The second entry in that line shows that the Democratic bias of comments on economic issues was 49—that is, 49 percent of those whose comments on economic issues had a partisan bias thought they counted for the Democrats (which means, of course, that 51 percent thought they counted for the Republicans).

A striking feature of the opinion summarized in Table 6 is its stability on several sets of issues. The Republicans were the continual victors in the ideological battles of this period. In every election, the roughly 30 percent of the voters who invoked ideological terms and themes in eval-

TABLE 6 Salience and Democratic Bias of Voters' Comments on New Deal Issues, 1952–1984

	1952		1956		1960		1964		1968		1972		1976		1980		1984	
Issue	S	DB	S	DB	S	DB	S	DB	S	DB	S	DB	S	DB	S	DB	S	DB
Economic issues	65	49	39	55	39	48	29	54	35	35	40	52	49	50	48	24	59	35
Governmental spending	25	10	7	12	16	17	12	13	24	13	7	25	15	11	8	14	10	12
Monetary and fiscal policy	22	8	10	76	12	45	9	44	—	—	18	57	17	63	13	36	33	43
Election's economic impact	44	80	29	58	23	67	13	91	17	69	22	66	28	70	32	20	33	29
Social Security, the aged, workers' welfare programs	10	93	4	92	9	80	21	88	10	82	9	64	3	79	7	79	18	87
Medical care	1	20	0	0	7	47	11	79	6	86	—	—	5	55	3	80	9	89
Farm policy	9	82	19	80	12	71	5	62	4	35	2	61	3	88	2	41	4	70
Labor, unions	13	85	8	79	9	77	9	68	6	75	6	55	7	43	8	59	9	55
Welfare, poverty	—	—	—	—	—	—	9	73	12	37	23	23	12	46	15	31	18	36
Ideological stance	31	39	21	46	25	42	38	39	34	34	31	33	31	32	32	37	38	37
Relation to big business, common man	43	84	48	83	41	83	41	88	37	87	41	89	45	90	40	85	43	89
Power, housing, and education	4	83	4	67	4	58	4	78	5	84	3	75	1	84	2	71	8	86
All New Deal issues	85	60	76	67	74	63	77	66	73	55	75	58	76	63	76	47	84	53

NOTES: Samples and sample sizes as in Table 2, except for deletion of respondents who voted for third- and minor-party candidates and respondents with New Deal scores of zero. Definitions of salience and Democratic bias as in Table 2.

uating parties and candidates (fewer voters in 1956 and 1960 than in other years) preferred that party's stance by a margin approaching two to one. Governmental spending, though less salient, was also a Republican issue in every year by a very large margin—six to one, on average. Welfare (here meaning mainly aid to the indigent) was a Republican issue in every year except 1964, when Lyndon Johnson's War on Poverty drew largely favorable comment.

Some issues were Democratic throughout. In each election from 1952 on, approximately 40 percent of all voters cited the association of the parties and candidates with either "big business" (or industry or Wall Street or special interests), or the common man (ordinary people, or working people) as something to like or dislike about the parties or candidates. On average, the pro-Democratic bias of such comments was six to one. Comments about Social Security, the problems of the aged, and workers' welfare programs were strongly biased toward the Democrats as well, and on occasion (for example, in the elections of 1964 and 1984), these issues were of reasonably high salience. Comments about labor, farm policy, and power, housing, and education were relatively infrequent but usually quite strongly pro-Democratic in their import. Medical care was a Democratic issue in 1964 and after.

Table 6 reveals the paucity, in the 1980 survey, of direct references to the specific changes in policy that Ronald Reagan was advocating. References to deregulation, reductions in federal spending, changes in welfare programs, or the lowering of taxes were not prominent in voters' evaluations of parties and candidates, either in absolute terms or relative to their frequency in other elections. Consider monetary and fiscal policy. Although a 30 percent, across-the-board tax cut was a central feature of the program that Reagan offered the American people, and although the tax cut promised voters direct, measurable, material benefits, the salience of monetary and fiscal policy in the election that gave Reagan the presidency was low (13 percent). References to governmental spending—another important issue in the Reagan platform—were fewer in 1980 than they had been in 1976, and slightly more Democratic in bias. These data, in short, provide almost no support for the view that the Reagan administration came to power as the result of an increasingly insistent popular demand for the economic and welfare policies Reagan had proposed. Of course, opposition to New Deal–like policies won some support for Reagan, but it had won support in roughly equal measure for all Republican candidates for president since 1952.

Nor is there any strong indication in Table 6 that voters viewed Reagan's new economic and welfare policies with greater interest and increased favor after four years of his leadership. The salience of monetary and fiscal policy increased considerably in 1984. This change doubtless reflects a campaign in which the Democratic candidate had promised an increase in taxes, but opinion on that issue was more favorable to the Democrats than it had been four years earlier. And both the salience and partisan bias of comments on every other area of policy listed in the table either remained roughly the same in 1984 as they had been in 1980 or became increasingly pro-Democratic.

So, why, insofar as they concerned New Deal issues, were the elections of 1980 and 1984 different from all other elections since 1952? Look at the figures for "election's economic impact" in Table 6. These data report the salience and bias of voters' comments about the impact of the election on employment, wages, salaries, working conditions, the cost of living, prices, and economic conditions generally. Between 1952 and 1976, the salience of these issues ranged between 13 and 44, to average 25. During the same period the average Democratic bias of comments on these issues was 72—that is, of all those who invoked these issues in saying what they liked and disliked about the parties and candidates in the elections from 1952 to 1976, an average of 72 percent counted them for the Democrats. Then came the 1980 and 1984 elections, in which about one-third of all voters invoked these bread-and-butter issues and an average of 76 percent of those who did counted them for the *Republicans*. The voters most concerned about their own or the nation's economic well-being withdrew their confidence from the Democrats, something that most such voters had failed to do, even in the Republican landslides of 1952, 1956, and 1972.

Of course, many observers have attributed Republican gains at the polls in 1980 and 1982 to changes in voters' evaluations of the major parties and their candidates as managers of the economy.[21] That the positions voters took on *other* New Deal issues changed so little, however, points to these conclusions:

1. If a connection exists between changes in economic and welfare policies since 1980 and the shift of voters' allegiances toward the Republicans in 1984, it is mainly an indirect one in which economic conditions were the intervening variable. Neither an increased demand for those particular policies nor a new appreciation of them, once they were instituted, contributed more than marginally to that shift.

2. If a direct link exists between New Deal issues and the movement of voters toward identification with the Republican party, that movement most probably occurred in two stages; many voters first lost confidence in the Democrats when the economy performed badly, then gained confidence in the Republicans when it began to perform well.

Evidence strongly supports the first conclusion; available evidence does not permit a strong test of the second conclusion, but it is surely a reasonable one.[22]

[21] See, for instance, Steven J. Rosenstone, *Forecasting Presidential Elections* (New Haven, Conn.: Yale University Press, 1983), pp. 128–29; J. Merrill Shanks and Warren E. Miller, "Policy Direction and Performance Evaluation: Complementary Explanations of the Reagan Elections," paper prepared for delivery at the annual meeting of the American Political Science Association, New Orleans, August 29–September 1, 1985; Steven J. Rosenstone, "Why Reagan Won," *Brookings Review*, Nov. 3, 1985; D. Roderick Kiewiet and Douglas Rivers, "The Economic Basis of Reagan's Appeal," in Chubb and Peterson, *The New Direction in American Politics*, pp. 69-90; and Donald R. Kinder, Gordon S. Adams, and Paul W. Gronke, "Economics and Politics in 1984," paper prepared for delivery at the annual meeting of the American Political Science Association, August 28–September 1, 1985, New Orleans.

[22] The second conclusion is consistent with the conception of party identification as a running tally of voters' retrospective evaluations; see Morris P. Fiorina, *Retrospective Voting in American National Elections* (New Haven, Conn.: Yale University Press, 1981), pp.

A Case Study of Democratic Change

What has been called the "realignment perspective"[23] is a helpful guide in interpreting the changes in partisan alignments in and since 1984, but what we have just learned about such changes also suggests some refinements in that perspective.

For brevity and clarity, V. O. Key's statement of its basic elements would be hard to improve upon. In *Politics, Parties, and Pressure Groups*,[24] he presents his view of partisan change as an antidote to pessimism about party politics: The appeals of the two major parties ordinarily have such a "bewildering sameness" (p. 220) that one may be led "to the inference that the party battle is meaningless"(p. 222). Such an inference ignores the cycles of innovation, resistance, and reconciliation that characterize the party battle over time, for on occasion "the electorate votes a party out of power in a decisive manner; it expresses clearly a lack of confidence in those who have been in charge of affairs" (p. 522). At such times the party that wins power makes substantial changes in

89–98. It is also consistent with Barry Sussman's interpretation of the *Washington Post*-ABC News poll of February 1985; see "Fragile Realignment: As the Economy Goes, So Goes the GOP," *Washington Post* National Weekly Edition, March 18, 1985, p. 37. Examining data from the University of Michigan's 1980 and 1984 National Election Studies, Warren E. Miller found some evidence of a relationship between *prospective* evaluations of the national economy in 1980 and 1984 and changes in party identification among young, unsophisticated voters, but none between *retrospective* evaluations of the economy and those changes ("Party Identification and Political Belief Systems: Changes in Partisanship in the United States, 1980–1984," manuscript). The latter finding is not telling evidence against the second conclusion, however, since retrospective evaluations that favored the Republicans in those years were, according to Miller, "pervasive." In such a situation, the absence of any correlation between changes in individual voters' partisan identifications and changes in their retrospective evaluations of the economy would be consistent with a shift of the entire distribution of partisan preferences in favor of the Republicans. For an elaboration of this point, see Gerald H. Kramer, "The Ecological Fallacy Revisited," *American Political Science Review*, March 1983, p. 94ff.; and my *Interpreting Elections*, pp. 64–70.

[23] The term is taken from Jerome Clubb, William H. Flanigan, and Nancy Zingale, *Partisan Realignment: Voters, Parties, and Government in American History* (Beverly Hills, Calif.: Sage, 1980).

[24] V. O. Key, Jr., *Politics, Parties, and Pressure Groups*, 5th ed., (New York: Thomas Y. Crowell, 1964). Some other important works on party realignment are: Walter Dean Burnham, *Critical Elections and the Mainsprings of American Politics* (New York: Norton, 1970); Everett Carll Ladd, Jr., with Charles D. Hadley, *Transformations of the American Party System: Political Coalitions from the New Deal to the 1970s* (New York: Norton, 1975); Kristi Anderson, *The Creation of a Democratic Majority, 1928-1936* (Chicago: University of Chicago Press, 1979); Gerald Pomper with Susan S. Lederman, *Elections in America*, 2d ed. (New York: Longman, 1980); John R. Petrocik, *Party Coalitions: Realignment and the Decline of the New Deal Party System* (Chicago: University of Chicago Press, 1981); James L. Sundquist, *Dynamics of the Party System* rev. ed. (Washington, D.C.: Brookings Institution, 1983), and Jerome Clubb, William H. Flanigan, and Nancy Zingale, *Partisan Realignment.*

policy, and, if these are both "technically successful" and "evocative of popular support," they "become embedded in the consensus by the impact of popular ratification in successive elections" (pp. 223–24). The new minority party at first resists, then accommodates to these changes, and finally assumes new functions: (1) reminding the majority leadership "that it is not really all the people" and assailing it for "ineptitude, arbitrariness, and crookedness"; (2) encouraging within minority ranks "an acceptance of modifications of the old order"; and (3) consolidating "sufficient strength to oust the government and to carry through the occasional thoroughgoing reorientation of the political order that circumstance and national conscience demand" (p. 226). This variant of thought about realignment may aptly be called a theory of democracy realized by fits and starts.

Key wrote somewhat ambiguously about the relationship between changes in policy and voters' preferences during realignment. He spoke of the "national conscience" demanding a "thoroughgoing reorientation of the political order"; but more typically, he saw the demands of voters as mainly a demand for change. An election may indicate "widespread unhappiness with past performance" (p. 522), but the "retrospective judgments by the electorate seem far more explicit than do its instructions for future action" (p. 543). Parties and their leaders "advocate great causes" and "devise and enact" new policies (p. 223); voters "ratify" such policies after the fact (p. 224). Thus, it is fair to say that Key saw parties and their leaders as *acting* in party politics and in the development of public policy and saw voters as largely *reacting*. He did not subscribe to Robert Michels' view that modern political organization makes inevitable the "dominion of the elected over the electors,"[25] but neither is Gerald Pomper's statement that voters during realignment "meddle decisively to change the political terms of reference"[26] quite in the spirit of Key's analysis. Key's view of the relationship between leaders and voters is more nearly akin to Thomas Ferguson's "investment" theory of realignment. Ferguson notes the high cost of acting politically and of obtaining the information required for effective political action, and the small incentive most of us have to pay such costs. He argues that political parties are more accurately regarded as "blocs of major investors who coalesce to advance candidates representing their interests"[27] than as vote maximizers. Ordinary voters can qualify as serious investors in party politics, he argues, only if they have easy access to open party organizations and independent secondary organizations "capable of spreading costs and concentrating small contributions" on political action; otherwise, elec-

[25] Robert Michels, *Political Parties* (New York: Dover, 1959), p. 401.

[26] Pomper with Lederman, *Elections in America*, p. 104.

[27] Thomas Ferguson, "Party Realignment and American Industrial Structure," in P. Zarembka, ed., *Research in Political Economy* (Greenwich, Conn.: JAI Press, 1983), p. 10.

tions become "contests between several oligarchic parties, whose major public policy proposals reflect the interests of large investors [e.g., large corporations], and which minor investor-voters are virtually incapable of affecting, save in a negative sense of voting (or nonvoting) 'no confidence'."[28] An important implication of this view is that the connection between the motivation for such votes of no confidence and what government subsequently does may be slight.

The evidence that we have reviewed indicates just such a loose connection between the economic and welfare policies of the Reagan administration and the Republican party's successes with voters in 1980 and 1984. In those elections, many voters demanded a better performance from the economy, not revision of New Deal policies unnecessary to the realization of that demand. In the event, however, Reagan's apparent success with the economy gave him leeway to introduce such revisions, just as similar circumstances (most probably) had allowed Roosevelt to undertake measures unsanctioned, or even unwanted, by the electorate. In democracy realized by fits and starts, evidently, elites retain considerable freedom of action.

This view of partisan change surely counts against Michelian pessimism about voters' ability to control government. Voters care about the state of the nation's economy and know a good deal about economic conditions from experience. One way to act politically in the hope of improving the economic situation can be stated simply: If times are bad, vote against the party that holds the White House; if times are good, vote for that party. By following this rule, voters run the risk of throwing the rascals in—the policies of a new administration may produce even worse results than did those of the old one—but, for politicians and their backers who know the rule is being followed, the incentive intentionally to ignore a vote of no confidence is slight. As Page puts it,

> even if the Great Depression and lack of recovery were not at all Hoover's fault, . . . it could make sense to punish him in order to sharpen the incentives to maintain prosperity in the future. . . . To err on the side of forgiveness would leave voters vulnerable to tricky explanations and rationalizations; but to err on the draconian side would only spur politicians on to greater energy and imagination in problem solving.[29]

Creating a strong incentive to maintain economic prosperity can accomplish a great deal, politically, for it puts significant constraints on the kinds of policies that rational politicians can adopt. Even with all the

[28] Ibid., p. 11.

[29] Benjamin I. Page, *Choices and Echoes in Presidential Elections* (Chicago: University of Chicago Press, 1978), p. 222.

resources that elites have at their disposal (the existence of which led Michels to such gloomy conclusions about democracy), it is hard by any art to convince unemployed men and women that their situation is satisfactory.

Such crude reward-and-punishment democracy, however, will not satisfy the aspirations of many democrats. Results in many areas of public policy are less easily observable and less keenly felt by ordinary voters than the results of policies affecting the economy, and thus are less likely to become cues for electoral reward or punishment. Moreover, popular control of policy, even economic policy, is far from perfect. To achieve economic results widely regarded as good is not necessarily to achieve optimal economic results. Politicians, to some degree, can and do manipulate the economy so that its performance at election time is better than its general performance,[30] and they may be unable to make the economy perform well, no matter what the electorate may do, because they do not know how, or because factors beyond their control make it perform badly, or because they cannot mobilize political support for effective policies.[31]

This last limitation on the efficacy of democracy through votes of no confidence is important now. The present system for nominating presidential candidates has weakened the ties between presidents and their party's other officeholders. Concurrently, as Martin Wattenberg has shown, voters' evaluations of candidates and of parties have become increasingly dissociated; evaluations of the former are much more frequent, fuller, and, by inference, a stronger influence on voting.[32] The governmental system of checks and balances and the relative weakness of parties have always made it difficult for presidents to organize support for positive and coherent programs and for voters—reasonably—to hold presidents responsible for what the government does. Of course, however weak the parties may become, voters can still hold a president accountable for the state of the economy *unreasonably*, without regard to his ability to control its performance. In so acting, however, they create an incentive for presidents to get results by constitutional hook or crook. Skilled or ethical leaders may not act on that incentive, but few observers of American politics have seen an adequate supply of skilled and ethical leaders as by any means a sure thing.

[30] On this point, see, for instance, Edward R. Tufte, *Political Control of the Economy* (Princeton, N.J.: Princeton University Press, 1978).

[31] Cf. Page, *Choices and Echoes*, pp. 229–31.

[32] See Martin P. Wattenberg, "Realignment without Party Revitalization," paper prepared for delivery at the 40th annual conference of the American Association for Public Opinion Research, McAfee, New Jersey, May 1985.

Lessons for Party Leaders

As they look to the future, what view should party leaders take of the evidence that we have been reviewing? The history of the New Deal party system suggests that Republican candidates now enter elections with a new and powerful appeal. Consider the theme of Reagan's 1984 campaign, conveyed in a television advertisement that included magnificent pictures accompanied by soft music and the following narrative:

> It's morning again in America. Today, more men and women will go to work than ever before in our country's history. With interest rates at about half the record highs of 1980, nearly two thousand families today will buy new homes, more than at any time in the past four years. This afternoon, sixty-five hundred young men and women will be married, and with inflation less than half of what it was, just four years ago, they can look forward with confidence to the future. It's morning again in America, and, under the leadership of President Reagan, our country is prouder, and stronger, and better. Why would we ever want to return to where we were, less than four short years ago?

Now consider the biting sarcasm with which F.D.R. met the pretensions of his "me-too" challenger in 1940:

> The American people have not forgotten the condition of the United States in nineteen hundred and thirty-two. We all remember the failures of the banks, the breadlines of starving men and women, the youth of the country riding around in freight cars, the farm foreclosures, the home foreclosures, the bankruptcy and the panic. . . . At the very hour of complete collapse, the American people called for new leadership; that leadership, this Administration and a Democratic Congress supplied. . . . The tears, the crocodile tears, tears for the laboring man and laboring woman now being shed in this campaign come from those same Republican leaders who had their chance to prove their love for labor in 1932, and missed it. . . . And in 1940, eight years later, what a different tune is played by them. It is a tune played against a sounding board of election day. It is a tune with overtones, which whisper "votes, votes, votes!" Yes, these same Republican leaders are all for the new progressive measures now. They believe in them. They believe in them so much that they will never be happy until they can clasp them to their own chests and put their own brand upon them.[33]

[33] From his campaign address in Philadelphia, October 23, 1940.

Clearly, a party that can believably claim to have saved the country from serious difficulties believably attributable to its opposition fights from a powerful rhetorical position; we are disinclined to reject our rescuers in favor of those from whom they have rescued us. In the face of such a claim, moreover, a me-too strategy—that is, matching the policies of the opposition—may be a poor one for the disadvantaged party, since it is the ability to achieve results, not policies as such, that is the issue.

Common sense, nonetheless, suggests limits on the ability of a party of recovery to preserve or extend its gains. It is reasonable to suppose that the strength of voters' attachments to such a party will be in rough proportion to the gravity of the problems it is credited with overcoming. Then, too, the extent to which voters assign lasting credit and blame to parties for overcoming or failing to overcome difficulties should reflect the extent to which the press, campaign propaganda, and circumstances focus attention on parties as agents of political action. Finally, parties bring much baggage from the past to any new era. Of these considerations, the first two should give comfort to the Democrats. Carter's stagflation is not Hoover's Great Depression, and the present era is one in which, as Martin Wattenberg has observed, "television coverage of politics virtually ignores parties."[34] The implications of the third consideration are more politically evenhanded. On the one hand, as we have seen, the Republicans have for some time enjoyed a sizable advantage among voters who cast their evaluations of candidates and parties in ideological terms; on the other hand, the Democratic party, for many, has been and remains the party that represents the interests of ordinary people.

Our evidence reveals no mandate to repeal New Deal policies; some of them have shown their vulnerability, but others continue to be very popular. Ferguson observes that "it is highly doubtful that a modest social security program, a minimum wage, savings guarantees, small agricultural programs and well-funded relief programs during depressions would have been any less popular among the citizenry as a whole in 1840 than they were in 1940."[35] This conclusion is true, probably, though it is not provable, but the ease with which politicians ignored calls for such programs before they were adopted clearly does not mean that contemporary politicians can abolish them with equal ease. My point is not only that our governmental system presents serious obstacles to any effort to change policy, but also that benefits imagined are, for most people, very different from benefits actually enjoyed. Arnold observes that

[34] Martin P. Wattenberg, *The Decline of American Political Parties, 1952–1980* (Cambridge, Mass.: Harvard University Press, 1984), p. 91.

[35] Ferguson, "Party Realignment," p. 30.

> no policy is evaluated in isolation; it is always compared, at least implicitly, with the status quo. Citizens, agencies, and firms come to expect that the current flow of benefits will continue into the future. Decreasing that flow imposes very serious costs: firms may have to lay off employees, agencies lose authority, and citizens suffer losses in income. They all forfeit what they have come to regard as the "necessities" of life. Increasing the flow delivers some very nice benefits, but these are (in the short term) "luxuries"—worth asking for, but not worth dying for.[36]

That a difference exists between the meaning of social security *proposed* and of social security *adopted* is surely an important reason why the two most recent presidential candidates to have expressed doubts about the desirability of the Social Security Program—Barry Goldwater and Ronald Reagan—ended up by declaring their unqualified support for it.

A final point is one that few politicians are likely to have overlooked. Key noted an important condition for the continued dominance of a party of recovery: Its changes in policy must be both "technically successful" and "evocative of popular support"; that is, they must both work and be seen to work. This observation would seem to apply with particular force to administrations that promise economic recovery, as did those of Roosevelt and Reagan. Thus, F.D.R. in March of 1938 was, in the words of one of his biographers, an "anxious man."[37] The economy had taken a sharp downturn the previous August. Acting on the advice of his secretary of the treasury, Henry Morgenthau, Jr., a perplexed Roosevelt had at first called for deep slashes in spending and a balanced budget, but by April he was ready to recommend large-scale spending and an election-year Congress was ready to approve it. If it had not been for these well-timed spending measures and the better economic conditions that followed them, we might remember the New Deal quite differently. Similarly, it seems unlikely that the movement of voters toward the Republicans in 1984 and since will survive a serious deterioration of the economy. Any persuasive assessment of the ability of the Republicans to maintain or improve their present position, therefore, depends as much on economic evidence as on political evidence—and most probably depends on more of both kinds than anyone can muster.

[36] Douglas Arnold, "The Logic of Congressional Action," manuscript, p. 26.

[37] William E. Leuchtenburg, *Franklin D. Roosevelt and the New Deal* (New York: Harper and Row, 1963), p. 256.

9

Immigration and the Welfare State

JOSEPH H. CARENS

"There are no frontiers for hunger. You have the right to look for opportunity wherever you can."[1] These are the words of Angel, a Mexican peasant who illegally entered the United States, worked for a few years, and was caught and deported. He was explaining to an American why he intended to return (illegally) again.

Angel was making a moral claim about human rights. He was claiming that the poverty and lack of opportunity in Mexico gave him a moral right to seek work in the United States or anyplace else, and that the United States had no moral justification for excluding him. There are millions of Angels in the world—needy people who want to find decent conditions of life for themselves and their families, who see no real prospects of doing so in their native lands, and who consequently seek to immigrate to the United States and other rich Western countries.

Do we have any answer to Angel? Is the United States justified in keeping him out? Leave aside the question of whether our answer is likely to dissuade Angel from coming. Is there an answer that is reasonable, an answer that persuades us that exclusion is morally justifiable?

In most debates over immigration policy, Angel's voice is not even heard. The conventional moral view is that a country is justified in restricting immigration whenever it serves the national interest to do so. Most people now believe that it is wrong to discriminate among potential immigrants on the basis of race or national origin, although that sort of discrimination was a deep and pervasive feature of past American immigration policy and people still disagree about what counts as discrimina-

Charles Beitz provided very detailed, thoughtful, and perceptive comments on an earlier version of this paper. They have aided me immensely in revising it, although I fear the revisions might still not satisfy him. I also wish to thank the participants in the Princeton Seminar on Democracy and the Welfare State, at which this paper was presented. Their comments and questions stimulated me to think further about these issues in ways that are only partially reflected here.

[1] *Newsweek*, August 12, 1985, p. 48.

tion.[2] Most people also think that the historic traditions and values of the United States (as symbolized by the Statue of Liberty) imply a special national obligation to accept a continuing flow of immigrants and refugees. But almost no one suggests that a policy of open admissions or even one of vastly increased admissions would serve the national interest.

I wish to explore in this paper one of the most common claims about immigration and the national interest: that restrictions on immigration are necessary to protect the liberal democratic welfare state. I should make clear at the outset that I am sympathetic to this argument. For all its limitations, the welfare state represents a significant, hard-won achievement that offers some protection to the most vulnerable members of American society against the worst harms of a capitalist order. And I think it is reasonable to believe that unrestricted immigration, or even greatly expanded immigration, would significantly weaken the welfare state, at least in the foreseeable future. The question, however, is whether concern for the welfare state is sufficient to justify restricting immigration, if Angel's claim is taken seriously. The inquiry has a broader goal as well: to examine the nature and purpose of political community and to raise questions about what forms of closure and what types of exclusion are justifiable for the sake of community.

Does Immigration Threaten the Welfare State?

What is meant by the "welfare state"? Following Donald Moon's argument in Chapter 2 of this volume, I take the welfare state to be based ultimately upon the liberal premise of the moral equality of all humans. As Moon puts it, "Basic human equality requires full membership in the community—or citizenship—for all." The achievement of full membership for all requires the extension of civil, political, and social rights to all citizens. These social rights are, of course, the distinctive feature of the modern welfare state, and they reflect a recognition of the "equal social worth" of all members of society. Moon places particular emphasis on the importance of self-respect and the links, in our culture, between self-respect and providing for oneself economically. Thus a central element of the welfare state is economic management. The government is expected to regulate the economy so as to ensure that all able and willing to work can find decent jobs that will allow them and their families to maintain a reasonable standard of material well-being. When the state provides serv-

[2] Current policy strongly emphasizes family reunification and thus works against potential immigrants from places such as Africa that have historically sent relatively few (voluntary) immigrants to the United States.

ices or benefits, it should do so on a universal basis or through schemes of social insurance to avoid invidious distinctions among members of the society.

Some people fear that large-scale immigration will undermine both the will to support the institutions of the welfare state and the capacity to do so. The will to support the welfare state comes, it can be argued, from a sense of common bonds, from a mutual identification by the members of the community. These feelings are more likely to emerge when people share a common language and a common culture and when they belong to groups that have developed habits of cooperation with other groups. As Brian Barry points out, in a provocative essay on the individualist case for nationalism, "the presence of fellow-feeling obviously facilitates co-operation on common projects and makes redistribution within the polity more acceptable. . . . [I]f trust and understanding have developed between the members of a state, this makes it more possible to carry out policies that apply universalistic criteria and have the result of helping certain regions or groups more than others because there is some expectation that other policies another time will have the effect of benefiting other groups."[3]

One need not have any sympathy for the prejudice, xenophobia, and racism that have often characterized reactions to new immigrants to recognize that immigrants do not usually share the cultural understandings and historic ties of the native-born population. In many ways, these differences are a strength of the immigrants, for such diversity enriches a community. But as the number of immigrants grows larger, their presence can weaken whatever political support the welfare state draws from the sense of common nationality. As Ari Zolberg, a sympathetic observer of immigration, notes, "even when considered in the most objective perspective, the incorporation of any new population presents difficulties, and will occasion some sort of strain for the receivers. It stands to reason that the degree of strain will grow with the size of the immigrant group and the concentration of the flow in time, as well as with the cultural distance of the immigrants from the mainstream of the receiving society."[4] One way to deal with the "strains of incorporation" is to provide social services to facilitate the adaptation and integration of the new immigrants, but it is precisely the willingness to fund such services that may diminish as the flow of immigrants increases.

An even deeper fear about large-scale immigration is that it will have an impact on the economic well-being of the poorest members of society

[3] Brian Barry, "Self-Government Revisited," in David Miller and Larry Siedentrop, eds., *The Nature of Political Theory* (Oxford: Clarendon Press, 1983), p. 141.

[4] Ari Zolberg, "Keeping Them Out: Ethical Dilemmas of Immigration Policy" (photocopy), p. 8.

and on the capacity of the society to improve or even maintain the economic position of the most disadvantaged. Consider first what we know about the economic effects of current immigration into the United States.[5] The United States admits each year more refugees and immigrants for permanent resettlement than the rest of the world combined. During the past several years, legal admissions have ranged from 400,000 to 500,000 people. There is, however, a substantial flow of illegal immigrants as well, mainly from Mexico; many of the rest come from other countries in Latin America and the Caribbean. Nobody knows exactly how many illegal immigrants there are, or how long they stay. Many observers estimate that four to six million illegal immigrants have already entered the United States and that the rate of illegal immigration equals the rate of legal immigration. Almost all of the illegal immigrants and many of the legal immigrants are unskilled people eager to find jobs of any kind and prepared to accept difficult, unpleasant work at rates of pay that are low by American standards (minimum wage or below) because these jobs are much better than whatever work (if any) they can find in their native land. In many cases their real alternative at home is unemployment (without unemployment benefits), poverty, and hunger.

What are the consequences of this level of immigration for the American welfare state? Economists disagree to some extent about the effect on the labor market. Some insist that the immigrants primarily take jobs that citizens are unwilling to accept (because the wages are so low and the working conditions so bad) and able to refuse (because of the general availability of welfare-state programs). Thus, they conclude, the immigrants—both legal and illegal—have little effect on the economic position of those who are already citizens.[6] Others argue that assuming that these claims about a segmented labor market are true, the presence of large numbers of unskilled and vulnerable foreign workers helps to perpetuate this segmentation, by depressing the wages and working conditions that would otherwise have to be improved in order to attract unskilled domestic workers. Moreover, they point out, many of these immigrants cannot press for enforcement of the regulatory standards of the welfare state (e.g., minimum wage and overtime pay provisions, safety requirements,

[5] Much of the informtion in the next few paragraphs is drawn from Michael Teitelbaum, "Right versus Right: Immigration and Refugee Policy in the United States," *Foreign Affairs* 59 (1980): 21–59; and Vernon Briggs, *Immigration Policy and the American Labor Force* (Baltimore: Johns Hopkins University Press, 1984).

[6] For statements of this position by two of its most prominent advocates, see Michael J. Piore, *Birds of Passage: Migrant Labor and Industrial Societies* (Cambridge: Cambridge University Press, 1979); and Wayne A. Cornelius, *Mexican Migration to the United States: Cause, Consequences, and U.S. Responses* (Cambridge, Mass.: Center for International Studies, Massachusetts Institute of Technology, 1978).

collective-bargaining opportunities) because of their legal vulnerability. Thus, directly or indirectly, these economists say, present patterns of immigration hurt the economic position of precisely those citizens whom the welfare state is supposed to help: the poor and disadvantaged.[7]

What about the effects of immigration on the social services provided by the welfare state? Here, too, there is disagreement. Legal immigrants, particularly refugees, tend to make considerable use of social services, particularly in the first few years after their arrival. At the same time, they work and pay taxes to support social services including some, such as Social Security, that provide them with no current benefits. Overall, if we assume that legal immigrants tend to occupy lower-income positions and that welfare-state programs fulfill their redistributive and egalitarian promises, the costs of providing welfare-state services for legal immigrants should tend to be greater than the taxes paid by them. This conclusion is reinforced if one considers the costs of special services that the welfare state should provide to facilitate the integration of new immigrants (e.g., bilingual education). The situation with regard to illegal immigrants is somewhat different since they usually pay taxes (such as sales and income taxes and the Social Security payments that are withheld), but are reluctant to use the services for fear of alerting authorities to their presence. Thus, some people argue, illegal immigrants actually subsidize the welfare state, by paying in more than they take out. Of course, if that is true, it is hardly consistent with the egalitarian ideals of the welfare state. Moreover, one study suggests that illegal immigrants make greater use of welfare-state programs (including income-transfer programs) than previously thought.[8] And in 1982 the United States Supreme Court declared that the children of illegal aliens are entitled to a free public education.[9] All this suggests that the welfare costs created by illegal immigrants are likely to rise.

Thus far I have talked about the economic effects of immigration on the welfare state in a context in which the United States formally limits yearly immigration to half a million or so, although lax enforcement of restrictions permits about another half million immigrants to enter illegally. What would happen if we accepted Angel's claim and legally ad-

[7] Two of the most prominent advocates of this position are Briggs (*Immigration Policy*) and Walter Fogel; see "Immigrants and the Labor Market: Historical Perspectives and Current Issues," in Demetrios G. Papademetriou and Mark J. Miller, eds., *The Unavoidable Issue: U.S. Immigration Policy in the 1980s* (Philadelphia: Institute for the Study of Human Issues, 1984), pp. 71–92.

[8] David S. North, *Government Records: What They Tell Us about the Role of Illegal Immigrants in the Labor Market and in Income-Transfer Programs* (Washington, D.C.: New Transcentury Foundation, 1981). North estimates that Los Angeles County saves almost $50 million a year by screening out illegal aliens from welfare applicants.

[9] *Plyler* v. *Doe*, 457 U.S. 202 (1982).

mitted him and all those like him? The potential demand for entry is staggering.[10] For example, Mexico's population in 1980 was 68 million. These people faced conditions of massive unemployment and poverty. By the year 2000, Mexico's population is expected to have increased by 60 million. Where will these people find work? How will they survive? It is estimated that in Latin America as a whole, the (potential) labor force will increase by between 86 million and 95 million in the period 1980–2000. No one thinks the economies of Latin American countries are capable of creating jobs for even a fraction of these people. And this says nothing about the potential demand from the rest of the Third World.

To put these numbers in perspective, consider that if the immigration flow into the United States were six million a year, the proportion of immigration in relation to population would be roughly twice that in 1907, the year when immigration was the highest it has been thus far.[11] In absolute numbers it would be much more than twice the previous highest flow. Given the size of the potential demand, six million a year is probably a modest estimate of the flow that would follow the lifting of legal barriers.

What would be the consequences of such a large flow? At best, the segmented labor market would expand with a vengeance. One example of potential developments can be found in the cities along the Mexican-U.S. border, where Mexicans cross daily to work (often illegally). Vernon Briggs remarks that "it is not uncommon in many border cities for even lower-middle-class families to have full-time maids. As North has so poignantly put it, 'There is no servant problem on the border.' "[12] The existence of such a vulnerable, exploited underclass is incompatible with the goal of creating a society in which all members are regarded as having "equal social worth" and equal social, legal, and political rights. Of course, this sort of class subordination exists now in the welfare state, but open immigration would vastly increase the severity and scope of the problem and render almost useless the conventional welfare-state techniques for dealing with it.

With open borders, no immigrants would be legally vulnerable in the way that current illegal immigrants are. But intense economic competition among unskilled workers would make welfare-state regulations governing work even more difficult to enforce, and enforcement would only further increase the large and increasing pool of unemployed. Here is a potential reserve army of unemployed greater than anything Marx could have imagined. Would unemployed immigrants be eligible for welfare-

[10] The demographic estimates in this paragraph are taken from Teitelblaum, "Right versus Right."

[11] I borrow this point from Zolberg, "Keeping Them Out," p. 7.

[12] Briggs, *Immigration Policy*, p. 237.

state benefits? If not, the promise of the welfare state to guarantee full membership for all would be broken. If they were eligibile, the incentives to immigrate would be stronger and the increased financial burden would be overwhelming. Even if benefits were not provided, most would come anyway, as long as their chances of finding work in the United States seemed better than their chances at home. (Most immigrants now come looking for work, not benefits, even when they are entitled to them.)

Currently disadvantaged minorities would be placed in a situation of permanent dependence. Their best hope is elimination of the segmented labor market and creation of meaningful opportunities for work. The massive influx of immigrants would widen the gap between the primary and secondary labor markets, leaving them no place to go. Even apart from unemployment benefits, the demand for welfare-state services (education, health care) would grow enormously because immigrants have families. And, as I noted earlier, poorly paid immigrants cannot bear the full costs of these services even if they are employed. Therefore, redistributive taxes would have to be increased. At the same time, the constant influx of poor, needy people with whom most native residents have no longstanding ties or affinities would undermine the sense of common bonds that makes the welfare state politically possible.

Whatever the merits of claims that current levels of legal and illegal immigration do no harm to the welfare state, one can hardly be optimistic about the effects of a policy of open borders. Defenders of the welfare state fear that the end result of open immigration might well be the demise of the welfare state and a return to a nineteenth-century laissez-faire social order (assuming that the process was not short-circuited by a nativist political backlash, perhaps reinforced by national security concerns, long before it had run its course). A less extreme consequence would be that the massive increase in poor people would make it impossible to maintain welfare-state benefits at anything approximating their current level and would make the promise of full equality of citizenship an even more distant goal. Clearly, there are too many uncertainties to predict the consequences of open immigration with any accuracy. Still, can anyone argue that those who care about the project of the liberal democratic welfare state have no good reason to fear open immigration? Why should we risk it? "One answer comes from the very liberal theory upon which your liberal democratic welfare state is founded."[13] So Angel might respond, if he had time to engage in political theory.

[13] The arguments in the next few pages are developed at greater length in Joseph Carens, "Aliens and Citizens: The Case for Open Borders," *Review of Politics* (Spring 1987). Some liberal theorists (e.g., Robert Nozick) argue that a proper understanding of liberal principles leads to the conclusion that the welfare state is not justifiable. In this paper, however, I assume the prima facie legitimacy of the welfare state. I therefore focus on liberal theories

The Liberal Case for Freedom of Movement

To say that a concern for the welfare state justifies restrictions on immigration is to focus only on the moral claims of those who are already citizens, or at least permanent residents. But this ignores Angel's conflicting claim that he has a moral right to enter the country if he wishes to do so. Liberal theory starts with an assumption about the moral equality of all human beings, not just the moral equality of citizens of a particular state. As Moon's paper in this volume shows, the case for *civic* equality is based on the recognition of *moral* equality, not vice versa. Angel asserts that the exclusion of people like him from rich welfare states like the United States violates this principle of the fundamental moral equality of all human beings. How might we assess this claim?

One approach is to consider two familiar contemporary liberal theories that are often seen as justifying the liberal democratic welfare state: contractarianism and utilitarianism. The contractarian theory is suggested by Rawls in *A Theory of Justice*.[14] I say "suggested" because Rawls restricts his theory to questions of justice within a hypothetically closed society so that questions about immigration do not arise. Indeed, in recent essays he has made it clear that he thinks his theory applies only to domestic justice in Western liberal democratic societies. I side with Beitz and Barry, however, in arguing that the deeper logic of Rawls's theory leads to a global view of the original position.[15] Regardless of whether that is correct as an interpretation of Rawls's theory, I want to ask what follows if one does adopt a global view of the original position. Those in the original position would be (representative) individuals prevented by the veil of ignorance from knowing their place of birth or what society they were really members of. If the rest of Rawls's argument is correct, individuals in a global original position would presumably choose the two (really three) principles of justice: (1) equal liberties, (2a) fair equality of opportunity, (2b) the difference principle. These principles would apply globally, and individuals would design institutions to implement them—still from the perspective of the original position. Whether such institutions would include sovereign states is debatable, to say the least, but if states existed, they

that are used primarily to defend the welfare state rather than to criticize it. For an exploration of the implications of libertarian principles for questions about immigration, see the article cited in this note.

[14] John Rawls, *A Theory of Justice* (Cambridge, Mass.: Harvard University Press, 1971).

[15] See Charles R. Beitz, *Political Theory and International Relations* (Princeton, N.J.: Princeton University Press, 1979); and Brian Barry, *The Liberal Theory of Justice* (Oxford: Clarendon Press, 1973). My own defense of a global veil of ignorance is elaborated in "Aliens and Citizens."

would be states constrained by the principles of justice. No state could restrict religious freedom, for example, except perhaps to restrict the intolerant in some ways in order to preserve the global system of equal liberties.

What about freedom of movement among states? Would it be regarded as a basic liberty in such a system, or would it be constrained? There is clearly an important liberty at stake here. To have the right to live and work where one chooses can be as vital to one's plan of life as the right to practice one's religion or to associate with whomever one chooses. Indeed, freedom of mobility is often a prerequisite for the effective exercise of other freedoms. Early liberals attacked both the feudal practices that tied people to particular areas of residence and the inherited statuses that restrictions on mobility made possible. The granting of citizenship as a birthright by modern nation-states has had much the same effect; inherited status decisively shapes a person's life chances, and states have forcibly prevented individuals from changing that status by choice and through their own effort. Behind the veil of ignorance, not knowing whether one was in Angel's position, one would no more agree to restrict freedom of movement than one would agree to restrict freedom of religion.

I assume that the Rawlsian arguments for a system of equal basic liberties and for the priority of liberty are sufficiently familiar that they need not be repeated here. Freedom of movement would be a basic element in the global system of basic liberties; states could not legitimately restrict that freedom except to preserve the global system of basic liberties. In a nonideal world, where some people do not act justly, states presumably could prohibit the entry of people whose aim was overthrow of the state and subversion of the principles of justice. And perhaps a particular state could limit immigration if the demand for entry became so great that it somehow threatened the capacity of the government to maintain public order. But maintenance of public order is not the same as maintenance of the welfare state.

Rights are trumps in this type of social contract theory. Considerations that we would normally regard as morally important are ignored because of the priority accorded to rights. Take the idea that people have a right to be a citizen of the country they are born in and no right to be a citizen of a country they are not born in (with minor exceptions). From a rights persepective, birthplace and parentage are irrelevant. They are exactly the sorts of factors that the veil of ignorance is intended to exclude from the original position because they are "arbitrary from a moral point of view."[16] Americans' concern for the economic well-being of those who

[16] Rawls, *A Theory of Justice*, p. 72.

are already citizens and their descendants is clearly a central motivation of those who want to restrict immigration in order to maintain the welfare state. But the priority of liberty in the Rawlsian version of social contract theory makes such a concern irrelevant. The freedom of some cannot be restricted in order to improve the economic well-being of others. Freedom can be restricted only for the sake of freedom. Moreover, if we did ask about economic well-being, we would ask about the effects of immigration on the least well off and we would also have to include potential immigrants in our survey. There are no principled grounds in this version of the theory for giving priority to the concerns of people who are already citizens. If the potential immigrants were less well off than the citizens and if their economic situation would be improved by permitting them to immigrate, the contractarian approach would require that they be admitted regardless of the effect on the position of the citizens (so long as no group of them was thereby placed in a worse economic situation than the one originally faced by the potential immigrants).[17]

In contrast to Rawlsian contractarianism, a utilitarian approach can take into account the negative effects of immigration on the welfare state. Of course, much depends on how "utility" is defined. Is it subjective or objective? Is it a question of happiness or welfare as in classical utilitarianism, or a question of preferences or interests as in some more recent versions? Do all preferences or interests count or only some? But any version of utilitarianism would presumably take the economic effects of immigration into account. If open immigration would hurt some citizens economically, that would count against an open immigration policy in a utilitarian theory.

On the other hand, if open immigration would help some citizens economically, that would count for open immigration. More important, utilitarianism requires that the effects on the aliens be taken into account, too. Like contractarianism, and unlike conventional morality, utilitarianism provides no fundamental basis for giving priority to those who are already citizens. In the calculus of affected interest, everyone counts for one and no one counts for more than one. So the benefits (and harms) of open immigration for noncitizens would have to be considered. To justify restrictions on immigration, it would have to be shown that more open immigration would result in a net loss overall. Certainly that would be true at some point. Totally open immigration might lead to the breakdown of public order. But again, public order and the welfare state are not equivalent. Perhaps defenders of the status quo could argue that the harmful effects of the erosion of welfare-state

[17] What about the effects of migration on those left at home? Perhaps they are really the worst off. For a discussion of this issue, see "Aliens and Citizens."

institutions would outweigh any benefits provided by open immigration. But under current conditions, when so many millions of poor and oppressed people feel they have so much to gain from immigration to the advanced industrial states, that seems a very difficult case to make. The advocates of restrictions have not even tried to make such a case at any length.[18] It is hard to believe that a utilitarian calculus that took the interest of aliens seriously could justify significantly tighter restrictions on immigration than the ones implied by the "public order" restriction of contractarian theory.

Even a public order restriction might exclude millions of potential immigrants, given the size of the potential demand. So Angel might not get in. Nevertheless, if the arguments developed here were accepted, they would require changes in both current immigration policies and conventional moral thinking about the question of immigration.

Perhaps that is all to the good. Perhaps the United States has no right to control immigration, at least not for the sake of the welfare state. Conventional moral thinking may be bankrupt, a self-deceptive and self-serving defense of privilege in the name of equality. Before we rush to that conclusion, however, we should ask whether common-sense morality might include some moral truth that is missing or obscured by the theories discussed thus far. To pursue that possibility, I want to discuss some cases in which some form of exclusion is practiced for the sake of maintaining welfare-state programs and where the exclusion seems to me intuitively justifiable. By exploring these cases I hope to illuminate some general features of the relationships among exclusion, political community, and social welfare. I shall then attempt to determine whether these analyses can provide any basis for conclusions about immigration different from the ones discussed earlier. Ultimately, any defense of exclusion must come to terms with the criticism that it is just one more attempt by the (relatively) privileged to defend their unjustified advantages against the moral claims of the have-nots. I intend not to let this criticism slip from sight as the inquiry proceeds.

Possible Justifications for Exclusion

I begin with a case in which an attempt to exclude proved unsuccessful, because it illustrates, by way of contrast, the circumstances under which exclusion might be justifiable. A story appeared on the front page of the *Toronto Globe and Mail* on November 21, 1985, about a sixty-nine-

[18] Henry Sidgwick does make this claim, but as Michael Walzer points out, his argument is not very persuasive. See Walzer, *Spheres of Justice* (New York: Basic Books, 1983), pp. 37–38.

year-old man who had originally been a Canadian citizen but who had emigrated from Canada to the United States in the 1940s and had become a United States citizen, thus giving up his Canadian citizenship. After developing serious medical problems in 1983, he returned to Canada for medical treatment, which was paid for by the Canadian government, and applied for landed immigrant status. His application was turned down by the Immigration Department on the basis of a section in the Canadian Immigration Act that stipulates that people with medical conditions likely to cause "excessive demand" on health or social services are inadmissible. Unfortunately for the bureaucrats in the Immigration Department (and fortunately for the man), the *Toronto Globe and Mail* discovered other elements of interest in the case. The first four paragraphs of the story, which appeared under the headline "Ailing Veteran Can't Remain, Ottawa Decides," were as follows:

> Fred Darwin is a veteran of the Second World War. As a young and proud Canadian, he joined the Essex Scottish Regiment and went overseas.
>
> On August 19, 1942, his regiment took part in one of the bloodiest and disastrous [*sic*] battles of the war—the Dieppe raid.
>
> Mr. Darwin was among almost 2,000 soldiers captured by the Germans. He spent the next 3-1/2 years in a prison camp.
>
> Mr. Darwin, now a U.S. citizen, wants to live out the last years of his life in Canada. But Employment and Immigration Minister Flora MacDonald and her senior officials do not want to let him remain in the country.

The story was accompanied by a front-page picture of Mr. Darwin in his wheelchair. The headline in the next day's paper was "Public Outcry Prompts Ottawa to Let Veteran Stay in Canada."

This story could be used to illustrate any number of topics (e.g., bureaucratic procedures, symbolic politics, interest groups and the media), but I want to focus on its implications for questions about the legitimacy of exclusion. One can see why a rule-oriented bureaucrat would have decided to exclude Darwin. He no longer had any real ties to Canada. It seems reasonably clear that he wanted to immigrate primarily because of the free medical care he could receive in Canada. As it turned out, he was legally entitled as a veteran to free medical care while in Canada; the only question was whether he would be allowed to stay to take advantage of this entitlement. Thus the exclusion had a Catch-22 quality. Moreover, admitting Darwin was obviously a low-cost precedent. (How many other ailing expatriate World War II veterans are there?) Therefore, the decision to exclude Darwin was obviously foolish regardless of whether it was justifiable or not.

Suppose that Darwin had not been a former prisoner of war or even a veteran, but just someone who had emigrated from Canada to the United States. Better still, suppose he had never been a Canadian citizen but was just an ordinary United States citizen with severe medical problems who wanted to take advantage of Canada's system of national health insurance. Assume, for present purposes, that this person was one of the millions of Americans without any health insurance or legal entitlement to health care services. Would it have been wrong to exclude this potential immigrant on the grounds that he would place excessive demands on the health services?

I think not. But what reasons can be offered to justify exclusion in this case? For the moment, let us suppose that the Canadian exclusionary rule applies only to citizens of the United States or other affluent countries. One argument for exclusion is fairness.

In some cases, this argument clearly applies even at the individual level. Suppose a person, age sixty, has lived for many years in the United States, earning a substantial income and paying lower taxes than Canadians because of the absence of a universal, publicly financed health care system. He now finds that he needs very costly medical care. It would clearly not be fair for him to come to Canada and expect the Canadians to pay for his care. He could have afforded to purchase health insurance in the United States and did not; Canadians should not be asked to pay the costs of his imprudence. He has not done his fair share in contributing to the Canadian health care system. This argument appeals to the sense of reciprocity that is implicit in social insurance schemes in the welfare state. It would not be fair for a citizen to opt out of social insurance arrangements for years and then opt in just at the moment when he knows that he needs a disproportionate share of the benefits provided. Of course, citizens are not permitted to do this. At the very least, the same principle of fairness would seem to justify excluding noncitizens who seek to join a community for the sake of obtaining welfare-state benefits just at the moment when they need those benefits.

The story I have just told treated the American as personally responsible for his predicament, because he had an adequate income and access to health insurance and chose not to spend his money on it. Suppose that were not the case, however. Suppose he were poor and could not afford health insurance, or that he had had insurance and had lost it through no fault of his own (e.g., as a result of losing his job). Would that affect the argument about whether the Canadians ought to admit him? Suppose he were a liberal Democrat who had always supported national health insurance and had simply been on the losing side of the political battles all these years. Would that strengthen his case for admittance? (And if he were a conservative Republican who opposed socialized medicine, should that count against him?) Suppose he were a young adult who had serious health problems. He had never even had the chance to decide whether to live in the United States or in Canada. He was not responsible for the fact that he was born and brought up in the United States rather than in Canada. Would it be justifiable to exclude him?

I think it would be. The question is why. In these cases one cannot appeal to a sense of fairness based on notions of individual responsibility. The individual is not responsible for his predicament. But there is also a sense of fairness based upon notions of collective responsibility. Crudely put, the central intuition here is that communities should look after their own. Recall that we are considering at the moment only affluent liberal democratic welfare states such as the United States and Canada. We have put aside temporarily the questions raised by vast inequalities among states. Given broadly comparable economic resources, it would be unfair for the members of one community to expect the members of another to bear the burden of providing for a social need such as health care that will emerge in every community. The principle of fairness based on collective responsibility also applies to other goods supplied by the welfare state, such as employment opportunities, education, and income support.

This view of fairness rests in part on the assumption that there is considerable room for legitimate collective self-determination even within the context of a commitment to the welfare state. Suppose, for the sake of argument, that all liberal democratic welfare states were expected to ensure certain minimum levels of health, education, and income support for all their citizens. Even assuming we could identify appropriate minimum levels for all welfare states, some communities might want to provide more than the minimum.

Consider provision of education, for example. Amy Gutmann (Chapter 5 in this volume) has argued that a liberal democratic welfare state ought to provide all children with the education necessary to enable them to participate effectively in the democratic process. But this allows the community to decide whether to devote more resources to education than are required by the minimum standard and also gives the community the task of interpreting that standard. Moreover, communities may choose to allocate their educational resources in different ways. One community may decide to provide free or heavily subsidized university and post-graduate education. If individuals were able to travel freely across borders to take advantage of subsidized higher education, it might prove far more costly for the community to maintain that program than it would be if only members of the community benefited from the subsidy. That realization would be an incentive for the community to cut back on its funding for higher education. Thus free access could undermine the capacity for collective self-determination in areas where different collective choices are morally permissible.

Consider income-support programs as another example. Suppose Canada decided to establish a guaranteed annual income that was much more generous than that guaranteed under similar programs in the United States (even if the U.S. programs met the minimum standards for a liberal democratic welfare state). Would Canada be morally obliged to admit all poor U.S. citizens who wanted to immigrate to take advantage of this program? If so, Canada's capacity to fund the program would be seriously threatened. The principle of free access seems to create perverse incentives, for it penalizes the most generous communities and rewards the most stingy. At best this would tend to shift welfare-state benefits downward; at worst it would reduce them to the lowest common denominator.

If the goal is to prevent people from migrating to obtain better welfare-state benefits, perhaps it is not necessary to restrict migration as such. Perhaps access to benefits could be restricted on the basis of membership, while leaving people free to move where they wished. Of course, if people travel to a community and settle there, they must at some point be regarded as full members of the community and entitled to all the benefits of membership. It would not be fair to expect them to pay taxes to support programs from which they were permanently and formally excluded. In any event, permanent distinctions between native members of the community and immigrants would be incompatible with the commitment to equal citizenship. But temporary barriers (e.g., the requirement that one must be a resident member of the community for a certain period before being entitled to benefits) might be compatible with a commitment to equal citizenship in the long run. Such an arrangement would also ensure freedom to immigrate, while respecting the right of the community to exclude those who seek to join merely to take advantage of benefits not available in their own (comparably affluent) community.

One crucial question for this approach is whether employment is to be considered a welfare-state benefit. If people are not entitled to look for work in the community where they settle, then the right to immigrate becomes a purely formal freedom for all but the rich, because most people have to earn an income in order to live (especially when they are not entitled to the benefits of income-support programs, unemployment compensation, and so on). But it should be remembered that in a welfare state, the government is expected to regulate the economy so as to ensure that all those who are able and willing to work can find decent jobs. No government is likely to be entirely successful at this task and some will perform it better than others, in part because of differences in priorities (e.g., controlling inflation versus reducing unemployment), in part because of differences in skill (and luck) in designing and implementing economic policies. In this light, it seems reasonable to regard job opportunities as one of the benefits likely to be differentially provided by different welfare states. If so, then the arguments presented earlier as justifying restricted access to education or to income-support programs would seem to justify restricting employment to members, or at least giving members preference in hiring. For example, Canada's practice of requiring employers to give preference to Canadian citizens over U.S. citizens would be legitimate.

Migration among Subnational Communities

The line of argument I developed in the preceding section is that, in some circumstances, it is justifiable for people to be "stuck" with the policies and programs of the political community to which they happen to belong. It is justifiable not because the individual is responsible for what his or her community has done or failed to do, but because other communities may have to enforce at least limited forms of exclusion in order to maintain their capacities to make collective choices and to set their own welfare-state priorities. Admittedly, this principle requires the needy members of less generous communities to make do with less, even though they may not bear any personal responsibility for their needy condition or their community's policies. But without the possibility of exclusion, no community would dare rise too far above the norm in at least some areas of welfare-state provision. Moreover, without the possibility of exclusion, some communities might deliberately underfund welfare-state programs in an attempt to shift their responsibilities to others. Therefore, an institutional arrangement permitting some forms of exclusion can be fair, even though some individuals may be disadvantaged by the arrangement, because overall many more people are made better off. This argument assumes that freedom of movement is not to be given absolute priority, but is to be considered one value among others. In sum, people do not have a right to move in order to take advantage of benefits provided by another democratic political community, when their own community could have provided the same benefits but chose not to do so.

In presenting these arguments about political community, I have deliberately used nation-states as an illustration. Would the arguments be as persuasive if the communities in question were not Canada and the United States but California and Oklahoma, or Minneapolis and Gary? It is striking how similar the problems seem, yet how different the practices are when one compares subnational political communities with nation-states. In many countries such as the United States and Canada, subnational political units (provinces, states, counties, cities) bear the primary responsibility for welfare-state programs. They establish the levels of benefits and provide much of the financing for them. Different units often establish quite different levels of benefits, and concerns often arise about the possibility that people will move from one community to another in order to take advantage of differences in benefits.

In the summer of 1985, for example, Minnesota officials noted a dramatic increase in the number of non-Minnesotans coming to Minneapolis and applying for welfare. One factor in the influx appeared to be the huge disparity between the level of welfare support in Minnesota and that in the nearby state of Indiana. More than a third of the new families had come from Gary, where welfare payments in some cases amounted to less than half of the amount that a family of the same size could receive in Minneapolis. Minnesota officials were obviously upset by this in-migration of needy people. As the chairman of the Hennipin County Board put it, "I think it's both morally and politically wrong for us to lie down and let other communities make wholesale transfers of their caseloads onto us."[19] This is precisely the sort of argument I have been discussing. Communities should look after their own. It is not fair for one community to have to bear another's welfare responsibilities. When one community is more generous than another and outsiders come in to take advantage of this generosity, the result is to undermine political support for the programs. Thus communities should be able to exclude outsiders in order to preserve their welfare programs. If this argument is applicable to countries, why should it not apply equally to counties?

Whether it should or not, it is important to realize that it does not in practice. The United States Supreme Court has ruled that the right to travel across state lines and to establish residence in any state is part of the personal liberty protected by the Constitution and therefore a right that may not be restricted by the states. In 1941, the Supreme Court struck down a California state law that made it a crime to help indigent people come to California. (The law was aimed at reducing the migration of poor people from Oklahoma to California during the 1930s).[20] The

[19] *New York Times*, September 22, 1985, p. 35. Despite the rhetoric about other communities making transfers of caseloads, there was no indication that officials in Indiana had encouraged people to move to Minnesota. Would it have been wrong for them to do so? I assume so. Again, the appeal is to the principle that it is the community's responsibility to take care of its own, at least under normal circumstances. It does not follow, however, that the individuals have to put up with that care. It does not seem wrong for them to move if they can get better treatment elsewhere.

[20] *Edwards* v. *California*, 314 U.S. 160. The majority opinion relied on the commerce clause, but several justices thought that inappropriate; their concurring opinions relied on the Fourteenth Amendment instead. In a 1966 case, *United States* v. *Guest*, 383 U.S. 745,

Court had previously declared that denial of the right to work in a community would be "tantamount to the assertion of the right to deny . . . entrance and abode," a right the states did not have with respect to the citizens of other states or even with respect to aliens.[21] In principle, states may favor their own residents in expending state funds, but they may not prevent people from becoming residents and in most cases they are not allowed to distinguish between new residents and old residents.

The decisive case here is *Shapiro* v. *Thompson*,[22] which merits detailed discussion because it is directly relevant to the issues with which we are concerned. Prior to this 1969 case, some states had required people to reside in the state for a fixed period before applying for public assistance. These states had argued that durational residency requirements were needed to preserve their fiscal capacity to provide for their own poor by preventing the influx of poor people from other states, especially states offering fewer or relatively inferior welfare benefits. The Court explicitly rejected this rationale:

> We do not doubt that the one-year waiting-period device is well suited to discourage the influx of poor families in need of assistance. An indigent who desires to migrate, resettle, find a new job, and start a new life will doubtless hestitate if he knows that he must risk making the move without the possibility of falling back on state welfare assistance during his first year of residence, when his need may be most acute. But the purpose of inhibiting migration by needy persons into the State is constitutionally impermissible.

The Court argued that because all citizens have a constitutional right to travel freely and to establish residence anywhere in the United States, a state cannot legitimately try to deter people from entering, even if the people come solely to obtain more or better welfare benefits. What about arguments based on fairness and reciprocity such as the ones I have presented? Again the Court's rejection in *Shapiro* was explicit:

> Appellants argue further that the challenged classification may be sustained as an attempt to distinguish between new and old residents on the basis of the contribution they have made to the community through the payment of taxes. . . . Appellants reasoning would logically permit the State to bar new residents from schools, parks and libraries or deprive them of police and fire protection.

The Court's argument here seems to suggest that any distinction between new and old residents is invidious and indefensible. Once a person be-

Justice Stewart declared that "freedom to travel throughout the United States has long been recognized as a basic right under the Constitution."

[21] *Truax* v. *Raich*, 239 U.S. 361 (1915) at 42.

[22] 394 U.S. 618 (1969).

comes a resident, he or she is automatically a full member of the community. (And, as we have seen, the Court has ruled that states may establish no barriers to prevent people from becoming residents.) This is a strong version of free migration indeed, although, as some commentators have noted, even requiring people to establish residency before they can qualify for benefits can be a significant constraint on people who need jobs or income support.[23]

In later cases the Court backed off a bit from the position as I have interpreted it here. Durational residency requirements for free medical care were struck down following *Shaprio*, but states have been permitted to impose durational residency requirements on those seeking reduced tuition at state universities and on those seeking divorce decrees in state courts. So, in some situations, the Court has been willing to allow states to distinguish between new and old residents in the allocation of benefits. Still, the dominant thrust is clear. Preservation of state and local welfare programs is not a good enough reason for exclusion, even through the indirect means of residency requirements. Perhaps this will reduce the experimentation by states or local communities with "unusually generous welfare programs," as Justice Harlan wrote in his dissent in *Shapiro* (although that particular fear seems a bit quaint today). That consideration is not important enough to restrict mobility. Minnesota officials cannot legally deny aid to the newcomers in an attempt to get them to go back where they came from.

The fact that the Supreme Court has largely decided in favor of open borders within the United States does not prove that the arguments for exclusion are wrong. Perhaps the cases were wrongly decided. Perhaps the cases were decided correctly but the Constitution is flawed by an excess of liberal individualism. Perhaps the cases simply reflect a political choice of more national government and less state government, more centralization and less decentralization. In this last view, the deep commitment to interstate mobility would not rest on firm philosophical foundations. It would simply be our choice as a political community to subordinate subnational units to national unity. Other nation-states could choose differently, permitting the subunits to erect barriers to movement, for reasons such as the ones we have considered, without violating any fundamental principles.

There is a good deal to be said for this argument. In Canada, for example, the provinces have most of the responsibility for social welfare programs. The new Charter of Rights and Freedoms guarantees individuals the right to move freely between provinces but explicitly permits

[23] Margaret K. Rosenheim, "*Shapiro* v. *Thompson*: The Beggars Are Coming to Town," in Philip B. Kurland, ed., *The Supreme Court Review* (Chicago: University of Chicago Press, 1969), pp. 303–46.

provinces to require people to satisfy durational residency requirements before they can claim social benefits. In this respect, Canada's choices regarding internal mobility are different from those of the United States. One could argue that they are unwise or undesirable (as one could with regard to U.S. policies), but it is hard to see why they should be regarded as fundamentally unjust.

Suppose that there were a liberal democratic welfare state in which the local governmental units had primary responsibility for welfare programs and in where there were no formal guarantees of freedom of mobility. Would the arguments for restricting mobility apply in that context? I think the answer is yes—equally as well as they apply in the international context. I see no reason why we should restrict the term "political community" to the nation-state or automatically invest the nation-state with special moral status. Of course, exclusion by subunits would reduce national integration and the identification of members of the state with one another. But is that always bad, or are the gains in local identification and integration never worth the cost? We should note that exclusion practiced by nation-states reduces international integration and the identification of members of the world with one another. Perhaps that is worth the cost, too. The important point is that the nation-state represents another form of localism—the dominant form today, perhaps, but not one with a dominant moral claim over all other forms of localism.

It may be tempting to try to draw a radical distinction between arguments for international mobility and arguments for mobility within the nation-state. The nation-state, it could be argued, is a community and free internal mobility is needed for the sake of the national community, as part of the meaning of national citizenship. There is no comparable international community or international citizenship for which free mobility is needed. It is true that mobility within the nation-state is sometimes defended on these grounds. (It is a claim that appears in the U.S. Supreme Court cases, for example.) But it is important to see that free internal mobility is not always essential to the nation-state. Indeed, restrictions on mobility can also be defended in the name of the national community. In China, for example, despite recent relaxations in some controls over movement, peasants are still forbidden to move to the larger cities because the Chinese want to avoid the sorts of urban problems that plague so many other Third World countries. These prohibitions are criticized by some as a denial of individual freedom. Moreover, the U.N. Covenant on Civil and Political Rights includes free mobility as one of the rights every lawful inhabitant of any state should enjoy. So, the right of free movement within a state is widely regarded as an important personal liberty and not just a necessary component of national citizenship.

Where Does All This Leave Us?

I began by arguing that a political community is entitled to impose residency requirements in order to limit the entry of people from comparably situated communities who might be tempted to move to take advantage of better welfare-state benefits. Even within the narrow parameters of the welfare state, different communities may legitimately choose different ways of life, and the right to exclude could be an essential means of maintaining such a way of life. That conclusion still stands. But the discussion of mobility within nation-states has made clear that freedom of movement is in fact an important personal liberty and thus that any restrictions on freedom of movement (even residency requirements) entail the subordination of an important liberal value to other concerns. We thus have a case for limited forms of exclusion by comparably situated communities under some circumstances.

Suppose that the communities are not comparably situated. Instead of approximate economic equality between the communities in question, there are vast inequalities. Angel, not Fred Darwin, seeks admission. How should that affect our views about the justifiability of exclusion?

On the one hand, inequality increases the urgency of restriction. It is the migration of the Angels of this world, not the Fred Darwins, that would actually threaten the welfare state (as I showed in the first section of this paper). On the other hand, vast economic inequalities undermine the argument that it is fair to restrict entry in order to preserve the capacity for collective self-determination. That argument seems plausible if the communities start with comparable resources. If one community chooses to spend more on welfare-state benefits than another, it seems reasonable to argue that the community that spends less should not be able to shift the burden of caring for its needy members to another community. But if the community that provides less is unable to provide more, the argument breaks down. The differences in provision do not reflect different collective choices but different capacities. Exclusion then becomes a means of protecting differences in resources rather than preserving the ability to make different choices. Perhaps differences in resources can also be defended, but the grounds for that argument are far from obvious. In the absence of such a defense, exclusion for the sake of maintaining the welfare state seems to protect collective privilege more than it protects collective choice. Therefore, despite my sympathy for the project of preserving the welfare state, I am driven back to the conclusion of my analysis of liberal theory. Preservation of the welfare state does not justify restriction of immigration from poor countries to rich ones. Angel wins the argument.

At least he wins this argument. I think it is possible to make more persuasive arguments for exclusion, arguments that do not focus primarily on the preservation of the welfare state but on the claims of communities to preserve their identities and distinctive ways of life. These arguments apply under some circumstances—but not, by and large, the circumstances in which the rich capitalist nations of the world find themselves today. What about rich nations other than the United States? Should they not be expected to open their doors and risk their welfare states as well? Yes, but there are plenty of poor people to go around. The argument about the consequences for the welfare state would not be affected much if the United States took only its "fair share" of immigrants. Could the transfer of resources serve as a substitute for the admission of immigrants? Perhaps, to some extent and in some cases.[24]

The reality, however, is that the United States will not transfer resources or open its borders to the extent that is morally required according to the arguments advanced here. Does this reality matter to a normative inquiry such as the one I am conducting, and if so how? In other words, where does political reality fit (if at all) in political theory?

Political Theory and Political Realities

Some would say that this is exactly where we should have started. In this view, the proper approach to political theory is to begin with an understanding of where we are now, of what the actual possibilities are, given the constraints imposed by history, social structures, and cultural norms. One could speak of the given historic posssibilities at this moment in the world capitalist system. Or one could put the point as Sidgwick did:

> The utilitarian, in the existing state of our knowledge, cannot possibly construct a morality de novo either for man as he is (abstracting his morality), or for man as he ought to be and will be. He must start, speaking broadly, with the existing social order, and the existing morality as a part of that order: and in deciding the question whether any divergence from this code is to be recommended, must consider chiefly the immediate consequences of such divergence, upon a society in which such a code is conceived generally to subsist.[25]

If we were to apply this approach to the question of immigration, we would start with the recognition that most people feel that a policy that puts the interests of the citizens of their own country ahead of the inter-

[24] I have explored this issue more fully in a paper entitled "Migration, Morality and the Nation-State."

[25] Henry Sidgwick, *The Methods of Ethics*, 7th ed. (1907; Indianapolis: Hackett, 1981), pp. 473–74.

ests of citizens of other countries is perfectly legitimate, and indeed that people will become very angry if they feel that in failing to do so, the policy causes significant harm in their own country. This is precisely the view of some writers on the subject of immigration policy. In one of the most influential articles on that topic, Michael Teitelbaum repeatedly argues that those pushing for more open immigration are being unrealistic and even foolhardy in not recognizing the danger of a backlash if large-scale immigration leads to extreme social dislocation.[26] The *New York Times* echoed this view in a 1985 editorial: "The question . . . is not whether this country will control the borders. We will. The question is how harshly. If we don't do so now with calm, humane concern, we will later with xenophobic venom, of a kind discernible in last year's Texas primary campaign."[27]

If these arguments about the likely consequences of large-scale immigration are correct, I think tighter restrictions on immigration (especially illegal immigration) are indeed appropriate. But the fundamental problem with such realism is that it obscures the underlying ideal. Surely we want to know not only whether a country will control its borders but whether it is morally entitled to do so. We want to know what the citizens' deepest convictions are or ought to be, even if they cannot act upon them.

Suppose that under the "existing social order" and the "existing morality," blacks were regarded as inferior to whites (as they have been throughout most of American history). It is easy to imagine circumstances under which attempts to change this situation would have been (and were) likely to provoke a backlash whose consequences were even worse than the status quo. Indeed, under some circumstances it might have been politically prudent to accept some racially oppressive measures in order to avoid still harsher ones later on. These are always difficult questions to judge, but one cannot assume that such situations have never occurred. But it was surely important then, as it is now, to distinguish between a necessary tactical concession to a deep-seated and powerful prejudice and a legitimate defense of an important and honorable value.

Despite his theoretical strictures, Sidgwick himself frequently distinguished between moral ideals and the moral realities of his age, precisely in discussions of the nation-state. The truly ideal political order, he argued, would be a world government capable of preventing war. Unfortunately, he said, people do not have a sufficiently developed consciousness of their common humanity to make that ideal politically possible.

[26] Teitelbaum, "Right versus Right," pp. 44, 48, 52, and 56.

[27] "Peter Rodino Rides to the Rescue," July 21, 1985, p. 20E.

The nation-state was the dominant ideal of the age, and any attempt to move beyond it under those circumstances would have been futile.[28]

It would be equally futile today. Nationalism remains the dominant political ideology of our time. Occasionally—and especially in times of crisis (famine, earthquake)—peoples' sympathetic identification with others reaches beyond the borders of the nation-state. For the most part, however, it is within the nation-state, and sometimes even more strongly within subunits of the state, that people see themselves as members of a community. We should recognize that reality in any discussion of immigration policy. But in discussing political theory we should also address the question of whether we should embrace that reality as an ideal or regard it as a limitation eventually to be transcended. I do not claim to have answered that question fully here, but I have attempted to show that a commitment to the welfare state is not a sufficient moral reason for limiting immigration.

[28] Henry Sidgwick, *The Elements of Politics* (London: Macmillan, 1891), pp. 209–10.

10

The Patriarchal Welfare State

CAROLE PATEMAN

According to Raymond Williams's *Keywords*, "the Welfare State, in distinction from the Warfare State, was first named in 1939."[1] The welfare state was set apart from the fascist warfare state, defeated in the Second World War, and so the welfare state was identified with democracy at the christening. In the 1980s most Western welfare states are also warfare states, but this is not ordinarily seen as compromising their democratic character. Rather, the extent of democracy is usually taken to hinge on the *class* structure. Welfare provides a social wage for the working class, and the positive, social democratic view is that the welfare state gives social meaning and equal worth to the formal juridical and political rights of all citizens. A less positive view of the welfare state is that it provides governments with new means of exercising power over and controlling working-class citizens. But proponents of both views usually fail to acknowledge the sexually divided way in which the welfare state has been constructed. Nor do most democratic theorists recognize the *patriarchal* structure of the welfare state; the very different way that women and men have been incorporated as citizens is rarely seen to be of significance for democracy.[2] Even the fact that the earliest developments of the welfare state took place when women were still denied, or had only just won, citizenship in the national state is usually overlooked.[3]

I am grateful to Amy Gutmann and Michael Walzer, and especially to Joan Scott and Theda Skocpol, for their comments on and criticisms of a draft of this paper. I was also helped in thinking about this subject by conversations with Nancy Fraser, Wendy Sarvasy, and Birte Siim at Stanford, 1984–1985.

[1] R. Williams, *Keywords: A Vocabulary of Culture and Society*, rev. ed. (New York: Oxford University Press, 1985), p. 333.

[2] I will present a theoretical elaboration of a modern conception of "patriarchy" as the systematic exercise by men of power over women in *The Sexual Contract* (Polity Press, forthcoming). For a brief discussion of some of the issues, see C. Pateman, "The Fraternal Social Contract," in J. Keane, ed., *The Rediscovery of Civil Society* (London and New York: Verso, forthcoming).

[3] Women were formally enfranchised as citizens in 1902 in Australia, 1920 in the United

I do not want to dispute the crucial importance of class in understanding the welfare state and democracy. To write about the welfare state is, in large part, to write about the working class. However, my discussion treats class in a manner unfamiliar to most democratic theorists, who usually assume that the welfare state, democracy, and class can be discussed theoretically without any attention to the character of the relation between the sexes. I shall suggest some reasons why and how the patriarchal structure of the welfare state has been repressed from theoretical consciousness. I shall also consider the connection between employment and citizenship in the patriarchal welfare state, the manner in which "women" have been opposed to the "worker" and the "citizen," and a central paradox surrounding women, welfare, and citizenship. By "the welfare state" here, I refer to the states of Britain (from which I shall draw a number of my empirical and historical examples), Australia, and the United States. In the more developed welfare states of Scandinavia, women have moved nearer to, but have not yet achieved, full citizenship.[4]

For the past century, many welfare policies have been concerned with what are now called "women's issues." Moreover, much of the controversy about the welfare state has revolved and continues to revolve around the question of the respective social places and tasks of women and men, the structure of marriage, and the power relationship between husband and wife. So it is not surprising that the Reagan administration's attack on the welfare state has been seen as prompted by a desire to shore up the patriarchal structure of the state; the Reagan budgets, "in essence, . . . try to restabilize patriarchy . . . as much as they try to fight inflation and stabilize capitalism."[5] The difficulties of understanding the welfare state and citizenship today without taking the position of women into account are not hard to illustrate, because contemporary feminists have produced a large body of evidence and argument that reveals the importance of women in the welfare state and the importance of the welfare state for women.

Women are now the majority of recipients of many welfare benefits. In 1980 in the United States for example, 64.8 percent of the recipients of Medicare were women, while 70 percent of housing subsidies went to

States, and 1928 in Britain (womanhood franchise in 1918 was limited to women over thirty).

[4] On Scandinavia see, e.g., H. Holter, ed., *Patriarchy in a Welfare Society* (Oslo: Universitetsforlaget, 1984), especially H. Hernes, "Women and the Welfare State: The Transition from Private to Public Dependence"; and E. Haavio-Mannila et al., eds., *Unfinished Democracy: Women in Nordic Politics* (Oxford and New York: Pergamon Press, 1985).

[5] Z. Eisenstein, *Feminism and Sexual Equality* (New York: Monthly Review Press, 1984), p. 125.

women, either living alone or heading households;[6] and by 1979, 80 percent of the families receiving Aid to Families with Dependent Children were headed by women (the number of such families having grown fourfold between 1961 and 1979).[7] A major reason why women are so prominent as welfare recipients is that women are more likely than men to be poor (a fact that has come to be known as "the feminization of poverty"). In the United States, between 1969 and 1979, there was a decline in the proportion of families headed by men that fell below the official poverty line while the proportion headed by women grew rapidly.[8] By 1982 about one-fifth of families with minor children were headed by women, but they constituted 53 percent of all poor families,[9] and female heads were over three times as likely as male heads to have incomes below the poverty line.[10] By 1980 two out of every three adults whose incomes were below the poverty line were women. The National Advisory Council on Economic Opportunity reported in 1980 that, if these trends continued, the entire population of the poor in the United States would be composed of women and children by the year 2000.[11] In Australia women are also likely to be poor. A survey for the Commission of Inquiry into Poverty in 1973 found that, of the groups with "disabilities," fatherless families were poorest; 30 percent of such families were below the poverty line, and another 20 percent only marginally above it.[12] Nor had the situation improved by 1978–1979: 41 percent of women who were single parents were then below the poverty line.[13]

[6] B. Nelson, "Women's Poverty and Women's Citizenship: Some Political Consequences of Economic Marginality," *Signs* 10, no. 2 (1984): 221.

[7] S. Erie, M. Rein, and B. Wiget, "Women and the Reagan Revolution: Thermidor for the Social Welfare Economy," in I. Diamond, ed., *Families, Politics and Public Policy: A Feminist Dialogue on Women and the State* (New York: Longman, 1983), p. 96.

[8] Ibid., p. 100.

[9] S. Kamerman, "Women, Children and Poverty: Public Policies and Female-Headed Families in Industrialized Countries," *Signs* 10, no. 2 (1984): 250.

[10] J. Smith, "The Paradox of Women's Poverty: Wage-Earning Women and Economic Transformation," *Signs* 10, no. 2 (1984): 291.

[11] B. Ehrenreich and F. Fox Piven, "The Feminization of Poverty," *Dissent* (Spring 1984), p. 162.

[12] L. Bryson, "Women as Welfare Recipients: Women, Poverty, and the State," in C. Baldock and B. Cass, eds., *Women, Social Welfare, and the State* (Sydney: Allen and Unwin, 1983), p. 135.

[13] B. Cass, "Rewards for Women's Work," in J. Goodnow and C. Pateman, eds., *Women, Social Science and Public Policy* (Sydney: Allen and Unwin, 1985), p. 92. Cass also notes that women and their children were overrepresented among the poor making claims on colonial and postcolonial charities in Australia (p. 70). Similarly, in Britain, from 1834 during the whole period of the New Poor Law, the majority of recipients of relief were women, and they were especially prominent among the very poor. See D. Groves, "Members and Survivors: Women and Retirement Pensions Legislation," in J. Lewis, ed., *Women's Welfare Women's Rights* (London and Canberra: Croom Helm, 1983), p. 40.

The welfare state is now a major source of employment for women. For instance, in Britain the National Health Service is the biggest single employer of women in the country; about three-quarters of NHS employees, and 90 percent of NHS nurses, are women.[14] In 1981 there were more than five million jobs in the public health, education, and welfare sector in Britain (an increase of two million from 1961) and three-fifths of these jobs were held by women.[15] In the United States in 1980 women occupied 70 percent of the jobs at all levels of government concerned with social services, which was a quarter of all female employment and about half of all professional jobs occupied by women. Employment is provided largely at state and local levels in the United States. The federal government subsidizes the warfare state where there are few jobs for women; only 0.5 percent of the female work force is employed on military contracts. One estimate is that, for each billion dollar increase in the military budget, 9,500 jobs are lost to women in social welfare or the private sector.[16]

Women are also involved in the welfare state in less obvious ways. Negotiations (and confrontations) with welfare-state officials on a day-to-day basis are usually conducted by women; and it is mothers, not fathers, who typically pay the rent, deal with social workers, take children to welfare clinics, and so forth. Women are also frequently in the forefront of political campaigns and actions to improve welfare services or the treatment of welfare claimants. The services and benefits provided by the welfare state are far from comprehensive and, in the absence of public provision, much of the work involved, for example, in caring for the aged in all three countries is undertaken by women in their homes (something to which I shall return).

Finally, to put the previous points into perspective, there is one area of the welfare state from which women have been largely excluded. The legislation, policy-making, and higher-level administration of the welfare state have been and remain predominantly in men's hands. Some progress has been made; in Australia the Office of the Status of Women within the (Commonwealth) Department of Prime Minister and Cabinet monitors cabinet submissions, and the Women's Budget Program requires all departments to make a detailed assessment of the impact of their policies on women.

[14] L. Doyal, "Women and the National Health Service: The Carers and the Careless," in E. Lewin and V. Olesen, eds., *Women, Health, and Healing* (London: Tavistock, 1985), p. 237, p. 253.

[15] H. Land, "Beggers Can't Be Choosers," *New Statesman* (May 17, 1985), p. 8.

[16] Ehrenreich and Fox Piven, "The Feminization of Poverty," p. 165; also Erie et al., "Women and the Reagan Revolution" pp. 100–103.

Hegel's Two Dilemmas

To gain some insight into why the welfare state can still be discusssed without taking account of these factors, it is useful to begin by looking at Donald Moon's account (Chapter 2 in this volume) of the welfare state as a response to "Hegel's dilemma." Hegel was the first political theorist to set out the moral dilemma that arises when citizenship is undermined by the operation of the capitalist market. The market leaves some citizens bereft of the resources for social participation and so, as Moon states, as "undeserved exiles from society." Citizens thrown into poverty lack both the means for self-respect and the means to be recognized by fellow citizens as of equal worth to themselves, a recognition basic to democracy. Poverty-stricken individuals are not and—unless the outcome of participation in the market is offset in some way, cannot be—full citizens. The moral basis of the welfare state lies in the provision of resources for what T. H. Marshall called the "social rights" of democratic citizenship. For Moon, then, Hegel's dilemma is concerned with the manner in which the participation of some individuals as workers in the capitalist economy (or, in Hegel's terminology, in the sphere of civil society) can make a mockery of their formal status as equal citizens. In contemporary terms, it is a problem of class or, more exactly, now that mass unemployment could well be a permanent feature of capitalist economies, a problem of an underclass of unemployed social exiles. There is no doubt that this is an important problem, but Moon's reading of Hegel focuses on only *part* of the dilemma with which Hegel was faced.

In addition to the category of citizens who become social exiles through the accident that they can find no one to buy their labor-power at a living wage, Hegel also had to deal with a category of beings who are exiles because they are *incapable* of being incorporated into civil society and citizenship. According to Hegel—and to almost all the modern theorists who are admitted to the "tradition of Western political philosophy"—women naturally lack the attributes and capacities of the "individuals" who can enter civil society, sell their labor-power and become citizens.[17] Women, Hegel held, are natural social exiles. Hegel therefore had to find an answer to *two* dilemmas, and his theory gives a moral basis to both class division and sexual division. The welfare state could not provide a solution to the problem of women. Hegel's response was simultaneously to reaffirm the necessity of women's exile and to incorporate them into the state. Women are not incorporated as citizens like men, but as mem-

[17] For examples see T. Brennan and C. Pateman, " 'Mere Auxiliaries to the Commonwealth': Women and the Origins of Liberalism," *Political Studies* 27 (1979): 183–200; and C. Pateman, " 'The Disorder of Women': Women, Love, and the Sense of Justice," *Ethics* 91 (1980): 20–34.

bers of the family, a sphere separate from (or in social exile from) civil society and the state. The family is essential to civil society and the state, but it is constituted on a different basis from the rest of conventional social life, having its own ascriptive principles of association.

Women have now won the formal status of citizens, and their contemporary social position may seem a long way removed from that prescribed by Hegel. But Hegel's theory is still very relevant to the problem of patriarchy and the welfare state, although most contemporary political theorists usually look only at the relation between civil society and the state, or the intervention that the public power (state) may make in the private sphere (economy or class system). This view of "public" and "private" assumes that two of Hegel's categories (civil society and state) can be understood in the absence of the third (family). Yet Hegel's theory presupposes that family/civil society/state are comprehensible only in *relation* to each other—and then civil society and the state become "public" in contrast to the "private" family.

Hegel's social order contains a double separation of the private and public: the *class* division between civil society and the state (between economic man and citizen, between private enterprise and the public power); and the *patriarchal* separation between the private family and the public world of civil society/state. Moreover, the public character of the sphere of civil society/state is constructed and gains its meaning through what it excludes—the private association of the family. The patriarchal division between public and private *is also a sexual division.* Women, naturally lacking the capacities for public participation, remain within an association constituted by love, ties of blood, natural subjection, and particularity, and in which they are governed by men. The public world of universal citizenship is an association of free and equal individuals, a sphere of property, rights, and contract—and of men, who interact as formally equal citizens.

The widely held belief that the basic structure of our society rests on the separation of the private, familial sphere from the public world of the state and its policies is both true and false. It is true that the private sphere has been seen as women's proper place. Women have never in reality been completely excluded from the public world, but the policies of the welfare state have helped ensure that women's day-to-day experience confirms the separation of private and public existence. The belief is false in that, since the early twentieth century, welfare policies have reached across from public to private and helped uphold a patriarchal structure of familial life. Moreover, the two spheres are linked because men have always had a legitimate place in both. Men have been seen both as heads of families—and as husbands and fathers they have had socially and legally sanctioned power over their wives and children—and as participants in public life. Indeed, the "natural" masculine capacities that enable them, but not their wives, to be heads of families are the same capacities that enable them, but not their wives, to take their place in civil life.

Moon's interpretation of Hegel illustrates the continuing strength of Hegel's patriarchal construction of citizenship, which is assumed to be universal or democratic citizenship. The exiles from society who need the welfare state to give moral worth to their citizenship are male workers. Hegel showed deep insight here. Paid employment has become the key to citizenship, and the recognition of an individual as a citizen of equal worth to other citizens is lacking when a worker is unemployed. The history of the welfare state and citizenship (and the manner in which they have been theorized) is bound up with the history of the development of "employment societies."[18] In the early part of the nineteenth century, most workers were still not fully incorporated into the labor market; they typically worked at a variety of occupations, worked on a seasonal basis, gained part of their subsistence outside the capitalist market, and enjoyed "Saint Monday." By the 1880s full employment had become an ideal, unemployment a major social issue, and loud demands were heard for state-supported social reform (and arguments made against state action to promote welfare).[19] But who was included under the banner of "full employment"? What was the status of those "natural" social exiles seen as properly having no part in the employment society? Despite many changes in the social standing of women, we are not so far as we might like to think from Hegel's statement that the husband, as head, "has the prerogative to go out and work for [the family's] living, to attend to its needs, and to control and administer its capital."[20]

The political significance of the sexual division of labor is ignored by most democratic theorists. They treat the public world of paid employment and citizenship as if it can be divorced from its connection to the private sphere, and so the masculine character of the public sphere has been repressed. For example, T. H. Marshall first presented his influential account of citizenship in 1949, at the height of the optimism in Britain about the contribution of the new welfare state policies to social change—but also at the time (as I shall show) when women were being confirmed as lesser citizens in the welfare state. Marshall states that "citizenship is a status bestowed on those who are full members of a community,"[21] and

[18] I have taken the term from J. Keane and J. Owens, *After Full Employment* (London: Hutchinson, 1986), p. 11.

[19] Ibid., pp. 15–18, 89–90.

[20] G.W.F. Hegel, *Philosophy of Right*, trans. T. M. Knox (Oxford: Clarendon Press, 1952), sec. 171.

[21] T. H. Marshall, "Citizenship and Social Class," reprinted in D. Held et al., eds., *States and Societies* (New York: New York University Press, 1983), p. 253.

most contemporary academic discussions of citizenship do not question this statement. But, as shown graphically and brutally by the history of blacks in the United States, this is not the case. The formal status of citizen can be bestowed on, or won by, a category of people who are still denied full social membership.

Marshall noted that the Factory Acts in the nineteenth century "protected" women workers, and he attributes the protection to their lack of citizenship. But he does not consider "protection"—the polite way to refer to subordination—of women in the private sphere or ask how it is related to the sexual division of labor in the capitalist economy and citizenship. Nor does the "in some important respects peculiar" civil status of married women in the nineteenth century inhibit his confidence in maintaining, despite the limited franchise, "that in the nineteenth century citizenship in the form of civil rights was universal," and that, in economic life, "the basic civil right is the right to work." Marshall sees the aim of the "social rights" of the welfare state as "class-abatement": this is "no longer merely an attempt to abate the obvious nuisance of destitution in the lowest ranks of society. . . . It is no longer content to raise the floor-level in the basement of the social edifice, . . . it has begun to remodel the whole building."[22] But the question that has to be asked is, are women in the building or in a separate annex?

Citizenship and Employment

Theoretically and historically, the central criterion for citizenship has been "independence," and the elements encompassed under the heading of independence have been based on masculine attributes and abilities. Men, but not women, have been seen as possessing the capacities required of "individuals," "workers," and "citizens." As a corollary, the meaning of "dependence" is associated with all that is womanly—and women's citizenship in the welfare state is full of paradoxes and contradictions. To use Marshall's metaphor, women are identified as trespassers into the public edifice of civil society and the state. Three elements of "independence" are particularly important for present purposes, all related to the masculine capacity for self-protection: the capacity to bear arms, the capacity to own property, and the capacity for self-government.

First, women are held to lack the capacity for self-protection; they have been "unilaterally disarmed."[23] The protection of women is undertaken by men, but physical safety is a fundamental aspect of women's welfare

[22] Ibid., pp. 250–51, 257.

[23] The graphic phrase is Judith Stiehm's, in "Myths Necessary to the Pursuit of War" (paper), p. 11.

that has been sadly neglected in the welfare state. From the nineteenth century, feminists (including J. S. Mill) have drawn attention to the impunity with which husbands could use physical force against their wives,[24] but women/wives still find it hard to obtain proper social and legal protection against violence from their male "protectors." Defense of the state (or the ability to protect your protection, as Hobbes put it), the ultimate test of citizenship, is also a masculine prerogative. The anti-suffragists in both America and Britain made a great deal of the alleged inability and unwillingness of women to use armed force, and the issue of women and combat duties in the military forces of the warfare state was also prominent in the recent campaign against the Equal Rights Amendment in the United States. Although women are now admitted into the armed forces and so into training useful for later civilian employment, they are prohibited from combat duties in Britain, Australia, and the United States. Moreover, past exclusion of women from the warfare state has meant that welfare provision for veterans has also benefited men. In Australia and the United States, because of their special "contribution" as citizens, veterans have had their own, separately administered welfare state, which has ranged from preference in university education (the GI bills in the United States) to their own medical benefits and hospital services, and (in Australia) preferential employment in the public service.

In the "democratic" welfare state, however, employment rather than military service is the key to citizenship. The masculine "protective" capacity now enters into citizenship primarily through the second and third dimensions of independence. Men, but not women, have also been seen as property owners. Only some men own material property, but as "individuals," all men own (and can protect) the property they possess in their persons. Their status as "workers" depends on their capacity to contract out the property they own in their labor-power. Women are still not fully recognized socially as such property owners. To be sure, our position has improved dramatically from the mid-nineteenth century when women as wives had a very "peculiar" position as the legal property of their husbands, and feminists compared wives to slaves. But, today, a wife's person is still the property of her husband in one vital respect. Despite recent legal reform, in Britain and in some of the states of the United States and Australia, rape is still deemed legally impossible within marriage, and thus a wife's consent has no meaning. Yet women are now formally citizens in states held to be based on the necessary consent of

[24] See especially F. Cobbe, "Wife Torture in England," *Contemporary Review* 32 (1878): 55–87. Also, for example, Mill's remarks when introducing the amendment to enfranchise women in the House of Commons in 1867, reprinted in S. Bell and K. Offen, eds., *Women, the Family, and Freedom: The Debate in Documents*, (Stanford: Stanford University Press, 1983), 1: 487.

self-governing individuals.[25] The profound contradiction about women's consent is rarely if ever noticed and so is not seen as related to a sexually divided citizenship or as detracting from the claim of the welfare state to be democratic.

The third dimension of "independence" is self-government. Men have been constituted as the beings who can govern (or protect) themselves, and if a man can govern himself, then he also has the requisite capacity to govern others. Only a few men govern others in public life—but all men govern in private as husbands and heads of households. As the governor of a family, a man is also a "breadwinner." He has the capacity to sell his labor-power as a worker, or to buy labor-power with his capital, and provide for his wife and family. His wife is thus "protected." The category of "breadwinner" presupposes that wives are constituted as economic dependents or "housewives," which places them in a subordinate position. The dichotomy breadwinner/housewife, and the masculine meaning of independence, were established in Britain by the middle of the last century; in the earlier period of capitalist development, women (and children) were wage-laborers. A "worker" became a man who has an economically dependent wife to take care of his daily needs and look after his home and children. Moreover, "class," too, is constructed as a patriarchal category. "The working class" is the class of working *men*, who are also full citizens in the welfare state.

This observation brings me back to Marshall's statement about the universal, civil right to "work," that is to paid employment. The democratic implications of the right to work cannot be understood without attention to the connections between the public world of "work" and citizenship and the private world of conjugal relations. What it means to be a "worker" depends in part on men's status and power as husbands, and on their standing as citizens in the welfare state. The construction of the male worker as "breadwinner" and his wife as his "dependent" was expressed officially in the Census classifications in Britain and Australia. In the British Census of 1851, women employed in unpaid domestic work were "placed . . . in one of the productive classes along with paid work of a similar kind."[26] This classification changed after 1871, and by 1911 unpaid housewives had been completely removed from the economically active population. In Australia an initial conflict over the categories of classification was resolved in 1890 when the scheme devised in New South Wales was adopted. The Australians divided up the population

[25] For more detail, see my "Women and Consent," *Political Theory* 8, no. 2 (1980): 149–68.

[26] D. Deacon, "Political Arithmetic: The Nineteenth-Century Australian Census and the Construction of the Dependent Woman," *Signs* 11, no. 1 (1985): 31 (my discussion draws on Deacon); also H. Land, "The Family Wage," *Feminist Review* 6 (1980): 60.

more decisively than the British, and the 1891 Census was based on the two categories of "breadwinner" and "dependent." Unless explicitly stated otherwise, women's occupation was classified as domestic, and domestic workers were put in the dependent category.

The position of men as breadwinner-workers has been built into the welfare state. The sexual divisions in the welfare state have received much less attention than the persistence of the old dichotomy between the deserving and undeserving poor, which predates the welfare state. This is particularly clear in the United States, where a sharp separation is maintained between "social security," or welfare-state policies directed at "deserving workers who have paid for them through 'contributions' over their working lifetimes," and "welfare"—seen as public "handouts" to "barely deserving poor people."[27] Although "welfare" does not have this stark meaning in Britain or Australia, where the welfare state encompasses much more than most Americans seem able to envisage, the old distinction between the deserving and undeserving poor is still alive and kicking, illustrated by the popular bogey-figures of the "scrounger" (Britain) and the "dole-bludger" (Australia). However, although the dichotomy of deserving/undeserving poor overlaps with the divisions between husband/wife and worker/housewife to some extent, it also obscures the patriarchal structure of the welfare state.

Feminist analyses have shown how many welfare provisions have been established within a two-tier system. First, there are the benefits available to individuals as "public" persons by virtue of their participation, and accidents of fortune, in the capitalist market. Benefits in this tier of the system are usually claimed by men. Second, benefits are available to the "dependents" of individuals in the first category, or to "private" persons, usually women. In the United States, for example, men are the majority of "deserving" workers who receive benefits through the insurance system to which they have "contributed" out of their earnings. On the other hand, the majority of claimants in means-tested programs are women—and women who are usually making their claims as wives or mothers. This is clearly the case with AFDC, where women are aided because they are mothers supporting children on their own, but the same is also true in other programs: "46 percent of the women receiving Social Security benefits make their claims as wives." In contrast, "men, even poor men, rarely make claims for benefits solely as husbands or fathers."[28] In Australia the division is perhaps even more sharply defined. In 1980–1981, in the primary tier of the system, in which benefits are employment-re-

[27] T. Skocpol, "The Limits of the New Deal System and the Roots of Contemporary Welfare Dilemmas," in M. Weir, A. Orloff, and T. Skocpol, eds., *The Politics of Social Policy in the United States* (Princeton: Princeton University Press, 1988).

[28] Nelson, "Women's Poverty and Women's Citizenship," pp. 222–23.

lated and claimed by those who are expected to be economically independent but are not earning an income because of unemployment or illness, women formed only 31.3 percent of claimants. In contrast, in the "dependents group," 73.3 percent of claimants were women, who were eligible for benefits because "they are dependent on a man who could not support them, . . . [or] should have had a man support them if he had not died, divorced or deserted them."[29]

Such evidence of lack of "protection" raises an important question about *women's* standard of living in the welfare state. As dependents, married women should derive their subsistence from their husbands, so that wives are placed in the position of all dependent people before the establishment of the welfare state; they are reliant on the benevolence of another for their livelihood. The assumption is generally made that all husbands are benevolent. Wives are assumed to share equally in the standard of living of their husbands. The distribution of income *within* households has not usually been a subject of interest to economists, political theorists, or protagonists in arguments about class and the welfare state—even though William Thompson drew attention to its importance as long ago as 1825[30]—but past and present evidence indicates that the belief that all husbands are benevolent is mistaken.[31] Nevertheless, women are likely to be better off married than if their marriage fails. One reason why women figure so prominently among the poor is that after divorce, as recent evidence from the United States reveals, a woman's

[29] M. Owen, "Women—A Wastefully Exploited Resource," *Search* 15 (1984): pp. 271–72.

[30] Thompson was a utilitarian, but also a feminist, cooperative socialist, so that he took his individualism more seriously than most utilitarians. In *Appeal of One Half the Human Race, Women, Against the Pretensions of the Other Half, Men, to Retain Them in Political, and thence in Civil and Domestic Slavery* (New York: Source Book Press, 1970 [first published in 1825]), Thompson, writing of the importance of looking at the distribution of interests, or "the means of happiness," argues that the "division of interests" must proceed "until it is brought home to every *individual* of every family." Instead, under the despotism of husbands and fathers, "the interest of each of them is promoted, in as far only as it is coincident with, or subservient to, the master's interest" (pp. 46–47, 49).

[31] As Beatrix Campbell has reminded us, "we protect men from the shame of their participation in women's poverty by keeping the secret. Family budgets are seen to be a *private* settlement of accounts between men and women, men's unequal distribution of working-class incomes within their households is a right they fought for within the working-class movement and it is not yet susceptible to *public* political pressure within the movement" (*Wigan Pier Revisited: Poverty and Politics in the 80s* [London: Virago Press, 1984], p. 57). Wives are usually responsible for making sure that the children are fed, the rent paid, and so on, but this does not mean that they always decide how much money is allocated to take care of these basic needs. Moreover, in times of economic hardship women are often short of food as well as money; wives will make sure that the "breadwinner" and the children are fed before they are.

standard of living can fall by nearly 75 percent, whereas a man's can rise by nearly half.[32]

The conventional understanding of the "wage" also suggests that there is no need to investigate women's standard of living independently from men's. The concept of the wage has expressed and encapsulated the patriarchal separation and integration of the public world of employment and the private sphere of conjugal relations. In arguments about the welfare state and the social wage, the wage is usually treated as a return for the sale of *individuals'* labor-power. However, once the opposition breadwinner/housewife was consolidated, a "wage" had to provide subsistence for several people. The struggle between capital and labor and the controversy about the welfare state have been about the *family wage*. A "living wage" has been defined as what is required for a worker as breadwinner to support a wife and family, rather than what is needed to support himself; the wage is not what is sufficient to reproduce the worker's own labor power, but what is sufficient, in combination with the unpaid work of the housewife, to reproduce the labor-power of the present and future labor force.

The designer of the Australian Census classification system, T. A. Coghlan, discussed women's employment in his *Report* on the 1891 Census, and he argued that married women in the paid labor market depressed men's wages and thus lowered the general standard of living.[33] His line of argument about women's employment has been used by the trade union movement for the past century in support of bargaining to secure a family wage. In 1909 motions were put to the conferences of Labour party and Trades Union Congress in Britain to ban the employment of wives altogether, and as recently as 1982 a defense of the family wage was published arguing that it strengthens unions in wage negotiation.[34] In 1907 the family wage was enshrined in law in Australia in the famous Harvester Judgment in the Commonwealth Arbitration Court. Justice Higgins ruled in favor of a legally guaranteed minimum wage—and laid down that a living wage should be sufficient to keep an unskilled worker, his (dependent) wife, and three children in reasonable comfort.

Of course, a great deal has changed since 1907. Structural changes in capitalism have made it possible for large numbers of married women to enter paid employment, and equal-pay legislation in the 1970s, which in principle, recognizes the wage as payment to an individual, may make it seem that the family wage has had its day. And it was always a myth for

[32] L. J. Weitzman, *The Divorce Revolution* (New York: Free Press, 1985), chap. 10, especially pp. 337–40.

[33] Deacon, "Political Arithmetic" p. 39.

[34] Cited in A. Phillips, *Hidden Hands: Women and Economic Policies* (London: Pluto Press, 1983), p. 76.

many, perhaps most, working-class families.[35] Despite the strength of the social ideal of the dependent wife, many working-class wives have always been engaged in paid work out of necessity. The family could not survive on the husband's wage, and the wife had to earn money, too, whether as a wage-worker, or at home doing outwork, or taking in laundry or lodgers, or participating in other ways in the "informal" economy. In 1976 in Britain the wages and salaries of "heads of household" (not all of whom are men) formed only 51 percent of household income.[36] The decline of manufacturing and the expansion of the service sector of capitalist economies since the Second World War have created jobs seen as "suitable" for women. Between 1970 and 1980 in the United States over 13 million women entered the paid labor force.[37] In Britain, if present trends in male and female employment continue, women employees will outnumber men in less than ten years.[38] Nevertheless, even these dramatic shifts have not been sufficient to make women full members of the employment society. The civil right to "work" is still only halfheartedly acknowledged for women. Women in the workplace are still perceived primarily as wives and mothers, not workers.[39] The view is also widespread that women's wages are a "supplement" to those of the breadwinner. Women, it is held, do not need wages in the same way that men do—so they may legitimately be paid less than men.

When the Commonwealth Arbitration Court legislated for the family wage, 45 percent of the male work force in Australia were single.[40] Yet in 1912 (in a case involving fruit pickers) Justice Higgins ruled that a job normally done by women could be paid at less than a man's rate because women were not responsible for dependents. On the contrary, while many men received a family wage and had no families, and breadwinners were given the power to determine whether their dependents should share in their standard of living, many women were struggling to provide for dependents on a "dependent's" wage. Eleanor Rathbone estimated that before and just after the Great War in Britain a third of women in paid employment were wholly or partially responsible for supporting depend-

[35] See M. Barrett and M. McIntosh, "The 'Family Wage': Some Problems for Socialists and Feminists," *Capital and Class* 11 (1980): 56–59.

[36] Ibid., p. 58.

[37] Smith, "The Paradox of Women's Poverty," p. 300.

[38] A. Phillips, *Hidden Hands*, p. 21.

[39] The perception is common to both women and men. (I would argue that women's perception of themselves is not, as is often suggested, a consequence of "socialization," but a realistic appraisal of their structural position at home and in the workplace.) For empirical evidence on this view of women workers see, e.g., A. Pollert, *Girls, Wives, Factory Lives* (London: Macmillan, 1981), and J. Wacjman, *Women in Control: Dilemmas of a Workers' Cooperative* (New York: St. Martin"s Press, 1983).

[40] C. Baldock, "Public Policies and the Paid Work of Women," in Baldock and Cass, *Women, Social Welfare, and the State*, pp. 34, 40.

ents.[41] About the same proportion of women breadwinners was found in a survey of Victorian manufacturing industries in Australia in 1928.[42] Nevertheless, the classification of women as men's dependents was the basis for a living wage for women, granted in New South Wales in 1918; lower wages for women were enshrined in law and (until a national minimum wage for both sexes was granted in 1974) were set at 50–54 percent of the male rate. Again in Britain, in the late 1960s and 1970s, the National Board for Prices and Incomes investigated low pay and argued that, as part-time workers, women did not depend on their own wage to support themselves.[43] In the United States, as recently as 1985, it was stated that "women have generally been paid less [than men] because they would work for lower wages, since they had no urgent need for more money. Either they were married, or single and living at home, or doubling up with friends."[44]

Women are prominent as welfare claimants because, today, it is usually women who are poor—and perhaps the major reason why women are poor is that it is very hard for most women to find a job that will pay a living wage. Equal-pay legislation cannot overcome the barrier of a sexually segregated occupational structure. Capitalist economies are patriarchal, divided into men's and women's occupations; the sexes do not usually work together, nor are they paid at the same rates for similar work. For example, in the United States, 80 percent of women's jobs are located in only 20 of the 420 occupations listed by the Department of Labor.[45] More than half of employed women work in occupations that are 75 percent female, and over 20 percent work in occupations that are 95 percent female.[46] In Australia in 1986, 59.5 percent of women employees worked in the occupational categories "clerical, sales and services." In only 69 out of 267 occupational categories did the proportion of women reach a third or more.[47] The segregation is very stable; in Britain, for example, 84 percent of women worked in occupations dominated by women in 1971, the same percentage as in 1951, and in 1901 the figure had been 88 percent.[48]

[41] Land, "The Family Wage," p. 62.

[42] B. Cass, "Redistribution to Children and to Mothers: A History of Child Endowment and Family Allowances," in Baldock and Cass, *Women, Social Welfare, and the State*, p. 62.

[43] Campbell, *Wigan Pier Revisited*, pp. 130–31.

[44] A. Hacker, " 'Welfare': The Future of an Illusion," *New York Review of Books* (February 28, 1985), p. 41.

[45] Ehrenreich and Fox Piven, "The Feminization of Poverty," p. 163.

[46] S. Hewlett, *A Lesser Life: The Myth of Women's Liberation in America* (New York: William Morrow, 1986), p. 76.

[47] Women's Bureau, Department of Employment and Industrial Relations, *Women at Work* (April 1986).

[48] I. Bruegel, "Women's Employment, Legislation, and the Labour Market," in Lewis, *Women's Welfare*, p. 133 and Table 7.4.

The economy is also vertically segregated. Most women's jobs are unskilled[49] and of low status; even in the professions women are clustered at the lower end of the occupational hierarchy. The British National Health Service provides a useful illustration. About one-third of employees are at the lowest level as ancillary workers, of whom around three-quarters are women. Their work is sex-segregated, so that the women workers perform catering and domestic tasks. As I noted previously, 90 percent of NHS nurses are female but about one quarter of senior nursing posts are held by men. At the prestigious levels, only about 10 percent of consultants are female and they are segregated into certain specialities, notably those relating to children (in 1977, 32.7 percent women).[50]

Many women also work part-time, either because of the requirements of their other (unpaid) work, or because they cannot find a full-time job. In Australia in 1986, 57.4 percent of all part-time employees were married women.[51] In Britain two out of every five women in the work force are employed for thirty hours or less. However, the hourly rate for full-time women workers was only 75.1 percent of men's in 1982 (and it is men who are likely to work overtime).[52] In 1980 women comprised 64 percent of the employees in the six lowest paid occupations.[53] During the 1970s women's earnings edged slightly upward compared to men's in most countries, but not in the United States. In 1984 the median of women's earnings as full-time workers over a full year was $14,479, while men earned $23,218.[54] The growth in the service sector in the United States has largely been growth in part-time work; in 1980 almost a quarter of all jobs in the private sector were part time. Almost all the new jobs appearing between 1970 and 1980 were in areas that paid less than average wages; in 1980 "51 percent [of women] held jobs paying less than 66 percent of a craft worker's wages."[55]

Women's Work and Welfare

Although so many women, including married women, are now in paid employment, women's standing as "workers" is still of precarious legitimacy. So, therefore, is their standing as democratic citizens. If an individ-

[49] "Skill" is another patriarchal category; it is men's work that counts as "skilled." See the discussion in C. Cockburn, *Brothers: Male Dominance and Technological Change* (London: Pluto Press, 1983), pp. 112–22.

[50] Doyal, "Women and the National Health Service," pp. 250–54; and A. Oakley, "Women and Health Policy," in Lewis, *Women's Welfare*, p. 120 and Table 6.3.

[51] *Women at Work.*

[52] Phillips, *Hidden Hands*, p. 15.

[53] Bruegel, "Women's Employment, Legislation and the Labour Market," p. 135.

[54] Hewlett, *A Lesser Life*, p. 72.

[55] Smith, "The Paradox of Women's Poverty," pp. 304, 307; the quotation, p. 306.

ual can gain recognition from other citizens as an equally worthy citizen only through participation in the capitalist market, if self-respect and respect as a citizen are "achieved" in the public world of the employment society, then women still lack the means to be recognized as worthy citizens. Nor have the policies of the welfare state provided women with many of the resources to gain respect as citizens. Marshall's social rights of citizenship in the welfare state could be extended to men without difficulty. As participants in the market, men could be seen as making a public contribution, and were in a position to be levied by the state to make a contribution more directly, that *entitled* them to the benefits of the welfare state. But how could women, dependents of men, whose legitimate "work" is held to be located in the private sphere, be citizens of the welfare state? What could, or did, women contribute? The paradoxical answer is that women contributed—welfare.

The development of the welfare state has presupposed that certain aspects of welfare could and should continue to be provided by women (wives) in the home, and not primarily through public provision. The "work" of a housewife can include the care of invalid husbands and elderly, perhaps infirm, relatives. Welfare-state policies have ensured in various ways that wives/women provide welfare services gratis, disguised as part of their responsibility for the private sphere. A good deal has been written about the fiscal crisis of the welfare state, but it would have been more acute if certain areas of welfare had not been seen as a private, women's matter. It is not surprising that the attack on public spending in the welfare state by the Thatcher and Reagan governments goes hand-in-hand with praise for loving care within families, that is, with an attempt to obtain ever more unpaid welfare from (house)wives. The Invalid Care Allowance in Britain is a particularly blatant example of the way in which the welfare state ensures that wives provide private welfare. The allowance was introduced in 1975—when the Sex Discrimination Act was also passed—and it is paid to men or to single women who relinquish paid employment to look after a sick, disabled, or elderly person (not necessarily a relative). Married women (or those cohabiting) are ineligible for the allowance.

The evidence indicates that it is likely to be married women who provide such care. In 1976 in Britain it was estimated that two million women were caring for adult relatives, and one survey in the north of England found that there were more people caring for adult relatives than mothers looking after children under sixteen.[56] A corollary of the assumption that women, but not men, care for others is that women must

[56] J. Dale and P. Foster, *Feminists and the Welfare State* (London: Routledge and Kegan Paul, 1986), p. 112.

also care for themselves. Investigations show that women living by themselves in Britain have to be more infirm than men to obtain the services of home helps, and a study of an old people's home found that frail, elderly women admitted with their husbands faced hostility from the staff because they had failed in their job.[57] Again, women's citizenship is full of contradictions and paradoxes. Women must provide welfare, and care for themselves, and so must be assumed to have the capacities necessary for these tasks. Yet the development of the welfare state has also presupposed that women necessarily are in need of protection by and are dependent on men.

The welfare state has reinforced women's identity as men's dependents both directly and indirectly, and so confirmed rather than ameliorated our social exile. For example, in Britain and Australia the cohabitation rule explicitly expresses the presumption that women necessarily must be economically dependent on men if they live with them as sexual partners. If cohabitation is ruled to take place, the woman loses her entitlement to welfare benefits. The consequence of the cohabitation rule is not only sexually divided control of citizens, but an exacerbation of the poverty and other problems that the welfare state is designed to alleviate. In Britain today,

> when a man lives in, a woman's independence—her own name on the weekly giro [welfare check] is automatically surrendered. The men become the claimants and the women their dependents. They lose control over both the revenue and the expenditure, often with catastrophic results: rent not paid, fuel bills missed, arrears mounting.[58]

It is important to ask what counts as part of the welfare state. In Australia and Britain the taxation system and transfer payments together form a tax-transfer system in the welfare state. In Australia a tax rebate is available for a dependent spouse (usually, of course, a wife), and in Britain the taxation system has always treated a wife's income as her husband's for taxation purposes. It is only relatively recently that it ceased to be the husband's prerogative to correspond with the Inland Revenue about his wife's earnings, or that he ceased to receive rebates due on her tax payments. Married men can still claim a tax allowance, based on the assumption that they support a dependent wife. Women's dependence is also enforced through the extremely limited public provision of child-care

[57] H. Land, "Who Cares for the Family?" *Journal of Social Policy* 7, no. 3 (1978): 268–69. Land notes that even under the old Poor Law twice as many women as men received outdoor relief, and there were many more old men than women in the workhouse wards for the ill or infirm; the women were deemed fit for the wards for the able-bodied.

[58] Campbell, *Wigan Pier Revisited*, p. 76.

facilities in Australia, Britain, and the United States, which creates a severe obstacle to women's full participation in the employment society. In all three countries, unlike Scandinavia, child care outside the home is a very controversial issue.

Welfare-state legislation has also been framed on the assumption that women make their "contribution" by providing private welfare, and, from the beginning, women were denied full citizenship in the welfare state. In America "originally the purpose of ADC (now AFDC) was to keep mothers out of the paid labor force. . . . In contrast, the Social Security retirement program was consciously structured to respond to the needs of white male workers."[59] In Britain the first national insurance, or contributory, scheme was set up in 1911, and one of its chief architects wrote later that women should have been completely excluded because "they want insurance for others, not themselves." Two years before the scheme was introduced, William Beveridge, the father of the contemporary British welfare state, stated in a book on unemployment that the "ideal [social] unit is the household of man, wife and children maintained by the earnings of the first alone. . . . Reasonable security of employment for the breadwinner is the basis of all private duties and all sound social action."[60] Nor had Beveridge changed his mind on this matter by the Second World War when his report, *Social Insurance and Allied Services*, appeared in 1942 and laid a major part of the foundation for the great reforms of the 1940s. In a passage now (in)famous among feminists, Beveridge wrote that "the great majority of married women must be regarded as occupied on work which is vital though unpaid, without which their husbands could not do their paid work and without which the nation could not continue."[61] In the National Insurance Act of 1946 wives were separated from their husbands for insurance purposes. (The significance of this procedure, along with Beveridge's statement, clearly was lost on T. H. Marshall when he was writing his essay on citizenship and the welfare state.) Under the act, married women paid lesser contributions for reduced benefits, but they could also opt out of the scheme, and so from sickness, unemployment, and maternity benefits, and they also lost entitlement to an old-age pension in their own right, being eligible only as their husband's dependent. By the time the legislation was amended in 1975, about three-quarters of married women workers had opted out.[62]

A different standard for men and women has also been applied in the operation of the insurance scheme. In 1911 some married women were insured in their own right. The scheme provided benefits in case of "in-

[59] Nelson, "Women's Poverty and Women's Citizenship," pp. 229–30.

[60] Both quotations are taken from Land, "The Family Wage," p. 72.

[61] Cited in Dale and Foster, *Feminists and the Welfare State*, p. 17.

[62] H. Land, "Who Still Cares for the Family?" in Lewis, *Welfare Women's Rights*, p. 70.

capacity to work," but, given that wives had already been identified as "incapacitated" for the "work" in question, for paid employment, problems over the criterion for entitlement to sickness benefits were almost inevitable. In 1913 an inquiry was held to discover why married women were claiming benefits at a much greater rate than expected. One obvious reason was that the health of many working-class women was extremely poor. The extent of their ill health was revealed in 1915 when letters written by working women in 1913–1914 to the Women's Cooperative Guild were published.[63] The national insurance scheme meant that for the first time women could afford to take time off work when ill—but from which "work"? Could they take time off from housework? What were the implications for the embryonic welfare state if they ceased to provide free welfare? From 1913 a dual standard of eligibility for benefits was established. For men the criterion was fitness for work. But the committee of inquiry decided that, if a woman could do her housework, she was not ill. So the criterion for eligibility for women was also fitness for work—but unpaid work in the private home, not paid work in the public market that was the basis for the contributory scheme under which the women were insured! This criterion for women was still being laid down in instructions issued by the Department of Health and Social Security in the 1970s.[64] The dual standard was further reinforced in 1975 when a non-contributory invalidity pension was introduced for those incapable of work, but not qualified for the contributory scheme. Men and single women are entitled to the pension if thay cannot engage in paid employment; the criterion for married women is ability to perform "normal household duties."[65]

Wollstonecraft's Dilemma

So far, I have looked at the patriarchal structure of the welfare state, but this is only part of the picture; the development of the welfare state has also brought challenges to patriarchal power and helped provide a basis for women's autonomous citizenship. Women have seen the welfare state as one of their major means of support. Well before women won formal citizenship, they campaigned for the state to make provision for welfare, especially for the welfare of women and their children; and women's organizations and women activists have continued their political activities around welfare issues, not least in opposition to their status as "dependents." In 1953 the British feminist Vera Brittain wrote of the wel-

[63] M. Davis, *Maternity: Letters from Working Women* (New York: Norton, 1978 [first published 1915]).

[64] Information taken from Land, "Who Still Cares for the Family?" pp. 263–64.

[65] Ibid., p. 73.

fare state established through the legislation of the 1940s that "in it women have become ends in themselves and not merely means to the ends of men," and their "unique value as women was recognised."[66] In hindsight, Brittain was clearly overoptimistic in her assessment, but perhaps the opportunity now exists to begin to dismantle the patriarchal structure of the welfare state. In the 1980s the large changes in women's social position, technological and structural transformations within capitalism, and mass unemployment mean that much of the basis for the breadwinner/dependent dichotomy and for the employment society itself is being eroded (although both are still widely seen as social ideals). The social context of Hegel's two dilemmas is disappearing. As the current concern about the "feminization of poverty" reveals, there is now a very visible underclass of women who are directly connected to the state as claimants, rather than indirectly as men's dependents. Their social exile is as apparent as that of poor male workers was to Hegel. Social change has now made it much harder to gloss over the paradoxes and contradictions of women's status as citizens.

However, the question of how women might become full citizens of a democratic welfare state is more complex than may appear at first sight, because it is only in the current wave of the organized feminist movement that the division between the private and public spheres of social life has become seen as a major *political* problem. From the 1860s to the 1960s women were active in the public sphere: women fought not only for welfare measures and for measures to secure the private and public safety of women and girls, but for the vote and civil equality; middle-class women fought for entry into higher education, and the professions and women trade unionists fought for decent working conditions and wages and maternity leave. But the contemporary liberal feminist view, particularly prominent in the United States, that what is required above all is "gender-neutral" laws and policies, was not widely shared.[67] In general, until the 1960s the focus of attention in the welfare state was on measures to ensure that women had proper social support, and hence proper social respect, in carrying out their responsibilities in the private sphere. The problem is whether and how such measures could assist women in their fight for full citizenship. In 1942 in Britain, for example, many women welcomed the passage in the Beveridge Report that I have cited because, it was argued, it gave official recognition to the value of women's unpaid

[66] Cited in Dale and Foster, *Feminists and the Welfare State*, p. 3.

[67] There was considerable controversy within the women's movement between the wars over the question of protective legislation for women in industry. Did equal citizenship require the removal of such protection, so that women worked under the same conditions as men; or did the legislation benefit women, and the real issue become proper health and safety protection for both men and women workers?

work. However, an official nod of recognition to women's work as "vital" to "the nation" is easily given; *in practice*, the value of the work in bringing women into full membership in the welfare state was negligible. The equal worth of citizenship and the respect of fellow citizens still depended on participation as paid employees. "Citizenship" and "work" stood then and still stand opposed to "women."

The extremely difficult problem faced by women in their attempt to win full citizenship I shall call "Wollstonecraft's dilemma." The dilemma is that the two routes toward citizenship that women have pursued are mutually incompatible within the confines of the patriarchal welfare state, and, within that context, they are impossible to achieve. For three centuries, since universal citizenship first appeared as a political ideal, women have continued to challenge their alleged natural subordination within private life. From at least the 1790s they have also struggled with the task of trying to become citizens within an ideal and practice that have gained universal meaning through their exclusion. Women's response has been complex. On the one hand, they have demanded that the ideal of citizenship be extended to them,[68] and the liberal feminist agenda for a "gender-neutral" social world is the logical conclusion of one form of this demand. On the other hand, women have also insisted, often simultaneously, as did Mary Wollstonecraft, that *as women* they have specific capacities, talents, needs, and concerns, so that the expression of their citizenship will be differentiated from that of men. Their unpaid work providing welfare could be seen, as Wollstonecraft saw women's tasks as mothers, as women's work *as citizens*, just as their husbands' paid work is central to men's citizenship.[69]

The patriarchal understanding of citizenship means that the two demands are incompatible because it allows two alternatives only: either women become (like) men, and so full citizens; or they continue at women's work, which is of no value for citizenship. Moreover, within a patriarchal welfare state neither demand can be met. To demand that citizenship, as it now exists, should be fully extended to women accepts the patriarchal meaning of "citizen," which is constructed from men's attributes, capacities, and activities. Women cannot be full citizens in the pres-

[68] I have discussed the earlier arguments in more detail in "Women and Democratic Citizenship," The Jefferson Memorial Lectures, University of California, Berkeley, 1985, Lecture 1.

[69] For example, Wollstonecraft writes, "speaking of women at large, their first duty is to themselves as rational creatures, and the next, in point of importance, as citizens, is that, which includes so many, of a mother." She hopes that a time will come when a "man must necessarily fulfill the duties of a citizen, or be despised, and that while he was employed in any of the departments of civil life, his wife, also an active citizen, should be equally intent to manage her family, educate her children, and assist her neighbours." *A Vindication of the Rights of Women* (New York: Norton, 1975), pp. 145, 146.

ent meaning of the term; at best, citizenship can be extended to women only as lesser men. At the same time, within the patriarchal welfare state, to demand proper social recognition and support for women's responsibilities is to condemn women to less than full citizenship and to continued incorporation into public life as "women," that is, as members of another sphere who cannot, therefore, earn the respect of fellow (male) citizens.

The example of child endowments or family allowances in Australia and Britain is instructive as a practical illustration of Wollstonecraft's dilemma. It reveals the great difficulties in trying to implement a policy that both aids women in their work and challenges patriarchal power while enhancing women's citizenship. In both countries there was opposition from the right and from laissez-faire economists on the ground that family allowances would undermine the father's obligation to support his children and undermine his "incentive" to sell his labor-power in the market. The feminist advocates of family allowances in the 1920s, most notably Eleanor Rathbone in Britain, saw the alleviation of poverty in families where the breadwinner's wage was inadequate to meet the family's basic needs as only one argument for this form of state provision. They were also greatly concerned with the questions of the wife's economic dependence and equal pay for men and women workers. If the upkeep of children (or a substantial contribution toward it) was met by the state outside of wage bargaining in the market, then there was no reason why men and women doing the same work should not receive the same pay. Rathbone wrote in 1924 that "nothing can justify the subordination of one group of producers—the mothers—to the rest and their deprivation of a share of their own in the wealth of a community."[70] She argued that family allowances would, "once and for all, cut away the maintenance of children and the reproduction of the race from the question of wages."[71]

But not all the advocates of child endowment were feminists—so that the policy could very easily be divorced from the public issue of wages and dependence and be seen only as a return for and recognition of women's private contribution. Supporters included the eugenicists and pronatalists, and family allowances appealed to capital and the state as a means of keeping wages down. Family allowances had many opponents in the British union movement, fearful that the consequence, were the measure

[70] Cited in Land, "The Family Wage," p. 63.

[71] Cited in Cass, "Redistribution to Children and to Mothers," p. 57. My discussion draws on Land and Cass. In the United States, during the same period, feminists supported the movement for mothers' pensions. Unlike mother eligible for family allowances, mothers eligible for pensions were without male breadwinners. The complexities of mothers' pensions are discussed by W. Sarvesy, "The Contradictory Legacy of the Feminist Welfare State Founders," paper presented to the annual meeting of the American Political Science Association, Washington, D.C., 1986.

introduced, would be to undermine the power of unions in wage bargaining. The opponents included women trade unionists who were suspicious of a policy that could be used to try to persuade women to leave paid employment. Some unionists also argued that social services, such as housing, education, and health, should be developed first, and the TUC adopted this view in 1930. But were the men concerned, too, with their private, patriarchal privileges? Rathbone claimed that "the leaders of working men are themselves subconsciously biased by prejudice of sex. . . . Are they not influenced by a secret reluctance to see their wives and children recognised as separate personalities?"[72]

By 1941 the supporters of family allowances in the union movement had won the day, and family allowances were introduced in 1946, as part of the government's wartime plans for postwar reconstruction. The legislation proposed that the allowance would be paid to the father as "normal household head," but after lobbying by women's organizations, this was overturned in a free vote, and the allowance was paid directly to mothers. In Australia the union movement accepted child endowment in the 1920s (child endowment was introduced in New South Wales in 1927, and at the Federal level in 1941). But union support there was based on wider redistributive policies, and the endowment was seen as a supplement to, not a way of breaking down, the family wage.[73] In the 1970s, in both countries, women's organizations again had to defend family allowances and the principle of redistribution from "the wallet to the purse."

The hope of Eleanor Rathbone and other feminists that family allowances would form part of a democratic restructuring of the wage system was not realized. Nevertheless, family allowances are paid to women as a benefit in their own right; in that sense they are an important (albeit financially very small) mark of recognition of married women as independent members of the welfare state. Yet the allowance is paid to women as *mothers*, and the key question is thus whether the payment to a mother—a private person—negates her standing as an independent member of the welfare state. More generally, the question is whether there can be a welfare policy that gives substantial assistance to women in their daily lives *and* helps create the conditions for a genuine democracy in which women are autonomous citizens, in which we can act *as women* and not as "woman" (protected/dependent/subordinate) constructed as the opposite to all that is meant by "man." That is to say, a resolution of Wollstonecraft's dilemma is necessary and, perhaps, possible.

The structure of the welfare state presupposes that women are men's

[72] Cited in Cass, p. 59.

[73] Ibid., pp. 60–61.

dependents, but the benefits help make it possible for women to be economically independent of men. In the countries with which I am concerned, women reliant on state benefits live poorly, but it is no longer so essential as it once was to marry or to cohabit with a man. A considerable moral panic has developed in recent years around "welfare mothers," a panic that obscures significant features of their position, not least the extent to which the social basis for the ideal of breadwinner/dependent has crumbled. Large numbers of young working-class women have little or no hope of finding employment (or of finding a young man who is employed). But there is a source of social identity available to them that is out of the reach of their male counterparts. The socially secure and acknowledged identity for women is still that of a mother, and for many young women, motherhood, supported by state benefits, provides "an alternative to aimless adoloscence on the dole" and "gives the appearance of self-determination." The price of independence and "a rebellious motherhood that is not an uncritical retreat into femininity"[74] is high, however; the welfare state provides a minimal income and perhaps housing (often substandard), but child-care services and other support are lacking, so that the young women are often isolated, with no way out of their social exile. Moreover, even if welfare-state policies in Britain, Australia, and the United States were reformed so that generous benefits, adequate housing, health care, child care, and other services were available to mothers, reliance on the state could reinforce women's lesser citizenship in a new way.

Some feminists have enthusiastically endorsed the welfare state as "the main recourse of women" and as the generator of "political resources which, it seems fair to say, are mainly women's resources."[75] They can point, in Australia for example, to "the creation over the decade [1975–1985] of a range of women's policy machinery and government subsidized women's services (delivered by women for women) which is unrivalled elsewhere."[76] However, the enthusiasm is met with the rejoinder from other feminists that for women to look to the welfare state is merely to exchange dependence on individual men for dependence on the state. The power and capriciousness of husbands is being replaced by the arbitrariness, bureaucracy, and power of the state, the very state that has upheld patriarchal power. The objection is cogent: to make women directly dependent on the state will not in itself do anything to challenge patriar-

[74] Campbell, *Wigan Pier Revisited*, pp. 66, 78, 71.

[75] F. Fox Piven, "Women and the State: Ideology, Power, and the Welfare State," *Socialist Review* 14, no. 2 (1984): 14, 17.

[76] M. Sawer, "The Long March through the Institutions: Women's Affairs under Fraser and Hawke," paper presented to the annual meeting of the Australasian Political Studies Association, Brisbane, 1986, p. 1.

chal power relations. The direct dependence of male workers on the welfare state and their indirect dependence when their standard of living is derived from the vast system of state regulation of and subsidy to capitalism—and in Australia a national arbitration court—have done little to undermine class power. However, the objection also misses an important point. There is one crucial difference between the construction of women as men's dependents and dependence on the welfare state. In the former case, each woman lives with the man on whose benevolence she depends; each woman is (in J. S. Mill's extraordinarily apt phrase) in a "chronic state of bribery and intimidation combined."[77] In the welfare state, each woman receives what is hers by right, and she can, potentially, combine with other citizens to enforce her rightful claim. The state has enormous powers of intimidation, but political action takes place collectively in the public terrain and not behind the closed door of the home, where each woman has to rely on her own strength and resources.

Another new factor is that women are now involved in the welfare state on a large scale as employees. The possibilities for political action by women now look rather different than in the past. Women have been criticizing the welfare state in recent years not just as academics, as activists, or as beneficiaries and users of welfare services, but as the people on whom the daily operation of the welfare state to a large extent depends. The criticisms range from its patriarchal structure (and, on occasions, especially in health care, misogynist practices), to its bureaucratic and undemocratic policy-making processes and administration, to social work practices and education policy. Small beginnings have been made on changing the welfare state from within; for example, women have succeeded in establishing Well Women Clinics within the NHS in Britain and special units to deal with rape victims in public hospitals in Australia. Furthermore, the potential is now there for united action by women employees, women claimants, and women citizens already politically active in the welfare state—not just to protect services against government cuts and efforts at "privatization" (which has absorbed much energy recently), but to transform the welfare state. Still, it is hard to see how women alone could succeed in the attempt. One necessary condition for the creation of a genuine democracy in which the welfare of *all* citizens is served is an alliance between a labor movement that acknowledges the problem of patriarchal power and an autonomous women's movement that recognizes the problem of class power. Whether such an alliance can be forged is an open question.

Despite the debates and the rethinking brought about by mass unem-

[77] J. S. Mill, "The Subjection of Women," in *Essays on Sex Equality*, ed. A. Rossi (Chicago: University of Chicago Press, 1970), p. 137.

ployment and the attack on the union movement and welfare state by the Reagan and Thatcher governments, there are many barriers to be overcome. In Britain and Australia, with stronger welfare states, the women's movement has had a much closer relationship with working-class movements than in the United States, where the individualism of the predominant liberal feminism is an inhibiting factor, and where only about 17 percent of the work force is now unionized. The major locus of criticism of authoritarian, hierarchical, undemocratic forms of organization for the last twenty years has been the women's movement. The practical example of democratic, decentralized organization provided by the women's movement has been largely ignored by the labor movement, as well as in academic discussions of democracy. After Marx defeated Bakunin in the First International, the prevailing form of organization in the labor movement, the nationalized industries in Britain, and in the left sects has mimicked the hierarchy of the state—both the welfare and the warfare state. To be sure, there is a movement for industrial democracy and workers' control, but it has, by and large, accepted that the "worker" is a masculine figure and failed to question the separation of (public) industry and economic production from private life. The women's movement has rescued and put into practice the long-submerged idea that movements for, and experiments in, social change must "prefigure" the future form of social organization.[78]

If prefigurative forms of organization, such as the "alternative" women's welfare services set up by the women's movement, are not to remain isolated examples, or if attempts to set them up on a wider scale are not to be defeated, as in the past, very many accepted conceptions and practices have to be questioned. Recent debates over left alternatives to Thatcherite economic policies in Britain, and over the Accord between the state, capital, and labor in Australia, suggest that the arguments and demands of the women's movement are still often unrecognized by labor's political spokesmen. For instance, one response to unemployment from male workers is to argue for a shorter working week and more leisure, or more time but the same money. However, in women's lives, time and money are not interchangeable in the same way.[79] Women, unlike men, do not have leisure after "work," but do unpaid work. Many women are arguing, rather, for a shorter working day. The point of the

[78] See S. Rowbotham, L. Segal, and H. Wainright, *Beyond the Fragments: Feminism and the Making of Socialism* (London: Merlin Press, 1979), a book that was instrumental in opening debate on the left and in the labor movement in Britain on this question.

[79] I am grateful to Helga Hernes for supplying me with a copy of her paper, "The Impact of Public Policy on Individual Lives: The Case of Chrono-Politics" (presented to the meeting of the International Society of Political Psychology, Amsterdam, 1986), in which she discusses the political implications of different time-frames of men's and women's lives.

argument is to challenge the separation of part- and full-time paid employment and paid and unpaid "work." But the conception of citizenship needs thorough questioning, too, if Wollstonecraft's dilemma is to be resolved; neither the labor movement nor the women's movement (nor democratic theorists) has paid much attention to this. The patriarchal opposition between the private and public, women and citizen, dependent and breadwinner is less firmly based than it once was, and feminists have named it as a political problem. The ideal of full employment so central to the welfare state is also crumbling, so that some of the main props of the patriarchal understanding of citizenship are being undermined. The ideal of full employment appeared to have been achieved in the 1960s only because half the citizen body (and black men?) was denied legitimate membership in the employment society. Now that millions of men are excluded from the ideal (and the exclusion seems permanent), one possibility is that the ideal of universal citizenship will be abandoned, too, and full citizenship become the prerogative of capitalist, employed, and armed men. Or can a genuine democracy be created?

The perception of democracy as a class problem and the influence of liberal feminism have combined to keep alive Engels' old solution to "the woman question"—to "bring the whole female sex back into public industry."[80] But the economy has a patriarchal structure. The Marxist hope that capitalism would create a labor force where ascriptive characteristics were irrelevant, and the liberal feminist hope that antidiscrimination legislation will create a "gender-neutral" work force, look utopian even without the collapse of the ideal of full employment. Engels's solution is out of reach—and so, too, is the generalization of masculine citizenship to women. In turn, the argument that the equal worth of citizenship, and the self-respect and mutual respect of citizens, depend upon sale of labor-power in the market and the provisions of the patriarchal welfare state is also undercut. The way is opening up for the formulation of conceptions of respect and equal worth adequate for democratic citizenship. Women could not "earn" respect or gain the self-respect that men obtain as workers; but what kind of respect do men "achieve" by selling their labor-power and becoming wage-slaves? Here the movement for workplace democracy and the feminist movement could join hands, but only if the conventional understanding of "work" is rethought. If women as well as men are to be full citizens, the separation of the welfare state and employment from the free welfare work contributed by women has to be broken down and new meanings and practices of "independence," "work," and "welfare" created.

[80] F. Engels, *The Origin of the Family, Private Property, and the State* (New York: International Publishers, 1942), p. 66.

For example, consider the implications were a broad, popular political movement to press for welfare policy to include a guaranteed social income to all adults, which would provide adequately for subsistence and also participation in social life.[81] For such a demand to be made, the old dichotomies must already have started to break down—the opposition between paid and unpaid work (for the first time all individuals could have a genuine choice whether to engage in paid work), between full- and part-time work, between public and private work, between independence and dependence, between work and welfare—which is to say, between men and women. If implemented, such a policy would at last recognize women as equal members of the welfare state, although it would not in itself ensure women's full citizenship. If a genuine democracy is to be created, the problem of the content and value of women's contribution as citizens and the meaning of citizenship has to be confronted.

To analyze the welfare state through the lens of Hegel's dilemma is to rule out such problems. But the history of the past one hundred and fifty years and the contemporary record show that the welfare of all members of society cannot be represented by men, whether workers or capitalists. Welfare is, after all, the welfare of all living generations of citizens and their children. If the welfare state is seen as a response to Hegel's dilemma, the appropriate question about women's citizenship is: How can women become workers and citizens like men, and so members of the welfare state like men? If, instead, the starting point is Wollstonecraft's dilemma, then the question might run: What form must democratic citizenship take if a primary task of all citizens is to ensure that the welfare of each living generation of citizens is secured?

The welfare state has been fought for and supported by the labor movement and the women's movement because only public or collective provision can maintain a proper standard of living and the means for meaningful social participation for all citizens in a democracy. The implication of this claim is that democratic citizens are both autonomous and interdependent; they are autonomous in that each enjoys the means to be an active citizen, but they are interdependent in that the welfare of each is the collective responsibility of all citizens. Critics of the class structure of the welfare state have often counterposed the fraternal interdependence (solidarity) signified by the welfare state to the bleak independence of isolated individuals in the market, but they have rarely noticed that both have been predicated upon the dependence (subordination) of women. In the patriarchal welfare state, independence has been constructed as a masculine prerogative. Men's "independence" as workers and citizens is their freedom from responsibility for welfare (except insofar as they

[81] See also the discussion in Keane and Owens, *After Full Employment*, pp. 175–77.

"contribute" to the welfare state). Women have been seen as responsible for (private) welfare work, for relationships of dependence and interdependence. The paradox that welfare relies so largely on women, on dependents and social exiles whose "contribution" is not politically relevant to their citizenship in the welfare state, is heightened now that women's paid employment is also vital to the operation of the welfare state itself.

If women's knowledge of and expertise in welfare are to become part of their contribution as citizens, as women have demanded during the twentieth cantury, the opposition between men's independence and women's dependence has to be broken down, and a new understanding and practice of citizenship developed. The patriarchal dichotomy between women and independence-work-citizenship is under political challenge, and the social basis for the ideal of the full (male) employment society is crumbling. An opportunity has become visible to create a genuine democracy, to move from the welfare state to a welfare society without involuntary social exiles, in which women as well as men enjoy full social membership. Whether the opportunity can be realized is not easy to tell now that the warfare state is overshadowing the welfare state.

11

Citizenship and Welfare

ROBERT K. FULLINWIDER

We can view citizenship as having a dual relation to welfare. Citizenship is a precondition for receiving benefits. Welfare services are instituted and organized by a state for its members. Citizenship is also a set of habits and attitudes on which the delivery and receipt of welfare services have tutelary effects, either supporting or undermining good habits and attitudes.

Consider first citizenship as a precondition for receiving welfare. The provision by the state of broad welfare services (education, unemployment insurance, income supplements) and the making of welfare investments (public health activities, regional development such as TVA) reflect a variety of motives and grounds. One aim of such services and investments is the development of human capital. Educated, healthy, undemoralized people are economically and socially productive. Welfare services may also contribute to a second aim, social peace. Crime and disorder can be minimized by income supplements, unemployment insurance, and other programs that prevent desperation and anger. Third, simple humanity motivates relief of extreme distress, apart from other considerations. Fourth, the welfare state can express a sense of communal solidarity, a feeling that we will not let any of our own go under. Finally, a system of welfare may be seen as a response to claims of justice. Joint cooperation in making possible the social product justifies a variety of claims for assistance or compensation by those cooperating.

Each of these grounds reflects a focus by the state on itself and its members: investing in its social and economic productivity, securing its social peace, taking care of its own, responding to claims arising from its organization as a collective enterprise. Thus, citizenship, roughly speaking,

This paper was written with support from the Exxon Education Foundation. I am grateful to my colleagues at the Center for Philosophy and Public Policy for their comments on an earlier version, and to Richard Mohr and Amy Gutmann. I owe a special debt to Claudia Mills.

constitutes the basis of eligibility for welfare. The state's welfare measures are for its members.

Consider next citizenship as a set of habits and attitudes that may be affected positively or negatively by welfare services. Citizenship means being socially responsible, self-supporting, law-abiding, civil, politically active. The way welfare is delivered and received can teach good or bad civic lessons. It can foster or undermine social responsibility.

These tutelary effects of welfare are the subject of current debates in the United States about imposing work or service requirements on the potential recipients of public aid as a condition of getting it. If income support, for example, is given to individuals without obliging them to work, then they will become habituated to welfare dependency. If such support instead carries with it a duty to work, the recipient learns a lesson about social obligation, and at the same time is spared having to feel that he is a parasite on the rest of society. So it is conjectured.

This sketch of the relation between citizenship and welfare is crude. If it is accurately to describe a modern society like the United States, many qualifications have to be made. For example, legal citizenship in the United States is not a condition of receiving the vast majority of social services. Resident aliens are entitled to most of the benefits American citizens may obtain and, with insignificant exceptions, are entitled to participate fully in the economy. Even illegal aliens and their children cannot be denied some important services. In addition, most civil burdens fall on all permanent U.S. residents, citizen and noncitizen alike, including such obligations as military service (in times of conscription).

In this paper I wish to develop the crude sketch of citizenship and welfare by discussing some of the other qualifications. In the next section I analyze the reasons for welfare and the significance of community membership. In the last section I consider two proposals for making welfare benefits better vehicles for teaching civic lessons. Although my general aim is to shed some light on the moral foundations of the welfare state, I also have three subsidiary aims. The first is to emphasize the plurality of grounds for welfare and the diversity of meanings of citizenship. The second is to examine some of the arguments of other contributors to this book. The third is to question the idea that the noninstrumental reasons for welfare lack support in a liberal conception of the state.

The Reasons for Welfare

Let us first inquire further into how the various grounds or justifications for welfare imply who should receive it. It is a mistake, I think, to try to reduce the foundations of the welfare state to a simple principle or ground. Different parts of the welfare state were established at different times for different reasons and this plurality of reasons is not reducible to a single value. Simple humanity prompts a society to devise some mechanisms to relieve extreme distress and deal with disasters. Beyond simple humanity, a range of communitarian motives come into play. Policies and programs of the welfare state that provide safety nets, redistribute income, and offer other forms of help to the least well off, as well as support development of talent, can express such attitudes of solidarity as: "I don't want my good to hinder your good"; "I don't want to profit while you don't"; "we're all in this together"; "your flourishing is a part of my own flourishing."

Much of the welfare state can be viewed as a form of human investment. Such investment has both negative and positive aims. Investment to secure for as many as possible the conditions and opportunities for legitimate work conduces to social peace and has the negative aim of minimizing crime and disorder without resort to draconian police-state measures. Investment in education, health, and opportunity has the positive aim of increasing social productivity.

Social justice provides substantial grounds for income redistribution and other welfare services. The standard of living of a society like the United States is made possible by the willingness of most people to accept an intricate array of social and economic regulations and arrangements whose benefits are paid for by imposing costs on certain people, usually the less well off. Imposition of sanitation requirements in restaurants and emissions controls in factories raises the cost of doing business, effectively barring potential providers who cannot meet that cost. Credential thresholds for professions and occupations bar individuals who would substitute cheap and enterprising services for advanced training. Such requirements, thresholds, rules, and restrictions are pervasive in society, and arguably they make life better for most of us. But the cost is diminished opportunities for those who have neither capital nor training, a cost that, to ensure justice, ought to be compensated. The various programs that constitute the "safety net," as well as other elements of the welfare state, can be viewed as compensation to the least well off for bearing the brunt of the exclusions from and restrictions on economic activity that benefit the rest of society.

Community, humanity, and social justice are noninstrumental reasons for providing welfare. These reasons underwrite aid to persons because they need it, because it is owed them, because they are one of our own, and not for some ulterior end. Social peace and human investment are instrumental reasons. They support aid to persons because it benefits society at large. Human investment, however, need not be strictly instrumental; the expansion of human capacities is not only a means to other goods but a good in itself. These diverse reasons interact and overlap to provide a web of justification for welfare-state activities.

Directed as they are to those within its territory, are the state's welfare services properly restricted to those who have legal citizenship status? The "natural" scope of application of the assorted reasons for the welfare state varies. Reasons of humanity apply to everyone within the state's jurisdiction—citizens and noncitizens, residents and visitors. Need is need. Human investment seems appropriately directed at long-term residents, whether citizens or not. At least from the point of view of productivity, productive noncitizen residents are as valuable as productive citizen residents. Social peace, likewise, is maximized by providing services to all long-term residents.

Social justice as a reason brings within its scope of application those who are sufficiently involved in the state's social and economic life. Sufficient involvement is vague; it means enough involvement that one counts as a cooperating and burden-sharing contributor to the social product. Such contributors need not be citizens. Finally, the reason of community points to communal members as the objects of solicitude. Communal membership can mean different things. Although it seems most natural to equate such membership with citizenship, this is not a necessary implication. Whatever other meanings it might acquire, membership generally implies residence.[1]

Is there warrant for not distributing benefits according to the "natural" scope of the reasons just examined? Although the reasons generally justify extending welfare benefits to all long-term residents, might we restrict them to citizens? This would narrow the distribution. And although the reasons presuppose the existence of an organized community and focus on its members, should we extend benefits to outsiders (nonresidents) as well? This would widen the distribution.

Let us consider the last question first. One answer is that the exigencies of the state system limit the extension of welfare benefits beyond a nation's borders. The sovereignty of nations makes direct welfare support a national affair. The United States, for example, cannot directly subsidize college loans to Indonesian students, or provide unemployment insurance for Brazilians, or build flood-control projects in Sri Lanka. (It can provide financial aid and technical assistance to the government of Sri Lanka to build dams, or to the government of Indonesia to establish educational

[1] Residence is central to communal membership because the world is organized on the basis of spatially based political communities (states). Michael Walzer discusses a conception of nationality in which the world is composed of "national corporations" on the model of churches. Such corporations admit members, tax them, provide services and benefits, and so on, but have no territorial dominion. He suggests that territoriality is a preferable basis for organization of the state. See *Spheres of Justice* (New York: Basic Books, 1983), p. 44.

subsidies. There are prudential and moral reasons for supplying some level of aid and assistance to foreign governments.)

This answer is too quick, however. If outsiders are allowed to become insiders, the answer will not apply. Distribution of welfare benefits can be widened by increasing the number of members rather than by giving to nonmembers. So the crucial question becomes: By what right do states limit membership?

A thorough discussion of this difficult question lies beyond the scope of this paper. If communities have the moral right to exist and define a common way of life and common institutions, then they cannot be required to admit outsiders promiscuously and indiscriminately. Nevertheless, the question still remains whether communities have a moral duty to take in *needy* applicants for admission.

But upon what ground can a needy applicant press a moral claim for admission? It is insufficient for him to argue that in an ideal (or at least a better) world, the system of nation-states would not exist, and the well-being of individuals would not depend upon what state they happened to be born in. Our world is not the best world. The absence of any alternative to the state system effectively moots the question of what moral claims might arise under a radically different arrangement. From a purely moral point of view, the family may likewise be a nonoptimal arrangement that would not exist in a better world. This fact, however, does not presently lend support to the moral claim of a poor child to be taken in by a better-off family.

If we leave aside any special relations an applicant might have acquired with the community or its government, the legitimacy of his moral claim to admission seems to rest on his need.[2] In short, his case rests on an appeal to simple humanity. Common humanity, however, obligates us only in limited ways to incur sacrifices to make others better off. Individually and collectively, we are bound to respond to disaster and extreme distress. Beyond this, individuals and collectivities have wide discretion in deciding how they might use their resources to aid those who are less

[2] Special relations might be rooted in special obligations undertaken or acquired by the receiving country. For example, if the United States is directly or indirectly responsible for the needy applicant's condition, it may as a consequence owe him admission. My interest, in this paper, is with the general condition of neediness and what sort of general obligation it imposes. On claims to admission grounded in special obligations, see Judith Lichtenberg, "National Boundaries and Moral Boundaries: A Cosmopolitan View," in Peter G. Brown and Henry Shue, eds., *Boundaries: National Autonomy and Its Limits* (Totowa, N.J.: Rowman and Littlefield, 1981), pp. 79–100; and Judith Lichtenberg, "Mexican Migration and U.S. Policy: A Guide for the Perplexed," in Peter G. Brown and Henry Shue, eds., *The Border That Joins: Mexican Migrants and U.S. Responsibility* (Totowa, N.J.: Rowman and Littlefield, 1983), pp. 13–30.

well off, and in any case are not required to accept burdens that interfere with their other legitimate activities.[3]

It is very difficult to translate these comments into special prescriptions for action or specific judgments of existing national policies. For one thing, there is no common intuitive basis to guide our interpretation of the moral force of simple humanity. We almost never encounter people, even strangers, whom we think of as "simply humans"; we encounter fellow citizens, coreligionists, neighbors, historic kinsmen, political confederates, allies in war, or guests. Our typical moral judgments and responses are almost always made in the context of some connection between us and others that goes beyond being members of the same species. Partly for this reason, it is difficult to be precise about the boundaries between what is strictly required by simple humanity, what is not strictly required (but refusal to provide it would be indecent or insensitive), and what is not required (but its provision would be praiseworthy).

Joseph Carens, in Chapter 9 of this book, appears to offer a ground other than simple humanity upon which the needy applicant can base his claim for admission: "the moral equality of all human beings." This assumption, from which "liberal theory starts," threatens, according to Carens, any privileged claim by the insider over the outsider to the state's benefits.

What does the moral equality of persons mean and what are its implications? Carens seeks to answer these questions by using Rawls's "original position" and giving it a global interpretation. In contrast to Rawls, he wants us to imagine the parties in the original position as representative members of the world's population who are ignorant of what society they will be born into. "If the rest of Rawls's argument is correct," says Carens, individuals in a global original position would presumably choose for the world the same strong principles of justice set out in *A Theory of Justice*,[4] principles that include freedom of movement as fundamental. Consequently, the outsider can found a claim in justice for entry into a state; "states could not legitimately restrict freedom of movement except to preserve the global system of basic liberties."

This extension of Rawls's argument from the original position is illegitimate. In Rawls's theory, the parties to the original position are to choose principles to regulate the basic institutions of a well-ordered society. This means that the choice is made on the assumption that the par-

[3] See James Fishkin, *The Limits of Obligation* (New Haven, Conn.: Yale University Press, 1982), p. 63ff.; Alan Donagan, *The Theory of Morality* (Chicago: University of Chicago Press, 1977), p. 85; Henry Sidgwick, *The Methods of Ethics* (New York: Dover, 1966), pp. 252-58.

[4] John Rawls, *A Theory of Justice* (Cambridge, Mass.: Harvard University Press, 1971), pp. 60–62.

ties will be associated under common institutions reflecting a common sense of justice.

This restriction on the choice situation is not an arbitrary, gratuitous limitation, as Carens appears to think. It is integrally related to the derivation of the principles of justice in *A Theory of Justice*. These principles reflect the parties' knowledge that because their institutions will reflect a common conception of justice, they will be entitled to make extensive claims upon one another.[5] Suppose that the parties to the original position do not have this knowledge, and are to choose principles to judge the claims that unrelated representatives of the world's population can make against one another. This would clearly change the choice of principles, if any determinate choice is possible now. The only general claims such unrelated representatives can make against one another are those rooted solely in common humanity. On this basis, the principles (governing what—personal duty? the state's foreign relations?) chosen by the parties will be weak. They will be more like the principles of natural duty in *A Theory of Justice*—principles of nonaggression and rescue. In short, moral equality, abstracted from any setting of community or association, amounts to simple humanity. The former implies no more than the latter, and is not a separate ground on the basis of which the needy outsider can apply for admission.

A claim to admission based on simple humanity provides the needy applicant with little moral leverage. The mere fact of his need does not negate the state's right to refuse him admission. However, the claim need not rest on what morality requires as a bare minimum. An expanded sympathy for the fate of others can make us ready to bear additional burdens. We may be unwilling to tell the needy applicant that he must be content with the cards fortune has dealt him, for it was not our doing that he must languish while we prosper. When Christ, for example, told the parable of the good Samaritan, he was not urging his listeners to remember their natural duty to relieve distress. He was proposing something more radical—that they view the victim beside the road to Jericho as a neighbor. The sense of duty that derives from such a viewpoint—or from an even stronger ideal also expressed in the Scriptures, the ideal of universal brotherhood—may prompt a community to maintain a generous admissions policy. Even here, though, there will be limiting factors, unless we are dealing with a population given to intense self-sacrifice. Duties to each other in a community will be undermined if too many resources are devoted to admitting outsiders.[6]

[5] Ibid., pp. 4–5, 11, 14, 53, 128.

[6] But what does it cost to admit the outsider? If each admittee is productive, he adds to as well as subtracts from the social pie. If what he adds is less than what he subtracts, admitting him is a cost. I assume that for any community or state, there is some level of immigration,

One limiting factor in particular, the principle of full membership, deserves our scrutiny. Up to this point we have been considering the second of the two questions posed earlier—whether we should distribute the welfare benefits of the state to outsiders by granting them admission. The first question was whether we may restrict the benefits to some insiders, namely, citizens. Those who adhere to the principle of full membership answer this question in the negative. The principle of full membership declares that if we allow immigrants to take up residence, we must offer them full citizenship, with all its rights and benefits.[7]

The principle of full membership limits a state's capacity to absorb needy immigrants by confronting the state with an all-or-nothing choice, thus foreclosing the option of admitting the applicant to some intermediate form of membership more palatable (because less costly) to the state.[8] Thus a state—even a generous state—that is committed to the full membership principle will turn away more needy applicants than a similarly situated and similarly disposed state not so committed.

Why is the principle of full membership a moral imperative? Some of its supporters appeal directly to a broad principle of human equality.[9] But the same comments are in order here that I made earlier in regard to the claims of applicants to be admitted to a state. "Human equality" in the abstract has very little content. It means we cannot be indifferent to the fact that other persons have interests and desires, but it tells us little about the arrangements by which those interests and desires might be promoted. We are not permitted to take advantage of the weakness of others to exploit them, to impose upon them usurious and unconscionable terms for obtaining our cooperation or help. But these restrictions leave open the possibility of making a variety of arrangements that fall short of granting them full membership. If we turn away the needy applicant on

or some rate, or some type, that proves to be a burden. I understand "burden," moreover, in a broad sense encompassing more than economic cost. Immigration can alter the cultural and political features of a community. I take no position here on how protective of its features a community rightfully may be. Some forms of protectiveness seem morally unworthy, such as excluding immigrants on racial grounds in order to maintain racial purity. The argument in this paper assumes that there is some threshold of threat to a community's cultural and political integrity that makes it morally legitimate to weigh self-protection against the claims of needy applicants.

[7] See Walzer, *Spheres of Justice*, pp. 52–61. Joseph Carens in Chapter 9 and Donald Moon in Chapter 2 of this volume make similar arguments.

[8] A parallel situation: Many intelligent and capable young scholars lose their academic jobs because, at the end of their sixth or seventh year, their universities are faced with an all-or-nothing choice—continue to employ them forever or fire them.

[9] Donald Moon (in Chapter 2 of this volume) roots the full membership requirement in the "moral equality of persons." Joseph Carens likewise views the requirement as a reflection of the "commitment to equal citizenship," which derives from the broader imperative of equality.

the grounds that we have no room for him as a full member, then in a sense we do not take his need seriously. We treat him as if what he needs is full membership when what he needs is the opportunity to put food on his table.

A state that feels it can advantageously accept many needy applicants as guest workers, though not otherwise, can give them substantial protections by subscribing to international conventions that determine the rights of migrant workers, entering into treaty arrangements with potential sending countries, and securing passage of appropriate domestic laws. Guest workers can be provided the general social benefits that attach to employment in the state, subjected to few restrictions (or none) on the kind of work they seek, given time if they lose a job to find another one, and protected against unjust termination of employment and discriminatory working conditions. Consequently, the terms of their admission, though limited to partial membership, can be made humane and decent.[10]

Michael Walzer claims that the full membership principle is a corollary of the principle of political justice: "men and women are either subject to the state's authority, or they are not; and if they are subject, they must be given a say, and ultimately an equal say, in what the authority does."[11] That the needy applicant may consent to being admitted as a subject without say is, for Walzer, not enough to make the admission legitimate. If subjects are not to be tyrannized, they must be able to affect the rules under which they live.[12] But Walzer's concerns can be satisfied in part by allowing guest workers to unionize, to organize lobbying groups, or even to vote in local or municipal elections, as now permitted in some states.[13] This would have the effect of making the guest worker more than a mere subject. Walzer never makes clear, however, why the guest worker's say must be equal to that of the citizens, or why the guest worker's consent to be admitted with limited political rights is not morally acceptable.

Providing legal protections, a range of welfare services, and limited political rights to guest workers raises the cost of admitting the needy applicant, but the cost may be less than that incurred by extending full membership. However, even if considerations of principle do not directly bar admission of needy applicants to less than full membership, there may be strong reasons for not adopting dual membership policies. Despite safeguards, a guest worker program runs the risk of encouraging, in practice,

[10] For a more detailed discussion of various protections and arrangements, see Elsa M. Chaney, "Migrant Workers and National Boundaries: The Basis for Rights and Protections," in Brown and Shue, *Boundaries*, pp. 37–79.

[11] *Spheres of Justice*, Walzer, pp. 60–61.

[12] Ibid., p. 58.

[13] For example, Sweden, Belgium, and some cantons of Switzerland. See Chaney, "Migrant Workers and National Boundaries," pp. 54–55.

development of a society with a despised servile class and a despising ruling class.[14]

These reflections do not lead us to any clear-cut answers to the two questions posed earlier in this section. Might we extend welfare benefits to outsiders by making them insiders? A state is not required by considerations of simple humanity or human equality to admit all needy applicants, but the only limits on its generosity in admitting them are the obligations it has to those who are already resident.

Might we restrict welfare benefits to citizens? Some of the reasons for welfare are less inclusive than others, but the total mix of reasons provides little basis for distinguishing among long-term residents. Although citizenship constitutes the basis for the fullest range of political rights and for permanent membership, extended residence and participation in the economy are the appropriate grounds for receiving most welfare services and benefits. Thus, the claim made at the beginning of this paper—that citizenship is a precondition for receiving welfare benefits—should be amended.

Welfare as a Part of Civic Education

If citizenship shapes welfare, it is also shaped by it. This is the second part of citizenship's dual relation to welfare. The kinds of welfare benefits distributed by the state, the modes of delivery, and the conditions for receipt can teach good or bad lessons in citizenship. Citizenship, here, means more than full legal membership in the state. It means a set of attitudes, habits, aspirations, and responsibilities. The focus in this section is on welfare as a part of civic education.

There are many reasons why we might want to impose special conditions on the receipt of welfare benefits. For example, government loans for medical education might come with an obligation that recipients devote some part of their future practice to areas where doctors are in short supply. The justification for this imposition would be better distribution of health care assistance throughout the nation's regions and populations. In this section I shall examine two proposals for conditioning benefits whose justification is their anticipated effects on civic attitudes. The first proposal would impose work requirements on able-bodied recipients of "welfare." The second would tie government-subsidized college loans to performance of public service.

"Welfare"—provision of money and in-kind services to those who are too poor to support themselves—is shaming. Part of the shame may derive from reformable features of welfare policy, but part inheres in the

[14] Walzer, *Spheres of Justice*, pp. 52–58.

condition of disabling poverty itself. The very poor are unable to meet one of the informal responsibilities of citizenship—to be self-supporting. Even in societies with generous provisions for the needy, the sense that a good citizen is one who can support himself and his dependents is deeply ingrained. People do not want to be a burden on others.

Contemporary critics of federal welfare programs charge that they erode this sense of citizenship and create long-term, habituated welfare dependency. In so doing, they harm the recipients they are supposed to help. Lawrence Mead argues that the central problem with federal programs has been their "permissive" character. They "award their benefits as entitlements, expecting next to nothing from the beneficiaries in return."[15] What is needed is to couple benefits "with serious work and other obligations that would encourage functioning and thus promote the [social and economic] integration of the recipients. . . . Even more than income and opportunity, [beneficiaries] need to face the requirements, such as work, that true acceptance in American society requires."[16]

Mead calls his approach a "civic conception" of welfare, since it aims to foster "the common obligations of citizenship" among welfare recipients. "The great merit of equal citizenship as a social goal," he says, "is that it is much more widely available than status. It is not competitive. It does not require that the disadvantaged 'succeed', something not everyone can do. It requires only that everyone discharge the common obligations, including social ones like work."[17]

A critic of the civic conception might argue that tying welfare to work requirements adds insult to poverty. The poor are already powerless; making them perform for their handouts further confirms their powerlessness. Unconditioned welfare entitlements allow the poor to regain some control over their own lives.

There is merit to this argument, but it is also something of a bluff. As long as the poor remain poor enough to need help, making that help un-

[15] Lawrence Mead, *Beyond Entitlement: The Social Obligations of Citizenship* (New York: Free Press, 1986,) p. 2.

[16] Ibid., pp. 3–4.

[17] Ibid., pp. 14, 12. See also Chapter 2 of this volume. Moon explains that "self-respect is not a matter of having a certain status or enjoying particular rights. Rather, it requires that one perform certain duties or, better, live up to some ideal. One cannot achieve self-respect simply by having one's rightful claims recognized. Indeed, the opposite may be more nearly true: to be able to assert one's rights depends upon one's having self-respect . . . feeling oneself to be worthy of exercising those rights. And that depends upon one's living up to the standards one holds. To have self-respect, we must be accorded the rights of citizens; to gain self-respect, we must perform the duties of citizens." For a different moral defense of work requirements, see Baruch Brody, "Work Requirements and Welfare Rights," in Peter G. Brown, Conrad Johnson, and Paul Vernier, eds., *Income Support: Conceptual and Policy Issues* (Totowa, N.J.: Rowman and Littlefield, 1981), pp. 247–57.

conditional does not change their basic powerlessness. What the poor need most is to be self-supporting.

If Mead is right, tying work requirements to welfare benefits will speed that development. The work requirement will reinforce in recipients the norm of citizenship and, moreover, will permit them, while on welfare, to feel they are living up to that norm. The work requirement will ensure that the able-bodied poor, in Michael Walzer's words, "experience something other than their own poverty."[18] Their experience of being on welfare will not be an experience of parasitism.

There is merit to this argument as well, but it likewise may be something of a bluff. In being required to perform make-work jobs, the welfare recipient *simulates* assuming the responsibility of being self-supporting. His experience of meeting a minimum requirement of citizenship is a pseudoexperience. Nevertheless, this may be enough to diminish welfare dependency and accomplish a transition to self-support.

Whether work requirements can produce self-support depends upon many factors, a point illustrated by Switzerland, which does not have a large problem of welfare dependency. Its social insurance and public aid programs are designed to keep people working and self-sufficient and are supported by a social system that encourages responsibility and competence. Most of the population lives in small communities; thus children grow up under community scrutiny, and truancy is noticed and dealt with. Almost every child completes education and occupational training.[19] Moreover, the problem of female-headed households in which the children receive no support from their fathers—which is so serious in the United States—is virtually nonexistent in Switzerland. Divorce is only with fault. Living together out of wedlock is against the law in several cantons. Fathers who do not live with their children, because they are divorced or have never married, cannot escape child-support payments. The government can attach wages or property to ensure payment, and it has little trouble finding the fathers to collect from since every male must register (for purposes of tax collection, voting, and military service) in the commune where he lives, and change his registration each time he moves. All tax returns in Switzerland are open to the public, so it is hard for a father to hide income or assets.

The public aid program is designed to take people off assistance as soon as possible. Each applicant for aid works out an individual "contract" with the local welfare agency, specifying how much aid is needed, for how

[18] See the paper by Michael Walzer, Chapter 1 in this volume.

[19] I have taken the details of Swiss society from Ralph Segalman, "Welfare and Dependency in Switzerland," *The Public Interest*, no. 82 (Winter 1986), pp. 106–21.

long, and what steps will be taken to enable him to become self-supporting again.

Welfare officers can vary the amount of aid according to a recipient's progress and can change the nature and extent of aid given to those who are insufficiently cooperative.

> [Almost] any aspect of the client's life, and that of his family, may be raised for discussion by the welfare worker. The worker has generally unlimited controls in requiring interviews with the client, or conducting collateral visits with the relatives, employers, teachers of the client's children, and others who may, in any way, affect the client's progress toward becoming independent. Thus, the welfare worker, both formally and indirectly as well, can shape the way in which public aid and public social services are used by the client and his family. If a client seeks to go beyond the case worker's constraints, or beyond the agency's constraints, he then comes face-to-face with community authorities who are almost always in agreement with the goal of self-reliance.[20]

In Switzerland, such aspects of society as educational requirements, military registration, living patterns, and public scrutiny combine with a highly paternalistic and discretionary public aid program to reduce the problem of welfare dependency. Swiss society thus contrasts sharply with American society. The highly mobile U.S. population is largely concentrated in crowded urban areas, and there is limited public scrutiny of children; rates of school dropout are higher. Divorce, cohabitation, and out-of-wedlock pregnancies are common, and there is frequent economic dislocation and regional depression. In this context, can changes in the welfare system effectively diminish welfare dependency by encouraging and supporting self-sufficiency?

Decentralizing services, combining aid and rehabilitation services into one program, and relaxing some of the restrictions on paternalistic intervention into welfare recipients' lives might be the necessary background conditions that would enable work requirements to have a positive effect. Nevertheless, work requirements as a vehicle for teaching lessons in civic responsibility and as an inducement to become self-sufficient cannot be expected to make a very great change in the absence of supporting and enforcing lessons in all other aspects of the welfare recipient's life. In the United States, work requirements press against the tide, not with it as they do in Switzerland. And it is the tide that produces the main effects.

The motivation of proposals to tie subsidized college loans to performance of some kind of national service is quite different. The reason for

[20] Ibid., p. 13.

tying work requirements to welfare is to prevent welfare aid from undermining the capacity of recipients to fulfill the responsibility of self-sufficiency. College loans, however, go to college-bound young people who are largely from the middle class and already showing themselves to be competent. The loans allow them to improve their situation and do not, apparently, make them worse off in the process. The ubiquity of the loans, moreover, keeps borrowers from feeling stigmatized. Tying college financial aid to national service is seen as a convenient device for leveraging large numbers of middle-class youth into programs to assist the elderly, clean up the environment, tutor poor students, train for military service, and so on. Apart from the benefit to the community, such service, it is thought, is needed to teach youths citizenship.

These are youths who have successfully completed twelve years of school and who will spend, or have spent, another two to four years or more in college. Why must they be induced or coerced to spend a year or so in national service—military service or some organized civilian activities, presumably at subsistence wages? William James supplied the answer at the beginning of the twentieth century: Youths are selfish.

The same answer is given by Morris Janowitz in *The Reconstruction of Patriotism*, which is the culmination of his thirty-year argument for national service.[21] If national service is to teach citizenship, what is it to teach and how? Janowitz's explicit definition of citizenship is political: the citizen is one who shares "in the civic life of ruling and being ruled in turn" (p. 2, quoting Aristotle). But in his specific discussion of national service, this notion of citizenship is peripheral. National service is essentially apolitical community activity. It is not direct training in either holding political office or collectively forging political platforms or participating in election campaigns.

Rather, the direct effects of national service are, in Janowitz's mind, to teach "the student to balance rights against obligations," "to balance the pursuit of economic self-interest against collective civic obligations," and to create in the student a feeling of being "a member of a larger collectivity" (pp. 144, 145, 172). Janowitz lists several obligations of citizenship: to pay taxes, pursue education for oneself and one's family, serve when

[21] Morris Janowitz, *The Reconstruction of Patriotism: Education for Civic Consciousness* (Chicago: University of Chicago Press, 1983), esp. p. 189. The specific proposal to tie college loans to national service requirements was made by Charles Moskos at the beginning of the 1980s; see "Making the All-Volunteer Force Work: A National Service Approach," *Foreign Affairs* 60 (Fall 1981): 22–34. The proposal is endorsed by Janowitz at pp. 202–3. It should be said that Moskos's interest in national service derives more from his concern with the quality of the armed forces than from a concern about the duties of citizenship generally. See also William James, "The Moral Equivalent of War," in John J. McDermott, ed., *The Writinqs of William James* (New York: Modern Library, 1968), pp. 660–71.

called for military service and jury duty, promote the welfare of the community, vote, join voluntary associations (p. 6). This is a heterogeneous list, and just as it is obscure how national service is supposed to teach political participation, it is obscure how it teaches citizens to fulfill obligations of jury duty or tax paying or pursuit of education, or the other obligations on the list.

What national service seems to teach is not this or that obligation but that there *are* obligations. A continuing theme in Janowitz's study is that since World War II, rights have been emphasized to the exclusion of obligations, producing a "grotesque" imbalance in the attitudes of youth (p. xiii). People pursue their own interests and jealously guard their rights, wanting not to be burdened by anything else. National service that is required, or expected, is an antidote to selfishness; it is a lesson not in obligations but in obligation.

Whether such a case can be made for national service depends upon the aspects of citizenship it might serve. We need initially to clarify three aspects implied in Janowitz's list of citizenship obligations: citizen-as-self-supporter, citizen-as-good-neighbor, and citizen-as-political-participant. The first has already been discussed in connection with welfare work requirements. It includes responsibilities to support oneself and one's family. There is little evidence that college students subsequently prove themselves to be deficient in this aspect of citizenship.

The second aspect, citizen-as-good-neighbor, includes a range of desirable communal activities such as keeping one's lawn mowed, joining the crime watch brigade, watching out for the neighbor's children, and taking a turn in the volunteer fire department. These activities, and the qualities they reflect, make neighborhood life pleasant; selfishness undermines neighborliness. The extreme selfishness that produces vandalism, neighborhood neglect, and other antisocial behavior is not generally an attribute of college-educated people. National service imposed on the college bound seems rather severe overkill, then, with respect to the first two aspects of citizenship.

It should be noted that the qualities included in the first two aspects have nothing to do with citizenship in a strict sense. They pertain mostly to living with other people. If I leave the United States to reside in Stockholm or Melbourne or London for several years, I should there support myself and my family, as well as mow my lawn, report crime, and watch out for the neighbor's children. These are not responsibilities that are somehow connected to my being a citizen of the United States, and that cease to apply when I reside elsewhere. Similarly, the duty of obey the law and pay taxes has to do with residence, not legal citizenship.

The third aspect has more direct relevance to legal citizenship, since usually only citizens have a right to vote in their nation's elections. Many

Americans do not vote; still fewer actively involve themselves in political campaigns. Perhaps a greater sense of civic duty would produce more voters, but lack of voter turnout is probably less a reflection of selfishness than of disgust with politics, dissatisfaction with the ballot choices, and a feeling that one's vote does not count. More likely, a high voter turnout reflects selfishness: Voters often show up to vote for the candidate who favors their pocketbook. The political virtue that seems desirable is less the duty to vote than the disposition to think in terms of the common good.

Favoring or opposing national service may appear to be a matter of calculating effects and alternatives, but in fact differing stands on national service may reflect different views of the nature of the common good. Let me extend this suggestion by sketching two crude alternatives: the liberal view, in which national service has no privileged place, if any place at all, as a means of civic education; and what I will call a martial view, which considers national service a model of the citizen-state relationship.

Benjamin Constant used the imagery of a highway to describe how a liberal understands the common good. Each traveler, though using the same highway, has his own itinerary. The liberal conceives of the common good as a common thoroughfare, not as a common destination. The common good is a framework of institutions and obligations that allows persons, singly and collectively, to define and pursue their own ideas of meaning, perfection, and salvation. The role of civic education is to foster the habits that sustain this framework: habits of self-sufficiency, neighborliness, and political participation. The good citizen must subordinate private will to the common good, but the subordination is partial. In a well-ordered state, by supporting the common good, the individual supports the conditions for his own, independent good. The moral citizen does not have to value subordination for its own sake, or value the intrinsic rewards of citizenship over the intrinsic rewards of other goods.

In contrast, the martial view of citizenship takes the common good to be a common goal to which individuals fully subordinate their wills. What the goal or destination is, is not as important as that it is common. In the martial state, the coincidence between common good and personal good arises not because the common good serves the independent ends of individuals but because individuals identify their own good with the goals of the state. The first function of civic education, then, is to ensure the requisite identification and to encourage the readiness of each individual to find fulfillment by subordinating his will to the collective goal.

I call this conception of citizenship martial because military service most clearly exemplifies its requirements. The extreme regimentation and arduousness of military service leave the soldier very little leisure time for personal projects. Uniforms, common living quarters, unit training and maneuvers, strict discipline, and physical hardship eliminate from the soldier's life the distractions of civilian life—commerce, family, politics.[22] The full energies of each soldier are devoted to preparation for, and success in, battle, ordeal that requires the complete sacrifice of self to the common purpose. In battle, "there is a lack of the sordidness, meanness and petty individualism that makes everyday life so unlovable."[23]

What society needs, proposed William James, is the "moral equivalent of war," the experience of sacrifice and suppression of "petty individualism" without the destruction of life and limb.[24] Universal military training, or national service with military and civilian components, serves this end. In the martial view of citizenship, national service (or military service) not only inculcates desirable habits of citizenship but is an experience of citizenship, or of what citizenship ought to be; and even apart from any more remote effects, the experience is valuable in itself.

Strong proponents of national service may be buying into some version of the martial ideal. "Defenders of the welfare state," comments Michael Walzer in Chapter 1 of this book, "seek to institutionalize and perpetuate the helpfulness born of collective crisis, the spirit of mutuality that arises among citizens confronting a flood or a storm or even an enemy attack." Tying benefits to national service or military service requirements is one way to institutionalize the solidarity forged by collective crisis. But why is it desirable to maintain feelings born of crisis in normal times? The answer, I think, flows from some sympathy, perhaps weak, for the martial view of citizenship. A permanent crisis, or some simulacrum of it, is needed to suppress selfishness—but not the selfishness that unfits individuals to be self-sufficient, or neighborly, or politically involved. There is not enough of that selfishness in college-bound young people to require a permanent crisis. The selfishness to be overcome is the individual's insistence on measuring the meaning of life by something other than political participation or public service or subordination to a collective goal.

If the debates about the usefulness of national service as a means turn out to reflect a contest between ideals of citizenship, the competition of ideals may reflect an even deeper concern about means. Underlying the martial view may be the fear that without a common goal, a humane social order cannot sustain itself. The common good viewed as a common highway is too limited a vision of civic association. It refers to a purely

[22] A frequent criticism of today's U.S. Army is that a large proportion of junior-level enlisted personnel are married. Critics also complain of the "civilization" of military life.

[23] Frederick Coudert, quoted in Michael Pearlman, *To Make Democracy Safe for America: Patricians and Preparedness in the Progressive Era* (Urbana: University of Illinois Press, 1984), p. 123.

[24] James, "The Moral Equivalent of War," pp. 666–69.

instrumental order in which "each person assesses social arrangements solely as a means to his private aims."[25] Persons do not care about the good of others and do not view their institutions as being good in themselves.

In such a society, the noninstrumental reasons for the welfare state—social justice, human development for its own sake, community—cannot remain sufficiently alive, and the instrumental reasons cannot be sufficiently strong, to support a full range of services. The wholly instrumental society ultimately will not even sustain the basic virtues of citizenship—self-sufficiency, neighborliness, and responsible political participation—that have been the focus of this section.

The metaphor of the common highway, however, need not be taken in this purely instrumental sense. It stands for a social order whose basic institutions allow all persons to realize their own ends; but these institutions need not be valued solely instrumentally, nor should their impact on others be viewed with indifference. In the liberal state, citizenship is built from the bottom up rather than from the top down.[26] Individuals define their own ends initially through family ties, personal relationships, and participation in valued collective enterprises beginning at the local level. To the extent that individuals find that the larger system of institutions permits them to achieve their chosen ends and supports their causes, and that it is predicated on an unconditional respect for their choices and causes, not on some overriding social goal that their choices just happen to further, they will come to value the system as good in itself, and to view the fate of their fellows as not unconnected to their own good.[27] There is no reason why the justifications for the welfare state cannot flourish in a liberal democratic polity, organized around common institutions, but lacking agreement on a common destination.

[25] Rawls, *A Theory of Justice*, pp. 521–22.

[26] I follow here Josiah Royce, *The Philosophy of Loyalty* (New York: Macmillan, 1918), pp. 243–48.

[27] Rawls, *A Theory of Justice*, p. 499.

NOTES ON CONTRIBUTORS

Joseph H. Carens is associate professor of political science at the University of Toronto. He is the author of *Equality, Moral Incentives, and the Market* (University of Chicago Press, 1980) and of articles on social and political theory. He is currently writing a book on immigration and political community.

Jon Elster is professor of political science and philosophy at the University of Chicago, and research director of the Institute for Social Research, Oslo. He is the author of *Making Sense of Marx* (Cambridge University Press, 1985) and of several other books on social theory. His current research interest is the intersection between the theory of collective action, bargaining theory, and theories of distributive justice.

Robert K. Fullinwider is a research associate at the Center for Philosophy and Public Policy of the University of Maryland, where his current work focuses on civic education. He is the author of *The Reverse Discrimination Controversy* (Rowman and Littlefield, 1980) and coeditor of the *The Moral Foundations of Civil Rights* (Rowman and Littlefield, 1986).

Amy Gutmann is Mellon Professor of Politics at Princeton University and director of the Program in Political Philosophy. She is the author of *Democratic Education* (Princeton University Press, 1987) and *Liberal Equality* (Cambridge University Press, 1980), and the coauthor of *Ethics and Politics: Cases and Comments* (Nelson-Hall, 1984).

Jennifer L. Hochschild is professor of politics and public affairs at Princeton University. She is the author of *What's Fair? American Beliefs about Distributive Justice* (Harvard University Press, 1981) and *The New American Dilemma: Liberal Democracy and School Desegregation* (Yale University, 1984), and a coauthor of *Equalities* (Harvard University Press, 1981). She is currently studying the relationships between race, class, and power and their implications for democratic theory and practice.

Stanley Kelley, Jr., is professor of politics at Princeton University. He is the author of *Professional Public Relations and Political Power* (Johns Hopkins University Press, 1956), *Political Campaigning* (Brookings Institution, 1960), *Interpreting Elections* (Princeton University Press, 1983), and of articles on voting and party politics.

Richard Krouse was associate professor of political science at Williams College before his death in August 1986. He wrote extensively on liberal theories of political economy and social philosophy.

MICHAEL MCPHERSON is professor of economics and chairman of the Economics Department at Williams College. He has written on morality and economics and on educational policy. He is coeditor of the journal *Economics and Philosophy.*

J. DONALD MOON is professor of government at Wesleyan University. He is the author of a chapter on the "Logic of Political Inquiry" in the *Handbook of Political Science*, as well as articles on the philosophy of social science and on the welfare state.

CAROLE PATEMAN is reader in government at the University of Sydney. She is the author of *Participation and Democratic Theory* (Cambridge University Press, 1970) and *The Problem of Political Obligation* (2d ed.; Polity Press/University of California Press, 1985), and coeditor of *Feminist Challenges* (Allen and Unwin/ Northeastern University Press, 1986). Her most recent book, *The Sexual Contract*, is forthcoming from Polity Press.

DENNIS F. THOMPSON is Whitehead Professor of Political Philosophy in the Government Department and the John F. Kennedy School of Government at Harvard University. He is also director of the universitywide Program in Ethics and the Professions. He is the author of *The Democratic Citizen: Social Science and Democratic Theory in the Twentieth Century* (Cambridge University Press, 1970), *John Stuart Mill and Representative Government* (Princeton University Press, 1976), and *Political Ethics and Public Office* (Harvard University Press, 1987).

MICHAEL WALZER is professor of social science at the Institute for Advanced Study, Princeton, N.J. He is the author of, among other books, *Interpretation and Social Criticism* (Harvard University Press, 1987), *Spheres of Justice* (Basic Books, 1983), *Just and Unjust Wars* (Basic Books, 1977), and *The Revolution of the Saints* (Harvard University Press, 1965). He is an editor of *Dissent* and a contributing editor of *The New Republic.*

INDEX

LIBRARY OF CONGRESS CATALOGING-IN-PUBLICATION DATA

Democracy and the welfare state.

(Studies from the Project on the Federal Social Role)
Includes index.
1. Public welfare—United States. 2. Democracy.
3. Welfare state. I. Gutmann, Amy. II. Series.
HV91.D462 1988 361.6′5 87–36055
ISBN 0–691–07756–8 (alk. paper)
ISBN 0–691–02275–5 (pbk.)